ATLAS OF RUSSIA AND THE INDEPENDENT REPUBLICS

ATLAS OF RUSSIA AND THE INDEPENDENT REPUBLICS

MOSHE BRAWER

SIMON & SCHUSTER

A Paramount Communications Company

New York   London   Toronto   Sydney   Tokyo   Singapore

Copyright © 1994 by Carta
The Israel Map and Publishing Company, Ltd.

Cartographic Editor: Pirhia Cohen
Text Editor: Barbara Ball
Annotated Bibliography: Linda S. Vertrees
Designed and produced by Carta, Jerusalem

Simon & Schuster
Academic Reference Division
15 Columbus Circle, New York, NY 10023

Printed in the United States of America

printing number
2 3 4 5 6 7 8 9 10

Library of Congress Cataloging-in-Publication Data
Brawer, Moshe, 1919–
    Atlas of Russia and the independent republics / Moshe Brawer.
        p.   cm.
    Includes bibliographical references and index.
    Includes information on the history, natural features, population,
and communications network of the former Soviet Union.
    ISBN 0-13-051996-0
    1. Former Soviet republics—Maps.   2. Baltic States—Maps.
I. Title.
G2110.B7   1994   ‹G&M›
912.47—dc20   94-21023
                                                            CIP
                                                            MAP

The paper in this publication meets the requirements of
ANSI/NISO Z39.48-1992 (Permanence of Paper).

Contents

Key to General Maps

~~~ River

––ⱴ– Canal

≝ⱼ Swamp

▲ 7440 Spot height in meters

— ·· — International border

BAKU Capital

⊡ **PERM** City (pop. 1,000,000 or more)

◉ **Lvov** City (pop. 500,000–1,000,000)

◎ Grozny City (pop. 200,000–500,000)

● Atyrau City (pop. 100,000–200,000)

○ Elista Town (pop. up to 100,000)

Key to City Maps

■ Building

○ Monument

⚓ Port

⛪ Church

▭ Stadium

✈ Airport

⊷▭⊶ Railway

✛ Cemetery

▨ Park, gardens

Abbreviations

°C	degree Celsius
CIS	Commonwealth of Independent States
cm	centimeter
cu.	cubic
°F	degree Fahrenheit
ft.	foot
in.	inch
km	kilometer
m	meter
mi.	mile
mm	millimeter
pop.	population
RSFSR	Russian Soviet Federated Socialist Republic
sq.	square
USSR	Union of Soviet Socialist Republics

Common Geographical Abbreviations

C.	Cape
I., Is.	Island(s)
L.	Lake
Mt., Mts.	Mount, Mountains
Pen.	Peninsula
R.	River
Res.	Reservoir

Flag color symbols

black   white   yellow   red   blue   brown   green

Preface

With the collapse of the Soviet Union in 1990–1991 there emerged fourteen sovereign states, in addition to Russia, that are gradually assuming full control of the territories within their boundaries. Many of the states have never, or at least not for a long time, been independent.

The Soviet Union, despite its vast size and great variety of physical features and peoples, was a country in which the division into constituent republics had little bearing on its actual government. This was particularly true of economic policies and development programs and projects, in which what the Soviet government considered as "national interests" had conspicuous priority over any local needs or interests. This also applied to the communications (land, water and air) network, as well as to many other aspects of government activities and services. Thus, under the practical system of government that prevailed in the USSR, the boundaries between the "republics" did not have even the functions that internal boundaries have in federal democratic states.

This atlas presents the physical and human characteristics of the emerging or reemerging states as independent entities. It provides information on the economic resources, facilities, capabilities, advantages and disadvantages of the individual states as they formulate their own economic policies.

Many of the vital statistics presented here are valid for late 1993. However, some states of the former Soviet Union have yet to produce independent, up-to-date surveys and statistical data on their population and economy. It was therefore necessary to depend largely on surveys and statistical publications of national and local Soviet institutions.

Nearly all the states are groping with numerous difficulties inherent in the transition from Soviet domination to independence. Changes in the political, economic and administrative organization of some states are likely to take place in the near future.

The atlas went to press in summer 1994, two and a half years after the dissolution of the Soviet Union. In those two and a half years the names of towns and geographical features that were given names of Communist personalities or events under Soviet rule reverted, in many cases, to their pre-Soviet names or were replaced by new names. In some of the Asiatic republics, Russian names dating back to tsarist times were replaced by names in the local language. The index at the end of the atlas lists the more important variant forms.

City streets whose names have only recently changed were unavailable at press time. The city maps presented here were based on the latest material available from the USSR.

The Cyrillic alphabet was used throughout the Soviet Union, except in the Baltic republics. Even those languages with their own alphabets—Georgian and Armenian, for example—were represented on Soviet maps in Cyrillic forms.

As a result, a distorted pronunciation (for English-speakers) of many place names was unavoidable. Thus, the Uzbeki or Turkmeni letter equivalent to the English g (as in George) or j (as in joy) was rendered by the Cyrillic letters for dzh. A name whose pronunciation could be rendered in Latin letters as Jarjur was transliterated from the Russian as Dzhardzhur. Such distortions can now be avoided by direct transliteration from the non-Russian languages of the former Soviet Union.

To continue to use a transliteration from the Cyrillic form of non-Russian names because they are still, in 1994, the only official ones available is unreasonable. Nearly all the Central Asian republics have decided to do away with the Cyrillic script, as have Azerbaijan and Moldova.

In this atlas, I have therefore used either the official spellings in Latin letters (for those republics that have already adopted the Latin alphabet) or a transliteration that represents the English pronunciation of the local name. Where the decision to replace the Cyrillic by the Latin alphabet has not yet been made, or where dominant and final forms have not yet been adopted, I have used the most suitable Latin-alphabet form.

I am indebted to Professor J. Dorfman (formerly of the University of Kiev) and to M. Benenson (formerly of the University of Moscow), both of whom are now at the Department of Geography at Tel Aviv University, for their invaluable help. I also wish to thank members of the Institute of East European (formerly Soviet) Studies at Tel Aviv University for their excellent advice and unfailing readiness to provide or check information required for the preparation of this atlas.

Moshe Brawer

INTRODUCTORY SURVEY

Natural Features of the Former Soviet Union

The Soviet Union prior to its breakup in 1991 covered an area of 8,600,660 square miles (22,275,700 sq. km), or nearly 15 percent of the total surface area of the world. It extended over 170°30′ of longitude (from 20°E to 169°30′W) and over 46° of latitude (from 35°N to 81°N). About 22 percent of this huge, continuous block of land lies beyond the Arctic Circle, where over much of the area the sun does not rise for weeks or months in winter and does not set in summer. Only less than 4 percent of its total surface area lies within the warmer parts of the earth. Of the 27,500 miles (44,000 km) of maritime borders, about 1,100 miles (1,800 km) are not frozen in winter. The Soviet Union covered much of eastern Europe and all of northern Asia. The traditional boundary between Europe and Asia is formed by the Ural Mountains, Ural River, Caspian Sea and Great Caucasus. The former Soviet Union has a great variety of physical features, landscapes, soils, climate, flora and fauna.

The former Soviet Union has three main types of terrain: plains and lowlands; plateaus and uplands; and mountains. The plains and lowlands occupy more than half the surface area of the former Soviet Union and are its widest and most continuous features. The European portion is almost entirely covered by plains and lowlands, with an average elevation of 574 feet (175 m). Small hilly areas exceed 1,000 feet (300 m) in elevation, with the highest peak at 1,310 feet (400 m). The elevations are very resistant rock formations, remnants of geologically ancient mountains or moraines (hills

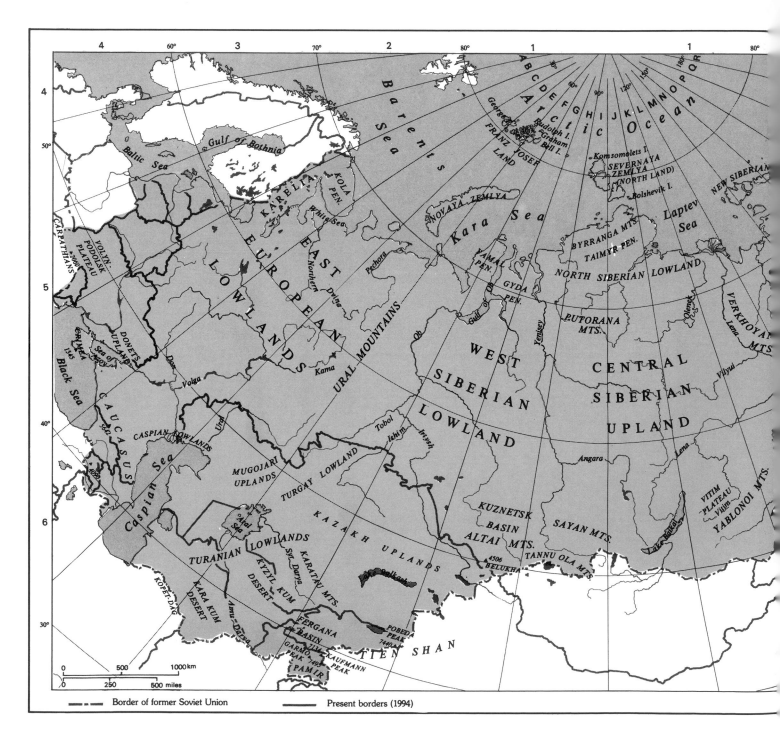

Border of former Soviet Union   Present borders (1994)

formed by glacial deposits). A thick mantle of glacial deposits covers the northern and central lowlands. Some of these elevations form the watershed between the main rivers, especially those flowing north to the Baltic Sea and Arctic Ocean and those flowing south to the Black and Caspian seas. In the southeast the East European Lowlands (or Plain) merge with the Caspian Lowlands, a substantial part of which lies below sea level. The narrow and long Kuma-Manych Depression separates this region from the lowlands and northern foothills of the Caucasus. The low-lying part of the Crimean

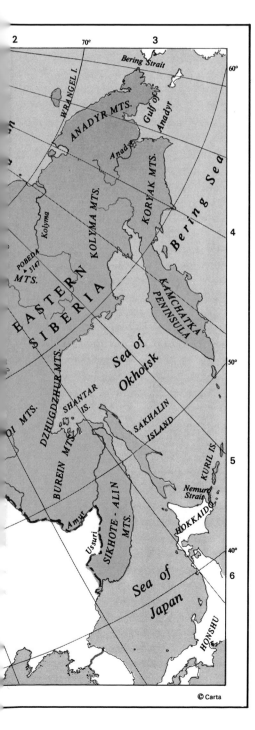

Peninsula is another southern extension of the East European Lowlands.

East of the Urals, on which the East European Lowlands border, there stretches the West Siberian Lowland, a very wide, level plain with a slight northward slope, which is largely swampy or waterlogged. It extends from the Arctic Ocean in the north to the Kazakh Uplands and Central Asian Highlands in the south. Its eastern margin is formed by the Yenisey Valley. Unlike the East European Lowlands, the West Siberian Lowland drains entirely northward to the Arctic Ocean, mainly by the Ob River and its tributaries. The comparatively narrow Turgay Lowland connects the West Siberian Lowland with the semiarid and arid Turanian Lowlands, another wide region of plains and hilly areas extending to the Caspian Sea and the mountains of Iran and Central Asia.

The Turanian Lowlands include the Kara Kum and Kyzyl Kum deserts, the most extensive desert areas of the former Soviet Union, and the Aral Sea and Lake Balkash Basin, the second largest inland basin after the Caspian. The two main rivers of the Turanian Lowlands, the Amu Darya and Syr Darya, were harnessed in major irrigation projects undertaken by the Soviet Union, thereby extending the desert's cultivable lands.

The North Siberian Lowland, which forms most of the northern part of Central Siberia, is another wide, flat, ill-drained plain, with some low ridges of hills. It is much smaller in area than the West Siberian Lowland. Other lowlands are mainly wide river valleys, such as those of the Lena-Vilyui, Amur-Ussuri, Kolyma, Indigirka and Anadyr rivers. These are small in extent, narrow in their upper parts and wider in their lower reaches.

The plateaus and uplands (which often have the characteristics of dissected plateaus) are ancient mountain systems, formed in early geological periods of orogenesis, or mountain-building processes—tectonic movements of folding, uplifting, faulting and sinking—occurring in the earth's crust. The oldest known mountain-building movements of the earth's crust are believed to have taken place over 700 million years ago (Precambrian), about 500 million years ago (Caledonian), 300 million years ago (Hercynian), 130 million years ago (Mesozoic) and, most recently,

50 million years ago (Alpine). Each of these processes was very slow and continued for millions of years. The ex-Soviet uplands belong mainly to the three oldest systems mentioned above. They are all extremely eroded, underwent great changes and in many cases are covered by more recent, particularly glacial, deposits.

The most resistant rock formations make up the more elevated outcrops of these ancient mountains, which rarely rise above 6,000 feet (1,800 m). The widest continuous area of such uplands is the Central Siberian Plateau (or Uplands). Another large area is the Kazakh Uplands (in central Kazakhstan). Other uplands of this type, which are generally smaller in extent, include the Khibin Massif (Kola Peninsula), the Volyn-Podolsk Plateau and the Donets Upland, the uplands of the Novaya Zemlya island and of the Taimyr Peninsula, the Mugojari Uplands (south of the Urals), the Kuznetsk Basin and surrounding ranges, the Vitim Plateau and the Aldan Plateau. Large areas which were subject to the same or similar geological processes are not part of the upland regions, but form lowlands or are buried under the extensive Russian and Siberian plains.

The mountainous regions are mainly situated along the southern and eastern fringes of the former USSR. Geologically, they are largely the creation of the two more recent mountain-making processes, especially the Alpine orogeny. These mountains are generally much higher, with many peaks above 16,000 feet (5,000 m), steeper, and in many areas still subject to strong repeated earthquakes and other volcanic activity. Some of the mountain systems in frontier areas are shared with neighboring states. Valleys and intermountain basins are often, insofar as human settlement and activities are concerned, the more important parts of the mountainous regions despite their relatively small extent.

The main mountain ranges are (highest peak in parentheses) a section of the northern Carpathians (6,760 ft./2,060 m); the mountains of southern Crimea (5,070 ft./1,545 m); and the Great Caucasus (18,498 ft./5,642 m) and Lesser Caucasus (13,400 ft./4,090 m) between the Black and Caspian seas. The Great Caucasus is largely covered with perpetual snow and glaciers. The legendary Mount Ararat (16,945 ft./

5,165 m) stands on the southern edge of the Lesser Caucasus (on the border with Turkey).

The Ural Mountains extend north to south for 1,600 miles (nearly 2,600 km) between the European and Asian parts of the ex-Soviet Union. Although the Urals are one of the most conspicuous physical features of the former Soviet Union, the highest peak is only 6,213 feet (1,893 m). While the ascent to the Urals from the European side is generally moderate, it is steep and often abrupt on the Asian side.

The Kopet-Dag Mountains extend eastward from the Caspian Sea along the boundary with Iran, where the range mostly lies. The Central Asiatic region, farther east, is the most mountainous part of the former Soviet Union. The highest and most inaccessible part of this area is the Pamirs ("the roof of the world"), in the south, with the highest elevations at Garmo (formerly Communism) Peak (24,585 ft./7,495 m) and Kaufmann (formerly Lenin) Peak (23,400 ft./7,134 m). The highest parts of the Pamirs are covered with large glaciers that feed some of the tributaries of the Amu Darya, a lifeline for the arid region to the northwest. Narrow valleys and the Fergana Basin separate the deeply dissected Pamir Mountains from the wide east-west Tien Shan Mountains (highest peak, Pobeda, at 24,400 ft./7,440 m), farther north, that stretch deep into western China. Two rivers, the Syr Darya and Ily, on which human survival in the arid lands farther

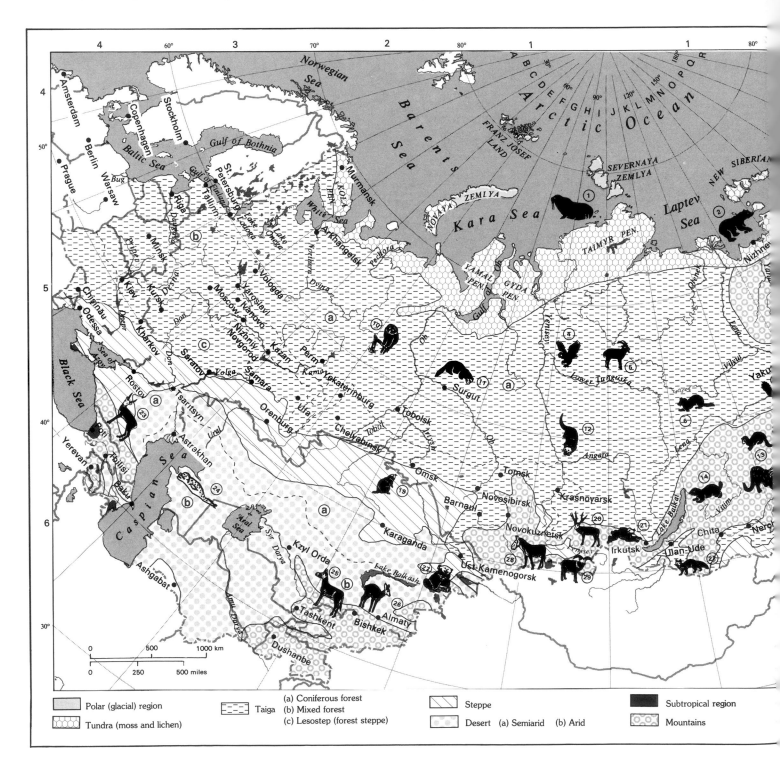

Polar (glacial) region		Taiga	(a) Coniferous forest	Steppe		Subtropical region
Tundra (moss and lichen)			(b) Mixed forest	Desert (a) Semiarid (b) Arid		Mountains
			(c) Lesostep (forest steppe)			

north depends, have their sources in the Tien Shan. Two of Central Asia's largest urban centers, Tashkent and Almaty (Alma-Ata), stand at the foot of these mountains.

The Altai mountain system to the northeast is another wide highland region, the natural resources of which played an important role in Soviet development projects. Two of the former Soviet Union's largest rivers, the Ob and Yenisey, have their sources here. The Altai is generally divided into four subsystems: the southern Altai; the inner Altai (which is the most elevated part of the system, rising to 14,774 ft./4,506 m); the eastern Altai (along the frontier with Mongolia); and the Mongolian Altai (which runs in a southeasterly direction and lies mostly within Mongolia and China).

The Sayan Mountains (highest peak, 11,446 ft./3,491 m), which lie between the Altai Mountains and Lake Baikal, present a gentler highland landscape with broader valleys and domelike summits. Some of the tributaries of the Yenisey River have their sources here. The southernmost part of the Central Siberian Uplands merges into the eastern Sayans. The lower and gentler nature of the latter is continued eastward of Lake Baikal (Transbaikalia). The main ranges of Yablonoi (8,090 ft./2,468 m) and Stanovoi (9,833 ft./2,999 m) run here in a northeasterly direction. The landscape is more deeply dissected. The large rivers of eastern Siberia, the Lena and Amur, have their headstreams in these highlands. They form the watershed between the areas drained to the Arctic Ocean and those drained to the Pacific Ocean.

The eastern (Far East region) and northeastern parts of the former Soviet Union are largely mountainous. Among the most prominent ranges are the Verkhoyansk (7,833 ft./2,389 m), Cherski (10,325 ft./3,147 m) and Kolyma (6,433 ft./1,962 m) mountains in the northeast and the Sikhote Alin Mountains (6,810 ft./2,075 m) in the southeast, along the coast of the Sea of Japan. The two parallel north-south ranges which occupy most of the Kamchatka Peninsula are not only the most elevated mountains (15,584 ft./4,750 m) of the Far East region but also the former USSR's main center of volcanic activity, with about twenty active volcanos.

The natural regions can be subdivided into six main latitudinal natural zones, using climate, soil, vegetation and terrain as criteria: (1) polar (glacial); (2) tundra; (3) forest; (4) steppe; (5) semiarid and arid; and (6) subtropical. These natural zones also appear in an altitudinal distribution in the high mountain regions.

1. The area under permanent ice or snow cover is small and confined to parts of the islands in the Arctic zone and to the most elevated parts of the high mountain ranges. This zone does not include the large part of the ex-USSR in which ground frost is permanent (permafrost), but where the surface soil (depending on location, topography and soil type) thaws to a depth of 12 to 60 inches (30 to 150 cm) each summer.

2. The tundra, in the extreme north, is a wide, generally flat expanse covered with moss and lichen. Its southern limits are not clearly defined and in some classifications include forests of dwarf trees (tundra forest). Tundra covers about 15 percent of the former Soviet territory.

— Present borders (1994)

- - - Border of former Soviet Union

© Carta

Geographical Zones; Flora and Fauna

Selected Fauna

1. *Odobenus rosmarus* (walrus)
2. *Thalarctos maritimus* (polar bear)
3. *Arctocephalus ursinus* (fur seal)
4. *Nyctea nyctea* (snowy owl)
5. *Capra sibirica* (Siberian ibex)
6. *Martes zibellina* (sable)
7. *Sciurus vulgaris* (squirrel)
8. *Ovis ammon* (mountain sheep)
9. *Latax lutris* (beaver)
10. *Syrnium uralense* (Uralian owl)
11. *Mustela putorius* (weasel)
12. *Lutra lutra* (otter)
13. *Mustela sibirica* (Siberian mink)
14. *Marmota sibirica* (Siberian marmot)
15. *Alces pfizenmayeri* (Ussuri elk)
16. *Leo tigris mongolicus* (Mongolian tiger)
17. *Cervus canadensis sibiricus* (Japanese deer, Canadian-Siberian deer)
18. *Panthera pardus villosa* (leopard)
19. *Marmota bobak* (bobac)
20. *Elaphurus davidianus* (deer)
21. *Lepus tolai* (hare)
22. *Alopex corsac* (corsac, Arctic fox)
23. *Capreolus pygargus* (wild goat)
24. *Phoca hispida caspica* (Caspian seal)
25. *Equus hemionus* (horse)
26. *Moschus moschiferus* (musk deer)
27. *Selenarctos tibetanus* (Asiatic black bear)
28. *Equus caballus przewalskii* (Mongolian horse)
29. *Pseudois nayaur* (sheep)
30. *Monodon monoceros* (narwhal)
31. *Delphinapterus leucas* (dolphin)

Winters in this zone are very severe, but somewhat mitigated on the eastern and western margins by the influence of the Pacific and Atlantic oceans, respectively. Summers are mild. Precipitation (annual average of 8 to 14 in./200 to 350 mm) falls mostly in summer.

3. The forest zone (also known as the taiga, its dominant subzone) is by far the largest of the latitudinal natural regions. It covers about 40 percent of the former Soviet Union and is generally divided into three subzones: (a) the taiga, in the north, with predominantly coniferous forests of spruce, larch, fir and stone pine; (b) mixed forests, farther south, with broad-leaved trees of oak, elm, maple, linden and ash, mixed with pine, aspen, birch, alder and other types; and (c) the lesostep (forest steppe), in the extreme south, a transitional zone to the steppe region. The mixed forests and forest steppe are increasingly interspersed with meadows. The forest zone has wide expanses of peat bogs, estimated to cover more than 10 percent of the area. The climate is highly diverse. Winters are cold to very cold. Extreme continental conditions prevail in the Siberian parts of the zone. Summers are temperate to warm, with temperatures of over 85°F (30°C) recorded in the south. An annual average precipitation of 16 to 20 inches (400 to 500 mm), which in some elevated areas rises to 24 to 28 inches (600 to 700 mm), falls mainly in summer.

4. The steppes are wide expanses with few trees and predominantly mixed herbaceous vegetation. This zone is estimated to cover 18 to 20 percent of the former Soviet Union. A large part of the zone is covered by fertile chernozem soil. Together with the southern part of the forest zone (the forest steppe), it had been the granary of the Soviet Union. The zone has a more temperate climate, continental conditions are less extreme and winters less severe. Summers are warm to hot and relatively dry. An annual average precipitation of 10 to 15 inches (200 to 375 mm) falls mainly in late spring and early summer. The southernmost parts of the European states of the former Soviet Union, with the exception of the Caspian Lowlands, belong to this zone.

5. The semiarid and arid zone includes the Caspian Lowlands, the Turanian Lowlands (in southern and southeastern Kazakhstan, most of Turkmenistan and Uzbekistan) and some basins and valleys on the southern fringes of Central Asiatic Russia. The vegetation is typically patchy, with dry steppe grasses, wormwood, fescues and xeraphytic grasses. This zone occupies about 14 percent of the former Soviet Union. The climate is characterized mainly by small amounts of precipitation, in most areas not exceeding an average of 10 inches (250 mm) annually and sometimes as low as 4 inches (100 mm). Typical continental, high diurnal and seasonal ranges of temperatures are also prevalent. Winters are cold and very low temperatures are not infrequent. Summer temperatures are relatively high, occasionally rising above 90°F (32°C).

6. The subtropical (Mediterranean) zone is very small and is confined to the coastal areas of the Black Sea and the Transcaucasian Lowlands. Winters are mild and rainy and summers are hot and dry. There are deciduous forests, woods of oak, hornbeam and beech, shrubs and, in some areas, typical Mediterranean vegetation.

The soil regions largely fit into the latitudinal natural regions and the corresponding altitudinal zones in the uplands and highlands. Tundra soils are in the extreme north, followed southward by podzol that dominates about half the land area. In central and eastern Siberia, podzol soils extend from the tundra to almost the southern boundaries of the former USSR. Chernozem covers most of the forest steppe and steppes, followed southward by a belt of chestnut soils and then brown soils that extend into the semiarid and arid zone. Sands cover large parts of the deserts of the Turanian Lowlands. Red soils cover some areas of the subtropical zone.

FAUNA

The vast expanse of the former Soviet Union is reflected not only in the great variety of natural features but also in the wealth and diversity of its wildlife. The world's richest variety of valuable, fur-bearing animals is found mainly in the huge forest zone, where hunting and collecting of furs are still an important occupation among the sparse rural population.

The typical animals of the tundra zone are the polar bear, hare, wild and domestic reindeer, lemming and the Arctic fox. The reindeer is the most important animal in the tundra. Many species of birds, including swans, geese and barnacle geese, fly into this zone in spring. The willow ptarmigan and snowy owl are among the permanent dwellers of the tundra forest.

Brown bear, marten, fox, squirrel, hare and elk are common in the taiga zone farther south. Sable and reindeer still exist in parts of Siberia. The most common birds are the capercaillie, hazel grouse and willow ptarmigan. In the mountain forests of Siberia, squirrel, fox, musk deer and mountain sheep are common, while steppe rodents, bobac and suslik dwell at higher elevations. The animals in the mountain forests of the Far East include black Himalayan bear, Ussuri elk, Japanese deer, sable, musk deer and goral. The Kamchatka Peninsula is noted for its diversity of large animals, including bear, fox, sable, reindeer and mountain sheep.

Farther south, the subzone of mixed forests and the transition region to the steppe zone have roebuck, elk, reindeer, squirrel, bobac, jerboa, bear, sable, wolf, suslik and mountain sheep. The Altai Mountains have a mixture of animals characteristic of the Mongolian steppes and the East Siberian taiga. These include bear, lynx, badger, deer, red deer, mountain goat, mountain sheep, sable, northern dhole, suslik, Mongolian mole and bobac.

The wolf, fox, most of the Altai animals, the spotted suslik, jerboa and hamster are characteristic of the steppe zone. Typical birds are the great and little bustard, crane, calandra lark, duck, heron and shore birds. Migratory locusts breed in reed thickets along some of the rivers.

The corsac is commonly found in the semiarid region, as are the white and yellow suslik, hamster and jerboa. There are many species of birds in the floodplains and river deltas. The fox, badger, red deer and hare are common in the Crimea, while wild boar, wildcat, roebuck and deer are characteristic of the lower parts of the Caucasus.

Extensive wildlife reserves are found throughout the former Soviet Union, mainly in the forest zone and some of the highland regions. They were set up especially to protect those animals which have become relatively rare because of their valuable furs.

Mean Temperature in January

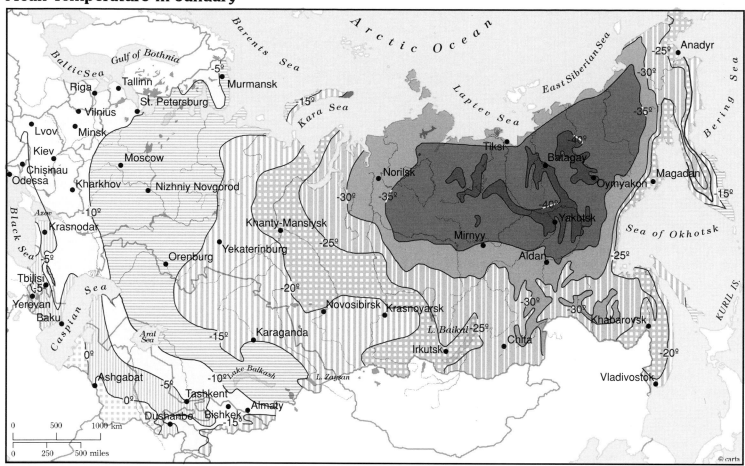

Mean Temperature in July

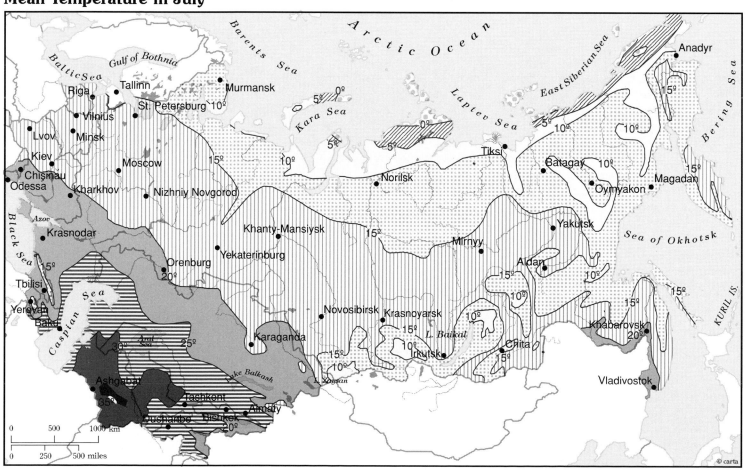

History of the Former Soviet Union

The Soviet Union was founded in November (October, according to the Julian calendar) 1917 with the formation of the Communist (Bolshevik) government, which succeeded the deposed tsarist regime and several short-lived interim governments. The constitution, which laid the foundation for the union, was adopted in 1918 by the Russian Soviet Federated Socialist Republic. Other constituent republics joined the RSFSR in 1922 to create the USSR.

At the time of the Communist Revolution (1917), the Russian Empire extended over 8,647,660 square miles (22,397,440 sq. km), from central Europe to the Pacific Ocean and from the Arctic Ocean to the fringes of the subtropics of Asia. The origins of this empire date back a thousand years, to the tenth century when Scandinavians, who came to settle and trade among Slavic tribes, established a fort at the site of present-day Kiev, which developed into a locally powerful principality. These Scandinavian "founding fathers" of Russia were known to the native inhabitants as Rus, from which the name Russia derived. Other Russian principalities followed, the most prominent of which were Novgorod, and later Moscow. Repeated invasions by hordes from the south and several centuries of subjugation by the Mongols brought stagnation and even decline to these principalities. It was only toward the end of the fifteenth century that their rise and expansion were resumed, this time under the leadership and later domination of Moscow. The sixteenth century saw the unification of the Russian principalities and great expansion eastward and southeastward across the Urals and to the Caspian Sea. Ivan IV, the first tsar of "all Russia," was crowned in 1547.

The expansion across central and eastern Siberia to the Sea of Okhotsk (Pacific Ocean) and the Amur Valley (Far East) was made in the seventeenth century, the period of greatest territorial gains for Russia. Further expansion followed in the eighteenth century: to the west, to the Baltic Sea and eastern Poland; to the south, to the Black Sea, the Crimea, areas east of the Sea of Azov, large areas of southern Siberia and the northern edge of Turkestan. In the northeast, Russia annexed the Chukot Peninsula, reaching the Bering Strait and gaining a foothold in Alaska (which led to its annexation in the early nineteenth century). The possession of some Arctic islands was also declared.

In the nineteenth century, Russia expanded into Europe with its possession of Finland, a larger part of Poland, Bessarabia (Moldova) and territories north of the Caucasus. The main expansion came, however, in Central Asia, the Caucasus, Transcaucasia and the Far East, where Russia reached the Sea of Japan and the Yellow Sea and occupied Sakhalin Island and the Kuril Islands. (For a more detailed summary of Russia's history, see the chapter on Russia.)

The military reversals in World War I, which led to the revolution and collapse of the tsarist regime, national movements for independence, uprisings and the civil war (1917–1921), also resulted in the overthrow of Russian rule in large areas of the empire inhabited by non-Russians. In accordance with a treaty (Brest-Litovsk) imposed by the German army on the Communist government in 1918, the independence of Finland, the Baltics, Poland and Ukraine was recognized. The independence of the Transcaucasian states was also envisaged. In the course of the civil war the Red Army, which consisted of Russian Communist forces and Communist organizations and supporters in various countries of the former tsarist empire (who fought with the Red Army, were integrated in it or formed local supporting militias), gained the upper hand and succeeded, by 1922, in imposing the authority of the central Russian Communist government on most of the non-Russian lands. The Communist "empire" had shrunk by 405,740 square miles (1,050,870 sq. km). The areas lost were Finland, the Baltic states, eastern and central Poland, Moldova (ceded to Romania) and the Kars District in Transcaucasia (ceded to Turkey). The civil war resulted in a severe scarcity of food, clothing, fuel and many other vital commodities. The famine claimed many victims.

Russia, the founding member of the Soviet Union, became a federal republic in 1918. Under its newly adopted constitution, some non-Russian lands were granted a (largely formal) degree of autonomy. They included most of the Central Asian territories that later (in the 1920s and 1930s) became constituent republics of the Soviet Union.

Ukraine, Belarus and Transcaucasia (the latter split in 1936 into the constituent republics of Georgia, Armenia and Azerbaijan) were the first to join the RSFSR as part of the Soviet Union. In 1924, the Uzbek Republic and the Turkmen Republic, which were previ-

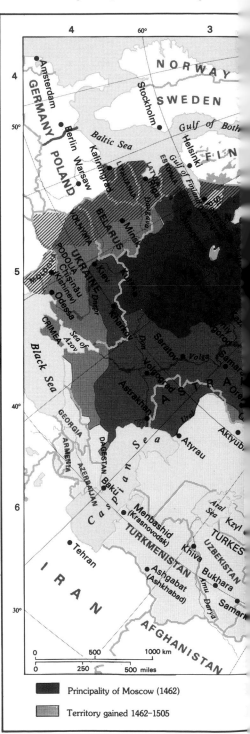

Principality of Moscow (1462)

Territory gained 1462–1505

ously autonomous republics within the RSFSR, became constituent members of the Soviet Union. Similarly, the Tajik and Kazakh republics became members in 1929 and 1936; they were formerly autonomous republics in the Uzbek Republic and the RSFSR, respectively.

The years following the civil war were characterized by strenuous efforts, sometimes by harsh means, to gear most aspects of life, especially the economy and public services, to the Communist ideology as interpreted and prescribed by the leadership. There was also in-tense, widespread indoctrination of this ideology and a compulsion to obey. At the same time significant achievements were being made in the development of agriculture, industry, transportation, public services and military power. Most of the population suffered much hardship during this period.

Beginning in World War II, the Soviet Union regained most of the territories it lost after World War I. Under a co-operation treaty with Nazi Germany in the summer of 1939 (shortly before the outbreak of the war), the Soviet Union annexed eastern Poland after the west-ern part was conquered by Germany. Under the same treaty, in 1940 it oc-cupied the Baltics and Moldova, incor-porating them as constituent republics. Part of the areas annexed from Romania were incorporated in Ukraine, namely, northern Bukovina (under Austria until the end of World War I) and the districts of Khotin, Akkerman and Ismail (the coastal area of Moldova and its access to the Danube delta). At the end of 1939 the Soviet Union invaded Finland and forced it to cede southern Karelia and

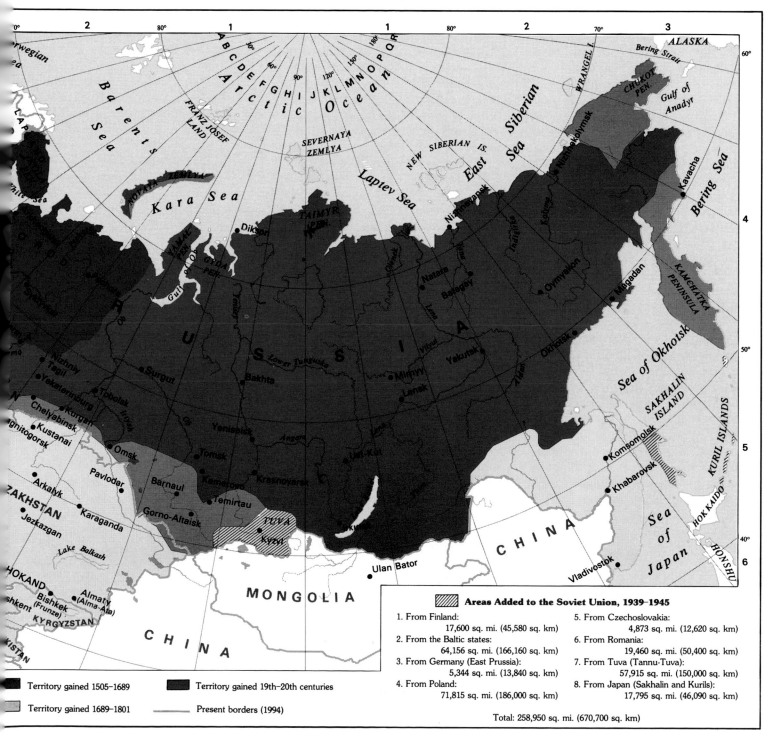

	Areas Added to the Soviet Union, 1939–1945
1. From Finland: 17,600 sq. mi. (45,580 sq. km)	5. From Czechoslovakia: 4,873 sq. mi. (12,620 sq. km)
2. From the Baltic states: 64,156 sq. mi. (166,160 sq. km)	6. From Romania: 19,460 sq. mi. (50,400 sq. km)
3. From Germany (East Prussia): 5,344 sq. mi. (13,840 sq. km)	7. From Tuva (Tannu-Tuva): 57,915 sq. mi. (150,000 sq. km)
4. From Poland: 71,815 sq. mi. (186,000 sq. km)	8. From Japan (Sakhalin and Kurils): 17,795 sq. mi. (46,090 sq. km)

Total: 258,950 sq. mi. (670,700 sq. km)

Territory gained 1505–1689
Territory gained 1689–1801
Territory gained 19th–20th centuries
Present borders (1994)

Finland's outlet to the Atlantic Ocean (Pechenga). This and areas of Karelia already in the Soviet Union first became the Karelo-Finnish constituent republic of the USSR, but in 1956 the status was changed to an autonomous republic within the RSFSR.

The Nazi German invasion in 1941 and the ensuing war had disastrous effects on the Soviet Union. The Germans occupied Belarus, Ukraine, the Baltics, Moldova and part of western Russia, all of which were devastated and suffered heavy losses of life. In their advance the Germans besieged Leningrad, reached the outskirts of Moscow, the banks of the Lower Volga, the foot of the Caucasus, and occupied the Crimea. The defeat of Germany in 1945 restored to the Soviet Union the territories it gained in 1939 and 1940. Moreover, it annexed (and included in Ukraine) Carpatho-Russia, a region in eastern Czechoslovakia during the interwar years. The Kaliningrad (Königsberg) province, formerly part of German East Prussia, was annexed to the Russian Republic as an enclave on the Baltic coast, between newly independent Poland and Soviet Lithuania. The Soviet Union also recaptured the southern half of Sakhalin Island (lost in 1905) and the Kuril Islands from Japan. Tuva (Tannu-Tuva), which was formally independent (but actually under Soviet suzerainty), was incorporated in the Russian Republic in 1944, first as an autonomous region and then as an autonomous republic.

Another consequence of the war was the subjugation of Russia's Eastern European neighbors to her political and economic dominance and military cooperation and aims (and in some cases presence) in what years later became known as the Warsaw Pact and Comecon. The Soviet Union occupied East Germany in 1945, as part of the postwar measures against Nazi Germany, and maintained its full military presence there until 1990.

The Soviet Union's postwar strategy, up to a few years before its disintegration, was first to overcome the ravages of the war and then to achieve rapid economic growth so as to catch up with Western Europe and North America. Externally, it strived to become politically and militarily the world's most influential and powerful state, during what became known as the Cold War with the United States and its allied Western powers. Relentless efforts, both open and clandestine, were made to bring Communist rule to as many countries as possible and to strengthen Communist activities in the non-Communist countries. The vast production of conventional and nonconventional arms and other military equipment weighed heavily on the Soviet Union's economic growth, domestic requirements and improvement of its living standards.

In 1954 the Crimean Peninsula, which had been part of the Russian Republic, was transferred to Ukraine.

The Soviet Union consisted of fifteen constituent republics with 129 territories and regions that were subdivided into 3,228 districts, 2,186 towns, 665 urban districts and 4,014 urban localities. To provide some recognition to small ethnic groups, twenty autonomous republics, eight autonomous regions and ten national districts were formed.

The Supreme Soviet, elected for a five-year term, was the highest legislative body of the Soviet Union. It consisted of two chambers: the Council of the Union and the Council of Nationalities, each with 750 members. An amendment to the constitution adopted in 1988 called for a People's Congress of 2,250 members to be elected in general elections. The Congress in turn would elect a 542-member Supreme Soviet.

The Council of the Union was elected by all Soviet citizens on the basis of national territories: thirty-two deputies for each constituent republic, eleven for each autonomous republic, five for each autonomous region and one for each national district. The actual running of the USSR was done by a Council of Ministers, about one hundred in number, appointed by the Supreme Soviet. The Supreme Soviet (both houses) elected a 39-member Presidium, or "inner cabinet," which was a kind of supreme legislative authority in almost permanent session.

The constituent republics each had similar legislative and governing bodies, as was the case, on a more limited and less authoritative basis, with autonomous republics, regions and areas. Local authorities of various types also had their elected council (Soviets). In 1988 there were 52,602 rural and urban councils (Soviets) with 2.3 million members. The Communist Party was the only legitimate political organization. The candidates it nominated for elections won nearly all the votes; there were hardly any dissenting votes. The supreme leadership of the Communist Party, known as the Politburo (Political Bureau), elected by the party's Central Committee, had been the actual power in the Soviet government, the policy- and decision-making body of the USSR. Only 9.3 percent of the adult population was admitted into the Communist Party and held elite status.

A liberalization (later known as perestroika) of the policies and practices of the Soviet government became apparent in 1985, following the election of Mikhail Gorbachev as leader of the Communist Party and Soviet government. A gradual departure from the strict totalitarian nature of the regime, more freedom of expression and of political dissension followed, as did more openness to foreign contacts and influences. This led step by step over the next five years to the development of internal and external (regarding European Communist countries) political processes that weakened the authority of the Soviet central government and of the party. In 1991 this resulted in the collapse of the Soviet Union and the dominance of the Communist Party.

In a referendum in 1991, the majority of the population voted for a Soviet Union that would be a federation of equal sovereign republics, in which democratic principles and human rights were guaranteed. This was followed within a few months by declarations of full independence by all the constituent republics, except Russia, which had, in fact, ruled the USSR.

In view of their deep-rooted interdependence, Russia, Ukraine and Belarus reached agreement at the end of 1991 to establish a framework of further close cooperation, to be called the Commonwealth of Independent States. The Commonwealth consists now of twelve republics of the former Soviet Union: eight (Armenia, Azerbaijan, Moldova, Kazakhstan, Turkmenistan, Uzbekistan, Kyrgyzstan and Tajikistan) joined the three founding states shortly after the Commonwealth was born; and one (Georgia) became a member in 1993. The three Baltic states (Estonia, Latvia and Lithuania) have so far stayed out of the Commonwealth.

Population of the Former Soviet Union

The population of the Soviet Union at the time of its breakup in 1991 was estimated to be 293.5 million. According to the last census in 1989, it was 286.7 million. The population more than doubled during the seventy-four years (1917–1991) of the Soviet Union's existence, despite the periods of famine and the heavy losses of life from the civil war (1917–1921) and World War II (1941–1945). The population was 139.3 million in 1914. It fell to 134 million by 1920, but rose to 170.5 million (81.7 million males and 88.8 million females) by 1939 and to 208.8 million (94 million males and 114.8 million females) in 1959. The population figures and the male/female ratio in 1939 and 1959 show clearly the effects of World War I, the ensuing civil war and World War II. The latter alone caused over 14 million deaths.

The birth rate and natural increase fell continuously even in times of peace, especially in the European part of the Soviet Union and among the people of European descent in the Asiatic part. The average annual natural increase in the 1930s for the USSR as a whole was 1.2 percent and in the 1970s and 1980s, 0.9 percent. The natural increase was only 0.6 percent in Soviet Europe for the latter decades and over 2 percent among the non-Europeans in Soviet Central Asia.

The rate of natural increase in some of the larger urban areas of the European republics was minimal. A mass migration of Russians and, to a lesser extent, Ukrainians and Belorussians to the Asiatic part of the Soviet Union occurred between the mid-1920s and the 1960s (particularly during the 1930s and World War II). This is clearly reflected in the increased proportion of Russians in the Asiatic republics of Georgia, Azerbaijan, Uzbekistan, Tajikistan and Turkmenistan between 1926 and 1970. A mass migration of Russians to the European Soviet republics took place mainly after World War II and continued almost to the time of the Soviet Union's collapse. During the same period many Russians (and others from Soviet Europe) migrated to Asiatic Russia (Siberia), especially to the areas that became highly industrialized. In 1989 over 25 million Russians (17.2 percent of all Russians in the Soviet Union) lived in the non-Russian republics, making up 18.2 percent of their total population (as opposed to 9.6 percent in 1926).

Much of this migration was involuntary. It was imposed by the Soviet government as a means of dispersing the population, strengthening the Russian presence in the Asiatic republics and, at times, as part of its russification policy. During and shortly after World War II, over 2 million people were forced to migrate from Soviet Europe to Soviet Asia. These included 525,000 Chechens and Ingush, 380,000 Germans, 220,000 Tatars, 217,000 Kabardi-

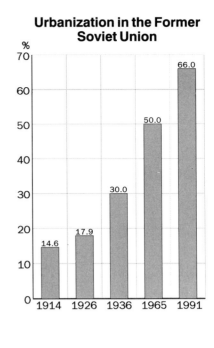

Urbanization in the Former Soviet Union

nians and Balkars, 141,000 Kalmyks and 80,000 Karachays. Of the Russians living in the non-Russian republics, the growth rate was often highest in the key cities of the main urban centers.

Urbanization increased rapidly under the Soviet Union. Nearly 13 percent of the population lived in urban areas at the turn of this century (in what was then the Russian Empire). The rate rose to 14.6 percent in 1914 and to 17.9 percent in 1926. It exceeded 30 percent by 1939 and 50 percent by 1965, reaching 66 percent in 1991. Apart from the massive growth of many cities, more than four hundred towns evolved (many of them completely new or villages and townships that grew into towns). At its birth the USSR had only two cities (Petrograd and Moscow) with a population of over 1 million and one city (Kiev) with 500,000 to 1 million; by 1990 there were twenty-four and thirty-five cities, respectively. The rural population reached its highest absolute number (120.7 million) in 1926, decreasing to 114.6 million by 1939, 106.3 million by 1970 and to 98.2 million in 1991. Nomadism and seminomadism, still prevalent in much of northern Siberia in the 1920s, have almost disappeared.

The rural population under the Soviet regime was organized in collective farms (kolkhozy) and state farms (sovkhozy). In 1917 there were 23.7 million small and medium-sized peasant farms, 99.3 percent of which were incorporated in 242,400 kolkhozy and 3,960 sovkhozy.

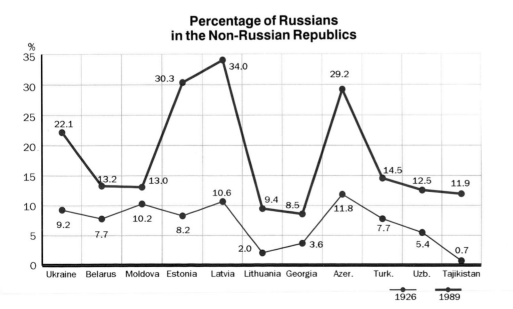

Percentage of Russians in the Non-Russian Republics

Distribution of Ethnic Groups

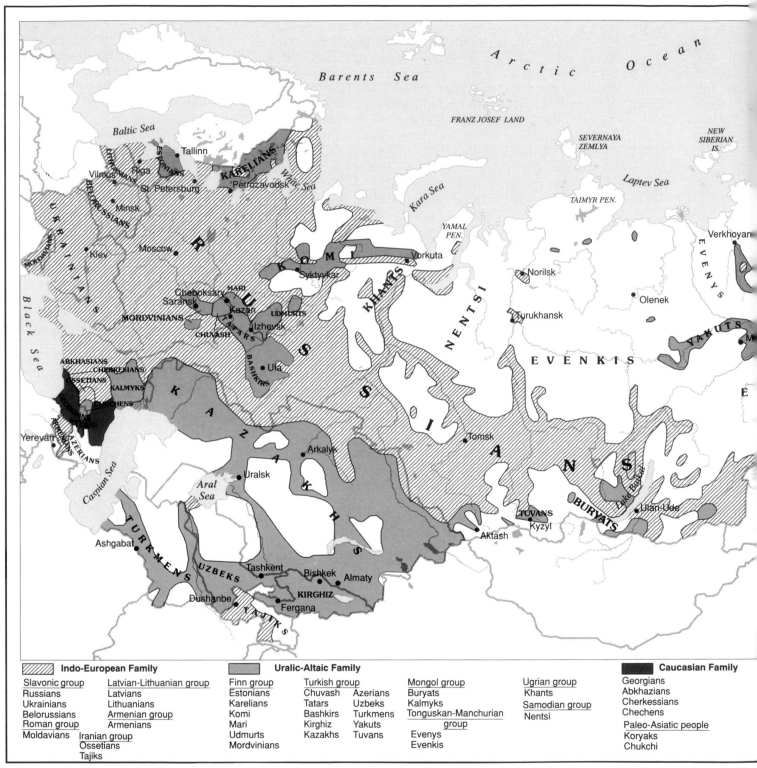

Indo-European Family

Slavonic group
Russians
Ukrainians
Belorussians
Roman group
Moldavians

Latvian-Lithuanian group
Latvians
Lithuanians
Armenian group
Armenians
Iranian group
Ossetians
Tajiks

Uralic-Altaic Family

Finn group
Estonians
Karelians
Komi
Mari
Udmurts
Mordvinians

Turkish group
Chuvash   Azerians
Tatars   Uzbeks
Bashkirs   Turkmens
Kirghiz   Yakuts
Kazakhs   Tuvans

Mongol group
Buryats
Kalmyks
Tonguskan-Manchurian group
Evenys
Evenkis

Ugrian group
Khants
Samodian group
Nentsi

Caucasian Family

Georgians
Abkhazians
Cherkessians
Chechens
Paleo-Asiatic people
Koryaks
Chukchi

Reorganization and development projects led to the unification of many kolkhozy. On the eve of the Soviet Union's disintegration, the farming population was organized in 27,900 kolkhozy and 23,300 sovkhozy.

The Soviet population consisted of over sixty ethnic groups, fifteen of which had constituent republics in the union and thirty-seven others had autonomous territories within one of the constituent republics. The twenty-two main ethnic groups and their percentage in the total population in 1989 (1926 figures in parentheses) were Russians, 50.6 (53); Ukrainians, 15.4 (21.2); Uzbeks 5.8 (2.7); Belorussians, 3.5 (3.2); Kazakhs, 2.8 (2.7); Azerians, 2.4 (1.2); Tatars, 2.3 (2); Armenians, 1.6 (0.9); Georgians, 1.4 (1.2); Moldavians, 1.2 (--); Tajiks, 1.5 (0.5); Lithuanians, 1.07 (--); Turkmens, 0.95 (0.52); Germans, 0.7 (0.84); Kirghiz, 0.9 (0.52); Chuvash, 0.64 (0.67); Jews, 0.5 (1.8); Bashkirs, 0.5 (0.5); Latvians, 0.5 (--); Mordvinians, 0.4 (0.9); Poles, 0.4 (--); and Estonians, 0.36 (--). Each of these nationalities totaled more than 1 million and altogether they formed over 95 percent of the total population. Some of the smaller ethnic groups numbered less than 100,000.

There are no statistics on religious affiliations in view of the anti-religious ideol-

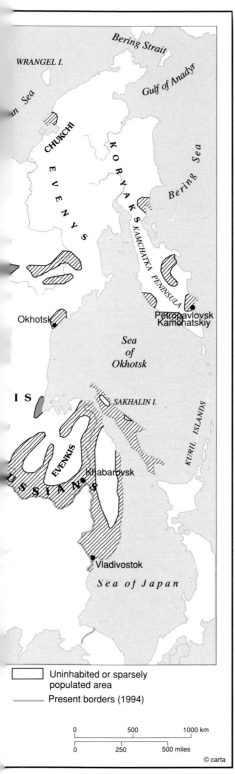

people of Muslim descent) formed about 18 percent of the total population in 1989. About 55 percent of the Muslims (Uzbeks, Kazakhs, Tajiks, Kirghiz, Turkmens, Buryats, Karakalpaks and smaller ethnic groups) live in Soviet Central Asia, 25 percent (Azerians, Ossetians, Chechens, Kabardinians, Ingush, Avars, Lezgins, Dargins, Abkhazians and several other small ethnic groups) live in the Caucasus, Transcaucasia and the surroundings, and nearly 20 percent (Bashkirs and Tatars) live in southeast European Russia and the southern Urals. Jews (many were not registered as such in the census) were nearly 1 percent of the population. Buddhism was and (to some extent) is the religion of the Kalmyks, Koreans and small ethnic groups in Central Asia and the Far East.

Illiteracy, which affected over 70 percent of the population (86 percent of whom were women) in 1914, was almost completely eradicated under the Soviet Union.

Distribution of the population is very uneven. Eight percent of the population (compared with 6 percent in 1939) live in over two-thirds of the total area of the former Soviet Union, while over 50 percent are concentrated in less than 10 percent of the area. The average population density for the Soviet Union as a whole was 33.7 persons per square mile (13 per sq. km) in 1991, compared with 17.8 (6.9) in 1926 and 20.7 (8) in 1939. The region with the highest density was the Moscow province (863 persons per sq. mi./333 per sq. km), followed by the Fergana Basin (in Uzbekistan), with 785 persons per square mile (303 per sq. km). In both these regions the density had more than quadrupled over the last seventy years. Large areas of northern Siberia, despite a similar growth in density, still contain less than one inhabitant per square mile. Thus, in the Sakha (formerly Yakutia) autonomous republic (1,197,760 sq. mi./3,103,200 sq. km), the density rose from 0.26 to 0.9 person per square mile (0.1 to 0.35 per sq. km) and in the Taimyr district (332,857 sq. mi./862,100 sq. km) it rose from 0.026 to 0.15 person per square mile (0.01 to 0.06 per sq. km). Of the former Soviet constituent republics, the highest rise in population density took place in Tajikistan (nearly 3.5 times) and the lowest (only by 14 percent) in Belarus (the worst ravaged by World War II). The comparative rise in population density in Soviet Asia was much higher than in the European part. However, the latter remains much more densely populated.

Main Caucasian Ethnic Groups

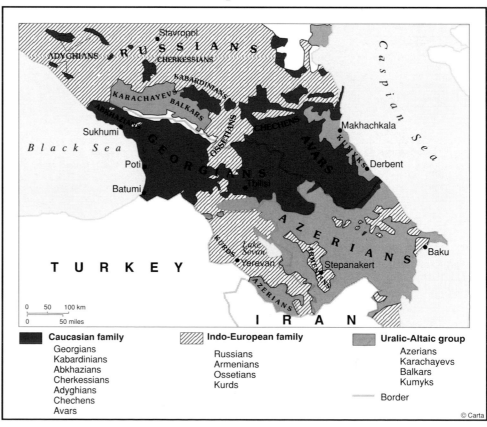

ogy guiding Soviet policy. It is estimated that nearly 80 percent of the people were Christians (or descendants of Christians). The great majority (Russians, Ukrainians, Belorussians, Georgians and some ethnic groups in northern Siberia) belonged to the Russian Orthodox church, with large numbers also affiliated with the Catholic and Protestant churches (mainly in the Baltics) and the Armenian church (Armenians). Muslims (and

Communications Network in the Former Soviet Union

The Soviet Union had one of the largest internal (second after the United States) and external transportation systems in the world. In 1991 there were 91,910 miles (147,700 km) of railroad tracks, 552,000 miles (883,000 km) of surfaced roads, 76,560 miles (122,500 km) of navigable internal waterways, 567,000 miles (907,200 km) of internal air routes, international airlines and a merchant fleet with regular services to all parts of the world. The development, production and acquisition of equipment for the internal and external transportation systems were centrally controlled and directed under tsarist Russia, when many of the major railway lines and roads were built. The centralized planning and running of the system became more extreme under the Soviet Union, when all means of public transportation were state-owned. The extensive expansion, development and repeated reorganization of the major types of transportation were based on an approach that the Soviet Union was one state. The constituent states could only undertake limited initiatives to develop some types of local transportation services.

The extreme interdependence in transportation services among the newly independent states of the former Soviet Union and their great difficulties in orga-

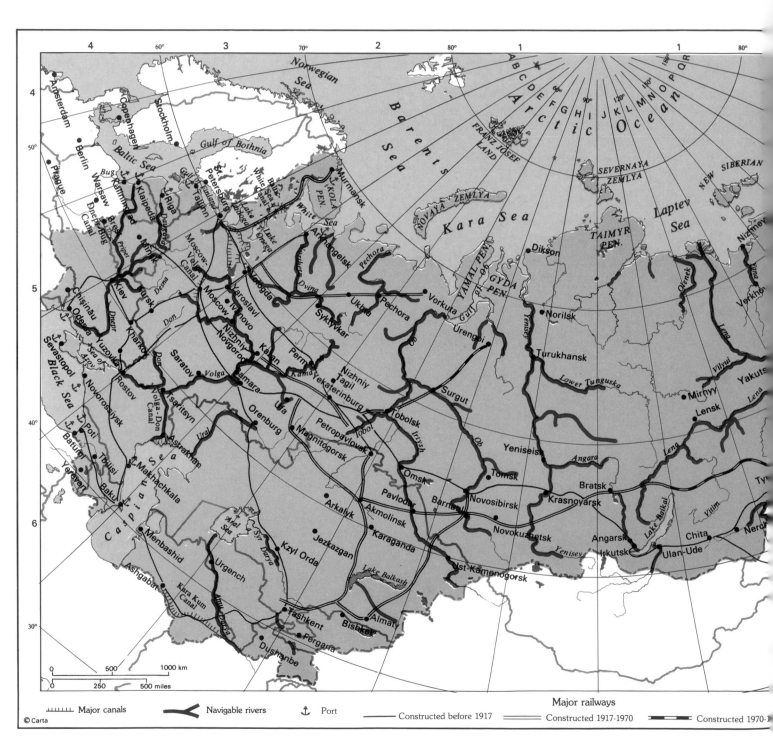

Major canals   Navigable rivers   ⚓ Port

Major railways
— Constructed before 1917   ═ Constructed 1917-1970   ▬ Constructed 1970-

© Carta

nizing transportation systems independently are the direct result of the policies of high centralization. Russia, by far the largest and most powerful of the successor states, dominates most of the transportation system of the former Soviet Union. It has, however, become largely dependent on ports of other successor states and on vital railway links that cross their territories. This is particularly crucial during the four to five months of winter when Russia has only short, remote stretches of coast that are accessible to shipping.

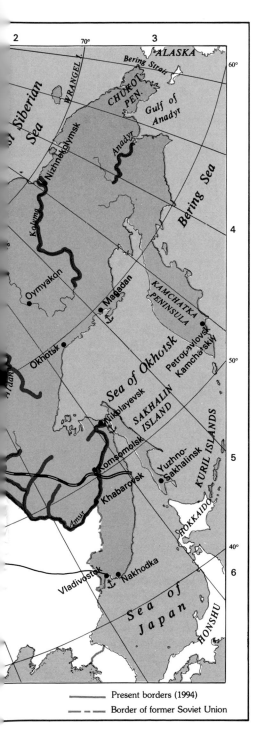

——————— Present borders (1994)
– – – – Border of former Soviet Union

Large railroad-building enterprises began in the mid-nineteenth century, under the tsarist empire, and continued into World War I. A railway network was formed between a number of urban centers and ports in the European part of the empire. The Trans-Siberian railroad (Moscow–Vladivostok), the world's longest railroad (5,775 mi./9,280 km), as well as the railway lines to Beijing and the Yellow Sea coast, the Transcaucasian (to Tbilisi and Baku), and the Trans-Turanian (to Samarkand and Tashkent) lines were also built. The total length of the railroads, many of them single-track, was 44,380 miles (71,000 km) in 1914. They were extended by 15,600 miles (nearly 25,000 km) by the mid-1930s and more than doubled in length by 1990. These included many new lines to or through the newly developed mining and industrial centers, as well as to some of the less inhabited regions of the Asiatic parts of the Soviet Union. In 1990, 47 percent of all domestic freight and 37 percent of passenger traffic were carried by the railways.

In 1914, the Russian Empire had nearly 17,000 miles (27,000 km) of metaled (hard-surfaced) roads. Many were military roads to or through frontier zones or to areas where uprisings and unrest occurred. The vast majority of the road network consisted of cart tracks. There were only 9,000 cars. The Soviet government made strenuous efforts to expand and improve the road system and the production of motor vehicles. By 1938 the Soviet Union had 54,700 miles (87,500 km) of hard-surfaced roads and 760,000 cars. The length of the motorways increased more than tenfold by 1991 and the number of vehicles (including trucks and buses), to 22 million.

The Soviet Union had the longest system of internal waterways, including all the major rivers, many of their tributaries, and modern linking canals for ships. Numerous sections of the rivers were improved. The connecting canals made internavigation possible between the Baltic, White (Arctic Ocean), Black and Caspian seas. Many of the rivers and canals are frozen in winter and therefore navigable only seven or eight months out of the year. The internal waterways played a very important role in commodities traffic, mainly in Soviet Europe. The total length of active waterways in the Russian Empire in 1914

was about 37,500 miles (60,000 km). It had more than doubled by 1991. Among the important shipping canals built by the Soviet Union are the Moscow-Volga Canal (which made Moscow an important inland port), the Baltic-White Sea Canal, the Volga-Don Canal and the Baltic-Dnepr Canal. Canals in Soviet Central Asia, mainly built for irrigation, are also used as local waterways. The ownership of over 19,000 vessels that operate on the inland waterways must be split between several of the Soviet Union's successor states.

The maritime fleet of the Soviet Union consisted (in 1991) of nearly 7,000 vessels, with a gross cargo capacity of 26 million tons (including the fishing fleet). The sharing of the maritime fleet and its continued functions in the service of the successor states are problems with which the CIS is faced.

Civil aviation started under the Soviet government (1922). Its development, both in internal and external services, came mainly after World War II. The building of passenger planes (six- and nine-seaters) began in the mid-1930s. Landing facilities and later airports were constructed on the outskirts of most large and medium-sized cities. Internal air routes totaled nearly 6,000 miles (9,500 km) in 1928; 66,000 miles (106,000 km) in 1938; 137,500 miles (220,000 km) in 1952; and 296,000 miles (474,600 km) in 1966. By 1991 the length of the network nearly doubled and the number of passengers (138 million) tripled. International air routes, which at first (in the 1940s and 1950s) were mainly confined to Communist and neighboring European states, had expanded to many countries throughout the world by the 1960s and 1970s. Aeroflot, the air carrier of the Soviet Union, became the largest civil air service system in the world. In 1991 it flew to 135 foreign destinations in 102 countries.

Most of the successor states of the Soviet Union have established their own national airlines, and already operate internal and international air services. The sharing of the Soviet Union's civil air fleet and the equipment required for its operation presented great difficulties. Most of the internal and international air services of the former Soviet Union, although reorganized, maintain most of their flight schedules under the aegis of a coordinating CIS aviation authority.

THE INDEPENDENT REPUBLICS

Russia

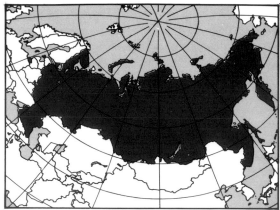

Area: 6,592,665 sq. mi. (17,075,000 sq. km)
Population (1993 estimate): 149,300,000
Natural increase (1990–1993): 0.2%
Capital city: Moscow

Population in Main Cities (1993 estimates):

Moscow: 9,000,000
St. Petersburg (Leningrad): 5,000,000
Nizhniy Novgorod (Gorki): 1,500,000

Novosibirsk: 1,500,000
Yekaterinburg (Sverdlovsk): 1,400,000
Samara (Kuibyshev): 1,300,000

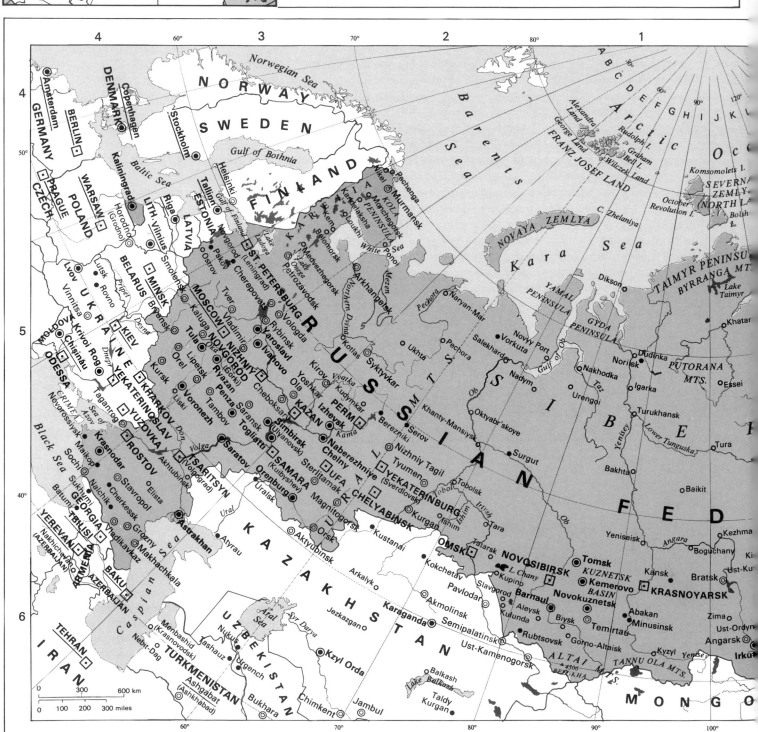

Russia is the largest state in the world. It covers 11.4 percent of the global land area and 76 percent of the area of the former Soviet Union. The country extends nearly halfway around the northern portion of the globe, including the whole of northern Asia and much of eastern and northeastern Europe. Its maritime borders touch the Atlantic Ocean and the Baltic, Barents, Black and Caspian seas on the west; the Arctic Ocean on the north; and the Pacific Ocean (Bering, Okhotsk and Japan seas) on the east.

The land borders touch Norway, Finland, Estonia, Latvia, Lithuania, Poland, Belarus and Ukraine on the west; and Georgia, Azerbaijan, Kazakhstan, Mongolia, China and North Korea on the south. It is separated from the United States (Alaska) in the northeast by the 56-mile (90-km) wide Bering Strait, and from Japan in the southeast by the 14-mile (22.5-km) wide Nemuro Strait. A small Russian enclave on the Baltic coast, around the city of Kaliningrad (formerly Königsberg), is separated from

the rest of the country by Lithuania and Belarus.

Because of its vast extent Russia has a great variety of natural landscapes, climatic conditions and peoples. Much of the area is uninhabited or only sparsely populated. The country spans eleven time zones. Russia includes seventeen ethnic, autonomous republics, five autonomous regions and ten national districts. Altogether, they make up 60 percent of Russia's land area (4 million sq. mi./10.36 million sq. km) and include 28 percent of the population.

NATURAL REGIONS

Russia is latitudinally divided into four main natural zones: the Arctic, tundra, forest (taiga) and steppes. A fifth, marginally small region—the Mediterranean (or subtropical) zone—is on the southwestern coast of the Black Sea. Views differ as to the extent of each of these natural zones and their subdivisions.

The Arctic zone in the extreme north includes most of the Russian islands and the elevated areas within the Arctic Circle: Franz Josef Land, Novaya Zemlya, Severnaya Zemlya, New Siberian Islands and the Byrranga Mountains on the Taimyr Peninsula. The ground here is frozen year round.

This is followed southward by the tundra zone, extending from the Norwegian and Finnish borders on the west to the Bering Sea on the east. Here the topsoil thaws in summer to a depth of 12 to 20 inches (30 to 50 cm) and, in some areas, to 40 inches (100 cm); deep, permanently frozen ground (permafrost) lies underneath. The tundra zone, depending on how the term is defined (whether one includes the treeless areas only or also the tundra forest), covers between 10 and 18 percent of Russia.

Much of the tundra region is marshy or waterlogged. The vegetation, which includes dwarf shrubs, berry bushes, mosses, lichens and carpets of flowers, flourishes after the summer thaw. The tundra is also characterized by swarms of mosquitos and many other insects. Utilizing the summer's long hours of sunshine, potatoes as well as certain grains and vegetables are grown in limited, well-drained areas in the south. Dwarf trees, mainly pines, are common

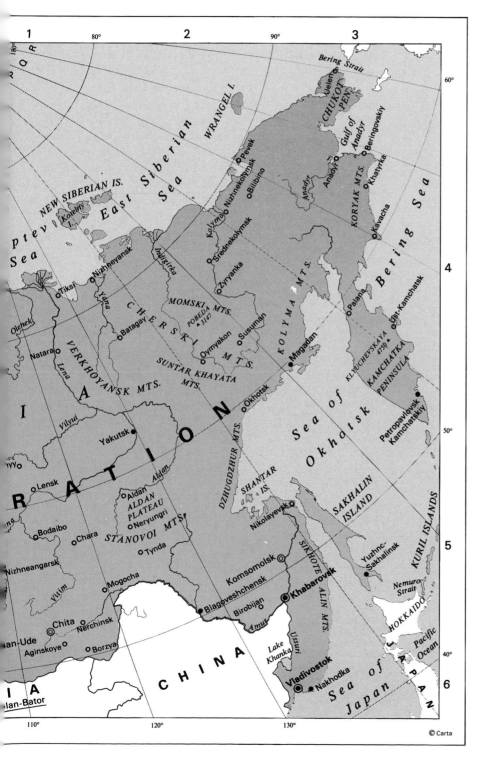

on the southern margins and form a transitional zone, known as the tundra forest, southward to the forest region.

The forest, or taiga, zone stretches across the entire country. Taken in its widest sense, the forest occupies about two-thirds of Russia, including central and eastern Siberia almost to its southern boundary. The forest zone is generally divided into the taiga (coniferous) forest proper and the belt of mixed forests along parts of its southern margin. The latter is widest in European Russia but almost absent in central and eastern Siberia. The taiga is the world's largest nontropical forest area. Pine, spruce, fir and larch are the commonest trees. Birch is widespread in the area's extreme south. The region freezes in winter and thaws to a depth of 40 to 80 inches (100 to 200 cm) in summer. Large areas are ill-drained due to the flatness of the large plains and river valleys that form much of the region. Bogs often containing extensive peat deposits are very prominent, especially in European Russia and in western Siberia. The forest zone is rich in fur-bearing animals.

The taiga region is largely unpopulated and, at most, only thinly inhabited. Only where mineral and lumber resources are extensively exploited are there concentrations of people. Agriculture is mainly practiced at the southern fringes of the region.

The steppe zone, the southernmost of the major regions, is not continuous. The steppes are widest in European Russia and southeastern Siberia, almost absent in central Siberia, and only partly present in eastern Siberia, in the areas adjoining Mongolia. The region in European Russia includes the semiarid lowlands that border the Caspian Sea on the northwest. In the north there is a transitional zone to the forest region known as the wooded steppe. Most of the steppe region is a wide, almost treeless expanse of grasslands. This is also the region of the rich black soil (chernozem), making it the most agriculturally productive part of Russia and one of the most fertile areas in the world. Before modern industrialization, this was the most populated region in Russia. Today it has the densest rural population.

The major natural zones can be subdivided into nine geographical regions, using physical and other natural characteristics as criteria.

Scandinavian Region

The Scandinavian region (Karelia and Kola Peninsula) lies in the northwest of Russia. Much of the region is a low plateau lined with hills of mostly glacial origin. An outlier of the Scandinavian highlands on the Kola Peninsula rises to 4,027 feet (1,208 m). The impact of the last European glaciation is evident everywhere. The region has numerous lakes, the largest of which are Ladoga (7,105 sq. mi./18,400 sq. km) and Onega (3,710 sq. mi./9,610 sq. km) in the extreme south. The region is largely covered with coniferous forests. The southwestern fringe (annexed from Finland in 1940) is part of Russia's outlet to the Baltic Sea.

Murmansk			
(46 m above sea level)			
Temperature		**Rainfall**	
−10°C	12.8°C	376 mm	All the year
Coldest month (average)	Hottest month (average)	Annual precipitation (average)	Main rainy season

Russian Lowlands

The Russian Lowlands extend east from the western borders to the Ural Mountains and from the Arctic Ocean south to the Caucasus and the Black and Caspian seas. The region is a largely wide, undulating plain intersected by several ranges of rounded, gently sloping hills on low plateaus, rising only a few hundred feet above the plain. These elevations are usually outcrops of old, very resistant rock formations. The most conspicuous of them are the Timan Hills (highest peak, 1,544 ft./471 m) in the northeast; the Valdai Hills (1,125 ft./343 m), the Smolensk-Moscow Ridge (1,046 ft./319 m), the Northern Uvali (960 ft./293 m) and the Middle Russian Ridge (960 ft./293 m) in the center; and the Volga Hills (1,079 ft./329 m) and Ergeni Hills (725 ft./221 m) in the south. The northern part of the region is covered by a mantle of glacial deposits with numerous moraines. Large areas in the north are also marshy or waterlogged. The Volga River drains a large part of the region to the Caspian Sea. The Don River drains the southwestern lowlands to the Sea of Azov (Black Sea). The Pechora, Mezen and Northern Dvina rivers drain the northern part of the region to the Arctic Ocean, while the

Western Dvina and Neva rivers drain the northwestern areas to the Baltic Sea.

Astrakhan			
(18 m above sea level)			
Temperature		**Rainfall**	
−6.9°C	25.1°C	190 mm	May–July
Coldest month (average)	Hottest month (average)	Annual precipitation (average)	Main rainy season

Caucasus Region

Russia includes the northern part of the Great Caucasus, extending northwest to southeast from the Black Sea to the Caspian. Its line largely follows the watershed formed between the rivers flowing north into Russia and those flowing south into the Transcaucasian states. The range's highest peaks (Elbrus [18,498 ft./5,642 m], Dykhtau [17,062 ft./5,204 m] and Kazbek [16,500 ft./5,033 m]) and glaciers are within Russia or cross its boundary. The mountains are deeply cut by numerous, almost parallel valleys that broaden and open northward. The piedmont and foothills extend into the Stavropol Uplands (highest peak, 2,723 ft./831 m), a moderately elevated, hilly area of the outlying highlands in the extreme north. The population is concentrated in the lower valleys and foothills, where numerous industrial towns have developed, utilizing the hydroelectric energy from the streams flowing from the high mountains and the mineral (namely oil and natural gas) and other resources available. The mountain slopes, up to an altitude of about 6,500 feet (2,000 m), are partly covered with forest. Areas up to 8,200 feet (2,500 m) are used for grazing in summer. Agriculture is practiced in the valleys and on the low spurs and foothills below 5,000 feet (1,500 m).

Ural Region

The Ural Mountains, with their northern (Pag Khog Range) and southern (Mugojari Uplands) extensions, stretch from the Arctic Ocean south toward the Aral Sea. The 1,900-mile (3,040-km) long system, which consists of a central range with noncontinuous, parallel chains, is the accepted frontier between Europe and Asia. Its slopes rise gently on the European side and are steeper and more abrupt on the Siberian side. Elevations only occasionally exceed 3,300 feet (1,000 m). The highest peaks are Narodnaya (6,213 ft./1,893 m) and Telposiz (5,302 ft./1,617 m) in the north, and Yamantau (5,377 ft./1,640 m) in the south. The system, which is 60 to 80 miles (100 to 130 km) wide, also forms the watershed between the rivers of European Russia (Volga and Pechora) and Siberia (Ob).

The Urals, especially the central and southern foothills, comprise one of the richest regions in mineral resources. It is one of Russia's largest and most varied industrial regions, giving rise to densely inhabited subregions. The northern Urals have Arctic and tundra characteristics, while the central Urals are clad with taiga forests. The lower areas of the southern Urals are steppe country and the region's main agricultural producers; above and to the north, lumbering is common.

Yekaterinburg			
(282 m above sea level)			
Temperature		Rainfall	
–15.6°C	17.2°C	462 mm	Apr.–Sept.
Coldest month (average)	Hottest month (average)	Annual precipitation (average)	Main rainy season

West Siberian Lowlands

The West Siberian Lowlands extend 900 to 1,100 miles (1,450 to 1,770 km) from the Ural Mountains (west) to the Central Siberian Highlands (east). The transition to and from the flat, slightly undulating plain in the west and east is an abrupt one. The Yenisey River Valley, which runs parallel and close to the western edge of the Central Siberian Uplands, is generally taken as the region's eastern frontier. The lowlands also extend from the Kara Sea (Arctic Ocean) south to the Kazakh Steppe, straddling two of the major latitudinal natural zones, the tundra and the taiga, and including some areas on the northern edge of the steppe region.

The lowland region is largely waterlogged or swampy, mainly because of its flatness, the small gradient of the riverbeds and the extensive glacial deposits (with numerous lines of moraines). The extensive marshy areas are augmented each spring by the early thaw in the south, while the northern river outlets remain frozen and clogged. Wide areas in the north and center are covered with peat bogs. The region is drained mostly by the Ob River (longest river in Russia and the fifth longest in the world) and its tributaries to the Arctic Ocean. The eastern fringes are drained by the Yenisey River (Russia's second largest river and the highest in discharge volume). The northern and central parts of the region remained largely unpopulated until the discovery of large oil and natural gas deposits. Today, it is one of the world's richest regions in oil and gas. Rich iron ore deposits have also been discovered in the northeast. Most agriculture is practiced in the extreme south. The region is also a major source of timber.

Salekhard			
(35 m above sea level)			
Temperature		Rainfall	
–24.4°C	13.8°C	465 mm	May–Oct.
Coldest month (average)	Hottest month (average)	Annual precipitation (average)	Main rainy season

Central Siberian Uplands

The Central Siberian Uplands extend from the Yenisey Valley east to the Lena (Russia's third longest river and second highest in discharge volume) Valley, and from the Arctic Ocean (Kara and Laptev seas) south to the Central Asian highlands. Much of the region is a low plateau deeply dissected by a dense network of rivers. Although most of the area never exceeds 1,200 feet (400 m) in elevation, the landscape has a hilly to mountainous nature because of the deep river valleys. The Putorana Mountains in the northwest are the highest part of the plateau, with areas rising from 3,000 to 5,577 feet (914 to 1,704 m).

The wide Taimyr Peninsula, dominated by the east-west Byrranga Mountains (highest peak, 3,760 ft./1,146 m), forms the northernmost part of the region, within the Arctic zone. This is followed southward by a broad east-west depression, the North Siberian Lowland, that separates the Taimyr Peninsula from the region's main upland areas. This depression, like the northern uplands, has typical tundra characteristics. The tundra gradually gives way to tundra forest and to the taiga, farther south. The latter covers almost the entire southern half of the region, which is very sparsely populated except for small areas in the valleys and along the larger tributaries of the Yenisey and Lena rivers. Natural gas, coal, ores and lumber are the main economic attractions.

Northeastern Siberia

Northeastern Siberia comprises the large peninsula between the Arctic (Laptev and East Siberian seas) and Pacific (Bering and Okhotsk seas) oceans, stretching from the Lena Valley in the west to the Bering Strait in the northeast. The region also includes the Arctic New Siberian and Wrangel islands, the northeast Pacific Commander (Komandor) Islands, and two main peninsulas—Chukot and Kamchatka. Northeastern Siberia is the most remote, desolate region of Russia. It has a very thin, widely dispersed population whose ethnic characteristics are largely preserved. The largely mountainous region includes a northern extension of the geologically young (Alpine) mountain systems of central and eastern Asia and much dissected plateaus. The most conspicuous ranges are the Verkhoyansk, Suntar Khayata, Cherski, Momski, Kolyma and Koryak. They rise from 6,000 to 10,000 feet (1,900–3,000 m), with the highest peak (Mount Pobeda in the Cherski Range) at 10,325 feet (3,147 m). The mountains of the Kamchatka Peninsula are outstanding in their volcanic nature and altitude. They include eighteen active volcanos, several rising above 11,000 feet (3,300 m); Mount Klyuchevskaya (15,584 ft./4,750 m) is one of the largest in the world.

Most of the region is drained northward to the Arctic Ocean by a series of rivers, the largest of which are the Lena, Yana, Indigirka and Kolyma. These flow in valleys that broaden northward into a wide lowland and large, flat deltas. Much of the lowland is marshy or waterlogged and, except along the rivers, inaccessible during the summer thaw. Most of the region has tundra characteristics, yet large parts of the mountains are permanently frozen and barren. The taiga extends only over the lower parts of the south and much of the Kamchatka Peninsula. There are few exploited mineral resources (mainly coal), although ore deposits (gold, copper, tin) are known to exist. Fishing is widespread along the coasts and main rivers in summer, as is hunting and lumbering in the south.

Anadyr			
(62 m above sea level)			
Temperature		Rainfall	
–22.7°C	10.5°C	260 mm	July–Oct.
Coldest month (average)	Hottest month (average)	Annual precipitation (average)	Main rainy season

Kotelny Island (sea level)			
Temperature		**Rainfall**	
−29.9°C	2.5°C	130 mm	May–Aug.
Coldest month (average)	Hottest month (average)	Annual precipitation (average)	Main rainy season

Irkutsk (469 m above sea level)			
Temperature		**Rainfall**	
−20.9°C	17.5°C	450 mm	June–Sept.
Coldest month (average)	Hottest month (average)	Annual precipitation (average)	Main rainy season

Russian Central Asia

Russian Central Asia (or South-Central Siberia) is a region of mountains, plateaus and foothills wedged between southeastern Kazakhstan, Mongolia and northern China. It includes the northern parts of some of Central Asia's high mountain ranges, from which all the great rivers of Siberia rise. The physical pattern of the region is very complex, with mountain ranges, often extremely broken, running in different directions and interspersed with basins, valleys, gorges and lakes. The most prominent ranges are the Altai (extending into Mongolia and including the region's highest peak, Mount Belukha, at 14,783 ft./ 4,506 m), Tannu Ola, West Sayan, East Sayan and Kuznets Alatau in the west; and the Yablonoi, Baikal, Barguzin, Daur and Borshchovochny ranges in the east. The much-dissected Angara Plateau, in the center, and the Vitim Plateau, in the east, have mountainous landscapes. The great bend of the Lena River Valley, above Yakutsk, forms a distinct frontier between this region and the Central Siberian highlands and plateaus to the north. Lake Baikal (12,162 sq. mi./ 31,400 sq. km), in the east, is the deepest (5,315 ft./1,620 m) lake in the world and Russia's largest freshwater lake. It is the source of the Angara River, a large tributary of the Lena and an important source of hydroelectric energy.

Taiga characteristics predominate much farther south here than in other parts of Siberia because of the elevation of most of the region. Tundra and arctic conditions prevail over the higher mountain ranges. Only the lower areas of the extreme south have steppe conditions— some semiarid valleys and basins. The region is rich in mineral resources, coal and hydroelectric energy. There are two main areas of population and economic activity: the Kuznetsk Basin (with its large coal deposits) in the west and the Baikal-Angara district in the east. This region has the most inhabited and industrialized areas in Asiatic Russia east of the Urals.

The Far East (Southeast Asiatic Russia)

The Far East region of Russia borders on northeast China, on North Korea (only a short section), and on the seas of Japan and Okhotsk. This region, Russia's outlet to the Pacific, includes the Kuril Islands and Sakhalin Island, extending toward Japan. The region contains Russia's southernmost coast and port (Vladivostok), but even these are frozen and inaccessible in winter. The region is largely mountainous with deeply dissected plateaus, rising from altitudes of 6,500 to 7,800 feet (2,000 to 2,400 m). The highest elevations are the Stanovoi Range (7,870 ft./2,400 m), Aldan Plateau, and Dzhugdzhur Range in the north; the Burein Range (7,816 ft./2,380 m) in the center; and the Sikhote Alin Mountains (6,810 ft./2,075 m) in the south.

The coast consists generally of a narrow, lowland strip that broadens near the river estuaries. The lowland areas are made up of small basins and river valleys, mainly those of the Amur River and its large tributaries (especially the Ussuri). The population and economic activities are mostly concentrated in and around these valleys. The Amur, which drains most of the region, is one of Russia's (and Asia's) longest rivers. Much of its course forms the frontier with China, while the lower course is in Russia. The lowlands also include the Lake Khanka Basin (shared with China) in the south, and northern Sakhalin Island. Nearly the entire region is part of the forest (taiga) latitudinal zone. The higher parts of the highlands have tundra characteristics. The Kuril Islands have numerous volcanos, while Sakhalin Island and the south are repeatedly subject to earthquakes.

Vladivostok (138 m above sea level)			
Temperature		**Rainfall**	
−14.6°C	20°C	725 mm	May–Sept.
Coldest month (average)	Hottest month (average)	Annual precipitation (average)	Main rainy season

CLIMATE

A wide variety of climatic conditions prevails over Russia's vast area. The climate varies according to latitude, elevation, proximity to oceanic influences and position. The major climatic regions correspond to the natural latitudinal zones. Except for marginal areas, Russia's climate is generally cool to cold, with various degrees of continental characteristics. Winters are mildest in the southwest along the Black Sea, where average temperatures for the coldest month (January) are a few degrees above freezing. Winters are most severe in the heart of northeast Siberia, where the average temperature for the same month is −58°F (−51°C) and minimum temperatures reach −96°F (−71°C). Winters are less cold in the extreme northwest (the Kola Peninsula coastal area) than in northeast Siberia. Summers are hottest in southeast European Russia (the Caspian Lowlands), in southwest Siberia, and in some of the valleys and basins in south-central Siberia, where temperatures may exceed 100°F (38°C). The mean daily range of temperatures in summer is particularly great over central, southern and northeastern Siberia; in some areas in July, it exceeds an average of 40°F (22°C).

Most of Russia has relatively dry winters. Large areas receive an average of less than 4 inches (100 mm) of precipitation, if any, during winter, while the average for more than three-quarters of the total area is less than 6 inches (150 mm). Only in parts of European Russia (mainly in the west and southwest), the Urals and some Siberian highland and northeastern coastal areas are those amounts exceeded. Although most of the precipitation derives from summer rainfall, a season which in many areas includes late spring and/or autumn, over two-thirds of Russia receives an average of less than 20 inches (500 mm) of rain annually. Much of southern Siberia and the Caspian Lowlands have an average annual precipitation of less than 10 inches (250 mm). Most of European Russia, part of the western and central and southern highlands of Siberia, and the Far East region receive an average precipitation of 20 to 40 inches (500 to 1,000 mm) annually. Only small areas of the high mountain ranges receive larger quantities. Parts of the Far East region benefit from summer monsoon rains.

POPULATION

The population is estimated at 149.3 million (1993), of whom nearly 108 million live in European Russia. It was 147.4 million at the 1989 census. The average annual rate of natural increase for the 1980s was 0.6 percent, decreasing to 0.1 percent in recent years; the rate was higher among several ethnic groups in the autonomous areas, and lower among Russians, especially in the large metropolitan areas. The high death rate in the first two decades of Communist rule and the heavy loss of life during the two world wars were mainly responsible for the slow increase in population in the first half of this century. Russia in its present boundaries numbered about 100 million inhabitants in the mid-1920s, 105 million in 1933, 114 million in 1951, 117.5 million in 1960 and 130 million in 1970. The proportion of Asiatic Russians in the total population has increased significantly, from about 10 percent in the mid-1920s to 28 percent at present.

In 1989, Russians were 81.5 percent of the population; Tatars, 3.8 percent; Ukrainians, 3 percent; Chuvash, 1.2 percent; Bashkirs, 0.9 percent; and Belorussians, 0.8 percent. Germans, Mordvinians, Dagestanis, Udmurts, Mari, Kazakhs, Jews, Armenians and over fifty other ethnic groups, each with its own language and culture, make up nearly 9 percent of the population. Most of these ethnic groups are concentrated in Asiatic Russia, where they lived long before they came under Russian sovereignty. Under Soviet rule, thirty-one ethnic groups in Russia had gained some form of autonomy. The percentage of Russians has declined from 83.3 percent in 1959 to 82.8 percent in 1970, especially in Asiatic Russia. Russians, Ukrainians, Belorussians, Germans and other nationalities of the Indo-European group form nearly 86 percent of the population. They make up nearly the entire population in most of European Russia and are a majority in most of the western, southern and southeastern (Far East) parts of Asiatic Russia. There are 25.3 million Russians living in the former Soviet republics outside Russia: 15 million in the European republics, where they form 20 percent of the population, and 10.3 million in the Asiatic states, where they are 16 percent.

The Caucasian group, which includes Abkhazians, Circassians, Chechens, Ingush, Adyghians, Avars, Nakhians, Dagestanis, Lezgins and Tabasarans, is concentrated in and around the northern Caucasus. The Uralic group includes the Karelians, Saamians, Komi, Komi-Permyaks, Udmurts, Mari and Mordvinians, who live mainly in the northern and eastern parts of European Russia, and the Khants, Mansi, Vengri, Nentsi (Nenets), Nganasans and Selkups, who live in northern Siberia. The Tatars of the Altaic group are the largest non-European minority; they live mainly in the Middle Volga (Kazan), southern Urals and southwest Siberia. This group also includes the Chuvash (who live in the Middle Volga Valley and southwest Siberia), the Bashkirs (southern Urals and southwest Siberia) and the Kalmyks (Caspian Lowlands, Lower Volga Valley). The Kumyks, Nogay, Balkars and

Main cities	Population
In European Russia	
Moscow	9,000,000
St. Petersburg (Leningrad)	5,000,000
Nizhniy Novgorod (Gorki)	1,500,000
Samara (Kuibyshev)	1,300,000
Kazan	1,100,000
Ufa	1,100,000
Perm	1,100,000
Rostov	1,000,000
Tsaritsyn (Volgograd)	1,000,000
Saratov	920,000
Voronezh	900,000
Izhevsk	640,000
Togliatti	640,000
Yaroslavl	640,000
Simbirsk (Ulyanovsk)	630,000
Krasnodar (Yekaterinodar)	625,000
Orenburg	550,000
Penza	550,000
Tula	540,000
Ryazan	520,000
Naberezhniye Chelny	500,000
In Asiatic Russia	
Novosibirsk	1,500,000
Yekaterinburg (Sverdlovsk)	1,400,000
Chelyabinsk	1,200,000
Omsk	1,200,000
Krasnoyarsk	1,000,000
Vladivostok	760,000
Irkutsk	630,000
Barnaul	620,000
Khabarovsk	610,000
Novokuznetsk	610,000
Kemerovo	530,000
Tomsk	510,000

Karachayevs live in the northern Caucasian districts. The Tuvans, Khakas, Shors and Altais live in southern Siberia and Russian Central Asia; small numbers of Yakuts, Dolgani and Tungus are widely dispersed over central, northern and northeastern Siberia. Other ethnic groups (Eskimos, Chukchi, Koryaks, Yukaghirs and Aleuts) live mainly on the fringes of northeastern Siberia, the Kamchatka Peninsula and Sakhalin Island.

The Russians, Ukrainians, Belorussians and some of the native people of Siberia are mostly followers (or descendants of followers) of the Russian Orthodox church. Islam is widespread among the non-European people of southern Siberia, southeast European Russia and the northern Caucasus. A growing revival of religious activity has taken place since the collapse of Communist repression.

About three-quarters of Russia is either thinly populated or virtually uninhabited. This is particularly true of northern European Russia and over 90 percent of Asiatic Russia. The average population density for the country as a whole is 3.4 persons per square mile (8.8 per sq. km). The average density

Ethnic Composition
1989

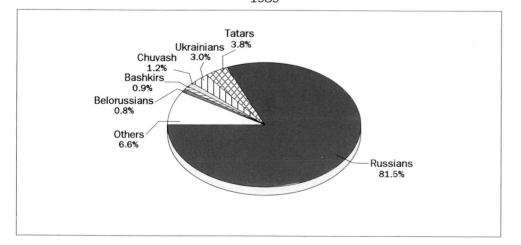

Tatars 3.8%
Ukrainians 3.0%
Chuvash 1.2%
Bashkirs 0.9%
Belorussians 0.8%
Others 6.6%
Russians 81.5%

for Sakha, formerly Yakutia (nearly 1.2 million sq. mi./3.1 million sq. km), in east central Siberia, is 0.9 person per square mile (0.35 per sq. km); in northeastern Siberia (1.5 million sq. mi./3.9 million sq. km) it is 0.8 person per square mile (0.2 per sq. km); and in the tundra region of central Siberia, only 0.16 person per square mile (0.06 per sq. km). Central European Russia, in a belt that narrows eastward toward the southern Urals, has the highest density: 863 persons per square mile (334 per sq. km) in the administrative region of Moscow (18,146 sq. mi./47,000 sq. km) and 202 persons per square mile (78 per sq. km) in the St. Petersburg region. The industrial subregions of the southern Urals, southern Siberia and Russian Central Asia have densities of 120 to 150 persons per square mile, and the southeast district of the Far East region has 210 persons per square mile.

Seventy-four percent of the population lives in urban areas. Urbanization expanded rapidly after World War II, with industrialization and the mechanization of agriculture. The urban population was estimated at nearly 15 percent in 1920. It was 33 percent in 1935, when there were only two cities (Moscow and St. Petersburg) with a population of over 1 million, nine cities with 500,000 to 1 million inhabitants, and sixteen cities with 250,000 to 500,000. It rose from 52 percent in 1959 to 62 percent in 1970. There are presently fourteen cities with over 1 million inhabitants; twenty-one cities with 500,000 to 1 million; and forty-seven cities with 250,000 to 500,000.

ECONOMY

Russia's economy was largely agricultural at the time of the Communist Revolution. It has since been transformed into the world's second largest industrial power. It also attained world prominence in the production of numerous mineral and energy resources, and made significant advances in the expansion, productivity, mechanization and organization of agriculture. All this was done within a Soviet framework of successive five-year government plans.

World War II had caused enormous material damage and loss of life. It took almost two decades to recover. Much of the postwar industrial development effort was channeled toward building up the Soviet Union's military and political influence. Russia's economy has been in a state of crisis and reorganization since the breakup of the Soviet Union. There has been a substantial fall in the output of important energy (oil, gas, coal) and mineral (iron, copper, bauxite) resources, as well as in industry and agriculture. Still, Russia is the world's richest country in mineral resources and one of the largest and most productive (albeit insufficiently modernized or efficient) industrial and agricultural powers.

Mineral Resources

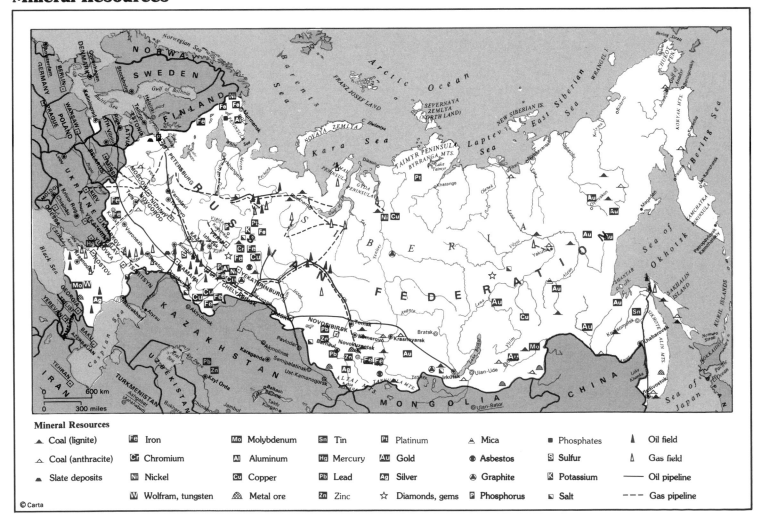

Mineral Resources						
▲ Coal (lignite)	Fe Iron	Mo Molybdenum	Sn Tin	Pt Platinum	⊿ Mica	■ Phosphates	⬛ Oil field
△ Coal (anthracite)	Cr Chromium	Al Aluminum	Hg Mercury	Au Gold	◉ Asbestos	S Sulfur	⬛ Gas field
▲ Slate deposits	Ni Nickel	Cu Copper	Pb Lead	Ag Silver	◎ Graphite	K Potassium	—— Oil pipeline
	W Wolfram, tungsten	⬙ Metal ore	Zn Zinc	☆ Diamonds, gems	P Phosphorus	⬚ Salt	--- Gas pipeline

© Carta

Agriculture

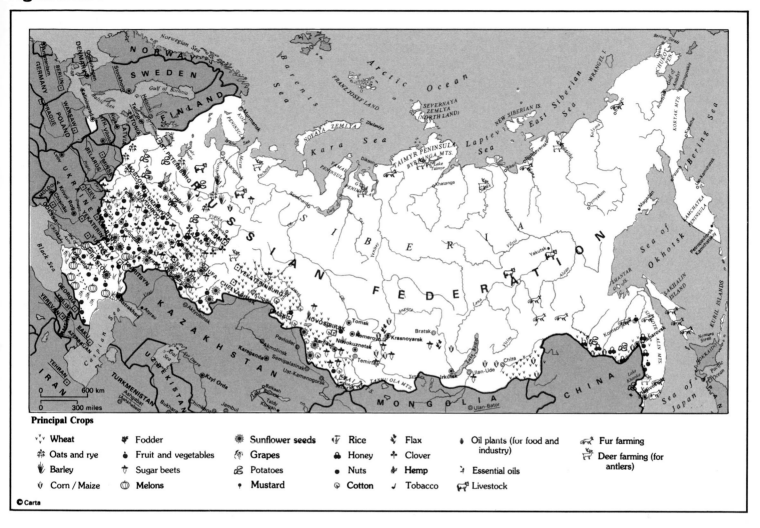

Principal Crops

Wheat	Fodder	Sunflower seeds	Rice	Flax	Oil plants (for food and industry)	Fur farming
Oats and rye	Fruit and vegetables	Grapes	Honey	Clover		Deer farming (for antlers)
Barley	Sugar beets	Potatoes	Nuts	Hemp	Essential oils	
Corn / Maize	Melons	Mustard	Cotton	Tobacco	Livestock	

© Carta

Agriculture

Russia's arable lands are nearly all confined to the steppe region, the southern forest region and small, isolated areas to the north. Climatic and soil conditions preclude about 70 percent of the land area from agriculture (except by artificial means and special technology). Only 15 percent of the land is cultivated, with a small, additional percentage used as seasonal pasture. Climatic conditions also limit the range of crops that can be grown. Nearly 90 percent of the farmland is devoted to cereals, maize, fodder and potatoes. Wheat is the main crop in the south, while rye, oats and fodder are more widespread in the north. The rich black-soil (chernozem) region in Russia produces a large share of the agricultural output, especially cereals. Rice is grown in the Lower Volga region and in the lowlands north of the Caucasus. Various fruits and vegetables are also widely grown. The main industrial crops are sugar beets, flax and sunflower seeds. Tobacco and cotton are grown in the extreme south. Russia is the world's largest producer of rye, oats, barley, potatoes and flax.

The breeding of cattle, pigs, sheep and goats is widespread and of primary importance in many farming communities. Large quantities of meat and milk are produced; in value, they are second to grains. There is large-scale breeding of reindeer in the north. Many farms, especially in Siberia, also breed fur-bearing animals.

Large, semidesert areas in southeast European Russia (Lower Volga region, lowlands north of the Caucasus) and on the southern fringes of Asiatic Russia (including the Far East) are under irrigation. Cultivated areas were expanded by the drainage of marshy and waterlogged lands, mainly in Asiatic Russia. Russia's forests are one of the world's largest sources of timber and pulp; they yielded 13,920 million cubic feet (392 million cu. m) of timber in 1989.

Mineral Resources

Russia has a great variety of minerals and is the world's wealthiest country in mineral output. For many years it was the world's largest oil producer (producing about 90 percent of the total output of the former Soviet Union). However, due to a substantial decrease in production in recent years, it fell to third place (after Saudi Arabia and the United States); 570 million tons of oil were produced in 1987 and 296 million tons in 1992. Seventy percent of the oil comes from fields in western Siberia, 13 percent from the southern Urals and 17 percent from European Russia (mainly the northern Caucasus and Lower Volga regions). Russia is the world's second largest producer of natural gas (after the United States); about 600,000 million cubic meters were produced in 1991. The main areas of production are in northwest Siberia and the southern Urals. Russia is also the world's third largest producer of coal (lignite and anthracite) (after China and the United States). Huge amounts of hydroelectric and atomic energy are produced and used, mainly in the inhabited parts of Russia.

Large quantities of iron ore are mined in the central and southern Urals, in Russian Central Asia and south of Moscow (Kursk). Russia is a leading producer of gold and platinum, mined in central and eastern Siberia and in the Urals.

It is also one of the largest producers of diamonds, silver and mercury. Other important minerals are nickel (Kola Peninsula, Urals), chromium, bauxite (aluminum), copper, lead, tin, zinc, tungsten (wolfram), cobalt, molybdenum and uranium. Mining is mostly carried out in the Urals, the highlands of south, central and eastern Siberia, the Caucasus and some of the hilly areas of European Russia. Russia is also rich in nonmetallic minerals, such as asbestos, phosphates, potassium and salt.

Industry

Russia has a vast and extremely diversified industry that plays a dominant role in the economy and pattern of employment, especially since the 1960s. Over 70 percent of the former Soviet Union's industrial production was either carried out in Russia or was largely dependent on it. The internal economic reorganization, underway since 1990, and the disintegration of the Soviet Union have affected many of Russia's

Industry

Main Industrial Products

- ◢ Metals
- ⊖ Farm machinery, tractors
- 🚗 Car assembly
- ✕ Oil refinery
- ⚗ Chemicals
- 🏭 Timber and wood products
- ⬛ Building materials, cement
- ⬛ Textiles
- ▽ Food and beverage
- ⌐ Fishery
- ⚓ Ships, dockyard
- ⚡ Nuclear power station
- ⚡ Hydroelectric power station
- ⚡ Thermal power station
- ⚓ Port

industries, slowed down production and paralyzed development.

The most important industry is metallurgy. It was often given priority in the Soviet industrial development programs and is the backbone of many other industries. The big centers are found near the main sources of iron (and other ores), coal and other forms of energy, as well as in areas that were already densely populated before large-scale industrialization began. These centers include the southern Urals, the western

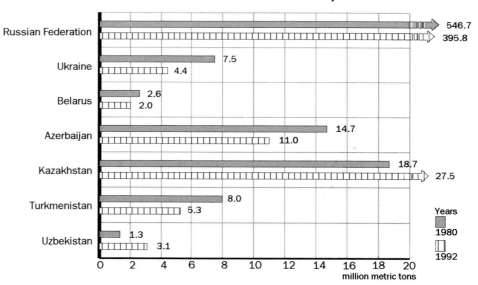

**Oil Production
in Russia and Other Selected Republics**

	million metric tons
Russian Federation	546.7 / 395.8
Ukraine	7.5 / 4.4
Belarus	2.6 / 2.0
Azerbaijan	14.7 / 11.0
Kazakhstan	18.7 / 27.5
Turkmenistan	8.0 / 5.3
Uzbekistan	1.3 / 3.1

Years
1980
1992

© Carta

part of Russian Central Asia (Kuznetsk Basin), Moscow and its environs, the Middle Volga Valley (Kazan, Samara), the Baikal region and the southern Far East. Apart from ferrous metallurgy, there is also a large, highly developed industry in nonferrous metals (especially aluminum). Virtually all types of machinery, vehicles (75 percent of the 1.9 million cars and trucks and the 500,000 tractors made in the Soviet Union in 1990 were produced in Russia), railway cars, agricultural equipment, ships, airplanes, engines, equipment for power stations, mining and oil refineries and iron and steel products are produced. A very large and highly developed military industry (much reduced in recent years) occupied a substantial share in the production capacity.

The chemical industry, which includes large petrochemical and gas-chemical enterprises, is concentrated mainly in the southern Urals, the Middle and Lower Volga Valley, the northern Caucasus and in and around Moscow. Many large plants are scattered over other, smaller industrial areas, as well. Fertilizers and other chemicals required for agriculture are an important sector of this industry. Synthetic fibers, rubber and plastics are produced on a large scale, as are various synthetic building and household materials; the main centers are in and around Moscow and St. Petersburg and in the southern Urals.

A wide range of fine instruments and electronics, mostly for industrial and military use and for public services, are produced mainly in Moscow and its surrounding area (within a radius of 100 miles), St. Petersburg and the Middle Volga region. The production of electric equipment and household goods, manufactured in most large industrial districts, has expanded considerably since the 1970s. The building materials industry (especially cement and bricks) is widespread; the main centers are central Russia, the Middle Volga region, the northern Caucasus and southwest Siberia.

Russia has one of the world's most extensive timber, wood products, pulp and paper industries. The centers are mostly located inside or on the fringes of the vast forests of northern Russia and Siberia, especially along the main rivers.

The textile, clothing and footwear industry, spread throughout the inhabited parts of the country, is an important sector in many of the smaller industrial centers. The food, beverage and tobacco industries are also widespread.

There is hardly any branch of industry that is not well represented in Russia. However, most branches lag conspicuously behind those in other industrial countries with regard to modernization, productivity and quality. The process of privatization, along with the influx of foreign capital, partners and know-how, is expected to bring about fundamental changes in the methods of operation and organization of many industries.

Employment of Russians in the Non-Russian Republics
Selected Branches (1987)

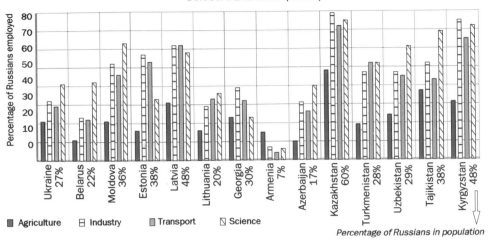

Percentage of Russians employed

■ Agriculture ⊟ Industry ▨ Transport ▧ Science

Percentage of Russians in population

Trade

Russia has a very large and extensive foreign trade. It is still the principal trading partner of the newly independent states of the former Soviet Union and of some countries that, until 1990, were members of Comecon (the Soviet economic bloc). The main trading partners outside the ex-Communist countries are Germany, Finland, the United Kingdom, the United States, Serbia, Italy, Japan, China and India. Main exports are oil and oil products; natural gas (piped directly to central and western Europe); coal; iron and steel products; vehicles; agricultural machinery; machines, machine tools and industrial equipment; textiles; timber and paper; chemicals; building materials; and food. Arms and military equipment are still important exports (though on a much smaller scale since the collapse of the USSR). Imports include raw materials (mostly from the ex-Soviet states), high technology, advanced industrial products and equipment, and food. Efforts are being made to expand trade mainly with western Europe, North America, China and Japan.

HISTORY

Eastern Slav tribes settled in what is now central European Russia and northern Ukraine between the fifth and seventh centuries. Russia's history is generally considered to begin in the late ninth century, when the Scandinavians (Varangians), known locally as the Rus, established the principalities of Kiev and Novgorod. The Varangians controlled the trade routes between the Baltic region and the Black and Caspian seas—in essence, between northeastern

Europe and the Mediterranean lands and the Middle East.

In the course of the tenth century, the Kiev principality expanded over most of the area inhabited by the southern Slavs (including small Russian principalities and towns controlled by the Varangians) and defeated the Khazar kingdom, which dominated the area between the Lower Dnepr and Lower Volga. By the end of the tenth century, it extended from the Baltic to the Black Sea and from the Volga to the Carpathians. It embraced Eastern (Greek-Byzantine) Christianity in 988. Russians became the ruling elite. The Kiev state reached its peak of power and prosperity in the early eleventh century, under the rule of Vladimir I and his successors. Kiev, now a grand duchy, declined in the twelfth century resulting from rivalries within the ruling dynasty and the growth of competing independent principalities. Three main centers emerged: Novgorod in the north; Suzdal (and later Vladimir) between the Upper Volga and Oka; and Halicz (Galicia) in the southwest.

The duke of Vladimir occupied and sacked Kiev in 1169 and assumed the title of Grand Duke. In 1224, Russia was invaded by the Tatars (Mongols), who, by 1240, conquered most of the country. The Russian principalities came under the suzerainty of the Tatar khanate of the Golden Horde, which levied them for tribute. This continued throughout the fourteenth century and well into the fifteenth. It was during this period that Moscow rose to become the leading Russian principality. The subjugation to the Tatars ended in 1480 after the decline of their empire and its breakup into the

three rival khanates of Crimea, Kazan and Astrakhan. The Russian principalities, however, were now faced with the rise of Lithuania, which gained control over parts of northern Russia.

The sixteenth century saw the expansion of the Muscovite state and its rise toward becoming the kingdom (tsardom) of all Russia. Several Russian principalities (such as Ryazan and Pskov) at first were annexed or regained from Lithuania (Smolensk), but under Ivan IV (the Terrible), the first duke of Moscow to assume the title of tsar, large areas of the Middle and Lower Volga region were conquered, including Kazan (1552) and Astrakhan (1556). The Russians also pushed into western Siberia (1583) and established their first settlements there, thus opening the way to further expansion that, by the end of the seventeenth century, brought them to the Amur Valley and the Far East. The Tatars, who reappeared briefly in central Russia in 1571, occupied and burned Moscow. The late sixteenth and early seventeenth centuries were a period of instability, unrest, rebellion and of invasions by Poles, Lithuanians and Swedes. A new dynasty, the Romanovs, who ruled Russia until the Communist Revolution (1917), gained the throne in 1613. Wars with Poland and Sweden, periods of internal upheaval, and incursions by Tatars and Turks in the south and southeast recurred in the seventeenth century. Russia managed to regain a large part of Ukraine but failed to gain access to the Baltic Sea. The clergy and nobility at this time became much more influential.

The period of Peter the Great (1689–1725) is generally taken as a turning point in Russian history. The tsar, in addition to expanding Russia's territorial domain in the Baltic region, southern Siberia and Kamchatka, introduced West European administrative and military concepts, technology, science and arts. Many foreign experts were put into key positions. Peter founded the city of St. Petersburg and made it his capital. His reforms affected the upper classes but hardly had any influence on the masses.

The ensuing period, in which six successors (mostly female) held the throne, is described as an eclipse in the rise of Russia and its monarchical role. This ended with the reign of Catherine II

(1762–1796), when some of the west-ernizing measures adopted by Peter the Great and the territorial expansion were resumed. Russia gained a major share in the final partition of Poland (1795) and a wide outlet to the Black Sea, including the Crimea, in two wars with Turkey. At this time the living conditions and rights of most of the rural population, especially the serfs, worsened considerably as the privileges and authority of the gentry grew. A revolt by the peasants and Cossacks (1772–1775) was brutally put down. Under Alexander I (1801–1825), the grand-son of Catherine II, Russia annexed Fin-land (1809) and Bessarabia (1812). Then came Napoleon's invasion of Russia, the conquest and burning of Moscow by the Russians, and Napoleon's retreat and defeat. Although the Napoleonic cam-paign in Russia lasted only six months, it had a very deep impact on the role Russia was to play in European and world affairs. The territorial gains made in Poland and on the western boundaries remained almost unchanged (except in Bessarabia) until 1917.

Russia's nineteenth-century history is marked by extensive territorial expan-sion in the Caucasus, Transcaucasia, Central Asia and the Far East; by in-volvement in a number of European wars; and by the suppression of internal rebellions and the growth of revolution-ary activities. The annexation of Trans-caucasia was completed in 1864, that of Uzbekistan and parts of Kyrgyzstan and Tajikistan by 1876, and of Turkmenistan and Kazakhstan by 1884. The eastern parts of the Amur Valley, the Ussuri Valley and the adjacent coast of the Sea of Japan came under Russian control by 1860, when Vladivostok was estab-lished, as did Sakhalin Island, in 1875. Russia gained a foothold in California in the early nineteenth century, but gave it up in 1841. Alaska (Russian America), to which Russia had claimed possession since the late eighteenth century, was sold to the United States in 1867.

The Crimean War (1853–1856), in which Russia faced Turkey, France and Britain, was another important landmark in Russia's nineteenth-century history. Russia's defeat was closely succeeded by the abolishment of serfdom (1861), along with restrictions on land rent and enabling peasants to redeem their plots. Other reforms that brought relief to most

of the rural population (94 percent of the total population) were also introduced. The period of Alexander II (1855–1881) also brought substantial economic devel-opment, the expansion of industry (es-pecially iron and steel) and the growth of urbanization. However, the pressure for further liberalization increased and revolutionary activities became more widespread.

The Russo-Japanese War (1904–1905) in Manchuria and Korea was another Russian defeat that deeply affected internal policies and developments. Rus-sia had practically gained control over

Manchuria and Korea (1896) and estab-lished a military base at Port Arthur on the Yellow Sea. It was forced by Japan, however, to abandon these gains and to cede Port Arthur and the southern half of Sakhalin. This re-sulted in widespread outbreaks of revolu-tionary activity, strikes, demonstrations and mutinies. The revolution was sup-pressed, but led to general elections for a parliament (Duma) that was promised limited legislative power. The Duma was dissolved a few weeks after it assembled (1906). A second Duma (1907) was sub-ject to the same fate.

St. Petersburg

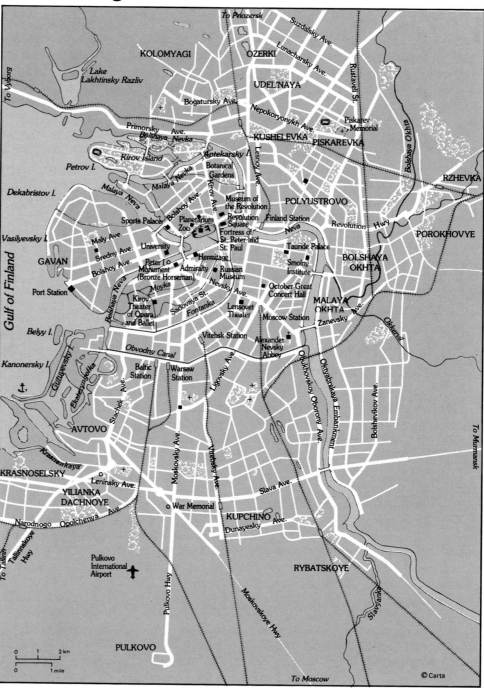

Russia's involvement and defeat in World War I (1914–1917) led to the outbreak of revolution and the collapse of the tsarist regime (1917). At first a provisional government was set up, in which moderate leftists gradually became the majority. The Bolsheviks (Communists), who formed the extreme left and had wide support among the working class, rebelled in what became known as the October Revolution, and gained control of the capital Petrograd (St. Petersburg), Moscow and many other centers. They established a government which, with the help of armed forces (the Red Army), set out to impose itself on all the country. A widespread civil war ensued between the Bolshevik forces (Red Army) and their opponents. Under a peace treaty with Germany (1918), the Bolshevik government gave up Finland, Estonia, Latvia, Lithuania, Moldova, Ukraine, Poland and Transcaucasia, all of which were to become independent states. By 1921 the Soviet Government (as the Bolshevik government officially became known) gained full control of what had been tsarist Russia, with the exception of Finland, the Baltic states, parts of Poland, Moldova (annexed by Romania) and the Kars District (annexed by Turkey). In 1922, Russia became the dominant constituent republic that joined with Ukraine, Belarus and Transcaucasia to form the Union of Soviet Socialist Republics. (For the history of the Russian Republic under the USSR, see introductory survey, pages 14–16.)

Under the Soviet Union, Russia formally lost all the territories that became constituent republics of the union, as well as the Crimea (ceded to Ukraine in 1954). It gained Karelia in 1940 (from Finland), Tuva in 1944, the province of Kaliningrad in 1945 (from Germany) and the southern part of Sakhalin and the Kuril Islands in 1945 (from Japan). Following the breakup of the Soviet Union in 1991, Russia became a founding member of the Commonwealth of Independent States.

GOVERNMENT AND POLITICS

Russia is a federal republic governed by an executive president, elected by popular vote for a five-year term. The first elected president, Boris Yeltsin, won 57.3 percent of the vote (against six op-

Russians in Capital Cities of Non-Russian Republics
1989

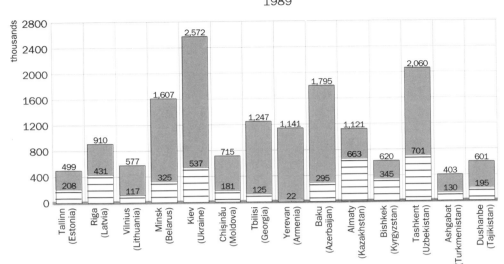

ponents) in elections held in 1991. His powers and functions were extended under an amended constitution that was approved by popular vote in December 1993. The legislature consists of two chambers, an upper house and a 444-member parliament (Duma). As a result of the general elections of 1993, three party groups (moderate socialists and liberals; Communists; and right-wing groups) are represented in the legislature, none of which received an absolute majority. The right-wing groups have the largest representation.

The federation consists of forty-nine provinces (oblast), six territories (krai), seventeen autonomous republics, five autonomous regions (oblast) and ten national districts (okrug). The autonomous republics each have their own elected legislature with limited local authority and functions. Many of the republics are striving toward much wider authority, in some cases requesting full independence.

Russia's westernmost province, Kaliningrad (5,830 sq. mi./15,100 sq. km; 880,000 inhabitants) is an enclave on the Baltic coast between Poland and Lithuania. It was annexed in 1945 from Germany.

The seventeen autonomous republics are:

1. Bashkiria: 55,430 sq. mi. (143,600 sq. km); pop. 4 million (40.3% Russians, 24.5% Tatars, 24.3% Bashkirs, 3.2% Chuvash); capital, Ufa (pop. 1.1 million); annexed in 1557.

2. Buryat: 135,650 sq. mi. (351,300 sq. km); pop. 1.1 million (72% Russians, 23% Buryats); capital, Ulan-Ude (pop. 360,000); annexed in 1689 and 1727.

3. Checheno-Ingush: 7,350 sq. mi. (19,300 sq. km); pop. 1.3 million (52.9% Chechens, 29.1% Russians, 11.7% Ingush); capital, Grozny (pop. 400,000); annexed in the 1850s. Separated into two republics—Chechenia and Ingushetia—in 1993.

4. Chuvash: 7,064 sq. mi. (18,300 sq. km); pop. 1.35 million (68.4% Chuvash, 26% Russians, 2.9% Tatars, 1.6% Mordvinians); capital, Cheboksary (pop. 430,000); annexed in the 16th century.

5. Dagestan: 19,416 sq. mi. (50,300 sq. km); pop. 1.9 million (over 30 nationalities, including 25.7% Avars, 15.2% Dargins, 12.4% Kumyks, 11.6% Lezgins, 11.6% Russians, 5.1% Laks, 4.4% Tabasarans, 4% Azerians); capital, Makhachkala (pop. 330,000); annexed in 1723.

6. Ingushetia: see Checheno-Ingush.

7. Kabardino-Balkar: 4,825 sq. mi. (12,500 sq. km); pop. 780,000 (45.6% Kabardinians, 35.1% Russians, 9% Balkars); capital, Nalchik (pop. 240,000); annexed in 1557.

8. Kalmyk: 29,300 sq. mi. (75,900 sq. km); pop. 330,000 (42.6% Russians, 41.5% Kalmyks, 6.6% Kazakhs, Chechens and Dagestanis); capital, Elista (pop. 90,000); annexed in the 17th century.

9. Karelia: 66,564 sq. mi. (172,400 sq. km); pop. 800,000 (71.3% Russians, 11.1% Karelians, 8.1% Belorussians, 3.2% Ukrainians, 2.7% Finns); capital, Petrozavodsk (pop. 270,000); ceded by Finland in 1940 and constituted as republic of the Soviet Union. Southern part annexed to Russia in 1946, and the rest annexed in 1956 as an autonomous republic.

10. Komi: 160,540 sq. mi. (415,900 sq. km); pop. 1.3 million (56.7% Russians, 25.3% Komi, 10.7% Ukrainians and Belorussians); capital,

Syktyvkar (pop. 240,000); annexed in the 14th century.

11. Mari: 8,955 sq. mi. (23,200 sq. km); pop. 760,000 (47.5% Russians, 43.5% Mari, 5.8% Tatars, 1.1% Chuvash); capital, Yoshkar Ola (pop. 250,000); annexed in 1552.

12. Mordvinia: 10,110 sq. mi. (26,200 sq. km); pop. 980,000 (59.7% Russians, 34.2% Mordvinians, 4.6% Tatars); capital, Saransk (pop. 320,000); subjugated by Russia in the 13th century.

13. North Ossetia: 3,088 sq. mi. (8,000 sq. km); pop. 650,000 (50.5% Ossetians, 33.9% Russians, 8.1% Ingushi and other Caucasian ethnic groups); capital, Vladikavkaz (formerly Ordzhonikidze; pop. 300,000); annexed in 1784.

14. Sakha (formerly Yakutia): 1,197,760 sq. mi. (3,103,200 sq. km); pop. 1.1 million (50.4% Russians, 36.9% Yakuts, 2.2% other northern tribes); capital, Yakutsk (pop. 190,000); subjugated by Russia in the 17th century.

15. Tatarstan: 26,250 sq. mi. (68,000 sq. km); pop. 3.7 million (47.7% Tatars, 44% Russians, 8.3% Chuvash, Udmurts and Mordvinians); capital, Kazan (pop. 1.1 million); annexed in 1552.

16. Tuva: 65,810 sq. mi. (170,500 sq. km); pop. 320,000 (60.5% Tuvans, 36.2% Russians); capital, Kyzyl (pop. 80,000); annexed in 1944.

17. Udmurt: 16,250 sq. mi. (42,100 sq. km); pop. 1.65 million (58.3% Russians, 32.2% Udmurts, 6.6% Tatars); capital, Izhevsk (pop.

650,000); annexed in the 15th and 16th centuries.

The five autonomous regions are:

1. **Adygei**: 2,934 sq. mi. (7,600 sq. km); pop. 440,000; capital, Maikop (pop. 150,000); in Krasnodar Territory.

2. **Gorno-Altai**: 35,740 sq. mi. (92,600 sq. km); pop. 195,000; capital, Gorno-Altaisk (pop. 40,000); in Altai Territory.

3. **Jewish Region**: 13,895 sq. mi. (36,000 sq. km); pop. 220,000 (84.1% Russians, 6.3% Ukrainians, 5.4% Jews); capital, Birobijan (pop. 82,000); in Khabarovsk Territory.

4. **Karachayevo-Cherkess**: 5,442 sq. mi. (14,100 sq. km); pop. 425,000; capital, Cherkessk (pop. 115,000); in Stavropol Territory.

5. **Khakass**: 23,855 sq. mi. (61,900 sq. km); pop. 580,000; capital, Abakan (pop. 155,000); in Krasnoyarsk Territory.

The ten national districts are:

1. **Agin-Buryat**: 7,336 sq. mi. (19,000 sq. km); pop. 78,000; capital, Aginskoye (pop. 8,000).

2. **Chukot**: 284,826 sq. mi. (737,700 sq. km); pop. 156,000; capital, Anadyr (pop. 7,700).

3. **Evenki**: 296,370 sq. mi. (767,600 sq. km); pop. 25,000; capital, Tura (pop. 3,500).

4. **Khanty-Mansi**: 201,970 sq. mi. (523,100 sq. km); pop. 1.3 million (mainly Russians but also Khants and Mansi); capital, Khanty-Mansiysk (pop. 30,000).

5. **Komi-Permyak**: 12,703 sq. mi. (32,900

sq. km); pop. 160,000; capital, Kudymkar (pop. 32,000).

6. **Koryak**: 116,410 sq. mi. (301,500 sq. km); pop. 40,000; capital, Palana (pop. 4,000).

7. **Nenets**: 68,224 sq. mi. (176,700 sq. km); pop. 55,000; capital, Naryan-Mar (pop. 20,000).

8. **Taimyr**: 332,857 sq. mi. (862,100 sq. km); pop. 55,000; capital, Dudinka (pop. 20,000).

9. **Ust-Ordyn-Buryat**: 8,648 sq. mi. (22,400 sq. km); pop. 140,000; capital, Ust-Ordynsk (pop. 15,000).

10. **Yamalo-Nenets**: 289,690 sq. mi. (750,300 sq. km); pop. 500,000; capital, Salekhard (pop. 30,000).

The six territories are:

a. **Altai**: 65,290 sq. mi. (169,100 sq. km); pop. 2.7 million; capital, Barnaul (pop. 700,000).

b. **Khabarovsk**: 318,378 sq. mi. (824,600 sq. km); pop. 1.85 million; capital, Khabarovsk (pop. 740,000).

c. **Krasnodar**: 29,344 sq. mi. (76,000 sq. km); pop. 4.8 million; capital, Krasnodar (pop. 780,000).

d. **Krasnoyarsk**: 903,360 sq. mi. (2,339,700 sq. km); pop. 3.1 million; capital, Krasnoyarsk (pop. 980,000).

e. **Primorye (Littoral Far East)**: 64,054 sq. mi. (165,900 sq. km); pop. 2.3 million; capital, Vladivostok (pop. 770,000).

f. **Stavropol**: 25,676 sq. mi. (66,500 sq. km); pop. 2.5 million; capital, Stavropol (pop. 380,000).

Administrative Division of Russia

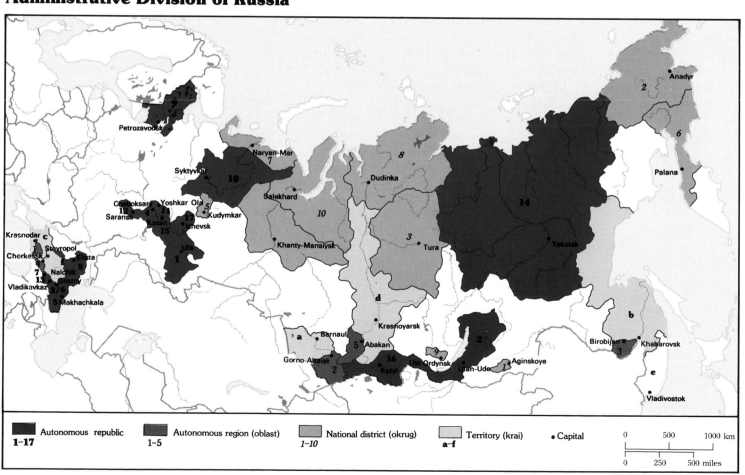

Autonomous republic	Autonomous region (oblast)	National district (okrug)	Territory (krai)	• Capital	0 500 1000 km
1-17	1-5	1-10	a-f		0 250 500 miles

THE CAPITAL

Moscow, with a population in 1993 of 9 million (9.2 million in the metropolitan area), is the largest metropolitan area in Russia, one of the largest cities in the world and the second largest in Europe. The city is built on an area of low hills (390–550 ft./120–168 m) on the banks of the Moscow River (a tributary of the Oka). The original settlement (where the Kremlin now stands) was founded on the hill above the confluence of the Moscow River with its small tributary, the Neglinaya—a site with defensive advantages and easily accessible by land or river. It lies well above the area affected by extreme spring flooding. Because of its central location in the heart of European Russia, Moscow developed into a focal point for important trade routes, an advantage that grew considerably with the advent of railways, inter-river canals and, more recently, air traffic.

The main growth of the city came when it became capital of the Soviet Union (1917). Its population was estimated at 349,000 in 1840; 463,000 in 1863; 979,000 in 1897; 1.1 million in 1908; and nearly 2 million in 1917. It fell to about 800,000 by 1920, due to severe famine and the civil war, but rose again in the early 1920s. The city numbered 3.7 million in 1933 and 4.1 million in 1939. The population decreased significantly during World War II but rose rapidly afterward. The population was 5 million in 1959 and 6.9 million in 1970. Russians constitute 89 percent of the population. Jews are the largest minority, followed by many nationalities of the former Soviet republics. The city's birth rate is very low, with hardly any natural growth rate since the 1960s; the population increase is almost entirely due to migration.

Moscow, first chronicled in 1147, was apparently a settlement on the Kremlin hill for some time before. It was fortified and became a market town in the late twelfth century, but remained part of the Vladimir principality until the end of the thirteenth century. The town was burned in 1237 and 1293 by the Tatars. In the early fourteenth century, Moscow gained control of the entire Moscow Basin, incorporated the principalities of Vladimir and Pereyaslavl, and became the political and religious center of northeast Russia. It was again captured by the Tatars in 1382. By the end of the fifteenth century, Moscow extended its rule over most of central and northern Russia; its ruler, Ivan III, claimed to be "ruler of all Russia." The expansion continued through the sixteenth century, with the capture of Novgorod, Pskov, Kazan and Astrakhan, but Moscow almost completely burned twice: in 1547 and in 1571, when occupied by the Tatars.

The transfer of the capital by Peter the Great to St. Petersburg in 1712 brought a period of decline to Moscow. The city suffered severe fires in 1739, 1748 and 1753. In 1812 came Napoleon's conquest and the destruction by fire of three-quarters of the city. Although the city was rebuilt and all its functions restored within a short period of time, it was only in the late nineteenth century that its growth and economic development took a conspicuous turn for the better. It became a center for industry, commerce and an expanding rail network, as well as a leading cultural, scientific and political center.

Moscow played an important role in the Communist Revolution. Its reinstatement as capital in 1917 and the continued Soviet efforts to develop the city gradually made Moscow into one of the world's great metropolises. World War II caused much destruction as the German army made strenuous but unsuccessful attempts to capture the city. The population has doubled since the war, with the addition of many suburbs and satellite towns.

The prominent feature of the city layout is the radial and ring network of the main avenues and streets. The Kremlin ("citadel"), the oldest and only part of the city to survive the many destructive conquests and conflagrations, stands at the heart of the city. This triangular fortress, surrounded by a high wall first built in 1300, is the seat of the central government. The Kremlin buildings, largely built between the fifteenth and seventeenth centuries, include the first royal palace, the residence of the Russian Orthodox church, churches, the great palace (built in the mid-nineteenth century), as well as government and residential buildings (former homes of the aristocracy), some dating to the eighteenth century. Several of the buildings are now museums. Next to the Kremlin is Red Square, containing the Vasily Cathedral and the Lenin Mausoleum.

The city is also known for its beautiful old cathedrals, churches and monasteries, some dating from the fifteenth to seventeenth centuries and repeatedly restored. Some cathedrals and churches were constructed and decorated by foreign architects and artists, many of them Italians. Moscow had 350 churches before the Communist Revolution. The city center, with its broad avenues and squares, has many tall, modern buildings alongside older and smaller ones, many of which were luxury residences of the aristocracy in the nineteenth century. The large residential quarters and suburbs that sprang up after the Communist Revolution, especially after World War II, consist mainly of large apartment blocks in typical Soviet style. Many people live in crowded conditions because of the continuous severe housing shortage. The city has an excellent transportation system and one of the world's finest subway networks.

Moscow, apart from its political, administrative and economic functions as the capital of Russia and the CIS, is the leading cultural center. It is the seat of the National Academy of Sciences; Russia's largest university (founded in 1755); over eighty scientific research and teaching institutions; technical colleges; and academies of music and arts. The number of persons employed in the scientific field is second to that of industry. The city also contains the Lenin Library, with one of the largest and richest archives in the world, museums, the famous Bolshoi Theater, opera, ballet and a philharmonic orchestra. It is one of the world's largest publishing centers of books, periodicals and newspapers, as well as the main center for Russian cinema and television.

Moscow is Russia's largest industrial city. It stands in the heart of a major industrial region, extending north to Tver and south to Tula. Nearly 30

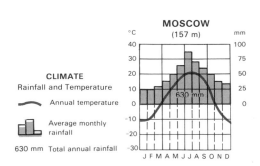

percent of the city's workforce is employed in industry and industrial research. Some of Russia's largest plants are located in or around Moscow. Metallurgy, metal processing and engineering (including car plants, machines and machine tools, and electrical equipment) are the largest industrial sector. Other large sectors are textiles, clothing and footwear; chemical and petrochemical industries; food; building materials; wood and paper products; military industries; electronic instruments and automation equipment; publishing and printing.

Moscow is Russia's main tourist attraction. For decades the city has received millions of visitors annually from all parts of the former Soviet Union. Foreign tourism, especially from western Europe and North America, has greatly increased since the 1980s.

Moscow

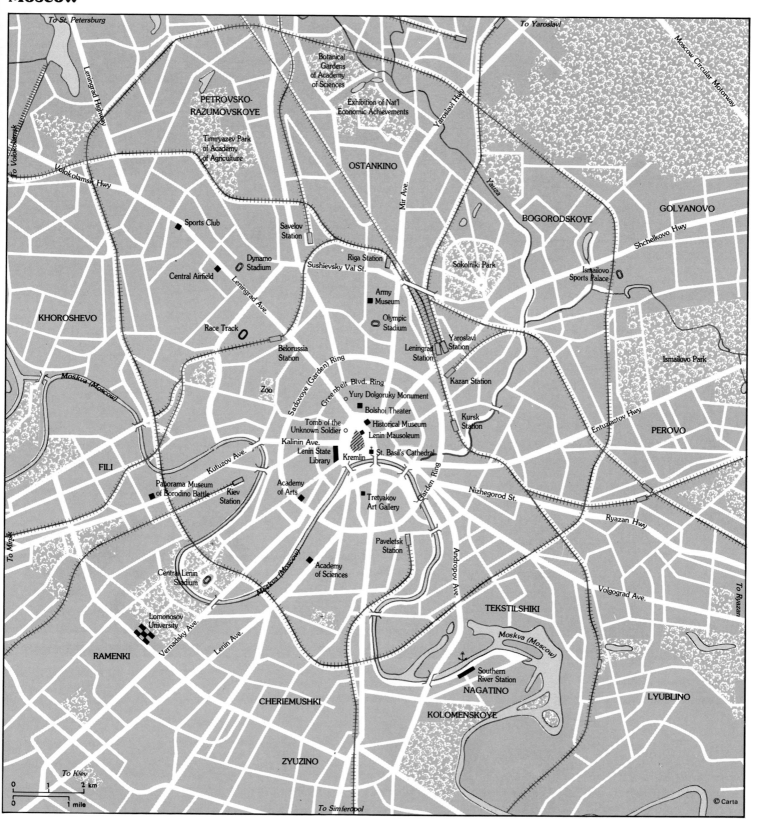

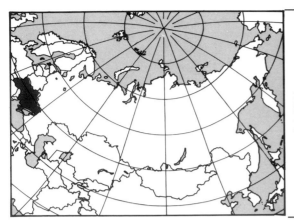

Ukraine

Area: 233,100 sq. mi. (600,700 sq. km)
Population (1993 estimate): 51,821,000
Natural increase (1990–1993): 0.1%
Capital city: Kiev (Kyyiv)

Population in Main Cities (1992 estimates):

Kiev: 2,600,000
Kharkov: 1,700,000
Odessa: 1,200,000

Yekaterinoslav (Dnepropetrovsk): 1,200,000
Yuzovka (Donetsk): 1,100,000

Ukraine is the second largest state (after Russia) in Europe and the second most populated state of the former Soviet Union. Industrially and agriculturally, it is one of the most developed and productive countries in eastern Europe. Most of Ukraine occupies the southwestern part of the great East European Plain, and includes nearly the entire warm-sea (not frozen in winter) outlet of the former Soviet Union. It is bordered by Russia on the east and north, by Belarus on the northwest, by Poland and Slovakia on the west, by Hungary, Romania and Moldova on the southwest and by the Black Sea and the Sea of Azov on the south. The Crimean Peninsula is in the extreme south. The country reaches into the valley of the Lower Danube in the south and the Hungarian Plain (Alföld) in the extreme southwest. Ukrainians constitute a large majority of the population; 84.6 percent of all Ukrainians in the former Soviet Union and 84 percent of the total in eastern Europe reside in Ukraine.

NATURAL REGIONS

The country's diversity of landscapes and the relief of the terrain do not lend themselves easily to a distinct division into natural regions, except in the extreme southwest (the Carpathian Mountains) and extreme south (the Crimean Mountains). Most of Ukraine, especially in the west between the Carpathian Mountains and the Dnepr (Dnieper) Valley, is a low (200–300 ft./60–100 m), much eroded plateau, elevated stretches of which form a gently sloping upland. Altitudes reach 1,200 to 1,300 feet (360 to 400 m), rising to 1,549 feet (472 m) at the highest point. This low plateau, though less wide, extends eastward beyond the Dnepr River, toward the Don Valley, and takes up most of southeastern Ukraine.

The plateau's western part, which extends from the Carpathian foothills in the west to the Dnepr in the east, is known as the Volyn-Podolsk Plateau. It is deeply dissected by a dense network of rivers, mainly tributaries of the Dnestr, Southern Bug and Dnepr, the main rivers which drain the country. It ends abruptly in the north toward the Polesye Lowland, a rolling, ill-drained plain extending into southern Belarus, a large part of which is covered by the Pripet Marshes. The Polesye Lowland differs from other parts of Ukraine, not only in its poor drainage but also in its soils and vegetation. In the south there is a gradual transition from the plateau to the Black Sea coastal plain, undulating and gently sloping southward and southeastward to the sea and the Lower Dnepr.

The elevated parts, or uplands, of the Volyn-Podolsk Plateau (Podolskaya Vozvyshennost and Pridneprovskaya Vozvyshennost) resemble chains of gently sloping hills, extending in a northwest-southeast direction for about 150 miles (240 km). The main areas of exposed bare rock, famous for their deep, fertile black soil, are found in the upper parts of the hills and on the banks of the deeply incised, narrow river valleys crossing them.

In the much narrower, eastern extent of the low plateau (beyond the Lower Dnepr), the main elevated hilly area, the Donets Upland (Donetski Kryazh), follows a similar direction but differs in its morphological and geological nature. Rising to a height of 1,203 feet (367 m), the hills are more rounded, with broader valleys. Another elevated belt at the southeastern fringes of the plateau, facing the coastal plain of the Sea of Azov, is the Priazov Upland (Priazovskaya Vozvyshennost), which extends in a southwest-northeast direction and presents a landscape of sharper, more distinct hills.

Northeastern Ukraine, east of the Middle Dnepr (from Yekaterinoslav to the border with Belarus), is a wide rolling plain, part of the extensive lowlands of central Russia. Much of this region was covered by the southernmost ice sheet of the Ice Age, leaving moraines and glacial deposits.

Crimea (Krym)

The Crimea, a peninsula extending southward into the Black Sea, has been administratively part of Ukraine since 1954. It is the country's only region which is not predominantly inhabited by Ukrainians. The Perekop Isthmus, whose narrowest point is only about 4 miles (6.5 km) in width, connects the peninsula with the mainland, from which it is separated mostly by shallow lagoons and narrow straits between spits. Its coast in the northeast and along most of the Sea of Azov is formed by the long, narrow Arabat Spit. The Kerch Peninsula, 70 miles (112 km) long, in the east, is separated from the Transcaucasian region of Russia by the narrow (2- to 9-mile-wide) Kerch Strait, connecting the Sea of Azov with the Black Sea.

About two-thirds of the Crimea (10,425 sq. mi./27,000 sq. km) consists of rolling plains and low hills, with small salt lakes in some coastal areas. The southern part of the peninsula is mountainous, with three almost parallel ranges, extending in a southwest-northeast direction and separated by deep valleys. Of the three ranges of the Crimean Mountains (also known as the Yaila Range), the southernmost, which runs parallel to and a short distance from the coast, is by far the highest, with peaks of more than 5,000 feet (1,500 m). The highest point is Mount Roman Kosh, at 5,070 feet (1,545 m). The southward-facing lower slopes of this range, and especially its foothills and the adjacent Black Sea shores, are famous for their mild ("Mediterranean") climate and their tourist and holiday resorts.

Carpathian Ukraine

The Carpathian Ukraine is a 160-mile- (255-km-) long section of the northeastern Carpathian Mountains, its forelands and small adjacent areas. The region was annexed by the Soviet Union from Poland (1939), Romania (1940) and Czechoslovakia (1945), and incorporated in the Ukrainian SSR.

The Carpathian Mountains, extending here in a southeast-to-northwest direction, consist of several ranges but no distinguishable lines of ridges. A few peaks exceed 6,500 feet (2,000 m), the highest point being Mount Hoverla (6,760 ft./2,060 m). Most peaks are below 5,000 feet (1,500 m) with numerous deep valleys, in which most of the population lives. Most of the mountains are densely forested and thus also known as the Forest Carpathians. Several of the chief tributaries of the Dnestr, Prut and Tisza rivers (the latter, tributaries of the Danube) have their origin in these mountains. Two mountain passes, the Veretski (in the north) and Yablonitsa (in the south), which are crossed by important and historically famous routes, have given this section of the Carpathians much of its political and strategic significance.

A small part of the Hungarian (Tisza) Plain lies southwest of the Carpathian foothills. This undulating plain, sloping gently westward, is an agriculturally rich area especially known for its vineyards.

The northern foothills and adjoining areas, which merge, farther east, into the Podolian Plateau, consist of medium (up to altitudes of 1,600 ft./500 m) and low hills with broad valleys. This is the most densely inhabited and economically productive part of the region. The cultural landscape of the region, in addition to its mountainous, physical nature, reflect its nineteenth- and early twentieth-century history (under Austria and later Poland, Czechoslovakia and Romania), giving Carpathian Ukraine its uniqueness.

Ukraine can be divided into three main natural zones, using climate, soil and natural vegetation as criteria.

(a) The Polesye, in the north, is a largely ill-drained lowland with extensive areas covered by swamps and peat bogs. A substantial part of this zone, approximately 20 percent of the country, is covered with mixed woodlands. This is the least inhabited part of Ukraine.

(b) The lesostep (forest steppe), in the center, contains the wide-open, main agricultural black-soil lands of Ukraine. It occupies about one-third of the total land area. Arable land covers nearly 70 percent of this agricultural zone, forests only 12 percent. Parts of the zone have Ukraine's densest rural population.

(c) The steppe zone is made up of the wide-open spaces in the south and especially the southeast. It comprises 40 percent of the land area. This is the drier and to some extent the less endowed part of the country, insofar as agricultural production and natural vegetation are concerned.

Almost the entire Ukraine (97 percent) drains to the Black Sea and the Sea of Azov. More than half the area is drained by the Dnepr River and approximately another quarter by the Dnestr and Southern Bug rivers. The Donets, a tributary of the Don River, drains a large area in eastern Ukraine. Some western areas are drained by tributaries of the Danube River, which flows about 100 miles (160 km) along the country's southwestern boundary.

CLIMATE

There are substantial climatic differences between the southern and southwestern parts of Ukraine and the northern and eastern parts. Climatically, Ukraine lies between the temperate continental zone of central Europe and the extreme continental climate of central and eastern Russia. Midwinter temperatures are cold, all below freezing point, except on the southern coast of the Crimea, where they are moderate. The average (and average minimum) temperatures for January are 19° to 21°F/−7° to −6°C (12° to 15°F/−11.2° to −9.5°C) in the north and east; 26° to 27°F/−2.5° to −3°C (21° to 22°F/−6° to −5.5°C) in the south and southwest; and 36° to 39°F/2° to 4°C (33° to 34°F/0.5° to 1°C) on the southern coast of the Crimea. The average (and average maximum) temperatures for the above regions for

July and August are 67° to 70°F/19° to 21°C (78° to 81°F/25.5° to 27.5°C); 71° to 73°F/21.5° to 23°C (79° to 82°F/26° to 28°C); and 75° to 76°F/24° (82° to 83°F/28° to 28.5°C), respectively. The average daily and seasonal range of temperatures is higher in the north and east than in the south. There are, on the average, 170 to 185 frost-free days annually in the north and east, 210 to 220 in the south and 250 in the southern Crimea.

Most of the precipitation falls during summer and autumn. June, July and August are the rainiest months. Snow falls from November to March. February is generally the driest month. The average annual precipitation is 21 to 28 inches (520 to 700 mm) in the north and west; 15 to 18 inches (380 to 450 mm) in the south and east; and 22 inches (550 mm) in the southern Crimea.

POPULATION

The number of inhabitants is estimated at 51,821,000 (1993). It was 51,452,000 at the last census in 1989; 49,757,000 in 1979; and 41,869,000 in 1959. The average annual increase over the 1980s was 0.4 percent, and in recent years 0.1 percent, one of the lowest rates in the former Soviet Union. The area within Ukraine's present boundaries was estimated to have a population of 40.3 million at the end of 1940. It suffered heavy losses during and shortly after World War II.

According to the 1989 census, 72.7 percent are Ukrainians, 22.1 percent Russians, 0.9 percent Belorussians and 1 percent Jews. There are also Poles, Romanians, Armenians, Bulgarians and

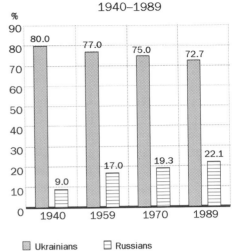

Ratio of Russians to Ukrainians
1940–1989

Tatars. Since World War II the percentage of Ukrainians has been steadily decreasing and that of Russians increasing. Ukrainians were 80 percent in 1940, 77 percent in 1959 and 75 percent in 1970, while Russians were 9 percent in 1940, 17 percent in 1959 and 19.3 percent in 1970. The Russians are concentrated mainly in the northeastern and eastern parts of the country, in the Crimea and in the large urban areas.

The majority of the population are followers (or descendants of followers) of the Greek Orthodox church. The Ukrainian Uniate and Roman Catholic churches have many adherents. Widespread revival of religious services and activities has taken place in recent years.

Ukraine is one of the most densely inhabited countries of the Commonwealth of Independent States (CIS) and the

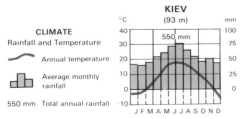

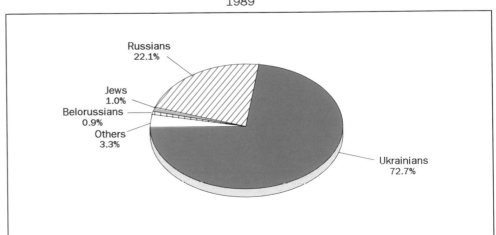

Ethnic Composition
1989

former Soviet Union. The average population density is 223 persons per square mile (86 per sq. km). The most densely inhabited part is the Donets industrial region (the Donets Basin), with 520 persons per square mile (200 per sq. km). The lowest density is in the area of the Polesye Lowland, in the north, with 120 to 140 persons per square mile (45 to 55 per sq. km).

Two-thirds of the population live in urban areas, mainly in the Donets Basin and the Dnepr Lowland. Urbanization has been growing steadily since the beginning of the century (when it was less than 20 percent) and especially after World War II, as a result of rapid industrialization and the mechanization of agriculture. It was about 30 percent in the late 1930s, 40 percent in the early 1950s and 55 percent in 1970.

Apart from the capital, Kiev, with its 2.6 million inhabitants, there are four other cities with a population of over 1 million: Kharkov (1.7 million); Odessa (1.2 million), the country's main seaport; Yekaterinoslav (formerly Dnepropetrovsk, 1.2 million); and Yuzovka (formerly Donetsk, 1.1 million). Other large cities are Zaporozhye (900,000 inhabitants); Lvov (800,000); Krivoi Rog (720,000); Mariupol (520,000); Nikolayev (510,000); Lugansk (formerly Voroshilovgrad, 500,000); Makeyevka (440,000); Vinnitsa (380,000); Sevastopol (360,000); and Kherson (360,000). There are ten towns with a population of over 250,000.

Ukrainian is the official language, but Russian is also widely used, even by many Ukrainians. The two languages belong, with Belorussian, to the East Slavic language family.

ECONOMY

Ukraine, relative to its share in the total area (2.7 percent) and population (18 percent) of the former Soviet Union, was economically one of the richest and most productive of the republics. It produced well over 20 percent of the Soviet Union's agricultural and industrial output and yielded a substantial part of its mineral products. With Europe's most extensive spaces of highly fertile land, large deposits of coal and iron ore, many other mineral resources, rivers with a high potential for hydroelectric energy, a long maritime coast with many ports and a dense network of railways, roads and internal waterways, Ukraine is endowed with many geographical and economic advantages, reflected mainly in its high industrial capacity. Industry is the dominant factor in the country's economy, although agriculture, on which its wealth depended until a few decades ago, continues to play an indispensable role. It took Ukraine over twenty-five years to recover from the devastation caused by Nazi Germany during World War II. Despite the impressive achievements in the modernization and expansion of agriculture and industrialization, there is considerable potential for further development.

Agriculture

The country as a whole is renowned for its fertility, but there are regional differences in productivity and in main crops,

Agriculture

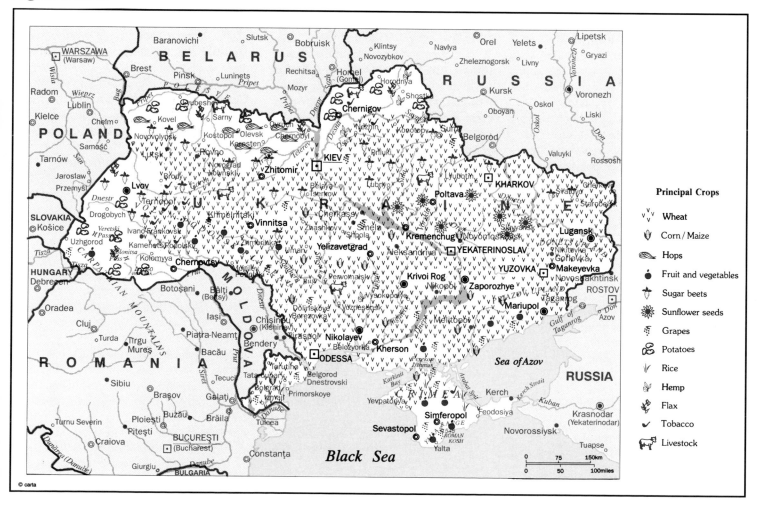

43

depending on soil and climatic factors. Mixed farming of grain, fodder crops, livestock, potatoes, vegetables and fruit is typical throughout most of the country. Sugar beets, sunflower seeds and flax are widely grown in the north and northeast. Tobacco, soya, cotton, koksagyz (a type of rubber plant) and grapes are grown in the warmer south, where wide areas are under irrigation. Over 70 percent of the country's total area is agriculturally utilized. About half of that area is devoted to growing grains (wheat, maize, rye, oats and buckwheat). Wheat, which was by far the leading grain until the 1950s, has gradually given way to maize, which has become almost equal in extent. Grain production in 1989 was 51.2 million tons (nearly 25 percent of the total production of the Soviet Union). Other main products in 1989 were sugar beets (51.9 million tons, or 53 percent of the USSR's total output), potatoes (19.3 million tons, or 27 percent), vegetables (7.4 million tons, or 26 percent) and sunflower seeds (2.9 million tons, or 41 percent). Production of grain has increased by 35 percent since 1960, sugar beets by 76 percent and potatoes by 2 percent.

There is much market gardening around the main urban and industrial centers. Fruit growing is important in the Carpathian and Crimean regions.

Livestock is the next important contributor to agricultural production. Cattle (25.2 million in 1990) and pigs (20 million) are raised in all parts of the country, while sheep and goats (9 million) are bred mainly in the south. Silver fox and other fur-bearing animals are bred on farms specializing in fur production. In 1989 Ukraine produced 24.4 million tons of milk (22.5 percent of the USSR's total

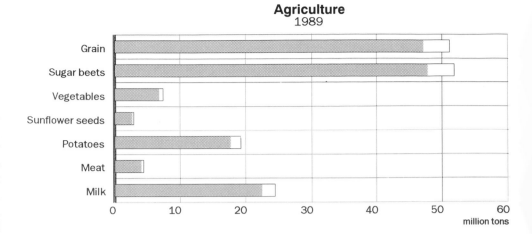

Agriculture
1989

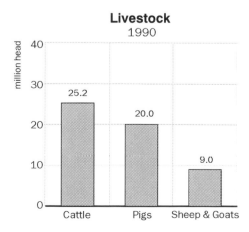

Livestock
1990

production) and 4.4 million tons of meat (22 percent), as well as large quantities of poultry and eggs.

In 1989, over 90 percent of the agricultural production was carried out in 7,451 collective farms and 2,466 state farms, which controlled nearly all the arable land. Reorganization and privatization have been in operation since 1991. Agriculture is undergoing a rapid transformation. Thirteen percent of the total land area is covered by forests.

Mineral Resources

The extensive coal and anthracite deposits in the Donets Basin are among the largest and richest in the world. They are believed to contain 60 percent of the coal reserves of the former Soviet Union. They provided in recent years about 25 percent of the coal production of the Soviet Union; 192 million tons were mined in 1988. Large coal deposits are known to also exist in the vicinity of Kharkov, Novomoskovsk and Lugansk. High-grade iron ore is mined at Krivoi Rog, which once provided a substantial part of its ore to the Soviet iron and steel industry. There are still large reserves at Krivoi Rog and other large ore deposits (though of lower grade) on the Kerch Peninsula (Crimea) and in the vicinity of Kremenchug and Belozyorka. Ukraine is also rich in manganese, mined in the vicinity of Nikopol. The mercury deposits in the Donets Basin (at Nikitovka) were the chief source of this mineral in the former Soviet Union.

Other minerals in large supply are salt (in the Donets Basin), graphite (near Mariupol), potassium, phosphorites, sulfur, kaolin, sands for glass making, gypsum, titanium (near Irsha), bauxite (at

Smela and Vysokopolye) and ozokerite (natural wax). Over seventy economically useful minerals are produced in Ukraine, mainly in the Donets Basin, the Crimea and the Carpathian region.

There are several oil and natural gas fields, mainly in the north, the west (Carpathian forelands) and the Crimea. Oil production totaled 5.4 million tons in 1988.

Hydroelectric power stations, mainly along the Dnepr River, provide large quantities of electricity. However, most of the required energy is produced by thermal and nuclear power plants.

Industry

Ukraine was represented in nearly every industrial branch of the Soviet Union and held a major position in leading industries, especially heavy equipment and food. The presence of large, high-quality iron ore deposits in proximity to coking coal and a wealth of other minerals and agricultural raw materials led to the development here of some of the first and most important industrial centers of eastern Europe and the Soviet Union. The iron and steel industry (54.8 million tons in 1989), which is the backbone of extensive and extremely varied metallurgical industries, has a leading role. Products include a wide range of machines, vehicles, locomotives, railroad cars, ships, airplanes, arms and military equipment, agricultural equipment, mining equipment, machine tools and industrial equipment, steel products, drilling and pumping equipment, pipes and irrigation equipment.

The chemical industry also covers a wide range of products, including fertilizers, sulfuric acid, caustic soda, pesticides, synthetic fibers, synthetic rubber, paints, pharmaceutical products and consumer goods. There is also a large building materials industry; 23.4 million tons of cement were produced in 1988. Glass and glassware, ceramics, porcelain and plastic ware are produced on a large scale.

The food industry is one of the country's largest and oldest industries. It is based largely on processing local agricultural products, including sugar (7 million tons in 1989, or 70 percent of USSR production), vegetable oil, dairy products, meat products, tinned vegetables and fruit, preserves, wine and alcoholic drinks and cereal products.

The manufacture of electronic products and consumer goods has expanded rapidly since the 1970s. These include television sets, refrigerators and washing machines. The textile, clothing, footwear, leather production and various woolen, cotton and linen production industries are scattered throughout most of the medium-sized and larger urban centers. There is also large production of timber products, pulp, paper and furniture.

There are six main industrial regions. The largest and most important is the Donets Basin, in the extreme east, where much of the heavy industry is concentrated. The main centers here are Yuzovka, Lugansk and Gorlovka. Farther north is the Kharkov industrial region, where chemicals, electronics and textiles are important industries, as is metallurgy. The Lower Dnepr industrial region is more dispersed, extending from Kremenchug to Kherson. Its main centers are Yekaterinoslav and Zaporozhye. The region includes the Dnepr's two large dams and hydroelectric power stations (at Yekaterinoslav and Kakhovka). Here again, iron, steel and other metals, as well as the chemical industry, are most important. Ukraine's capital, Kiev, is

Mineral Resources

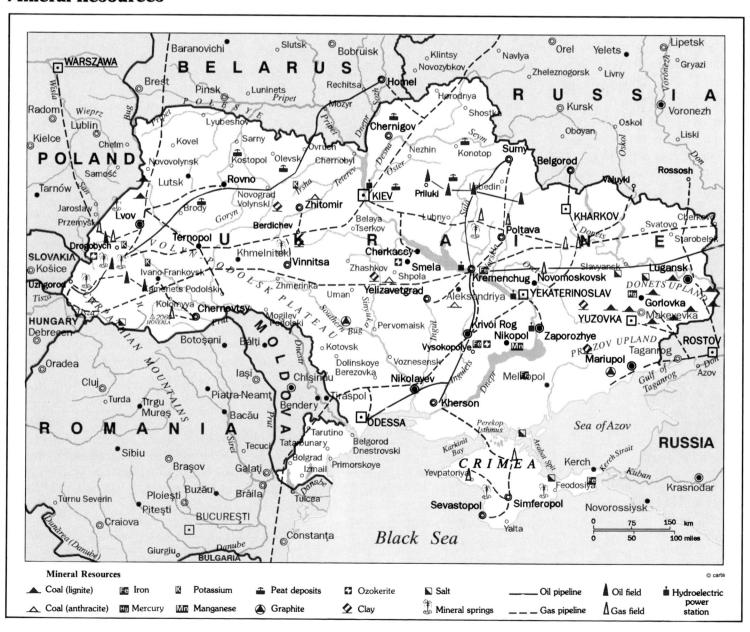

Mineral Resources

| ▲ Coal (lignite) | **Fe** Iron | **K** Potassium | ⬛ Peat deposits | ▣ Ozokerite | ◨ Salt | —— Oil pipeline | ⬥ Oil field | ⬛ Hydroelectric power station |
| △ Coal (anthracite) | **Hg** Mercury | **Mn** Manganese | ⬤ Graphite | ◈ Clay | ⚓ Mineral springs | - - - Gas pipeline | △ Gas field | |

© carta

Industry

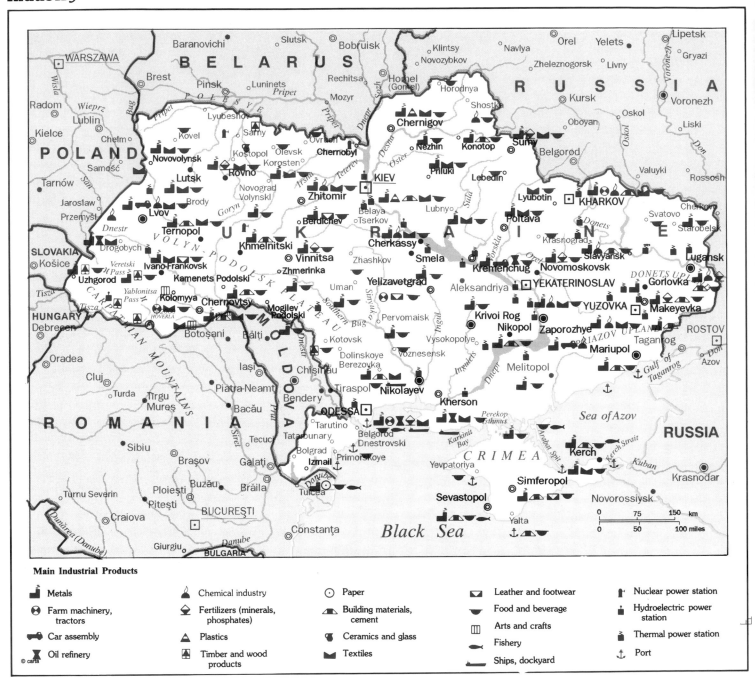

Main Industrial Products

Metals	Chemical industry	Paper	Leather and footwear	Nuclear power station
Farm machinery, tractors	Fertilizers (minerals, phosphates)	Building materials, cement	Food and beverage	Hydroelectric power station
Car assembly	Plastics	Arts and crafts	Fishery	Thermal power station
Oil refinery	Timber and wood products	Ceramics and glass	Ships, dockyard	Port
		Textiles		

© carta

the main center of the Middle Dnepr region, where food products, textiles and clothing, building materials and chemical products are prominent. The western region, with Lvov as its main center, is the most dispersed, composed of many small industrial towns. Production is highly varied, with food, wood products, clothing and chemicals dominant in most areas. The Odessa industrial region is confined to its urban area and immediate surroundings. Here the emphasis is on engineering, vehicles, ship-yards, chemical products and textiles.

Small industrial centers are dispersed in other parts of the country. Most urban centers have at least some industries, mainly for the processing of agricultural products.

Trade

Ukraine exports a large proportion of its agricultural and industrial products and mainly imports raw materials and some manufactured goods. Most of its trade is with countries of the former Soviet Union, former Comecon (Communist) countries, Germany, Finland and some Asian countries that had close links with the Soviet Union. Much of the foreign trade was carried out through Soviet trade channels. Since 1991 the handling of foreign trade has been undergoing reorganization and reorientation. Efforts to expand trade with western Europe and American countries have already met with some success.

HISTORY

The Ukrainians (also known as Little Russians) were already settled in the western and central parts of Ukraine by the seventh century. The earliest medieval Russian state came into being here with Kiev as its capital. Between the ninth and thirteenth centuries, it consisted of many small principalities under the suzerainty of the Grand Duchy of Kiev. The eastern part of the country (east of the Lower Dnepr) was then still an "open steppe" inhabited by people and tribes who were often on the move and subject to invasions from the east. The Tatars overran Ukraine in the mid-thirteenth century, controlling much of the area for over a century. The Lithuanians, who captured Kiev and its surroundings in 1320, later extended their rule south to the Black Sea and to most other parts of the country. Ukraine was part of the Polish-Lithuanian kingdom from the end of the fourteenth century to 1667, when the territories east of the Dnepr were ceded to Russia. Until the end of the eighteenth century, the word "okraina" meant "borderland" and was used to characterize the region known as Rus. It was during the Polish-Lithuanian rule that many Ukrainians settled in the steppes east of the Dnepr to escape oppression and exploitation. They established the Cossack communities, which gradually grew, expanded and, from the late sixteenth century, played an important role in the history of the region. With the partition of Poland in 1793 and 1795, Ukraine was annexed by Russia except for the westernmost districts (Galicia) that were incorporated in the Austrian Empire.

A short-lived independent Ukrainian Republic was established in 1917–18 with the collapse of the Russian and Austrian empires at the end of World War I. However, after two years of instability and armed struggle, most of Ukraine came under Russian Communist control and became a constituent republic of the Soviet Union (1922). The area of the Ukrainian Soviet Socialist Republic was 171,770 square miles (445,000 sq. km). The newly independent Poland occupied and annexed a large part of western Ukraine. Small parts of western Ukraine were also incorporated into Romania and in Czechoslovakia.

In the early stages of World War II, under an agreement with Nazi Germany, the Soviet Union annexed western Ukraine (33,980 sq. mi./88,000 sq. km) from Poland (1939); it also annexed northern Bukovina and parts of Bessarabia (c. 3,860 sq. mi./10,000 sq. km) from Romania (1940). The Carpathian region of Ukraine, Ruthenia, was annexed from Czechoslovakia in 1945. Ukraine was occupied by Nazi Germany in 1941 and largely devastated, with the agricultural and industrial base of the economy almost completely destroyed. The Crimean Peninsula was transferred from the Russian Republic and incorporated in Ukraine in 1954.

Ukraine declared its independence in 1991, with the dismemberment of the Soviet Union, and became a member of the CIS. Ukraine has been a member of the United Nations since 1945, one of the two Soviet republics (the other is Belarus) that were given a seat in the U.N. in addition to the Soviet Union.

GOVERNMENT AND POLITICS

The government is headed by an executive president, elected by popular vote for a five-year term. The last elections were held in 1990. The single-chamber legislature consists of 450 members, also elected for five years. The declaration of independence in 1991, which affirmed the democratic character of the state, transformed the former Supreme Soviet into a free parliament. Members of the former Communist Party, which won 239 seats in the 1990 elections, are now members of several democratic parties. The main opposition party is "Rukh" (Popular Movement for Freedom). The president and most members of government, appointed by the president, are former active members of the Communist Party.

The country is divided into twenty-four provinces, each of which is divided into a number of administrative districts. The Crimea (population, 2.5 million) is an autonomous region (oblast). The total number of administrative divisions includes 476 rural districts, 387 cities and 865 urban settlements (towns and townships).

THE CAPITAL

The capital, Kiev, known to Russians as the Mother of Cities, is one of the oldest and, for over a thousand years, one of the most important urban centers in eastern Europe. With a population of 2.6 million (1992), it is the largest metropolitan area in Ukraine and the third largest in the former Soviet Union. It is built on both sides of the Dnepr River, mainly on the terraces and hilly grounds of the right (west) bank, where it rises 300 feet (90 m) above the river, well above its spring flood level. This has been a convenient crossing point of the river, which divides here into two arms. The city is situated at the northern fringe of the fertile black-soil zone and at the southern edge of the forests and partly swampy areas farther north. The river, now dammed both north and south of the city, was turned into large reservoirs flooding the lower parts of the river valley.

It is believed that a settlement and trading post had existed on this site long before it was first mentioned in historical documents. Scandinavian (Varangian) tribes took control of the settlement in about the middle of the ninth century, developed it into a trade center on the route between the Baltic and Black seas and later (in 880) made it the capital of a Varangian-Russian principality, whose suzerainty extended over a number of small Russian states. In 988 it became the first seat of the Russian Orthodox metropolitan, after the adoption of Byzantine (Greek Orthodox) Christianity by the ruling prince. By the twelfth century Kiev was the capital of a powerful principality, and a wealthy city renowned for its beautiful buildings and churches, as well as for its markets.

It was captured and largely ruined in 1240 by the Tatars, who held the

Education
1989–1990

	No. of Institutes	No. of Students
Primary & Secondary Schools	21,700	7,100,000
Higher Education	147	888,800
Technical Colleges	88	44,100

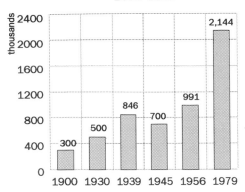

Population of Kiev
1900–1979

city until 1320, when it passed into the hands of Lithuania. It was under Polish rule from 1569 to 1654 and incorporated in Russia in 1686. Its importance as a commercial and industrial center (mainly for the processing of agricultural products) grew mainly in the second half of the nineteenth century, when it also became a focal point of rail, road and river communications. It also became the main center of Ukrainian national and cultural activities. It was the capital of the independent Ukrainian Republic from 1917 to 1920, during which time, however, it was occupied by the Red Army, the German Army, White Russians, Polish forces and, finally, the Soviet Army. Kharkov was first made the capital of the Ukrainian Soviet Socialist Republic, but in 1934 the capital was moved to Kiev. Germany captured the city in the autumn of 1941, and occupied it for two years. The city suffered devastation during the German invasion of the Soviet Union.

The city's population, which was 300,000 at the turn of the century, rose to 500,000 by 1930 and to 846,000 by 1939. It fell to under 700,000 during World War II, but rose again to 991,000 by 1956 and to 2,144,000 by 1979.

The old part of Kiev is famous for its churches, monasteries and public buildings, some of which date to the Middle Ages, although rebuilt repeatedly since then. These include St. Sophia Cathedral, the oldest in what was the Soviet Union (originally built in the eleventh century), St. Andrew's Church (eighteenth century), St. Michael's Monastery (originally eleventh century), All Saints Church (seventeenth century) and the Opera House (nineteenth century). There are also many remains of

other medieval structures, including the Golden Gate (an eleventh-century bastion). Much of the pre–World War II city was rebuilt with many modern public buildings in typical postwar Soviet style, as were the new suburbs of the largely expanded urban areas. The city has many public gardens and wide avenues, and is surrounded by forests and open spaces.

Kiev is one of the most important industrial centers in eastern Europe with a large variety of products. The industrial areas, including numerous large plants, are mainly situated east of the river. Iron and steel, engineering, machinery, chemicals, various electrical instruments and household goods, foodstuffs, and

processing of agricultural raw materials, textiles and clothing, leather products, building materials, glass and pottery, wood products, printing and publishing are the chief industries. In addition to its administrative functions, the city is a cultural and scientific center. It is the seat of the Ukrainian Academy of Sciences, a large university, many research institutes, an atomic research plant, technical and professional high schools, museums, an academy of music, opera and ballet, a philharmonic orchestra, theaters and film studios. It is also Ukraine's leading religious center, where the activities of a number of theological institutes have recently been revived.

Kiev

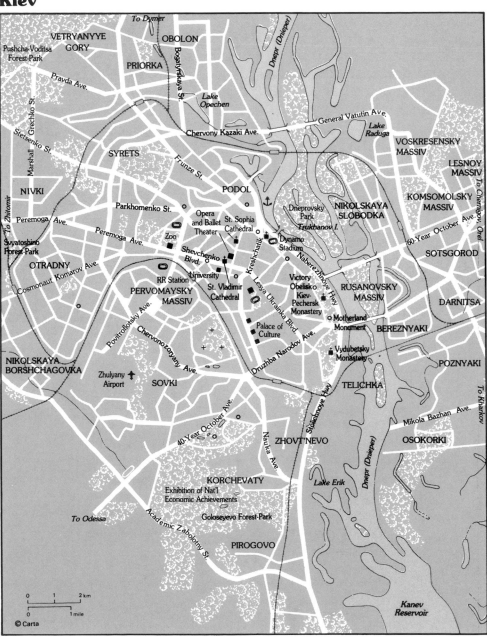

48

Belarus

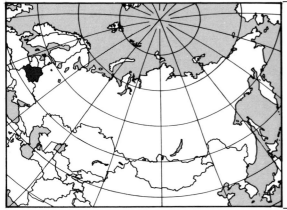

Area: 80,134 sq. mi. (207,600 sq. km)
Population (1993 estimate): 10,400,000
Natural increase (1990–1993): 0.34%
Capital city: Minsk (Mensk)

Population in Main Cities (1992 estimates):

Minsk: 1,700,000	Horodno (Grodno): 270,000
Homel (Gomel): 500,000	Brest: 260,000
Mohilev (Mogilev): 360,000	Bobruisk: 225,000
Vitebsk: 350,000	

Belarus (Belorussia or Byelorussia) is the third largest (in area and population, after Russia and Ukraine) of the European states of the former Soviet Union. It is a landlocked, largely flat country, with no conspicuous relief features or variety of landscape. Its entire surface is dominated by the residue of glaciation from the last European Ice Age. Belarus is bounded on the west by Poland, on the south by Ukraine, on the east and northeast by Russia, on the north by

Latia and on the northwest by Lithuania. In the north, it is only about 150 miles (240 km) from the Baltic Sea, the nearest large seaports being Kaliningrad, Klaipèda and Riga. Economically, Belarus is one of the most developed states of the former Soviet Union. Of all eastern Europe, Belarus is the country that suffered the worst destruction during World War II and has since been subject to extensive reconstruction efforts.

NATURAL REGIONS

The country's main natural landscape components are moraines, a dense network of rivers and brooks, numerous small lakes, large swampy areas and extensive forests that cover almost one-third of the country. The country is covered with a thick mantle of glacial deposits. The underlying topographical features contribute to the position and height of the lines of moraines, which mostly extend in a southwest-northeast direction. Maximum altitudes reach 1,000 to 1,135 feet (300 to 346 m), while the average elevation is only 400 to 500 feet (120 to 150 m). The gently sloping moraines are separated by wide, shallow valleys with small lakes, mainly in the northern half of the country, and poorly drained basins, mainly in the south. The main lines of moraines are known as the Belorussian Ridge (Belorusskaya Gryada), the eastern extension of which, into central Russia, is called the Smolensk-Moscow Ridge. They form the watershed between the rivers flowing northward into the Baltic Sea—in this case, mainly the Western Dvina, the Neman and the Bug (a tributary of the Visla)—and those flowing southward to the Black Sea—the Dnepr River and its tributaries.

While this drainage divide is often a basis for dividing the country into two natural regions—a northern and a southern one—their major characteristics remain nearly identical. Except for the low, hilly belts formed by the above-mentioned moraines, most of the country consists of low, undulating plains, whose average elevations are between 400 and 600 feet (120 and 180 m). Some of these plains, especially in central and eastern Belarus, are well drained and covered with fertile soil (loess and sandy loam) used for agriculture. These areas have been extended considerably by drainage and soil improvement projects since World War II. The better drained parts of the country, where most of the agricultural production takes place, are also the most densely inhabited. Many of the urban and rural settlements were established and developed on moraines and comparatively lofty ground to avoid the risk of flooding. Belarus's main urban and industrial center, Minsk, is situated on high ground (685 ft./210 m) of morainic origin. Over large areas, comparatively small differences in altitude (often less than 100 ft./30 m) and gradient of slope played a decisive role in the location of settlements and the distribution and nature of land use for agriculture.

The southernmost part of Belarus—the valleys of the Pripet River (a tributary of the Dnepr) and its tributaries—forms one of Europe's largest continuous swamplands known as Polesye, part of which is in Ukraine. It is an extensive, low-lying and ill-drained belt, 200 to 330 feet (60 to 100 m) wide, extending in an east-west direction. It is a thinly populated and partly desolate area. Much of this subregion is covered by forests and dense marsh vegetation. The navigation canal connecting the Dnepr River with the Visla River (Black and Baltic seas) through their respective tributaries, the Pripet and Bug rivers, runs through this marshy lowland.

Because of the small differences in elevation and land features, the extensive forests, in their composition, age

Polesye

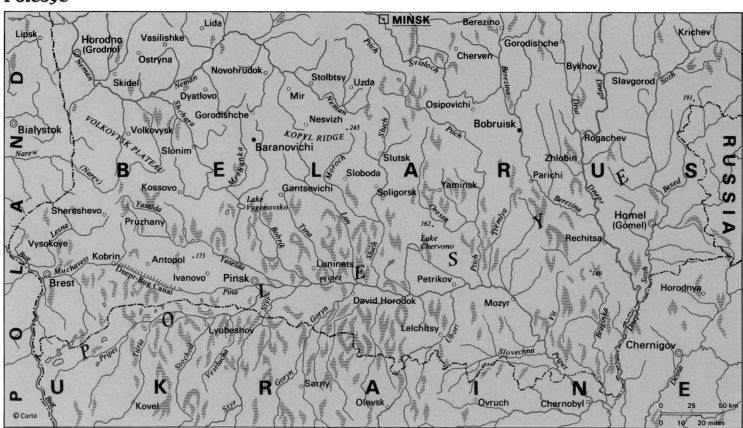

and dispersion, play an important role in the changing landscape. Mixed deciduous (oak, ash) and evergreen (pine, fir, birch) forests are common in the southern part of the country. These give way to a predominance of conifers in the north. The forests and swamps harbor a wealth of wildlife, some of them valuable to the economy.

CLIMATE

Because of the country's geographical position and the openness of the northern East European Plain, Belarus enjoys a comparatively mild continental climate with small differences in temperature between the northwest (the areas nearest the Baltic Sea) and the extreme east. The average daily and seasonal range of temperatures is also moderate. The average daily minimum temperatures for the coldest month are 16°F (-9°C) in the north and 14°F (-10°C) in the southeast, while average maximum temperatures for the hottest month (July) are 73°F (23°C) and 76°F (24.5°C), respectively. Minimum temperatures of -13° to -16°F (-25° to -27°C) and maximum temperatures of 94°F (34°C) have been recorded. The average annual precipitation is 22 inches (550 mm) in the north and 28 inches (700 mm) in the south. Rain falls mainly in spring and summer; there are no dry months. Rivers and lakes are frozen four to five months out of the year. There are, on the average, 210 to 220 frost-free days annually.

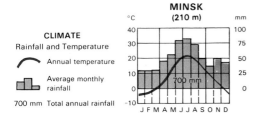

CLIMATE
Rainfall and Temperature

Annual temperature

Average monthly rainfall

700 mm Total annual rainfall

MINSK
(210 m)

POPULATION

The population of Belarus was estimated at 10,400,000 in 1993 and was 10,151,806 at the 1989 census. The average annual rate of natural increase in recent years has been 0.34 percent; during the 1980s it was 0.6 percent. The population was 8.1 million in 1959. It numbered 10.4 million in 1940, after the annexation of the eastern regions of pre–World War II Poland. The size of the population has only recently recovered from the ravages of the war.

According to the 1989 census, 78 percent of the population were Belorussians, 13 percent Russians, 4 percent Poles, 3 percent Ukrainians and 1 percent Jews. The composition was similar in 1949, when Belorussians were 80 percent, Russians 9 percent, Poles 7 percent, Ukrainians 2 percent and Jews 2 percent; however, the share of Poles and Jews in the population was much higher (12 and 11 percent, respectively) in 1940, following the annexation of former Polish territories. Many Poles emigrated to Poland after the war, while most of the Jews were exterminated during the German occupation (1941–1944). The postwar economic development, especially in industry, was responsible for the large increase in the number of Russians.

The predominant church in Belarus was the Russian Orthodox, before its suppression by the Communist regime. Russian Orthodox is again believed to be the dominant religion today, with the revival of religious freedom and activity. The once large Catholic (Uniate) community is also showing signs of revival.

The most densely inhabited parts of the country are the central districts, especially that of the capital, Minsk, and its hinterland, where the population density is 207 persons per square mile (80 per sq. km). The density is lowest in the south, where in some subdistricts it is less than 80 persons per square mile (30 per sq. km), and in the northeast, where it is 90 persons per square mile (35 per sq. km). The average density for the country as a whole is 131 persons per square mile (50 per sq. km).

Urbanization has made rapid progress since World War II. It was less than 20 percent in the mid-1930s, 43 percent in 1970, 52 percent in 1980 and, at present, nearly 60 percent. There are over 80 cities and towns, as well as 120 settlements officially classified as urban. In addition to the Minsk metropolitan area, with a population of 1.8 million, there are several large cities: Homel (Gomel), with 500,000 inhabitants; Mohilev (Mogilev), 360,000; Vitebsk, 350,000; Horodno (Grodno), 270,000; Brest (Brest-Litovsk), 260,000; Bobruisk, 225,000; Baranovichi, 160,000; and Borisov, 145,000.

The official spoken language is Belorussian, which is closely akin to Russian. Russian is also widely spoken.

ECONOMY

Belarus's economy is based mainly on its extensive and varied industrial production, although agriculture, which until the 1940s was the main source of livelihood of the majority of the population, continues to provide a substantial share of the country's produce. Both agriculture and industry were totally restored after World War II, during which time they suffered almost complete destruction. Most of the towns and villages were in ruins and had to be rebuilt. Belarus's central location in eastern Europe gives it many advantages. It controls the main rail and road communication lines between Russia and central and western Europe as well as vital links with the Baltic areas. It has easy access to both the Baltic Sea and the Black Sea.

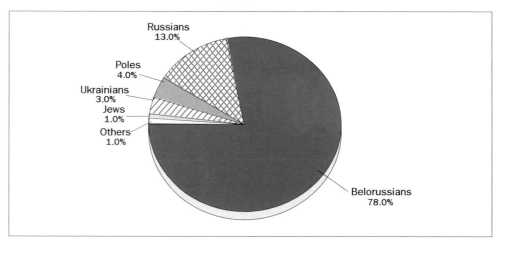

Ethnic Composition
1989

Much of the industry is dependent on the supply of raw materials and energy from the countries of the former Soviet Union, to which most of the products are also exported.

Agriculture

Belarus continues to produce mainly the products for which its agriculture has been known for generations, though with advanced modern methods, techniques, equipment and organization. Grains, fodder, flax, potatoes, sugar beets and vegetables are grown. Rye and oats are the main grains and take up a large part of the arable land in the central and southern parts of the country. Flax, potatoes and sugar beets are grown in the north, while hemp and some vegetables are grown in the south. Fodder crops are grown in all parts of the country, utilizing nearly one-third of the arable land. In 1989, agriculture produced 7.4 million tons of grain, 11.1 million tons of potatoes, 1.8 million tons of sugar beets and 900,000 tons of vegetables.

Livestock is raised on a large scale. There were 7.2 million cattle, 5.2 million pigs and 0.5 million sheep and goats in 1989. Livestock produced 1.2 million tons of meat and 7.4 million tons of milk. Livestock products make up about half the market value of agricultural production. Foxes and other fur-bearing animals are bred in a number of farms specializing in fur production.

Until the collapse of Communism in

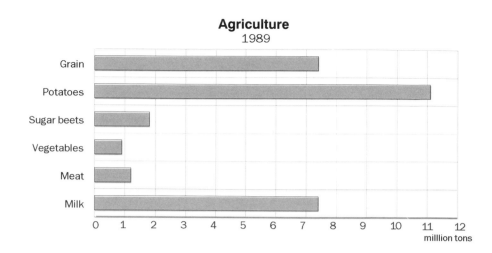

Agriculture
1989

million tons

Agriculture

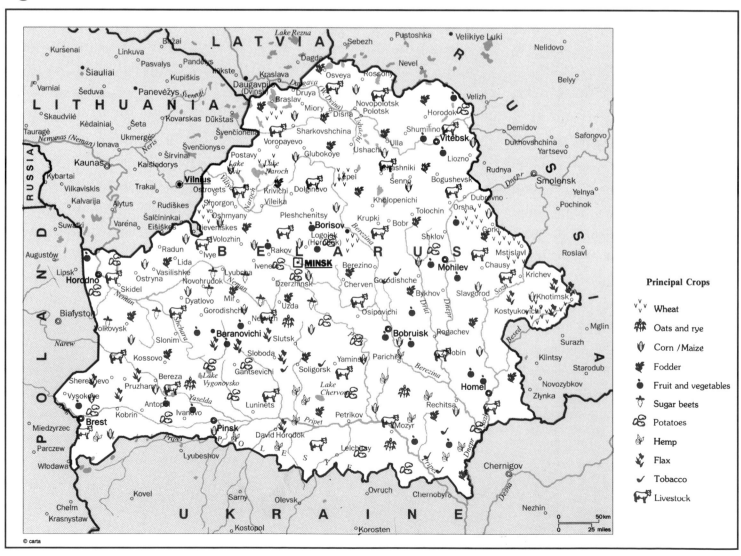

Principal Crops

v v v Wheat
& Oats and rye
& Corn / Maize
& Fodder
• Fruit and vegetables
& Sugar beets
& Potatoes
& Hemp
& Flax
✓ Tobacco
& Livestock

Industry and Mineral Resources

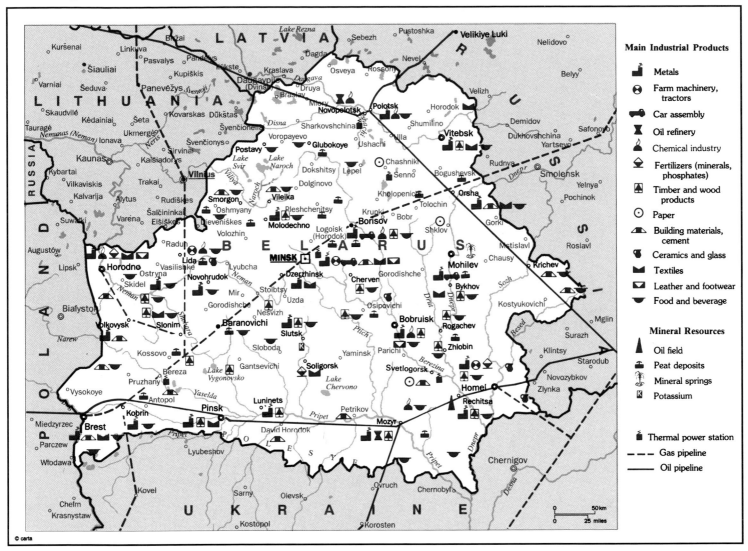

The following legend accompanies the map:

Main Industrial Products

- Metals
- Farm machinery, tractors
- Car assembly
- Oil refinery
- Chemical industry
- Fertilizers (minerals, phosphates)
- Timber and wood products
- Paper
- Building materials, cement
- Ceramics and glass
- Textiles
- Leather and footwear
- Food and beverage

Mineral Resources

- Oil field
- Peat deposits
- Mineral springs
- Potassium

- Thermal power station
- - - - Gas pipeline
- ———— Oil pipeline

1991, agriculture was organized in 1,675 collective farms and 913 state farms, which controlled nearly 60 percent of the total land. Since 1991 agriculture has been undergoing a process of reorganization and privatization.

The forests provide large quantities of timber. Part of it is used by local industries and some is exported.

Mineral Resources

The main mineral resources are peat and rock salt, both of which are found in great abundance. The mining and utilization of peat as a source of energy are making rapid progress. A modest oil field is in operation in the southeast, southwest of Homel. Quartz sands in

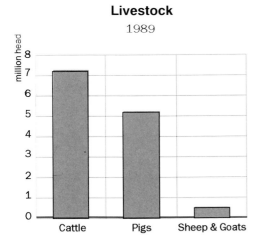

Livestock
1989

(Bar chart, million head: Cattle ~7.2, Pigs ~5.2, Sheep & Goats ~0.5)

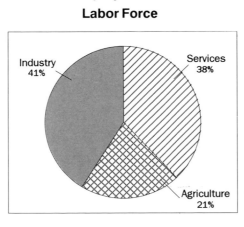

Employment of Labor Force

(Pie chart: Industry 41%, Services 38%, Agriculture 21%)

Main Industrial Products
1989

Product	Amount
Steel	1,100,000 tons
Rolled ferrous metals	700,000 tons
Timber	6,800,000 cu. m
Paper	203,000 tons
Cement	2,300,000 tons
Fabrics	512,000,000 sq. m
Knitwear	154,200,000 items
Hosiery	174,400,000 pairs
Footwear	44,800,000 pairs
Butter	158,000 tons
Granulated sugar	354,000 tons
Preserves	790,000,000 jars

this same region are used for high-quality glass production. Deposits of brown coal and phosphates are known to exist.

Industry

Industrially, Belarus is among the most developed and productive of the former Soviet states. The country experienced a very rapid and varied industrial expansion in the postwar period, giving it a leading position in a number of fields in the USSR. The most important industries are iron, steel and engineering, which are concentrated mainly in and around Minsk, Homel, Mohilev and Brest. They produce cars, trucks, tractors, heavy equipment, machinery and machine tools, industrial and agricultural equipment and iron and steel products. The chemical industry, with centers in Horodno, Soligorsk, Novopolotsk, Mozyr and Homel, produces fertilizers, various chemicals for industrial and agricultural use, paints, synthetic fibers, plastics, synthetic rubber and pharmaceutical products. There are oil refineries and associated factories for by-products. The electronics industries, including the manufacture of computers and various instruments, are among the most developed in the former Soviet Union. Electric tools and commodities are also produced.

The textile and clothing industry, with centers in Minsk and Homel, produces a large variety of cotton, linen, wool and synthetic fiber goods. Linen products are mostly manufactured in the north, where flax is grown. Footwear and a variety of leather and rubber products are produced in Minsk, Homel, Mohilev, Brest and some of the small industrial towns.

The food industry, largely dependent on local agricultural products, is scattered over most parts of the country. It produces sugar, canned foods, meat and milk products, preserves and alcoholic beverages. Wood products, including furniture, matches, tools, household goods, paper and paper products, are another well-developed field of industry. Building materials and bricks are also noteworthy.

The urban centers are all highly industrialized, but there are numerous factories in small townships and even rural areas. Many of the industries are closely linked with large industrial enterprises in Russia, Ukraine and the Baltic states.

Trade

As is the case in other states of the former Soviet Union, most trade in Belarus has been with other Soviet republics or through central Soviet international trade organs. Belarus maintains direct trade links with some foreign countries, mainly former Communist Eastern European states. Belorussian products continue to reach many countries, especially the developing ones. Economic ties with the former Comecon (Communist) states have been growing steadily since 1991.

HISTORY

The Belorussians are descendants of Eastern Slav tribes who were already in control of much of what is today Belarus by the beginning of the ninth century. A number of Belorussian principalities, based on towns such as Smolensk, Polotsk, Minsk, Vitebsk and Drutsk, came into being during the tenth and eleventh centuries. Most of them were under the suzerainty of the Grand Duchy of Kiev by the twelfth century. Much of the country came under Lithuanian rule by the early fourteenth century and, with the union of Lithuania and Poland in the sixteenth century, came under Polish rule. In subsequent periods, Belorussia repeatedly became a battleground between Polish and Russian rulers and between the Russian Orthodox and local Catholic (Uniate) churches. Poles were encouraged to settle in Belorussia to reinforce Poland's hold over the country. The nobility was mainly Polish, while the peasant masses were Belorussians. The three partitions of Poland (in 1772, 1793 and 1795) brought the entire country under Russian rule. Napoleon's armies marched through Belorussia on their way to Moscow and, on their retreat, suffered serious defeat in the Berezina Valley.

Much of Belorussia was occupied by the German army during World War I. In 1918 an attempt was made to establish an independent Belorussian national republic, but in early 1919 the country again became a battleground between Polish forces (who advanced eastward to the Berezina Valley) and Russian forces. The Red Army managed in 1920 to expel the Polish forces and the country became the Belorussian Soviet Socialist Republic (a constituent republic of the Soviet Union). Western Belorussia

was incorporated in Poland under an agreement (1921) between both countries. Under an agreement with Nazi Germany (1939), the Soviet Union occupied and annexed western Belorussia (41,700 sq. mi./108,000 sq. km with 4.8 million inhabitants), incorporating it in the Belorussian SSR and thereby doubling its area and population.

The Germans overran Belorussia within the first four weeks of their invasion of the Soviet Union, in June 1941, and held it for three years until it was reoccupied by the Soviet Army in July 1944. The war operations and the German occupation brought severe devastation to the country and a high loss of life. Reconstruction and redevelopment took nearly thirty years.

Belorussia became a founding member of the U.N. in 1945. The country declared its independence in 1991 as the Republic of Belarus and became a founding member of the Commonwealth of Independent States (CIS) after the breakup of the Soviet Union.

GOVERNMENT AND POLITICS

The country is governed by an executive president, who in 1991 was elected by parliament for a four-year term. Following the declaration of independence in 1991, the Supreme Soviet became the democratic legislature of the country. It consists of 380 members, nearly all of whom are former Communists and now members of several democratic parties. The president is also a former leading member of the Communist Party. The Socialist Party won nearly all the seats of the legislature in the first free general elections held in 1990. The two opposition parties, the Democratic Club and

Education
1989–1990

	No. of Institutes	No. of Students
Primary & Secondary Schools	5,600	1,500,000
Higher Education	33	189,400
Technical Colleges	145	147,100

the Popular Front, have not attracted much support so far. The government, appointed by the president, requires the confidence of parliament. The country is divided into six administrative regions, each consisting of a number of urban and rural districts.

THE CAPITAL

The capital, Minsk, has a population of 1.7 million (1992) and over 1.8 million in the metropolitan area; it is not only the largest urban center in Belarus but also one of the most important economic and communications centers of the European part of the former Soviet Union. Its administrative, economic, cultural and other functions extended well past the boundaries of Belarus and continued, to some extent, to do so even after neighboring territories had won their independence. The city is situated almost in the geographic center of the country, on the banks of the Svisloch River, a small tributary of the Berezina, at an altitude of 685 feet (210 m) in an area elevated by thick glacial deposits. It is surrounded by a fertile agricultural belt that was the source of the city's initial industrial and commercial activities. The site has been the meeting point of local, regional and continental routes for over a thousand years. The advantages of the city's location were also the cause of the repeated devastation it experienced.

Minsk is first mentioned in eleventh-century documents as Menesk, a station on the trade route between the Black and Baltic seas. In 1101 it became the capital of a principality of the same name. In the thirteenth century it became a Lithuanian fief and in the fifteenth century, part of Poland. It was captured and plundered by the Tatars in 1505 and by the Russians in 1508. The Swedes and the Russians conquered the city several times during the eighteenth century before it finally passed into Russian hands in 1793. The city was badly damaged in the Napoleonic invasion of Russia in 1812.

Minsk became an important and busy railway center in the last decades of the nineteenth century; it was the meeting point between the Berlin-Warsaw-Moscow line and the main line from the Baltic ports to Ukraine and the Black Sea ports. Its population, which was approximately 50,000 in the 1870s, doubled by the turn of the century and rose to over 200,000 by the mid-1930s. The city suffered much devastation during World War I. It was taken and held by the Germans (1917) and later (1919) by the Poles. Minsk became the capital of the Belorussian Soviet Socialist Republic upon its establishment in 1922. It was an important garrison town and military base in the pre- and interwar years of the two world wars. It was devastated to a great extent (three-quarters of the buildings were destroyed or damaged beyond repair) as a result of the German invasion and occupation (1941–1944) in World War II. It was almost totally rebuilt into a modern city. It has also grown enormously since the end of the war, when its population was estimated at 100,000 (240,000 in 1940). It rose to 916,000 by 1970 and to 1.3 million by 1980.

Minsk is primarily an industrial center. About one-third of Belarus's industrial products are manufactured in and around Minsk. These products include cars, trucks, tractors, various types of machinery, iron and steel products, industrial and agricultural tools, electrical instruments, communications equipment, furniture, textiles and clothing, wood products, food, chemicals, ceramics, printing and publishing.

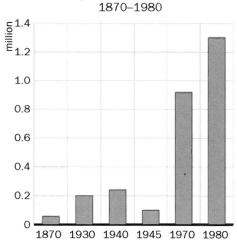

Population in Minsk
1870–1980

The capital is the seat of the Belorussian Academy of Sciences and numerous institutions of research and higher learning, a university (founded in 1921), an atomic reactor, an advanced computer center, various technical colleges, academies of arts and music, museums and theaters. Massive public buildings in typical post–World War II Soviet style are conspicuous in the central part of the city, as well as in many of the large residential suburbs.

Minsk

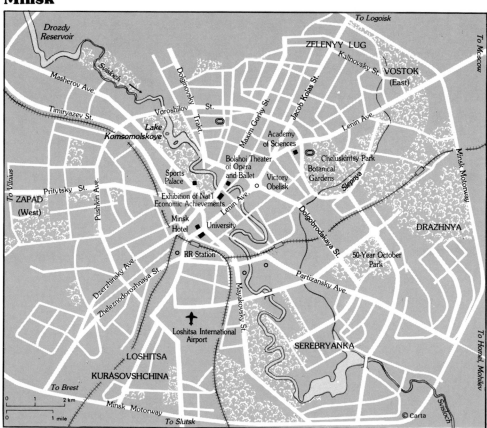

Moldova

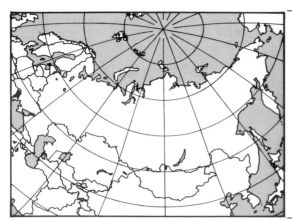

Area: 13,000 sq. mi. (33,700 sq. km)
Population (1993 estimate): 4,460,000
Natural increase (1990–1993): 0.4%
Capital city: Chişinău (Kishinev)

Population in Main Cities (1992 estimates):
Chişinău: 685,000
Tiraspol: 190,000
Bălţi (Beltsy): 165,000
Bendery: 133,000

Moldova is the smallest but most densely inhabited of the European states of the former Soviet Union. It is a landlocked country situated in the extreme southwest of the former USSR, bounded by Romania on the west and by Ukraine on the north, east and south. The greater part of the country is hemmed in between the valleys of the Prut and Dnestr (Dniester) rivers, which flow to the Black Sea in the southeast, only a short distance away. The Prut is the last large tributary of the Danube, to which Moldova has access in its southwestern corner. A narrow strip of territory east of the Dnestr (known as the "left bank" or "Trans-Dnestr") was the only area of Moldova which remained in the USSR

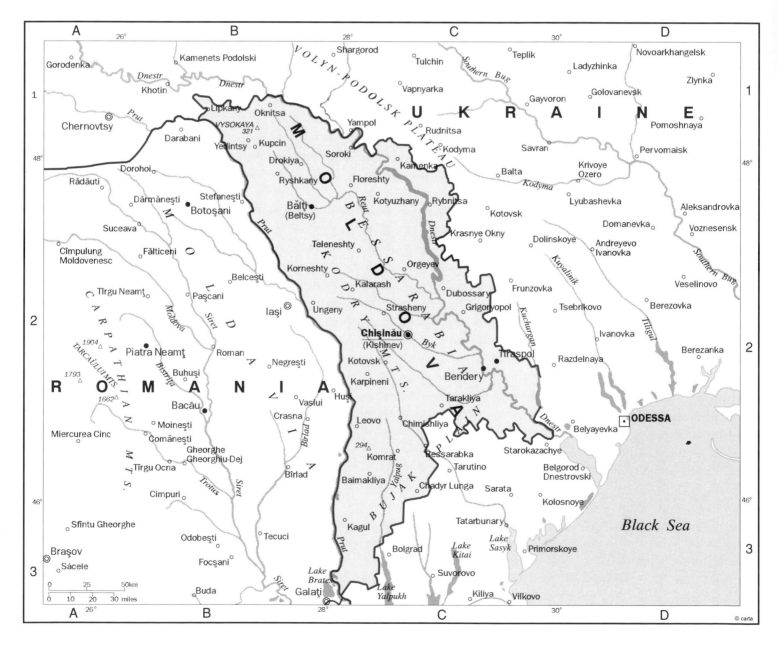

during the period between 1918 and 1940, while the rest of the country was part of Romania. It is a country of low relief (average elevation, approximately 480 ft./145 m) with gently sloping hills, broad valleys and occasional, deeply incised river ravines.

NATURAL REGIONS

Because of the small variations in elevation, landscape and climatic conditions, the country as a whole can be included in one natural region. It is, however, generally divided into four subregions: the north, center, south and "left bank" (east of the Dnestr). The valleys of the two main rivers, the Dnestr and Prut, and of their Moldavian tributaries are, in fact, the predominant physical features; to a large extent they affect the pattern of human settlement and the distribution of population. The entire area of Moldova drains into the Black Sea through the Dnestr and Prut rivers, and in part through the strip of Ukraine that separates Moldova from the Black Sea.

Structurally, most of Moldova is considered part of the eastern forelands of the Carpathian Mountains. The north is largely an undulating plain, 500 to 700 feet (150 to 200 m) in elevation, which is dissected by numerous small rivers with several lines of low hills rising above them. The hills, 200 to 400 feet above the plain, are partly formed by outcrops of hard rocks, apparently remnants of outliers of the Carpathian Mountains. The highest point is Mount Vysokaya, at 1,053 feet (321 m). Rivers cutting into these hills form deep, narrow ravines in some areas. Much of the north is covered by deep rich black soils (chernozem), the main source of the land's high agricultural fertility.

The central subregion is the most elevated and hilliest part of the country. Much of it is taken up by the Kodry Mountains, whose average height is 1,200 feet (370 m), the highest point being 1,410 feet (429 m). Some of the hills culminate in sharp ridges or form steep escarpments, especially along the river valleys. This is the case along much of the Dnestr Valley, which in this part of the country is bordered by a high, right (western) bank. Broad valleys, gentle slopes and flat river terraces are also common. Many of the valleys and lower slopes are covered by the rich black soils mentioned above and form most of the agriculturally utilized lands. Most of the area is covered by forests or used as grazing grounds.

The south consists mainly of the gently southward-sloping Bujak Plain; it is flat and slightly undulating, with some hills reaching a height of 980 feet (300 m), mainly in the west. The plain is dissected by numerous rivers and brooks, some of which form gullies. The depth and quality of the soils of this subregion are less than those farther north. Black soils do extend into some areas here, but are often mixed with sediments deposited by rivers, especially in the valleys and low-lying lands. Some areas in the extreme south are covered with saline and marshland soils.

The narrow strip of land east of the Dnestr River—the "left bank"—is the western fringe of the Volyn-Podolsk Plateau (or elevated plain) that takes up much of western Ukraine. Here, it is dissected by numerous tributaries of the Dnestr River, some of which form deep (down to 300 ft.), steep, narrow canyonlike valleys. The land's natural characteristics make it part of the adjoining region of western Ukraine. Rich black soils cover most of this subregion.

CLIMATE

There are climatic differences between the slightly warmer (especially in winter) and drier south and the more continental climatic conditions of the north. The average temperature for the coldest month (January) is 23°F (-5°C) in the north and

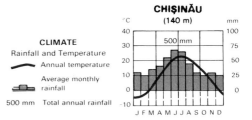

27°F (-3°C) in the south, with average minimum temperatures of 17°F (-8°C) and 21°F (-6°C), respectively. Absolute minimum temperatures of -27°F (-33°C) and -16°F (-27°C), respectively, have been recorded. The average temperatures for the hottest month (July) are 67°F (19.5°C) in the north and 73°F (23°C) in the south, with average maximum temperatures of 73°F (24°C) and 81°F (27°C), respectively. Absolute maximum temperatures of 90°F (32°C) and 102°F (39°C) were recorded. Average annual precipitation ranges from 18 to 22 inches (450 to 550 mm) in the north to 12 to 16 inches (300–400 mm) in the south. Most of the rain falls between April and September. Most of the rivers freeze over in winter for at least several weeks.

POPULATION

The number of inhabitants is estimated to be 4,460,000 (1993). It was 4,335,360 at the 1989 census. The average annual natural increase in the 1980s was 0.6 percent, and in recent years it has been 0.4 percent, one of the lowest rates in the former Soviet Union. According to the 1989 census, Moldavians

Ethnic Composition
1989

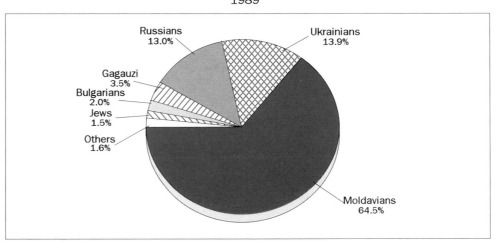

made up 64.5 percent of the population, Ukrainians 13.9 percent, Russians 13 percent, Gagauzi (a Turkic people) 3.5 percent, Bulgarians 2 percent and Jews 1.5 percent. The population has increased by 63 percent since 1940, when the republic in its present boundaries was formed. The increase was partly due to an influx of Ukrainians and Russians, although the proportional share of the various ethnic groups has not significantly changed. The proportion of Moldavians declined from 70 percent in 1940 to 64.5 percent at present; the Ukrainians and Russians increased from approximately 18 percent to 27 percent; Jews decreased from 10 percent to 1.5 percent and Germans from 3 percent to very few (they were evacuated by Nazi Germany after the annexation of Moldova by the USSR).

The Ukrainians and Russians are the majority (53 percent) in the subregion of the "left bank" (east of the Dnestr), where the Moldavians are estimated to form only about 30 percent of the population. The Gagauzi and Bulgarian minorities are concentrated in the south. Over 90 percent of the Moldavians belong to or are descendants of adherents of the Eastern (Russian, Ukrainian and Romanian) Orthodox church. A revival of religious activities is taking place today, mainly among the rural Moldavian population.

Moldova's average population density is 340 persons per square mile (131 per sq. km), the highest for any of the republics of the former Soviet Union. The density is much higher in the eastern part of the central subregion, where the capital, Chişinău (Kishinev), is located, and is least in the extreme south. Urbanization has made rapid progress, mainly due

to extensive industrialization since 1940, when over 87 percent of the population was rural; by 1970 nearly 35 percent of the population resided in towns and by 1989, the proportion had risen to about 50 percent.

The capital, Chişinău (Kishinev), with a population of 685,000 (1992), is by far the largest urban center. Other main cities are Tiraspol (190,000 inhabitants), Bălţy (165,000) and Bendery (133,000).

ECONOMY

Although industry is the most important economic branch, as a result of extensive industrialization that has taken place over the past forty years, agriculture remains the backbone of the economy, providing the raw materials for much of the manufactured products. Agriculture has undergone great changes since World War II. In addition to collectivization, it gradually underwent high mechanization, coupled with a far-reaching shift from grains and basic food commodities to industrial raw materials and products for export to other parts of the Soviet Union and to foreign countries. This shift was mainly based on taking much more advantage of the favorable soil and climatic conditions of the country than before. The extensive development and diversification of both agriculture and industry have made Moldova one of the economically wealthiest lands of the former Soviet Union.

Agriculture

Moldova is one of Europe's richest agricultural countries. Despite its small size (only 0.15 percent of the area of the ex-USSR), it played an important role in the production of several agricultural commodities, such as wine (20 percent

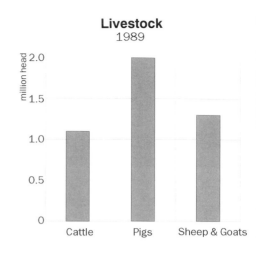

Livestock
1989

of Soviet Union output), tobacco, some vegetables and fruit. Nearly 80 percent of the area is agriculturally utilized for various crops, fodder, orchards, vineyards and horticulture, as well as for extensive grazing grounds for the large number of livestock raised.

The main agricultural products (output in 1989) are grains—3.3 million tons (chiefly wheat and corn), sugar beets—3.6 million tons, vegetables—1.2 million tons, fruit—2.2 million tons (including 1 million tons of grapes), tobacco, sunflower seeds and potatoes. Grains and sugar beets are mainly grown in the north, while tobacco, sunflower seeds and grapes are mainly grown in the south and center. Livestock, raised throughout the country, includes cattle (1.1 million in 1989), sheep and goats (1.3 million) and pigs (2 million). Livestock breeding accounts for nearly one-third of the agricultural production, including (in 1989) 356,000 tons of meat and 1.5 million tons of milk and milk products.

Agricultural production under the Soviet Union had been carried out almost entirely by 368 collective farms and 473 state farms. Steps to change the system and introduce privatization have been in progress since independence (1991). There is also a growing tendency to redirect agricultural planning to enable the expansion of exports to countries other than the states of the former Soviet Union.

Mineral Resources

Moldova has very few mineral resources of economic value. There are small deposits of lignite, phosphorites and gypsum. Slate and limestone are quarried for use and production of building materials.

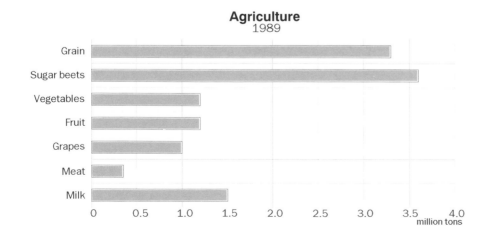

Agriculture
1989

Agriculture

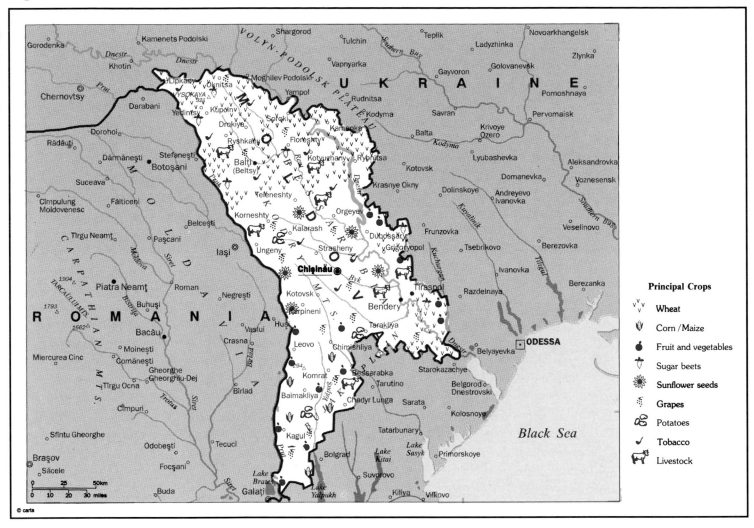

Principal Crops

ᵛᵛᵛ	Wheat
🌽	Corn / Maize
🍒	Fruit and vegetables
🥕	Sugar beets
✼	Sunflower seeds
⁞	Grapes
🥔	Potatoes
✓	Tobacco
🐄	Livestock

Industry

Since the late 1960s industry has become the country's main economic activity, largely engaged in the processing of agricultural raw materials and products. There are also many heavy industrial enterprises which depend on raw materials and components imported from other states of the former Soviet Union.

The leading food industries are sugar refining, oil pressing, winemaking, canning of vegetables and fruits, meat processing, dairy products, confectionary goods and fruit juices. There is also a large textile, clothing, footwear and leather products industry. Heavy industries include steel sheets and products, machinery, tractors, mechanized agricultural equipment and building materials (especially cement). Other industries produce various electric consumer goods, timber and wood products and tobacco products. There are several large hydroelectric power stations which, to-

gether with a number of thermoelectric power stations, meet domestic requirements and supply electricity to neighboring areas in western Ukraine.

Most industries are concentrated in and around the main urban centers that have grown rapidly as a result of industrial development. The capital, Chişinău, is the main industrial center, followed by Bendery, Bălţy and Tiraspol. Rybnitsa is a leading producer of building materials. Many industrial plants, especially for processing agricultural products, are in small townships in rural areas, from which they derive their raw materials.

Trade

As with other states of the former Soviet Union, Moldova's trade had been with other Soviet republics or through Soviet trade organizations. Moldova exports mainly agricultural products and industrial products manufactured from its agricultural raw materials. Major imports

were raw materials, fuels (oil, gas and coal), vehicles and a wide variety of industrial products. Since independence in 1991, growing efforts are underway to develop trade links with countries other than the former states of the USSR.

Main Industrial Products	
1989	
Steel	685,000 tons
Rolled ferrous metals	700,000 tons
Timber	63,000 cu. m
Cement	2,300,000 tons
Fabrics	224,000,000 sq. m
Knitwear	67,900,000 items
Hosiery	41,100,000 pairs
Footwear	23,200,000 pairs
Butter	29,000 tons
Granulated sugar	446,000 tons
Preserves	1,748,000,000 jars

Industry

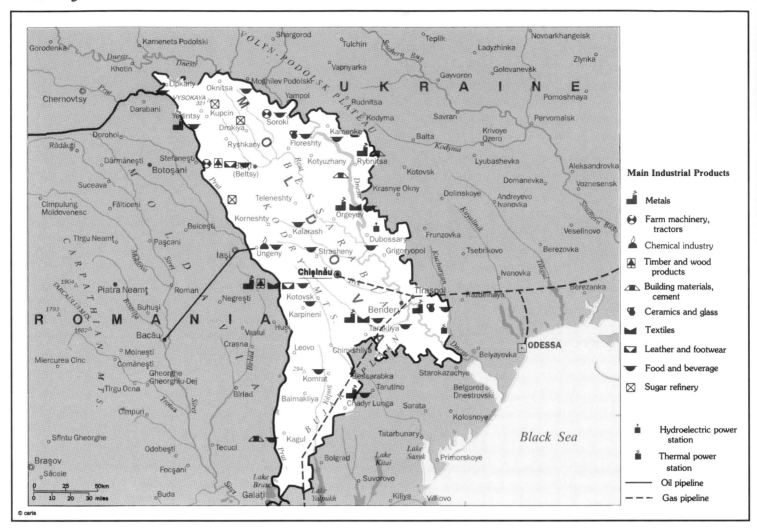

Main Industrial Products

- Metals
- Farm machinery, tractors
- Chemical industry
- Timber and wood products
- Building materials, cement
- Ceramics and glass
- Textiles
- Leather and footwear
- Food and beverage
- Sugar refinery

- Hydroelectric power station
- Thermal power station
- Oil pipeline
- Gas pipeline

© carta

HISTORY

Scythians were the earliest known tribes to inhabit the region of which Moldova is part. Much of Moldova was incorporated in the Roman province of Dacia in A.D. 106. The period in which the inhabitants were under Roman rule gave them one of their main ethnic characteristics—the Romanian language. The Romans were driven out by Goth tribes in 278. Various peoples and tribes (Slavs, Magyars and others) passed through Moldova and temporarily settled there during the first centuries of the medieval period. In the eleventh century, a large part of Moldova was annexed by the Principality of Kiev and in the middle of the fourteenth century, it became part of a Walachian (Romanian) kingdom known as Bessarabia (a name which probably derived from the Walachian dynasty Basarab). Bessarabia was later confined to a much smaller

region: the area between the rivers Prut and Dnestr, from the Danube River and Black Sea to Bukovina (a small country northwest of Moldova). Moldova presently extends over about 70 percent of the region known as Bessarabia.

The Principality of Moldova was founded in 1367. It extended over a much larger area than the present state and continued to exist until 1812, although it came under Turkish suzerainty toward the end of the fifteenth century. In 1812 most of Moldova was annexed by Russia (except the extreme south, the Bujak Plain, which Russia occupied from 1829 to 1856 and finally annexed in 1878).

During the Communist Revolution (1917), the local national movement declared the establishment of an autonomous republic within the Russian Soviet Federated Socialist Republic, but later (1918) declared itself independent. This was followed a few months later by a decision to become part of

Romania. However, the area east of the Dnestr which remained under the Soviet Union became, in 1924, a Moldavian autonomous republic within the Ukrainian Soviet Socialist Republic. This autonomous republic, with a population of 650,000 in 1939, extended over an area of 3,200 square miles (8,288 sq. km).

Under an agreement with Nazi Germany, the USSR occupied and annexed Moldova (Bessarabia) in 1940 and united it with the Moldavian autonomous republic (east of the Dnestr), to form the Moldavian Soviet Socialist Republic (MSSR), a constituent state of the USSR. The country suffered much destruction during World War II when it was under German occupation (1941–1944). The Germans formally ceded it back to Romania. After reoccupation by the Soviet Union, the northernmost (Khotin) district and southernmost (Black Sea) district of historic Moldova were incorporated in the Ukrainian SSR and Soviet

60

Education
1989–1990

	No. of Institutes	No. of Students
Primary & Secondary Schools	1,600	700,000
Higher Education	9	55,500
Technical Colleges	51	52,100
Academies of Sciences	17	1,264*

*research workers

Moldova was given its present boundaries. In 1991, following the breakup of the Soviet Union, Moldova declared its independence. At the end of that year it became a member of the Commonwealth of Independent States (CIS).

GOVERNMENT AND POLITICS

The country is governed by an executive president, who in 1990 was elected by popular vote for a four-year term. The constitution adopted in 1979 has been heavily amended since independence. The government consists of a single-chamber legislature made up of 380 seats—the Supreme Soviet. It became a democratic parliament after the declaration of independence. The Moldavian Popular Front, led by former Communists, won a large number of seats in the first free general elections held in 1990. Five other parties, some also led by former Communists, are also represented in the legislature, as are representatives of smaller parties and many independents. The government is appointed by the president but requires the support of a majority in parliament.

The Russian-speaking population in the subregion east of the Dnestr River is striving toward separation from Moldova and the formation of the Republic of Trans-Dnestr. Acts of violence by rebel groups have taken place in an effort to achieve this goal.

The country is administratively divided into 36 rural districts, 21 towns and 45 urban settlements. Romanian (Moldavian) is the official language, but Russian is widely used. The Roman alphabet was restored in 1989. Moldavian was written in Cyrillic during Soviet rule.

THE CAPITAL

Chişinău (pronounced Kishinau; in Russian, Kishinev or Kishinyev) is Moldova's largest urban industrial and communications center. It has a population of 685,000 (1992). It is situated on the banks of the Byk River, a tributary of the Dnestr, at an altitude of 130 feet (40 m) above sea level. The older part of the city, built on a low river terrace, was frequently subject to flooding. Most of the modern city is built well above the floodwater level (up to an altitude of 450 ft./140 m, above the river). Moldavians form less than half the population, which is largely made up of Ukrainians, Russians, Jews and other minorities. On the eve of World War II, Jews were the largest ethnic group, forming nearly half the city's population. Chişinău was badly damaged during World War II and was to a great extent rebuilt in typical postwar Soviet style.

Chişinău was founded in 1436 and remained a small market township until the middle of the nineteenth century. It grew rapidly after it became a rail and trade center. By 1900 its population had approached 100,000 and in 1935 it was 116,000.

Extensive industrialization and expanded functions as an administrative, communications and cultural center after World War II resulted in the city's rapid growth. By the 1959 census, it had 214,000 inhabitants and by 1970, 357,000. It has nearly doubled since.

Chişinău and its surrounding area have a wide variety of industries, the most important of which are engineering works, producers of tractors, machine tools, refrigerators and refrigeration equipment, washing machines, electrical instruments and processors of agricultural products, a wide variety of food products, wine, preserves and tobacco products. There are also many textile and clothing enterprises, manufacturers of leather goods and wood products, printers and publishers.

The city is the seat of the Moldavian Academy of Sciences, a university, research institutes, colleges and institutes for advanced training in various technical subjects, arts, music and drama. Its suburbs and surroundings are known for their gardens and orchards.

Chişinău

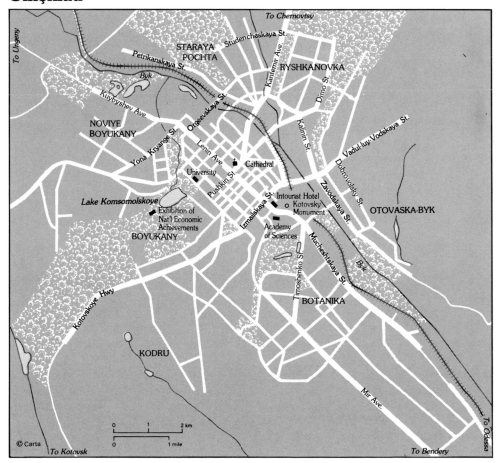

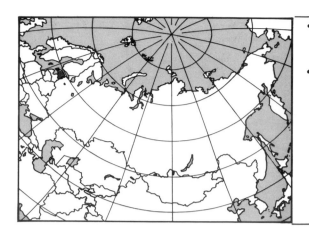

Estonia

Area: 17,413 sq. mi. (45,100 sq. km)
Population (1993 estimate): 1,610,000
Natural increase (1990–1993): 0.5%
Capital city: Tallinn (Reval)

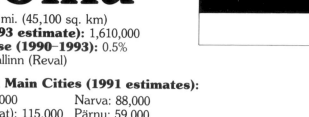

Population in Main Cities (1991 estimates):

Tallinn: 505,000	Narva: 88,000
Tartu (Dorpat): 115,000	Pärnu: 59,000
Kohtla-Järve: 90,000	

Estonia is the northernmost of the three Baltic states that regained their independence in 1991, after the breakup of the USSR. The country is bordered on the north by the Gulf of Finland, on the west by the Gulf of Riga, on the south by Latvia and on the east by Russia. Most of the boundary with Russia runs across Lake Peipsi and along the Narva (Narova) River to its outlet to the Baltic Sea. Hundreds of islands, most of them very small, are strewn along the much indented coast, taking up nearly a tenth of Estonia's area (1,610 sq. mi./ 4,120 sq. km). The two largest islands are Saaremaa (formerly German Ösel) (1,010 sq. mi./2,616 sq. km) and Hiiumaa (Dagö) (371 sq. mi./961 sq. km). Hundreds of lakes, most of them very small, cover nearly 6 percent of the area, of which Lake Peipsi, whose western half is in Estonia, makes up two-thirds. Swamps and waterlogged areas further reduce the country's dry lands.

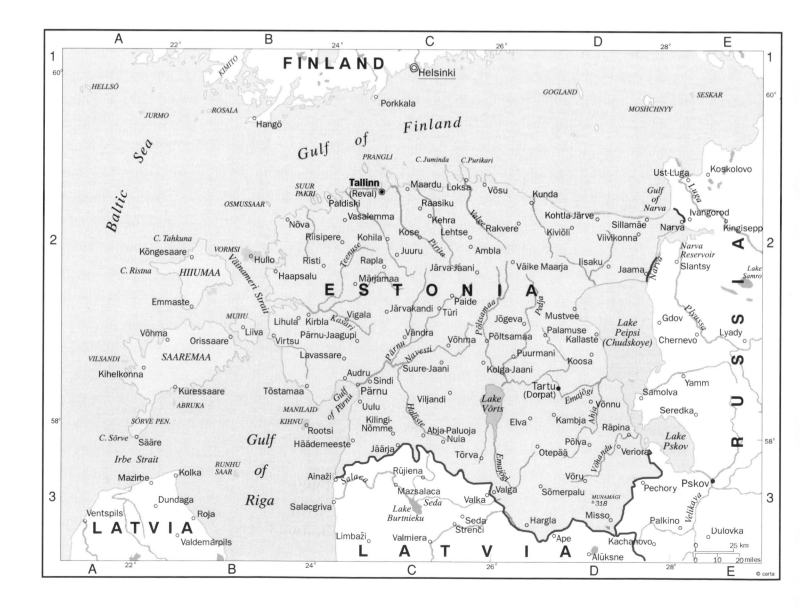

NATURAL REGIONS

Most of Estonia consists of a low, rolling plain with low, rounded, gently sloping hills. The country's surface is made up of a thick mantle of glacial deposits brought down by glaciers from Scandinavia during the last European Ice Age. The plain has a mean altitude of 160 feet (50 m) above sea level and a maximum height of 300 feet (90 m). Some moraines rise above 500 feet (150 m), especially in the southeast where Estonia's highest point, at 1,042 feet (318 m), is situated.

Just behind the flat, highly indented coast, a steep escarpment rises abruptly. It has an average height of 100 to 120 feet (30 to 35 m). Its highest point (150 ft./ 46 m) is in the vicinity of the capital Tallinn. The escarpment retreats several miles inland opposite the easternmost part of the coast, near the town of Narva.

The differences in the nature of various parts of the country are so small that a division into natural regions would be artificial. There are mainly climatic differences between the coastal areas and those farther inland. Large areas with poor natural drainage suffer from extensive flooding, especially in late spring. The country is largely drained by numerous small, shallow rivers, most of which flow directly to the Baltic Sea, and others into lakes with outlets to the sea. Forests occupy large areas (22 percent of the country). A substantial part of the swamps and waterlogged lands subject to drainage projects has already been reclaimed.

CLIMATE

Winters are cold, with temperatures well below freezing. The average temperatures for January are 25°F (–4°C) on the western coast and 18°F (–8°C) inland in the southeast. The sea along the coast is frozen on an average of eight to twelve weeks out of the year. The summer is mild and rainy. The average temperatures for July are 61°F (16°C) in the coastal areas and 63°F (17°C) inland. Precipitation, which averages 22 to 24 inches (550 to 600 mm) annually, occurs year round but is heaviest from June to August. Snow falls between November and March, and constitutes approximately 25 percent of the annual precipitation. With regard to natural vegetation Estonia is at the northern fringe of the mixed forest zone.

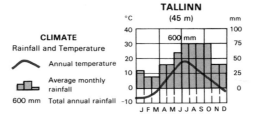

TALLINN (45 m)

CLIMATE
Rainfall and Temperature

Annual temperature

Average monthly rainfall

600 mm Total annual rainfall

POPULATION

The population of Estonia was estimated at 1.61 million in 1993. The last census, held in the USSR in 1989, recorded 1,565,000 inhabitants. The average annual increase for the 1980s was 0.7 percent and in recent years it has been 0.5 percent. In 1989 the ethnic composition of the population was 61.5 percent Estonians, 30.3 percent Russians, 3.1 percent Ukrainians, 1.8 percent Belorussians and 1.1 percent Finns. The Estonian population actually decreased while the country was under Soviet domination. According to the 1934 census, Estonians formed 88.2 percent of the total population of 1,126,000; Russians were only 8.5 percent. In 1970, Estonians dropped to 68 percent in a population of 1,356,000 (24.7 percent were Russians and 2.1 percent Ukrainians).

The great majority of Estonians are Lutheran (according to estimates, over 80 percent). The Russians and Ukrainians have their religious roots in the Orthodox church. The restoration of full religious freedom has led to a wide revival of religious activities.

The average population density is 90 persons per square mile (35 persons per sq. km). However, it is much higher in the northern part of the country where most of the cities and industries are concentrated, and much lower in the central and southern parts of the country, which are mainly agrarian. Seventy percent of the population lives in towns and urban settlements. The urban population has more than doubled over the last fifty years. The main urban centers are Tallinn (Reval) with 505,000 inhabitants (1991); Tartu (Dorpat), 115,000; Narva, 88,000; Kohtla-Järve, 90,000; and Pärnu, 59,000.

The Estonians are of Ural-Altaic origin, and in this respect are similar to their northern neighbors, the Finns. Finnish is a near relative to the Estonian language. Estonian is the official language, but Russian is also widely spoken.

Education
1989–1990

	No. of Institutes	No. of Students
Primary & Secondary Schools	600	200,000
Higher Education	6	26,300
Technical Colleges	36	19,900

Ethnic Composition
1989

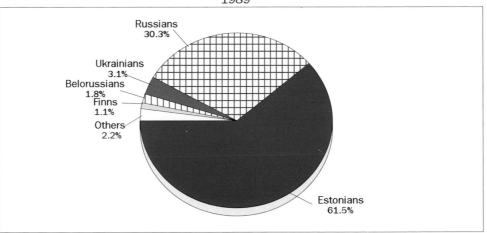

Russians 30.3%
Ukrainians 3.1%
Belorussians 1.8%
Finns 1.1%
Others 2.2%
Estonians 61.5%

ECONOMY

Estonia, which had a mainly agrarian economy, became highly industrialized under the USSR, with a well-developed agriculture. Industry and extraction and processing of mineral resources have become the dominant factors in economic activity and production. Both industrial and agricultural production were geared to USSR requirements and economic planning. Since the restoration of independence in 1991, efforts have been made to redirect the economy, especially foreign trade, and to bring about privatization in most fields of activity that were hitherto government owned and run. Agreements for economic cooperation with other Baltic states should provide the basis for plans to reorganize the economy.

Agriculture

Dairy farming, fodder, grains (mainly wheat and rye) and potato growing are the main occupations. Fruits, vegetables and flax are also widely grown. Nearly 60 percent of the area is under cultivation or improved pasture. There are substantial surpluses for export in milk and milk products, meat, potatoes and some vegetables. There is much fishing activity along the coast and a number of fish-processing plants. The forests provide large quantities of timber and raw materials for a variety of industries.

Mineral Resources

Estonia is rich in bituminous shale, which is an important source of fuel and of raw materials for the chemical industry. Large quantities of shale (23.3 million tons in 1988) are mined in the northeast for the production of gas, part of which is exported by pipe to St. Petersburg (formerly Leningrad), and oil. The bituminous shale and peat deposits give Estonia the largest local fuel resources in the Baltic region. Phosphorites are mined in the neighborhood of Tallinn, where uranium is also produced.

Industry

Shale and phosphorite processing, engineering, metalworking, shipbuilding and machine building are the most important industries and employ nearly 40 percent of the industrial labor force. These include the manufacture of mining machinery, excavators, agricultural machinery and implements, and refining equipment. The wide variety of other industries—food, paper, furniture, matches and wood products, building materials (mainly cement) and chemicals—is based mainly on local raw materials. Technical and scientific instruments, electronics, textiles and leather products are also manufactured.

Tallinn is the main industrial center. Other centers are Narva, Kunda, Kohtla-Järve, Tartu and Pärnu. There were 5,600 industrial enterprises in 1990, 51 percent of which were state-owned and 32 percent owned and run by cooperatives. These included all the big industries.

Trade

Until 1991, trade was mainly with other parts of the USSR or through its international commercial operations. Most trade is still with Russia and with neighboring states of the former USSR.

HISTORY

In the early Middle Ages, Estonian (or Esth) tribes settled in the region between the Gulf of Finland and the Gulf of Riga. Early sources describe them as wild, aggressive pagan tribes. They were first subdued by the Danes in the early thirteenth century, and then by German knights. They embraced Christianity in the late thirteenth century. They became, to a large extent, serfs when most of the land of what is present-day Estonia came under the control of German land-

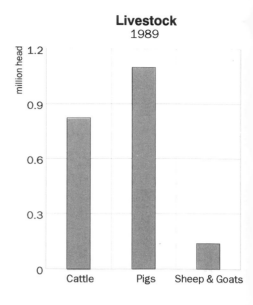

Livestock
1989

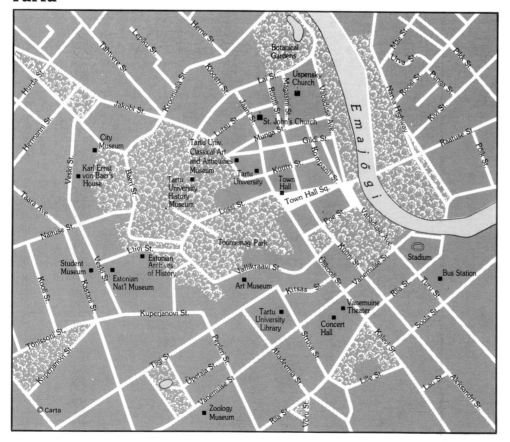

Tartu

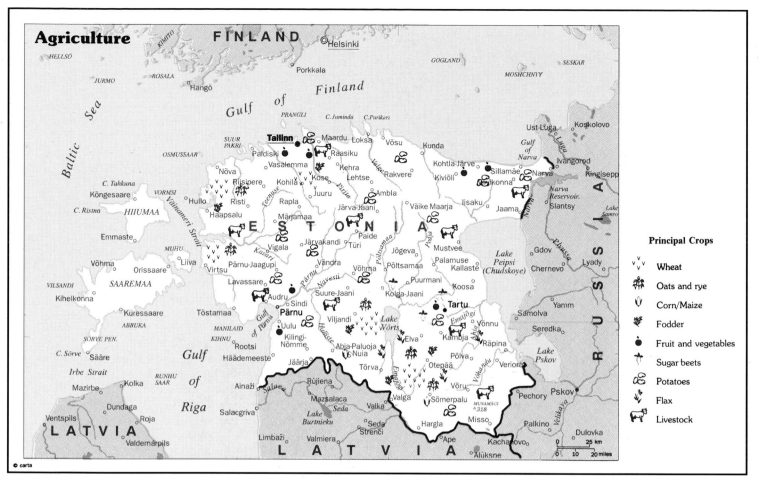

Agriculture

FINLAND

HELLSÖ
JURMO
ROSALA
KIMITO
Helsinki
Hangö
Porkkala
GOGLAND
SESKAR
MOSHCHNYY

Baltic
Sea

Gulf of Finland

PRANGLI
C. Juminda C. Purikari
Ust-Luga Koskolovo
Gulf of Narva
Ivangorod
Kingisepp

SUUR PAKRI
Tallinn Maardu Loksa Võsu Kunda
OSMUSSAAR
Paldiski
Vasalemma Raasiku Kohtla-Järve Sillamäe Narva
Nõva Kehra Rakvere Kiviõli Viivikonna
C. Tahkuna Risti Riisipere Kohila Lehtse Ijsaku Jaama
Kõngessaare VORMSI Kose Juuru Ambla Väike Maarja Narva Reservoir. Slantsy Lake Samro
C. Ristna HIIUMAA Hullo Haapsalu Rapla Järva-Jaani Mustvee Gdov Chernevo Lyady
Emmaste MUHU Märjamaa Paide Jõgeva Lake Peipsi (Chudskoye)
Võhma Liiva Vigala Järvakandi Türi Põltsamaa Palamuse Kallaste
Orissaare Virtsu Pärnu-Jaagupi Vändra Võhma Puurmani Koosa
VILSANDI SAAREMAA Lavassare Suure-Jaani Kolga-Jaani Samolva Seredka
Kihelkonna Kuressaare Audru Sindi Viljandi Tartu Võnnu Räpina Lake Pskov
ABRUKA Tõstamaa Pärnu Lake Võrts Elva Kambja Veriora
SÕRVE PEN. MANILAID Uulu Emajõgi
C. Sõrve Sääre KIHNU Kilingi-Nõmme Abja-Paluoja Otepää Põlva Lake Pskov
Irbe Strait Rootsi Nuia Tõrva Võru Pechory Pskov
Mazirbe Kolka RUNHU SAAR Häädemeeste Jäärja Valga Sõmerpalu Palkino
Dundaga Roja Ainaži Rūjiena MUNAMÄGI △318 Misso Dulovka
Ventspils Salacgriva Mazsalaca Valka Hargla Kachanovo
LATVIA Valdemārpils Lake Burtnieku Seda Seda Strenči Ape Alūksne
Limbaži Valmiera LATVIA

Gulf of Riga

RUSSIA

Principal Crops

ᵛᵛ	Wheat
🌾	Oats and rye
🌽	Corn/Maize
🌿	Fodder
●	Fruit and vegetables
🥕	Sugar beets
🥔	Potatoes
🌾	Flax
🐄	Livestock

© carta

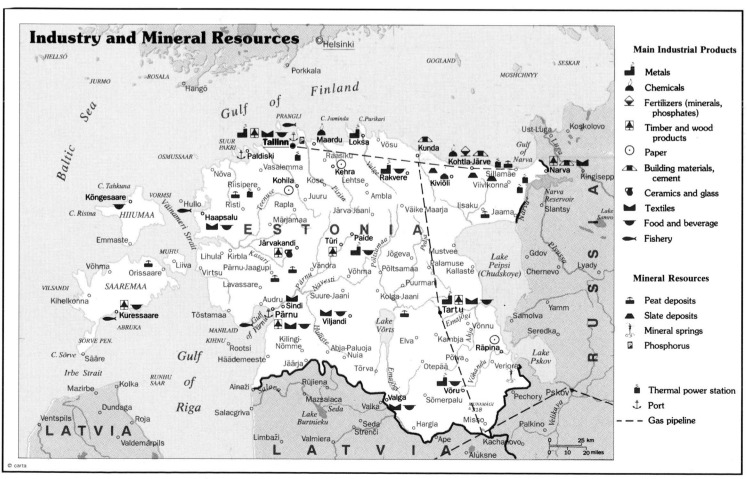

Industry and Mineral Resources

Helsinki

HELLSÖ
JURMO
ROSALA
Hangö
Porkkala
GOGLAND
SESKAR
MOSHCHNYY

Baltic Sea

Gulf of Finland

PRANGLI
C. Juminda C. Purikari
Ust-Luga Koskolovo

SUUR PAKRI
Tallinn Maardu Loksa Võsu Kunda
OSMUSSAAR
Paldiski Vasalemma Kohtla-Järve Gulf of Narva
Nõva Kehra Raasiku Rakvere Kiviõli Sillamäe Narva Kingisepp
Kõngessaare Kohila Kose Lehtse Viivikonna
C. Tahkuna VORMSI Risti Riisipere Juuru Ambla Ijsaku Jaama
C. Ristna HIIUMAA Hullo Haapsalu Rapla Järva-Jaani Väike Maarja Narva Reservoir. Slantsy Lake Samro
Emmaste Märjamaa Türi Paide Jõgeva Mustvee Gdov Chernevo Lyady
MUHU Lihula Kirbla Järvakandi Põltsamaa Palamuse Kallaste Lake Peipsi (Chudskoye)
Võhma Liiva Vändra Võhma Puurmani
Orissaare Virtsu Pärnu-Jaagupi Suure-Jaani Kolga-Jaani Samolva Seredka
VILSANDI SAAREMAA Lavassare Viljandi Tartu Võnnu
Kihelkonna Kuressaare Audru Sindi Pärnu Lake Võrts Elva Kambja Räpina Veriora Lake Pskov
ABRUKA Tõstamaa MANILAID Kilingi-Nõmme Põlva
SÕRVE PEN. KIHNU Abja-Paluoja Otepää
C. Sõrve Sääre Rootsi Nuia Tõrva Võru Pechory Pskov
Irbe Strait Häädemeeste Jäärja Valga Sõmerpalu Palkino
Mazirbe Kolka RUNHU SAAR Ainaži Rūjiena MUNAMÄGI △318 Misso Kachanovo
Dundaga Roja Salacgriva Mazsalaca Valka Hargla Velikaya Dulovka
Ventspils Limbaži Lake Burtnieku Seda Seda Strenči Ape Alūksne
Valdemārpils Valmiera LATVIA

Gulf of Riga

LATVIA

RUSSIA

Main Industrial Products

🔨	Metals
⚗	Chemicals
⚱	Fertilizers (minerals, phosphates)
🪵	Timber and wood products
☉	Paper
⛰	Building materials, cement
🏺	Ceramics and glass
⊔	Textiles
▽	Food and beverage
🐟	Fishery

Mineral Resources

⚒	Peat deposits
▲	Slate deposits
⚲	Mineral springs
℗	Phosphorus
█	Thermal power station
⚓	Port
- - -	Gas pipeline

© carta

Agriculture
1988

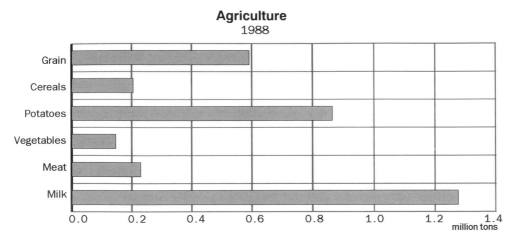

Categories of Industrial Output
1988

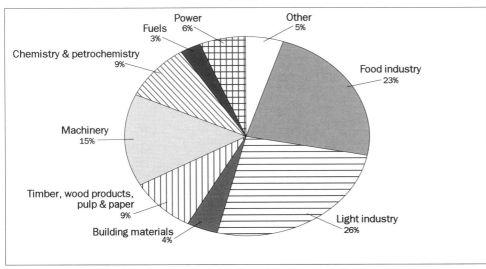

the autumn of 1944. Coupled with the economic, especially industrial, development since the 1950s, many Russians and Ukrainians settled in Estonia. They now comprise more than one-third of the total population and about half the urban population. Estonia regained its independence in 1991 with the disintegration of the USSR.

GOVERNMENT AND POLITICS

Under a new constitution that came into force in 1992, Estonia became a democratic republic. The government consists of a single-chamber legislature, the national assembly, with 101 members who are elected by proportional representation. An executive president is elected by the national assembly. Following general elections held under the new constitution in 1992, the parties represented in the national assembly are the Fatherland Front, 29 members; Safe Home, 16; Popular Front, 15; Moderate Party, 12; National Independence Party, 10; Estonian Citizens, 8; Royalist Party, 8; and small parties, 3. The Estonian parties support an amendment to the constitution which will deny the parliament vote to Russians (and their descendants) who settled in Estonia after its incorporation in the USSR in 1940. The flag and national anthem of pre-1940 free Estonia were restored.

The country is divided into fifteen districts and has thirty-three towns with municipal status.

lords. After a period under Swedish rule, the country became part of the Russian Empire in 1721 until the establishment of its independence in 1917. Serfdom was abolished in 1817. Attempts to Russify the Estonians were made during the last decades of Russian rule.

A Communist regime took control with the declaration of independence, but was replaced in 1919 by a democratic regime with the help of foreign intervention. This regime was overthrown in 1934 and replaced by a dictatorship. The 1939 German (Nazi)–Soviet pact ceded Estonia to the Soviet sphere of influence, and in fact to Soviet suzerainty. Soviet military bases were established on Estonian territory. The country was occupied in 1940 by Soviet troops and later incorporated into the USSR as one of its republics. Estonia was occupied by Nazi Germany in the summer of 1941 and retaken by the Soviet army in

Distribution of Labor Force
1989

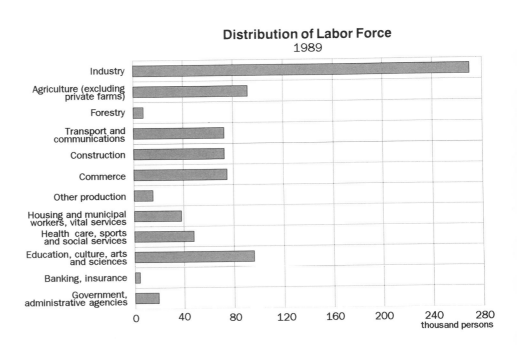

THE CAPITAL

Tallinn (Reval in German) is by far Estonia's largest city and main seaport. Its satellite towns and townships form a metropolitan area of over 600,000 inhabitants, well over half of Estonia's urban population. It is situated on a small bay on the southern shores of the Gulf of Finland. The sea here is frozen for an average of fifty days a year at the height of winter. It is the economic and industrial heart of the country. A wide variety of industries, including some of Estonia's largest enterprises, are concentrated in and around Tallinn. These include nearly all branches of industry listed above in the survey of Estonia's economy. The rapid growth of the city (its population tripled) and the expansion of its industrial production have taken place mainly since World War II. Tallinn, in addition to its political and administrative functions, is the cultural and scientific core of the country, although the main institution of higher education is in Tartu (the University of Tartu). An estimated 45 percent of the inhabitants are not Estonians, but mainly Russians.

Tallinn consists of a small, picturesque, walled old town and a spaciously planned, modern part. The old town, with two Gothic-style, thirteenth-century churches and an old Danish citadel, has many fifteenth- to seventeenth-century buildings and is similar in pattern and style to northern German towns of that period. Much of the modern part resembles the typical post–World War II Soviet urban architecture. The hilly landscape, the bay, the high cliffs along the coast and the popular bathing beaches make Tallinn one of the most attractive cities in the Baltic region.

A settlement is known to have existed on the site of Tallinn in the eleventh

Tallinn

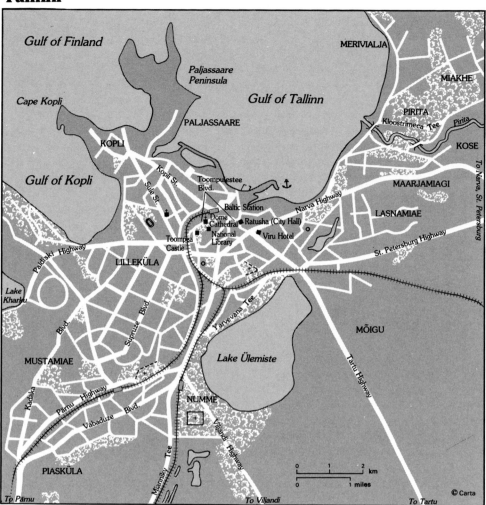

century. It was inhabited by Danes who later built a citadel in the thirteenth century. It became a German trading base and a port of the Hanseatic League in 1285, but later came under the control of an order of German knights (1346). The Swedes took the city in 1561, and later ceded it to the Russians (under Peter the Great) in 1710, when it became the base of the Russian Baltic fleet. Its population numbered approximately 70,000 in 1918, when it became the capital of the Estonian Republic, and 145,000 in 1940, when Estonia lost its independence. Under Nazi German occupation (1941–1944), it suffered serious damage as a result of Allied air raids. As the capital of the Estonian Soviet Socialist Republic and an important outlet to the Baltic Sea for the USSR, Tallinn attained, in the postwar period, unprecedented growth and economic development.

Latvia

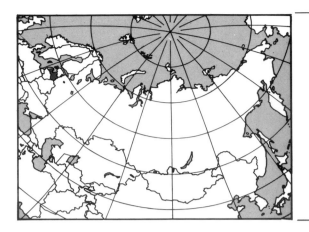

Area: 24,595 sq. mi. (63,700 sq. km)
Population (1993 estimate): 2,740,000
Natural increase (1990–1993): 0.5%
Capital city: Riga

Population in Main Cities (1990 estimates):

Riga: 917,000
Daugavpils (Dvinsk): 127,000
Liepāja: 114,900

Jelgava: 75,100
Jūrmala: 66,400
Ventspils: 50,400

Latvia is the middle of the former three Baltic republics of the USSR that regained their independence in 1991. The country is bordered on the north by Estonia, on the east by Russia, on the southeast by Belarus, on the south by Lithuania and on the west by the Baltic Sea and the Gulf of Riga. Its natural, human and historic characteristics are similar to those of the other ex-Soviet Baltic states but it is considered to be the most russified of them.

NATURAL REGIONS

Differences in natural characteristics between the various parts of the country are small, expressed mainly in the coastal landscapes with lower ranges of temperatures as opposed to an undulating plain and low, rounded hills inland, with somewhat greater climatic extremes. As in the other Baltic states, the thick mantle of glacial deposits, which covers most of the country, dominates the surface. The hills are mainly moraines. The many small lakes, the largest of which is about 30 square miles (78 sq. km), marshy

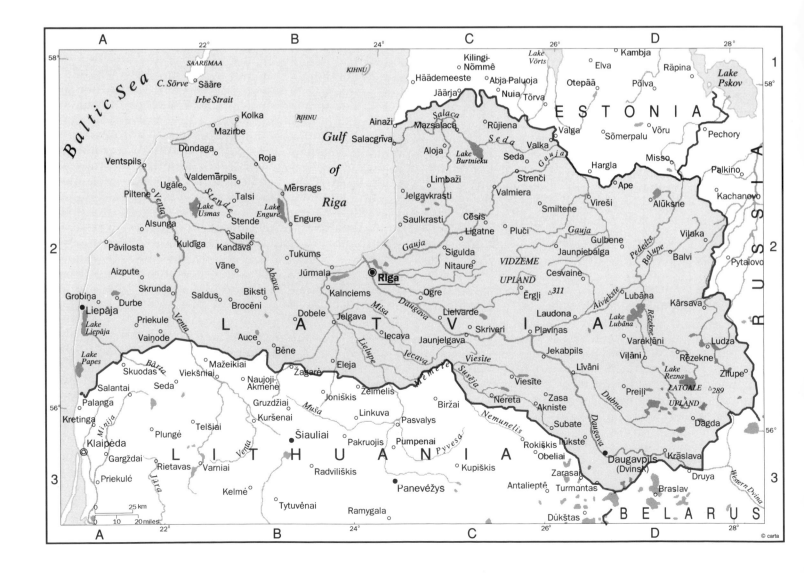

Urban and Rural Population

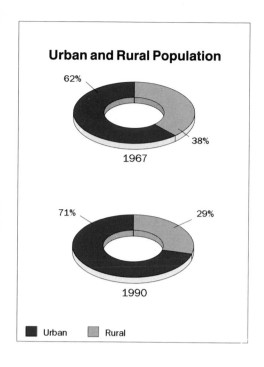

62% 38%
1967

71% 29%
1990

■ Urban ■ Rural

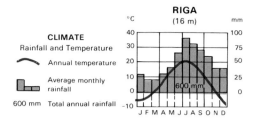

RIGA
(16 m)
°C   mm
CLIMATE
Rainfall and Temperature
⌒ Annual temperature
▭ Average monthly rainfall
600 mm Total annual rainfall
J F M A M J J A S O N D

areas and numerous stony lands are typical features of this mantle. Large-scale projects to improve poor drainage have substantially reduced the extent of the marshes and waterlogged areas.

The coast is mostly flat, with long stretches of sandy beaches and few indentations. The deep and wide Gulf of Riga is the only major deviation from the generally south-north direction of the shoreline.

The main hilly area is the Vidzeme Upland in central Latvia. It rises to 1,027 feet (311 m) and slopes gently in all directions. Another elevated area, the Latgale Upland in the southeast, is only slightly lower, reaching 948 feet (289 m). The area between the two uplands, known as the Latvian Depression, contains one of Latvia's larger lakes and much marshland and peat bogs.

Latvia's main watercourse, the Daugava (Western Dvina) River, which runs into the Baltic Sea at Riga, drains a large part of the country. It is navigable throughout Latvia and well into Belarus. It is connected by canals with Russia's inland waterway system, with the Neva, Volga and Dnepr rivers. The northwestern and southwestern parts of the country are drained by a number of small rivers directly to the sea.

CLIMATE

Latvia, like the other Baltic states, has a temperate climate with much cloudiness, comparatively little sunshine and high humidity. Average temperatures for the midwinter months are below freezing. Precipitation during these months falls in the form of snow. The average temperatures for January are 25° to 27°F (–4° to –3°C) along the coast and 14° to 19°F (–8° to –7°C) in the southeast. Temperatures below 0°F (–18°C) are not infrequent. The Gulf of Riga is ice-bound from December to March, but the Baltic coast, in the southwestern part of the country, is accessible to shipping almost throughout the winter. Average July temperatures are 61° to 63°F (16° to 17°C) in the coastal areas, 63° to 66°F (17° to 19°C) inland. Temperatures above 86°F are occasionally recorded. The average annual precipitation is 22 to 30 inches (550 to 750 mm), and the highest quantities fall on the Vidzeme Upland. Rainfall is heaviest in summer (July and August), while the spring has relatively low precipitation. Rivers generally rise in late spring and early summer, and flood some areas along their courses.

POPULATION

The population is estimated at 2,740,000 (1993). According to the 1989 census, it was 2,667,000. The average annual increase over the 1980s and in recent years has been 0.5 percent. Latvia had one of the lowest birth rates in the former USSR; the low birth rate and natural increase have prevailed since the 1930s. Fifty-two percent of the inhabitants were Latvians (or Letts), 34 percent Russians, 4.5 percent Belorussians, 3.5 percent Ukrainians, 2.3 percent Poles, 1.3 percent Lithuanians and 0.9 percent Jews.

Non-Latvians form the majority of the population in the main urban centers. The percentage of Latvians in the rural population is well above the average for the entire community. The large influx of Russians, Belorussians and Ukrainians after World War II, especially during the period of economic development and industrial expansion under the USSR, greatly reduced the Latvian majority. At the time of the incorporation of Latvia into the Soviet Union (1940), Latvians formed 77 percent of the country's population, while the Russians, Belorussians (and Ukrainians, if there were any) made up only 12 percent. The Latvian population actually decreased numerically during the fifty years of subjugation to the USSR. Latvians numbered nearly 1.6 million (out of nearly 2.1 million) in 1939 and only 1,387,000 in the 1989 census. Russians (as in other former Soviet republics) increased during that same period, from 250,000 to 1,150,000. In 1966, Latvians were 66 percent of the population and Russians 27 percent.

The Latvians are (or were) mainly Lutherans. The Catholic church also has a large following. Several other Protestant churches have substantial numbers

Ethnic Composition
1989

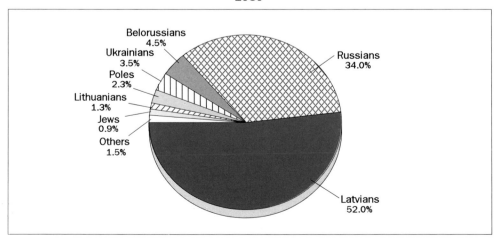

Belorussians 4.5%
Ukrainians 3.5%
Poles 2.3%
Lithuanians 1.3%
Jews 0.9%
Others 1.5%
Russians 34.0%
Latvians 52.0%

of adherents. The Russians, Belorussians and Ukrainians belong to (or are descendants of adherents of) the Russian Orthodox church. A revival and expansion of religious activity by all churches has taken place in recent years.

The proportion of the urban population has more than doubled over the last fifty years. It was 35 percent in 1939, 62 percent in 1967 and nearly 71 percent in 1990. Nearly 35 percent of the country's inhabitants live in the capital, Riga, and over 40 percent in the Riga metropolitan area. Other important urban centers are Daugavpils (formerly Dvinsk), with 128,200 inhabitants (1990); Liepāja, the main southwestern coastal port, 114,900; Jelgava, 75,100; Jūrmala, 66,400; and Ventspils, 50,400. There are fifty-seven towns and thirty-seven urban settlements.

Latvian (Lettish) is the official language, but Russian is widely spoken and used. Latvian is unique among the Baltic languages. It is of Indo-European origin, related to Lithuanian and old Prussian with an admixture of remnants of old Finnish dialects. The Latvian (or Lettish) spoken today is a dialect which has be-

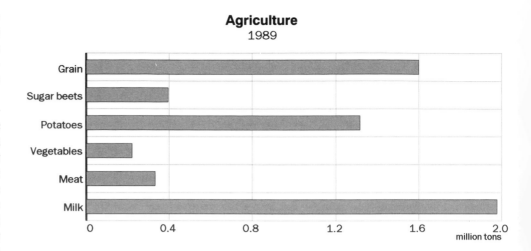

Agriculture
1989

come dominant over the past seventy years, while other Latvian dialects have almost died out.

ECONOMY
Latvia's economy, which was largely agricultural when it came under Soviet control in 1940, has since become mainly industrial. Industry produces two-thirds of the national income. Agriculture, which has also been modernized somewhat, is now in the process of reorganization and privatization. Forestry and timber production are traditionally important. Transit trade through Latvia's Baltic port, which was domestic under the USSR, has recently become international and serves mainly Belarus and Russia.

Agriculture
Cattle and dairy farming, as well as the growing of grains, potatoes and fodder, are the main occupations. Grains grown are rye, wheat, barley and oats. Potatoes, sugar beets, vegetables, fruit

Agriculture

Industry and Mineral Resources

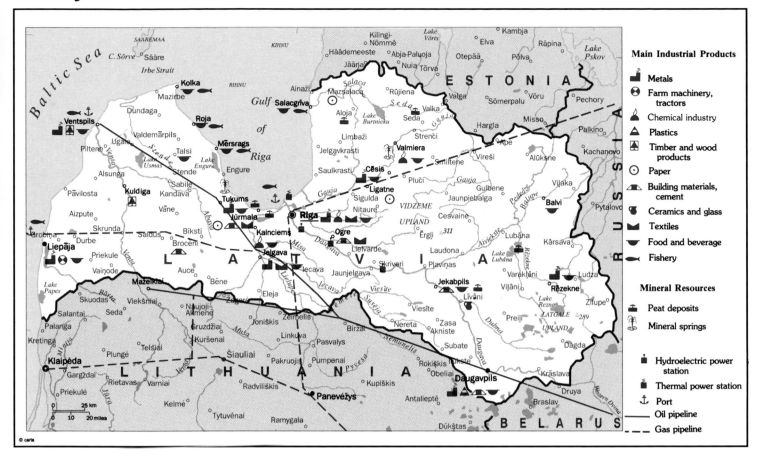

and flax are prominent in agricultural production. Improved pasture extends over large areas, including much drained marshland. Milk, milk products and meat are the main agricultural exports. In 1990, livestock included 1.5 million cattle, 1.6 million pigs and 167,000 sheep and goats. Poultry is also widely bred.

Forests cover 38 percent of Latvia and are the source of much timber (4.2 million cu. m in 1990), paper and other products. The forests are chiefly coniferous. Fishing is important along the Baltic coast, and supports a fish processing and canning industry.

Mineral Resources

Peat deposits cover nearly 10 percent of Latvia, and are largely exploited as fuel. Small quantities of gypsum are mined. Coastal areas are an important source of amber.

Industry

Modern industrialization has taken place mainly since the 1950s as part of the large-scale industrial development program of the Soviet Union. The major industrial center is in and around Riga, where most large and important enterprises are located. Daugavpils and Liepāja are other main centers. Hydroelectric power stations along the Daugava River and power stations using local peat are the main local sources of energy.

Heavy industry takes the lead in industrial output. Plants include shipbuilding, metal engineering, machine building, streetcars and railway passenger cars (of which Latvia was a major producer in the USSR), agricultural machinery and tools, diesel engines, scooters and motorcycles. Other products include refrigerators, washing machines, electrical instruments and telephone exchanges. The chemical industry produces fertilizers, pharmaceuticals and various consumer goods. The textile and clothing industry produces mainly fabrics, hosiery, woolen goods and footwear. Timber and timber products, paper, matches and furniture are industries with a well-established local tradition. Cement and other building materials are also produced. The food industry is widely spread throughout the country; its major products are sugar, butter and other milk products, meat products and preserves. Like other branches of the economy, industry has been undergoing a reorganization in management and ownership since 1990.

Livestock
1990

(bar chart: million head on vertical axis, scaled 0 to 12)

Category	Value
Cattle	~1.5
Pigs	~1.6
Sheep & Goats	~0.2
Poultry	~11.3

Distribution of Labor Force
1989

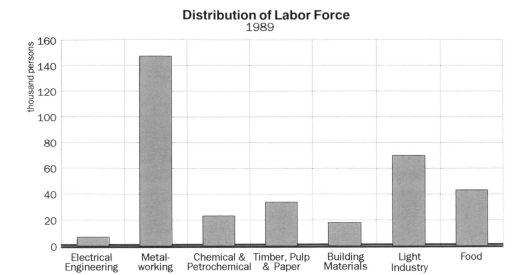

	thousand persons
Electrical Engineering, Metal-working, Chemical & Petrochemical, Timber, Pulp & Paper, Building Materials, Light Industry, Food

Main Industrial Products	
1989	
Steel	555,000 tons
Rolled ferrous metals	800,000 tons
Timber	2,400,000 cu. m
Paper	138,000 tons
Cement	776,000 tons
Fabrics	125,000,000 sq. m
Knitwear	43,000,000 items
Hosiery	78,800,000 pairs
Footwear	10,200,000 pairs
Butter	47,000 tons
Granulated sugar	248,000 tons
Preserves	504,000,000 jars

Employment of Labor Force

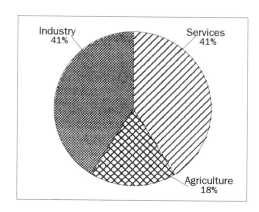

Industry 41%
Services 41%
Agriculture 18%

Trade

Before the annexation of Latvia by the USSR in 1940, trade was mainly with Germany, Britain and the other Baltic states. Exports consisted mainly of timber (40 percent), butter (23 percent) and flax (6 percent). As part of the Soviet Union, trade was with other parts of the USSR or via its international trade networks. Most trade is still with Russia, Belarus and other former republics of the USSR. An agreement for economic cooperation with Lithuania and Estonia was signed in 1990.

HISTORY

The Baltic tribes that later became the Latvian (or Lettish) people are believed to have settled in this area in the sixth and seventh centuries. They were partly of Indo-European origin and partly of Finno-Ugrian descent. In the twelfth century, the country came under German rule, mainly that of bishops and knights, who turned the local inhabitants into serfs. Christianity replaced paganism. Riga was founded at the mouth of the Daugava River, and became an outpost of the Hanseatic League. Two local, German-dominated states came into being—Livonia and Courland. German rule came to an end in 1562 and was replaced in Courland (southern Latvia) by Poland, while Livonia (northern Latvia) was contested by Sweden. It became subject to Swedish rule from 1629 to 1721, when it was taken over by Russia. Russian rule was extended also to Courland (and thus to the entire area of Latvia) in 1795 and lasted until 1918, when Latvia became an independent republic following World War I. Latvia lost 40 percent of its population and suffered great material damage during World War I. The agrarian reform that had been implemented in the early 1920s abolished the landowning nobility (mainly of German origin) and considerably improved the standard of living of the peasantry. Hardly had Latvia recovered from the ravages of World War I when it came under Russian domination again in 1940, following the 1939 German-Soviet accord, which put it under Soviet influence. Latvia became a Soviet Socialist Republic incorporated in the USSR. It was occupied by Nazi Germany in 1941 and retaken by the USSR in 1944. The damaging effects of World War II were significant. In addition to much devastation, the country lost 20 percent of its population. The German minority (approximately 60,000) was evacuated by Germany in 1940. Seventy thousand Latvians retreated with the German army in 1944, never to return. Over 200,000 Latvians were exiled by the Soviet authorities to Siberia and other parts of the Soviet Union because they had cooperated with Nazi Germany or for other political reasons. Many Russians were encouraged to settle in Latvia in the post–World War II period. Latvia regained its independence in 1991 with the disintegration of the USSR, and became a member of the United Nations.

GOVERNMENT AND POLITICS

The 201-member legislature, elected in 1990 as the Supreme Soviet, has become the parliament (Saeima) of sovereign Latvia. It restored the 1922 constitution, under which parliament is elected for a three-year term by universal, direct elections based on proportional representation. Parliament also elects the president of the state for a three-year term; the president has executive powers. He appoints a prime minister and is chief of the armed forces.

The Popular Front won a majority (121 seats out of 201) in the 1990 elections. Its leader, A. V. Gorbunovs, who was first elected as the chairman of the Presidium of the Supreme Soviet, has become the first president. There is also a Congress of Latvia, elected only by ethnic Latvians, the aim of which is to safeguard the Latvian character of the country. The country is divided administratively into twenty-six districts.

THE CAPITAL

Riga, with a population of 917,000 (1990) and a metropolitan-area population of about 1.1 million (40 percent of Latvia's population), is not only the largest city in Latvia but one of the larger and economically important urban centers in the Baltic region. It is situated near the entrance of the Daugava (Western Dvina) River on the Gulf of Riga. It is located on a slightly elevated plateau at the outlet to the sea of a wide internal, navigable waterway system that stretches over much of what was the European USSR and extends to the Caspian and Black seas. It is also the focal point of East European railway lines and roads. The port serves a wide area of Belarus and northwestern Russia. It has an outlying port, Daugavgriva, on the gulf, for large ships.

Riga, in addition to its administrative and political functions as a capital, is the economic heart of the country, with by far the largest concentration of industrial enterprises. Industries include shipbuilding, machine building, metal engineering, railway cars, streetcars, motors, scooters, electrical equipment and instruments, telephone equipment, scientific instruments, chemical products, pharmaceuticals, rubber and plastics, textiles and clothing, leather products, wood products, paper, building materials and a variety of food products.

Most Latvian cultural activity is concentrated in Riga. It is the seat of the university (founded in 1919), institutes of higher learning, research and arts, technical colleges, various museums, theaters, a philharmonic orchestra and scientific and general publishing enterprises.

The old town, on the right bank of the river, has preserved to some extent the pattern and architectural characteristics of a sixteenth- to seventeenth-century north German town with remnants of buildings from the thirteenth to fifteenth centuries: Gothic-style churches, a castle and some other public buildings.

Riga was founded in 1158 by German merchants. It became a base for church activity (Catholic) and the seat of a bishopric in 1201. It joined the Hanseatic League in 1282 and became one of the most active commercial centers of the Baltic region. Its citizens enjoyed a certain amount of autonomy, which was respected when the town passed into Polish hands in 1581, Swedish hands in 1621 and finally to Russia in 1710. Most of its inhabitants became Protestant in the sixteenth century.

Riga had a population of 300,000 in 1900. In 1918, it became the capital of independent Latvia and in 1940 of Soviet Latvia. Its population, which numbered 393,000 in 1939, decreased significantly during World War II, and grew rapidly after the war, due mainly to the influx of Russians, Belorussians and Ukrainians. Economic development and especially industrialization attracted many people from Latvia's rural areas. The population rose to 605,000 in the 1959 census and to 835,000 by 1979.

Education
1989–1990

	No. of Institutes	No. of Students
Primary & Secondary Schools	900	400,000
Higher Education	10	45,600
Technical Colleges	57	38,100
Academies of Science	15	1,812

Riga

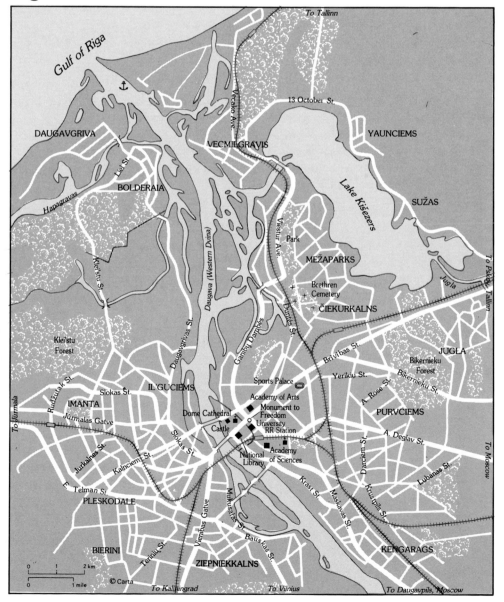

Lithuania

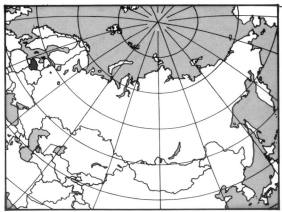

Area: 25,170 sq. mi. (65,200 sq. km)
Population (1993 estimate): 3,820,000
Natural increase (1990–1993): 0.76%
Capital city: Vilnius

Population in Main Cities (1992 estimates):
Vilnius: 593,000   Šiauliai: 150,000
Kaunas: 430,000   Panevėžys: 130,000
Klaipėda: 210,000

Lithuania is the westernmost and the largest, in both area and population, of the three Baltic states of the former Soviet Union. It is the only Baltic state in which the native ethnic group forms a dominant majority and the Russians a small minority. It is also the only one of these states which benefited from sub-stantial territorial expansion while part of the Soviet Union. The state is bounded on the north by Latvia, on the east by Belarus, on the south by Poland and Russia (the isolated province of Kaliningrad) and on the west by the Baltic Sea—mainly along the northern part of the Kurian Lagoon (Kurisches Haff, Kur-šių Mareš, Kurskiy Zaliv). The only pre–World War II boundary Lithuania had retained upon regaining its sovereignty in 1991 was that with Latvia. Economically, and with regard to some vital services, Lithuania is still largely dependent on the other European states of the former USSR.

NATURAL REGIONS

Lithuania consists of low-lying, undulating plains with ranges of low, gently sloping hills rising above them. Almost the entire country is covered with thick glacial deposits that drifted from the north during successive periods of extensive glaciation. The hilly areas, formed by moraines, are studded with numerous (over two thousand) small lakes, a phenomenon typical of glacial landscapes.

The Lithuanian coastal area is formed by the northern parts of the Kurian Spit (Kuršių Kopos or Kurische Nehrung) and Kurian Lagoon, and by a narrow belt of sand dunes along almost the entire mainland coast. The Kurian Spit is a sand spit 60 miles (97 km) long and from 1,300 feet to 2.5 miles (400 m to 4 km) wide; except for a narrow strait near its northern end, it cuts off the freshwater Kurian Lagoon from the Baltic Sea. The southern, larger part of the spit and lagoon is included in the Russian enclave of Kaliningrad, wedged between Poland and Lithuania. The sandy beaches of the spit and of the Lithuanian mainland coast have long been popular bathing resorts. The coastal region is actually the western fringe of the low, undulating plain extending over most of the country.

The western morainic hilly region rises about 25 miles (40 km) east of the coast. The Samogitian (Žemaičių) Upland forms the central part of western Lithuania; it rises generally to 400 to 600 feet (120 to 180 m) and slopes gently to the low, surrounding plain. This region, which includes the legendary Mount Medvegalis (672 ft./234 m), is noted for its forests and numerous lakes.

Another, slightly more elevated, morainic hilly region occupies the southeastern and eastern parts of the country. It is part of the Baltic Ridge (Baltiyskaya Gryada) that extends into neighboring countries. The highest peak here is 958 feet (292 m). The southeastern and northeastern parts of this hilly region are rich in small lakes and swampy valleys. The thick mantle of heavy glacial clays covering both the plain and the valleys of the hilly regions, as well as the very low gradient of the slopes of much of the country, are responsible for the poor natural drainage of extensive areas that are seasonally (especially in spring

and early summer) or perennially waterlogged or marshy. Extensive projects were undertaken under Soviet rule to improve the drainage of large areas and swamps, affecting almost 40 percent of the total area.

Most of the country is drained by the Nemunas (Neman) River, which rises in Belarus and is navigable for over 300 miles (500 km) throughout its course in Lithuania. Its main tributary, the Neris (Viliya), on which the capital, Vilnius, stands, is also navigable throughout much of its course. The northern part of the country drains to the Western Dvina River or directly to the Baltic Sea.

Forests, largely in the hilly areas, cover about 20 percent of the country and form one of its main natural resources. The forests are predominantly pine, but oak and birch are common in some parts of the country. Forests were much more extensive until the latter part of the nineteenth century, when they extended over half the total area.

CLIMATE

Western Lithuania has a somewhat milder winter climate than the other Baltic states farther east. The ports, namely Klaipėda, are generally free of ice and accessible even at the height of winter. They were and are used extensively for transit trade with Belarus and northwestern Russia. Average temperatures for the coldest month (January) range from 26°F (-3.3°C) in the extreme west to 22°F (-5.6°C) in the east. The average minimum temperatures for the same month range from 13° to 16°F

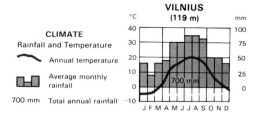

(-10.6° to -9°C), respectively. Temperatures below -20°F (-29°C) have been recorded. The average temperatures for the warmest month (July) are 62° to 65°F (16.7° to 18.3°C), and the average maximum 65° to 71°F (20.5° to 21.7°C). Temperatures exceeding 90°F (30°C) have been recorded. Precipitation occurs throughout the year (snow in winter), with an annual average precipitation of 22 to 25 inches (550 to 630 mm). August and September are usually the rainiest months.

POPULATION

Official estimates put the population in 1993 at 3,820,000; it was 3,675,000 at the 1989 census and 3,128,000 in 1970. The average annual natural increase in recent years has been 0.76 percent, and over the ten-year period 1979–1989 it was 0.7 percent. In 1930, Lithuania's population numbered 2,340,000 (it then excluded the eastern region with the capital, Vilnius, which was held by Poland). The annual rate of natural increase in the 1930s was 1.2 percent. In 1993, 80.1 percent of the population were Lithuanians, 8.6 percent Russians, 7.7 percent Poles and 1.5 percent Belorussians. The percentage of Lithuanians has remained

Ethnic Composition
1993

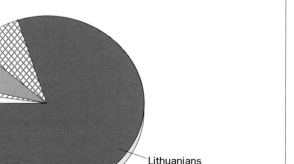

75

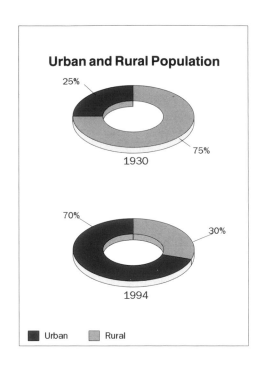

Urban and Rural Population

25%

75%

1930

70%

30%

1994

■ Urban ■ Rural

almost unchanged since the country gained its independence after World War I; it was 80.1 percent in 1930. Substantial changes did, however, take place in the composition of minorities during and after World War II. Jews then formed 7.3 percent of the population; Germans, 4.1 percent; Poles, 3 percent; and Russians and Belorussians, 2.5 percent. The Jews were almost totally exterminated in World War II under the Nazi German occupation. The Germans fled or were driven out of the country at the end of the war. Large numbers of Russians and people from neighboring Soviet republics settled in Lithuania during the postwar period, when it was part of the Soviet Union. The Polish population increased mainly as a result of the incorporation of the Vilnius district, which was part of Poland from 1920 to 1939.

Eighty percent of the population is Catholic (the great majority of them Lithuanians and Poles), about 10 percent is Greek Orthodox or of Orthodox descent (Russians and most of the Belorussians and Ukrainians) and about 7 percent Protestants (the Lithuanian Lutheran church). The regaining of independence in 1990 was followed by a large-scale revival of religious activity, especially among Catholics.

Seventy percent of the population is urban, more than twice its proportion in the late 1940s. It was only 25 percent urban in the mid-1930s. There is a steady move from the rural areas to towns, mainly to the larger cities. There are over ninety cities, towns and townships. In addition to the capital, Vilnius, four towns have a population of more than 100,000 inhabitants: Kaunas (or Kovno, the Lithuanian capital between the two world wars), with 430,000 inhabitants; Klaipėda (Memel), the main port, with 210,000 inhabitants; Panevėžys (Poneviej), 130,000; and Šiauliai (Shauli), 150,000. A number of smaller, newly planned towns to function as subregional centers were developed in the 1960s and 1970s, such as Alytus (in the southeast), Mažeikiai (in the northwest) and Utena (in the northeast).

Industry and Mineral Resources

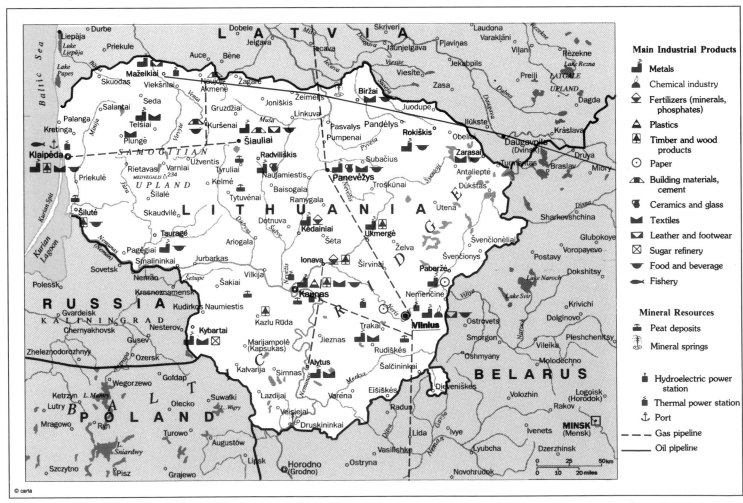

Main Industrial Products

⬛ Metals

♨ Chemical industry

⬗ Fertilizers (minerals, phosphates)

△ Plastics

⬛ Timber and wood products

⊙ Paper

◸ Building materials, cement

♔ Ceramics and glass

⋈ Textiles

◩ Leather and footwear

⊠ Sugar refinery

▽ Food and beverage

✕ Fishery

Mineral Resources

⬚ Peat deposits

⬚ Mineral springs

⬛ Hydroelectric power station

⬛ Thermal power station

⚓ Port

--- Gas pipeline

— Oil pipeline

© carta

Agriculture

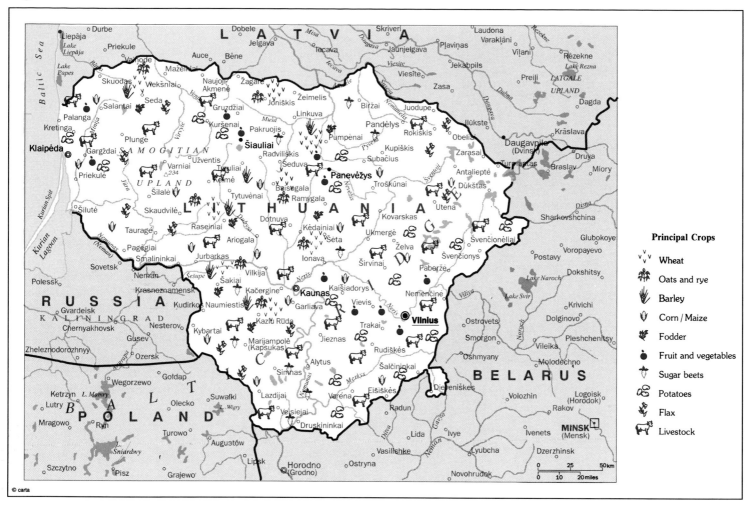

The southeastern region and parts of the southern and coastal regions are the most densely inhabited, while the western hilly region and large parts of the plain have a comparatively thin rural population. The average population density for the country as a whole is 150 persons per square mile (58 per sq. km).

Lithuanian is the official language but Russian is widely used.

ECONOMY

Lithuania is still largely agrarian, although industrial development during the period of Soviet rule has given industry a predominant role in the economy. The main urban areas and their surroundings have become industrial centers. Lithuania, since regaining its independence in 1990, has been trying to establish direct economic relations with countries outside the former Soviet Union. It is, however, still largely dependent on the former USSR states—especially Russia—for a supply of raw materials and essential commodities, as well as for the export of its products. A treaty with Russia, signed in 1991, governs these economic relations and special arrangements concerning the Russian Kaliningrad enclave. There is also an agreement for close economic cooperation with the neighboring former Soviet Baltic states of Estonia and Latvia.

Agriculture

Nearly 70 percent of the total area is utilized for cultivation or improved grazing. The main products are grains (mostly rye, wheat, oats and barley), fodder crops, potatoes, sugar beets, vegetables, fruit and flax. Grains are grown mainly in the southern and central regions, while cattle and pigs are raised mainly in the north and west. Meat, milk, poultry and their products form a substantial part of Lithuania's agricultural exports.

Agricultural activities under the Soviet Union were carried out in 737 collective farms and 311 state farms. Before the Soviet occupation in 1940, small and middle-sized farms (of 10 to 50 acres) were responsible for the great majority of agricultural production. A program to reprivatize agriculture is now being carried out. Many collective farms were divided into small landholdings and put at the disposal of farming families.

Mineral Resources

Lithuania is poor in mineral resources. Small quantities of oil are produced in the northwest (Kretinga). Large quantities of peat are quarried. Lithuania is an important source of amber.

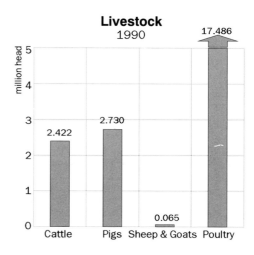

Livestock
1990

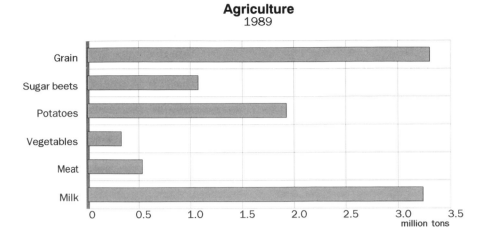

Agriculture
1989

Grain
Sugar beets
Potatoes
Vegetables
Meat
Milk

0   0.5   1.0   1.5   2.0   2.5   3.0   3.5
million tons

Industry

The main urban centers and their surroundings have become largely industrialized since the 1950s, as part of the framework of USSR economic development programs. Vilnius, Kaunas, Klaipèda and Siauliai are the focal points of a variety of industries, including a number of large enterprises. Agricultural products and the extensive forests provide raw materials for many of the industries. There is also shipbuilding (at Klaipèda), engineering, agricultural and industrial tools, electronics, chemicals, building materials (mainly cement), textiles, footwear, leather products, paper, timber products, fish processing, sugar and various food products. Privatization of many industries is in progress. Hydroelectric power stations and a nuclear power station provide most of the country's energy.

Trade

Trade is still mainly with the neighboring states of the former Soviet Union. However, a substantial growth in an exchange of goods with other European countries has already been recorded. Close economic cooperation with Latvia and Estonia has been in operation since 1990.

HISTORY

The Lithuanian's earliest ancestors are believed to have settled here about two thousand years ago, in the lower part of the Neman Basin. They were called Aestii by the first-century Roman historian Tacitus, who described them as efficient agriculturalists. To the second-century Greek geographer, Ptolemy, they were Galindae and Sudeni tribes. The Lithuanian language belongs to an ancient, almost extinct, Baltic branch of the Indo-European language family, which uniquely preserves its Sanskrit and Greek roots. The first recorded mention of Lithuanian tribes appears in the eleventh century, when they were still pagans faced with continuous pressure from Slavic invaders from the south and later (in the twelfth and thirteenth centuries) from German Teutonic knights. It was only then that the Lithuanian tribes united under a common rule (of a grand duchy) and military organization. They were converted to Western Christianity in the thirteenth and fourteenth centuries.

The fourteenth and fifteenth centuries witnessed a period of consolidation, expansion and the assumption of a leading political and military role in eastern Europe. Lithuania's domain extended over White Russia (Belarus) and a large part of Ukraine, reaching the shores of the Black Sea. A union with Poland in 1385— formally, a dynastic union—gave it a dominant position in eastern Europe. The union had a common sovereign (from 1501) and legislature (from 1569). The rise of Russia in the east and of Prussia in the west (seventeenth and eighteenth centuries) resulted in the loss of territories and power. The union saw its total collapse and loss of independence with the division of Poland (in 1795) among Russia, Prussia and Austria. Nearly the entire area of Lithuania became part of the Russian Empire.

The Lithuanians suffered extreme suppression under tsarist Russia, including prohibition of the use of their language in print and restrictions on educational and religious activities. The country suffered much devastation during World War I, when it was under German occupation for three years. It gained its independence in 1918, but lost its eastern part, with the capital, Vilnius, which Poland occupied (1920) and annexed (1922). Initially, under a treaty with the Soviet Union, the country's area extended over 32,000 square miles (83,000 sq. km), but was soon reduced to 21,490 square miles (55,660 sq. km) following the loss of its eastern region to Poland.

The democratic regime established in 1919 was overthrown in 1926 and replaced by a dictatorial regime. In 1939, Nazi Germany occupied and annexed Lithuania's main port, Klaipèda (Memel), which had been, since 1923, an autonomous town under Lithuanian sovereignty. The Soviet Union restored the region and city of Vilnius to Lithuania in October 1939, following the division and occupation of Poland by Germany and the Soviet Union. The German-Soviet treaty of September 1939 placed Lithuania within the sphere of Soviet influence and paved the way to its forced incorporation as a republic in the Soviet Union (1940). Germany, with the active help of the local population, occupied Lithuania within a few days after its invasion of the Soviet Union in June 1941, an occupation which lasted until July/August 1944, when the Soviet army regained control over the country. Large numbers of Lithuanians withdrew with the German army, while others who actively assisted the Germans were expelled to other parts of the USSR. The Soviet authorities encouraged the settlement of large numbers of Russians and Belorussians in Lithuania. Collectivization of agriculture was enforced in 1949. Lithuania regained its independence in 1990 with the collapse of the Soviet Union.

GOVERNMENT AND POLITICS

The 141-member Supreme Soviet, elected in February 1990, became the country's democratic legislature upon declaring its independence a fortnight later. New elections and a referendum to approve a new constitution were held in October 1992. The election results were as follows: the Democratic Labor Party (former Communist Party), 73 seats; the National Front Sajudis Party, 30 seats; Christian Democrats, 8 seats; Union of Poles, 4 seats; and smaller parties

Education
1989–1990

	No. of Institutes	No. of Students
Primary & Secondary Schools	2,200	500,000
Higher Education	12	69,400
Technical Colleges	66	51,700

and independents, 10 seats. In 1993, the chairman of the Democratic Labor Party, Algirdas Brazauskas, was elected the country's president with wide executive powers. The government consists of members of the same party. The country is administratively divided into forty-four rural and twenty-two urban districts.

THE CAPITAL

The capital, Vilnius (Vilna, Wilno), is Lithuania's main economic, industrial and cultural center, as well as a major national and international focus of communication. The city is built on river terraces and on several hills around the confluence of the Neris and Vilnele (Vilejka) rivers; it lies about 390 feet (119 m) above sea level and 165 miles (265 km) from the Baltic coast. Its population of 593,000 (1992) had nearly tripled over the last forty years and had increased fivefold since World War II, at the end of which it was reduced to less than 120,000. World War II also brought far-reaching changes in the composition of the population. At the beginning of the century, Lithuanians made up only 15 percent of the city's population, while Jews were 40 percent and Poles 31 percent. Poles formed the majority of the population on the eve of and during World War II. They were 53 percent in a census carried out in 1942; the Lithuanians were then only 18 percent. There has also been a substantial increase in the percentage of Russians and Belorussians, who make up about one-fourth of the city's population.

It is believed that the first settlement on this site was established in the tenth century, when a small fort was built. The city, which was destroyed or badly damaged by wars and fires several times

in its long history, was actually founded in 1323 when the then Grand Duke of Lithuania, Gediminas, made it the country's capital. In the fifteenth century, it became a prominent Christian religious and cultural center. The first cathedral was built in 1387. The first books in Polish and in Belorussian were printed in Vilnius. The university founded here in 1578 was closed in 1832 (by the Russian authorities) and reopened in 1919. Vilnius was made the capital of an administrative region in 1795, when Lithuania came under Russian rule. The city was occupied by the German army in 1915 and held for three years. It became the capital of independent Lithuania at the end of 1918. After a short spell of occupation by the Polish army (1919) and later by the Soviet army (1920), it was ceded back to Lithuania for seven weeks before it was reoccupied and annexed by Poland. Vilnius was restored along with the surrounding region to Lithuania in the autumn of 1939, and reinstated as its capital, which it has been ever since.

The old section of the city has preserved some of its characteristics from the seventeenth and eighteenth centuries, when it was surrounded by a wall and had narrow, tortuous lanes. A gate and remnants of the wall and old fort have been preserved. In addition to two cathedrals (restored in the nineteenth century), there are numerous churches and some public buildings in Gothic and Baroque style, dating back to the seventeenth and eighteenth centuries. Much of the more modern parts of the city, 40 percent of which was demolished or severely damaged during World War II, was rebuilt or became modern suburbs with the city's rapid growth after the war.

Apart from the university, Vilnius has a variety of institutions of higher learning and scientific research, academies of art and music, museums and theaters. The city and its surroundings are Lithuania's main industrial center, producing a variety of metal and engineering products, chemicals, clothing, footwear, food products and a printing industry.

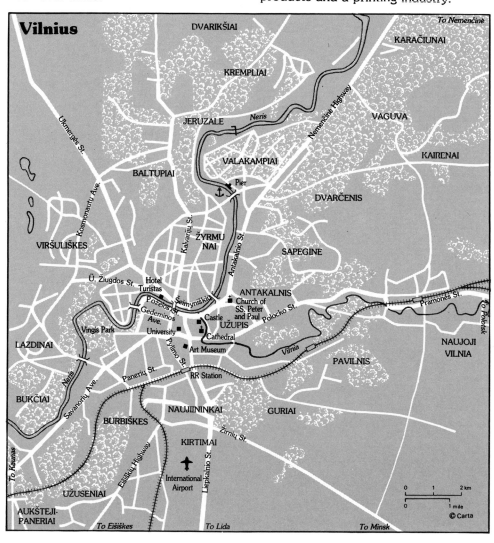

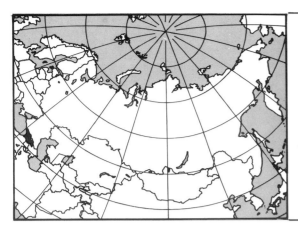

Georgia

Area: 26,900 sq. mi. (69,700 sq. km)
Population (1993 estimate): 5,640,000
Natural increase (1990–1993): 0.85%
Capital city: Tbilisi

Population in Main Cities (1990 estimates):

Tbilisi: 1,280,000   Batumi: 136,000
Kutaisi: 235,000   Sukhumi: 121,000
Rustavi: 160,000

Georgia is the westernmost of the three Transcaucasian states of the former Soviet Union. The country is largely mountainous (over 80 percent of the total area). It has a rich variety of natural landscapes, climatic and vegetation zones, as well as a diversity of ethnic groups, cultures and religions. The country is bounded on the north by Russia, on the northeast by Azerbaijan, on the southeast by Armenia, on the southwest by Turkey and on the west by the Black Sea, providing

Georgia with the longest warm-sea coast in the former Soviet Union. Five autonomous Caucasian ethnic regions are situated along Georgia's long and tortuous boundary with Russia; they are (from west to east) Karachayevo-Cherkess, Kabardino-Balkar, North Ossetia, Checheno-Ingush (which was separated into two republics, Chechenia and Ingushetia, in April 1993) and Dagestan. Three similar autonomous ethnic regions are within Georgia: Abkhazia, Adjaria and South Ossetia. Since

Georgia gained its independence in 1991, Abkhazia and South Ossetia have declared their desire for independence and have been in armed rebellion toward that end. There has also been much internal unrest and instability.

NATURAL REGIONS

Three natural regions can be distinguished: the main (or Great) Caucasus range in the north, by far the largest and

most dominant of the natural regions; the Lesser Caucasus in the south; and the lowlands and main river valleys and basins in the center. Although the smallest of the three regions, the latter is the core of the country and the most populated.

The western part of the Caucasus mountain system is divided between Georgia and Russia. To a large extent the boundary runs along the line of the highest ridges of the main range. This roughly corresponds to the watershed formed between the rivers flowing northward and those flowing southward into the Georgian central valleys and lowlands. The Georgian Caucasus therefore extends over the southern slopes of the main range, running from northwest to southeast, and contains the highest peaks and a large proportion of the glaciers. The boundary with Russia cuts across a long (over 150 mi./240 km) line of glaciers, including the largest in continental Europe. The highest mountains of this frontier zone include the extinct volcano Kazbek (Utsinkvari) (16,510 ft./5,047 m), Shkhara (16,627 ft./5,068 m) and Rustaveli (16,273 ft./4,960 m).

The Georgian Caucasus region consists mostly of ranges running almost parallel to and south of the central range, and of numerous spurs at right angles to the main trend of this mountain system, separated by narrow, deep river valleys. Some of the inner valleys are isolated and not easily accessible, making them a refuge for different ethnic groups, who were able to preserve their identity and way of life when the region came under various conquerors, especially the Russian Empire. The river valleys become broader as they approach the central lowlands, and the slopes of the adjoining mountain spurs become more gentle, thus attracting agricultural and more settlement activity than in other areas. Much of the area, up to an altitude of 6,000 to 7,000 feet (1,800 to 2,100 m), is covered by forests and brushwood.

The most important pass, which crosses the Caucasus in eastern Georgia, is the Daryal Pass (altitude, 7,805 ft./2,380 m), through which the historically famous Georgian Military Road runs, as does the main road link between Georgia and Russia. The Mamison Pass (9,270 ft./2,828 m), farther west, is another well-known and much-used route.

The western Lesser Caucasus, which forms the southern mountainous region of Georgia, has a more moderate relief than that of the Great Caucasus. The peaks are much lower (the highest, Didi Alul, is 10,830 ft./3,304 m) and gentle slopes are much more frequent. It also runs in a generally east-west direction. In the east, the region assumes the character of a dissected plateau that extends into northern Armenia and is known as the Armenian Plateau. Here again, the broader river valleys and the lower parts of the slopes of the main ranges are the main inhabited areas. This is particularly true of the valleys of the Kura River and its larger tributaries. The region has many small lakes, some of which are known for their picturesque landscapes. Features that owe their origin to volcanic activity are common in the eastern part of the region.

The central lowlands are divided into two main natural subregions by a spur of the Caucasus, the Suram Mountains, that form a highland link with the Lesser Caucasus. The watershed between the Kura River, flowing to the Caspian Sea, and the Rioni River (and its tributaries), flowing to the Black Sea, runs along the Suram Mountains. It is also a climatic divide between the more temperate, Mediterranean-like climate of the western part of the lowlands and the more arid and continental character of the areas to the east. The western lowlands consist mainly of the Black Sea coastal plain. The plain is widest at its center (over 20 mi./30 km), narrowing considerably at its northern and southern ends. The central part of the coastal lowlands, known as the Kolkhida Plain (the Colchis Plain of the ancient Greeks), was largely covered by swamps. Over the last fifty years the plain had been largely drained and subject to intensive cultivation of subtropical fruit and field crops.

The lowlands east of the Suram Mountains consist of the Kura Valley and the valleys and small basins adjoining it. This part of the lowlands is much narrower and more elevated than the western lowlands. It is considered by some geographical surveys as an intermontane basin or valley instead of part of the central lowlands. The capital, Tbilisi, is situated a short distance east of what is seen as the eastern edge of this basin, beyond another spur of the Caucasus which almost links it with the Lesser Caucasus.

CLIMATE

The proximity of the Black Sea, to the west, and the unbroken barrier of the Great Caucasus, to the north, play a predominant role in the country's climate. The climate varies greatly according to position and altitude. There are substantial differences in the range of temperatures and precipitation between the western and eastern parts of the country, especially in the lowlands. Winters are mild (up to an altitude of 2,000 ft./600 m). The Black Sea coast of Georgia has the warmest winter of any state in the former Soviet Union. The summers are warm, with typical Mediterranean temperatures. Rain (and snow) fall mainly in autumn and winter in the west, and in spring and autumn in the east. The average temperatures and average minimum temperatures for the coldest month (January) are, respectively, 42° to 43.5°F (5.5° to 6.5°C) and 20° to 23°F (−6.8° to −5.3°C) on the coastal plain; 30° to 33°F (−1° to 0.5°C) and 34° to 36°F (1.4° to 2.2°C) in the eastern lowlands (altitude, 1,300 ft./400 m); and 25°F (−4°C) and 17.5°F (−8°C) in the eastern part of the country (altitude, 3,000 ft./900 m). The average temperatures and average maximum temperatures for the hottest month (July/August) in the same above areas are 73° to 75°F (22.8° to 24°C) and 82° to 84°F (27.5° to 29°C); 75° to 77°F (24° to 35°C) and 87° to 88.5°F (30.5° to 31.5°C); and 71°F (21.7°C) and 81°F (27.5°C), respectively. Temperatures of over 95°F (35°C) are recorded occasionally in the valleys and basins, especially in the eastern part of the country.

The average annual precipitation ranges from over 100 inches (2,500 mm) on the westward-facing slopes in the west to 16 inches (400 mm) in the eastern valleys. Tbilisi, in the more arid part of the country, has an average of 20.5 inches (510 mm) of precipitation annually. The perpetual snow line is approximately 10,800 to 11,500 feet (3,300 to 3,500 m).

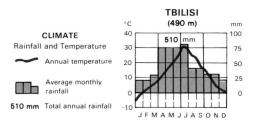

POPULATION

Georgia has an estimated population of 5.64 million (1993). The population was 5,449,000 at the 1989 census and 5,016,000 in 1979. The average annual rate of natural increase in recent years has been 0.85 percent. It was 0.8 percent during the 1980s, slightly below the average for the Soviet Union as a whole for the same period. The population growth rate has been low since World War II. The total population of Georgia was 3,542,000 in 1939 and 4,049,000 in 1959. The population was approximately 2 million in 1900.

According to the 1989 census, Georgians were 70.1 percent of the population; Armenians, 8.1 percent; Russians, 6.3 percent; Azerians, 5.7 percent; Ossetians, 3 percent; Abkhazians, 2.8 percent; Greeks, 1.9 percent; and Ukrainians, 1 percent. There are several other smaller minorities, including Adjarians, Germans and Jews. The percentage of Georgians has risen considerably since World War II. In 1969, Georgians were 64 percent of the population; Russians, 11 percent; Armenians, 11 percent; and Azerians, 4 percent.

The Georgians, Armenians and Russians are followers (or descendants of followers) of the Georgian Orthodox, Armenian church and Russian Orthodox church, respectively. The Azerians, Abkhazians, Ossetians and Adjarians are Muslims, forming about 11 percent of the population in 1993. There has been an apparent revival of religious activity since the declaration of independence in 1991.

The population is concentrated in the lowlands and in some of the valleys. More than 90 percent of the people live in areas below 3,300 feet (1,000 m), or in less than 20 percent of the country's total area. The mountain zones, between 3,300 and 5,300 feet (1,000 and 1,600 m) in altitude, are only sparsely populated. The average population density for the country as a whole is 208 persons per square mile (80 per sq. km). However, the density is well over 300 persons per square mile (120 per sq. km) in parts of the lowlands, especially in the eastern Kura Valley and the northern coastal plain. There has been a rapid increase in urbanization, particularly after World War II, with the industrialization of the main urban centers. The urbanization rate is presently 55 percent, as compared to approximately 35 percent in the 1930s. About 25 percent of the people live in and around the capital of Tbilisi. The other main towns are Kutaisi (235,000 inhabitants in 1990), Rustavi (160,000), Batumi (136,000), Sukhumi (121,000), Gori (59,000), Poti (54,000) and Tskhinvali (34,000).

The country's official language is Georgian, an ancient Caucasian language with its own alphabet. Russian is also widely used. The minorities each speak their own language in addition to Georgian and/or Russian.

ECONOMY

Georgia is rich in mineral and energy resources. It has climatic advantages and fertile lowlands and valleys. The country's geographical position, on the shores of the Black Sea, and its control of the most-used passes through the Caucasus have provided it with eco-nomic advantages. The economy is now primarily based on a modern, highly diversified industry and the utilization of the mineral and energy resources. Agriculture, which was the predominant source of livelihood for many years, has become of secondary importance despite its extensive modernization, mechanization and expansion over the last decades. The development of the communications network and port facilities has considerably increased the country's role in the transport of goods to and from the neighboring states of the former Soviet Union.

Agriculture

The cultivation of crops is mostly confined to areas below 4,200 feet (1,300 m). With the expansion of the land under cultivation, the intensification of agriculture and improvements in efficiency and productivity there came a continuous gradual shift from subsistence to commercial crops. While Georgia now exports large quantities of agricultural (mainly subtropical) products, it has become dependent on the imports of basic foods, such as wheat and other grains.

The coastal plain and the adjacent valleys and slopes are the main agricultural region. It is there that the most important commercial crops are grown: tea (over 90 percent of the former Soviet Union's production), citrus and other fruit, vegetables, tobacco, and certain trees and plants for the production of essences and special oils (for example, tung, rose, geranium, jasmine, eucalyptus). The lowlands and valleys farther inland, especially around Kutaisi, are the main wine-producing area. In the former Soviet Union, Georgia held a leading position in the production of good wines, for which it has a long tradition. Other crops

Education
1989–1990

	No. of Institutes	No. of Students
Primary & Secondary Schools	3,700	900,000
Higher Education	19	93,100
Technical Colleges	88	44,100

Ethnic Composition
1989

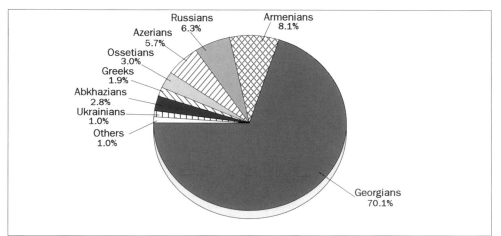

- Russians 6.3%
- Armenians 8.1%
- Azerians 5.7%
- Ossetians 3.0%
- Greeks 1.9%
- Abkhazians 2.8%
- Ukrainians 1.0%
- Others 1.0%
- Georgians 70.1%

include grains (mainly wheat), potatoes and sugar beets. The main products (and their production figures for 1989) are tea (packaged, 49,000 tons), grapes (514,000 tons), citrus (94,000 tons), vegetables (515,000 tons), grain (500,000 tons) and potatoes (332,000 tons). Cattle (1.4 million in 1990), sheep and goats (1.8 million) and pigs (1 million) are widely bred in the highlands, where seasonal movement to summer and winter pastures is practiced. In 1989, 712,000 tons of milk and milk products, 179,000 tons of meat and 6,400 tons of wool were produced.

Until the breakup of the Soviet Union, Georgian agriculture was organized within the framework of 719 collective farms (which controlled 66 percent of the agricultural land) and 594 state farms (34 percent of the land). The reorganization of ownership and production has been in progress ever since.

Mineral Resources

The manganese deposits near Chiatura in central Georgia are among the best in the world, in both quality and quantity. They are Georgia's most valuable mineral resource. There are large coal deposits in the same region (farther west) and in the northwest, near Tkvarcheli;

1.4 million tons of coal were mined in 1988. Brown coal, mined in the northeast (at Mirzaani), supplies a large part of the domestic needs. There are also deposits of gold, iron, mercury, tungsten, molybdenum, arsenic, baryta and diatomite shale. Marble, talc and clays are also quarried.

The many rivers that flow down from the Great and Lesser Caucasus provide an abundant source of energy. Numerous hydroelectric stations, especially along the Inguri, Kodori, Rioni and its tributaries, Kura, Aragui, Alazani and Khrami rivers, produce huge quantities of electric power required for industrial-

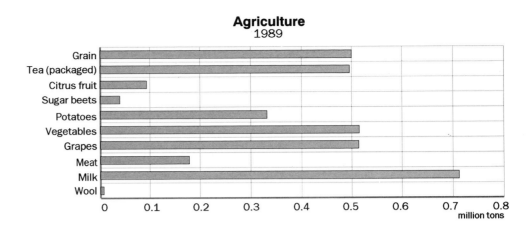

Agriculture
1989

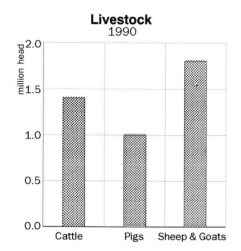

Livestock
1990

Agriculture

Main Industrial Products
1989

Steel	1,400,000 tons
Rolled ferrous metals	1,200,000 tons
Timber	304,000 cu. m
Paper	28,000 tons
Cement	1,500,000 tons
Fabrics	123,000,000 sq. m
Knitwear	56,200,000 items
Hosiery	31,900,000 pairs
Footwear	16,500,000 pairs
Butter	1,000 tons
Granulated sugar	32,000 tons
Preserves	727,000,000 jars

ization and other aspects of economic growth. There are also thermoelectric power stations operated by local fuel resources.

Industry

Georgia's large and varied industry developed mostly since the 1950s. The metallurgical and machine industries, with Rustavi and Zestafoni as the main centers, are prominent, producing iron, steel and a wide range of iron and steel products. Output in 1989 totaled 1.4 million tons of steel and 1.2 million tons of other ferrous metals. There is a large copper-smelting and refining combine. Heavy vehicles, locomotives, earth-moving equipment, various machines and machine tools, agricultural machinery and tools, and precision in-struments are manufactured. There is also a large chemical industry, whose main products include fertilizers, phar-maceutical products, fibers and house-hold commodities. The large building materials industry produces cement (1.5 million tons in 1989), slate, bricks, tiles and prefabricated structures. The textile and clothing industry manufac-tures wool, cotton, silk and synthetic fibers, knitwear, hosiery, other items of clothing, footwear and a variety of leather products.

The large food industry is mainly en-gaged in the production of wine and other alcoholic beverages, tea process-ing and packing, canning (of fruit, vege-tables, meat and dairy products), oils, sugar and sweets. There is also a tobacco industry.

Industry and Mineral Resources

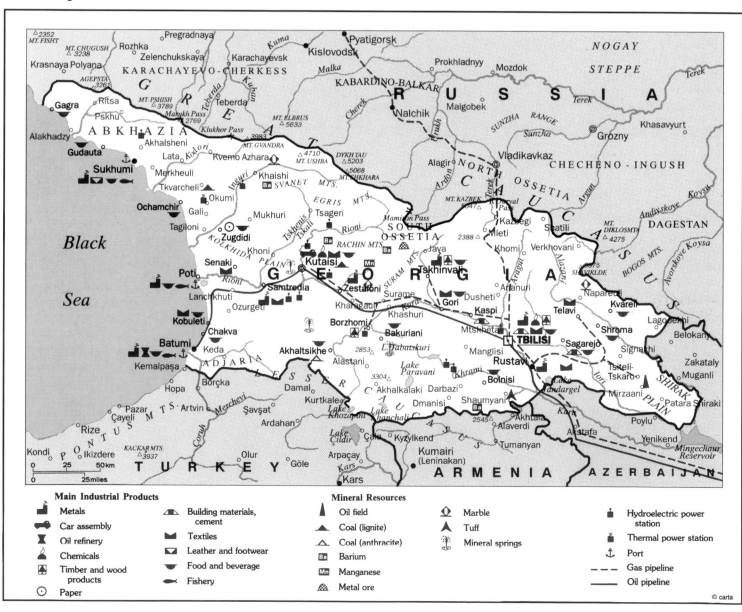

© carta

The industrial activity is largely concentrated in and around the main urban areas. Tbilisi is by far the largest industrial center. Rustavi, Kutaisi, Batumi and Sukhumi are next in importance. The districts of Tbilisi and Kutaisi are the most industrialized parts of the country.

Trade

Much of Georgia's industrial and agricultural production is intended for export. In 1990, nearly 94 percent of the exports went to other republics of the former Soviet Union—mostly to Russia, which supplied 76 percent of Georgia's imports. Since independence, the country's economic policy has placed much emphasis on increasing its foreign trade to countries outside the former Communist states.

HISTORY

Georgia (in Georgian, Skartvelo; in Russian, Gruziya) is one of the oldest states of the Caucasus region and the former Soviet Union. It was a kingdom first established over two thousand years ago. The Georgians are believed to be descended from tribes who migrated from Asia Minor (Turkey) and settled in the western part of the Caucasus region. They had formed two states by the fourth century B.C.: Egrisi (Colchis, to the ancient Greeks) in the west, and Korteli (Greek Iberia) farther east. Both states were released from Persian suzerainty by Alexander the Great. For several centuries Egrisi was under the influence of the Hellenistic world and later the Roman Empire, while Korteli was under Persian influence. The area of present-day Georgia was one of confrontation between the Roman (and later Byzantine) Empire and the Persian kingdoms during the first centuries A.D. The country under Byzantium embraced Christianity in the fourth century. The Georgian church was established and became predominant in the fifth century. The Arabs conquered eastern Georgia in the mid-seventh century (643–645), and Tbilisi became the seat of the governor of the Muslim caliphate.

Georgia gained its independence and for the first time its unity in 978 as a kingdom under the Bagratid Dynasty. The kingdom, after this known as Sakartvela, had its golden age in the twelfth and first half of the thirteenth centuries, when its domain extended from the Black to the Caspian seas. In 1234, it became part of the Mongol Empire, under which the Mongols employed Georgian troops in their military campaigns, including the conquest of Jerusalem (1303). After the withdrawal of the Mongols, the country broke up into a number of small kingdoms and princedoms that became subject to Persian or Turkish suzerainty (fifteenth to eighteenth centuries). The rulers and some of the inhabitants of these principalities converted to Islam during this period.

Russian expansion and increased interest in the Caucasus region at the time of Peter I (the Great) prompted the ruler of one of the Georgian states (Kakhetia-Karthelia) to put his country under Russian protection (1783). This did not prevent the Persians from invading eastern Georgia and leaving Tbilisi in ruins (1795). The entire area of Georgia was gradually annexed by tsarist Russia (1799–1804). The districts of Batumi and Kars were ceded to Russia by Turkey in 1878 (the Kars District reverted to Turkey after World War I) and were incorporated in Russian Georgia. There were several anti-Russian rebellions (in 1809, 1812, 1841 and during the 1905 revolution); all were crushed by the Russian army. The Russians abolished the autonomous Georgian church and incorporated it into the Russian Orthodox church.

During the Communist Revolution (1917–1919), Georgia was occupied first by the German army (1918) and later by a British expeditionary force (1919). After the withdrawal of the British, Georgia had a short spell of independence that at first was recognized by the Soviet government. The autonomous Georgian church was revived during this period. The Red Army occupied Georgia in February 1921. From 1922 to 1936, Georgia was part of the Transcaucasian Soviet Federated Socialist Republic. In 1936, it became a constituent republic of the Soviet Union and regained its independence in 1991, following the disintegration of the USSR.

GOVERNMENT AND POLITICS

The country is governed by an executive president who is elected by popular vote under a constitution that had been amended and adopted after the declaration of independence in 1991.

The president appoints the government, which requires the support of the legislature. The single-chamber legislature, originally the Supreme Soviet, turned into a democratic parliament with 235 deputies. This number was reduced to 134 in 1992. Following general elections in the autumn of 1992, the composition of the legislature was as follows: Peace Party—29 deputies; 11 October Party—18; Unity Party—14; National Democrats—12; Green Party—11; and Democratic Party—10. Forty additional seats are held by smaller parties and independent deputies. The president elected in 1991 was deposed the following year and replaced by the parliamentary chairman, who was appointed as provisional president. The country has been in a state of civil war since 1992. The government also faces armed rebellion in the autonomous regions of Abkhazia and Ossetia.

Georgia includes three autonomous regions (two have the status of republics), which were created under the Soviet Union to provide national aspirations for minority ethnic groups:

(1) Abkhazia, in the northwest, with an area of 3,320 square miles (8,600 sq. km) and 540,000 inhabitants (1992). Abkhazians (Muslims) make up 28 percent of the population, Georgians 44 percent and Russians 16 percent. The Abkhazians are a majority in the part of the country that controls a large section of Georgia's Black Sea coast. Their capital is Sukhumi. (2) Adjaria, in the southwest on the Black Sea coast and bordering Turkey, with an area of 1,160 square miles (3,000 sq. km) and 385,000 inhabitants (1992). Adjarians make up about half the population, Georgians 15 percent, Armenians 8 percent and Russians 8 percent. The capital is Batumi. (3) South Ossetia, in the central part of the Great Caucasus (North Ossetia is across the Caucasus, in Russia), with an area of 1,505 square miles (3,900 sq. km) and 100,000 inhabitants (1992), 65 percent of whom are Ossetians and 29 percent are Georgians. The capital is Tskhinvali.

The Abkhazians declared their independence in 1992 and managed to gain military control of most of their region in 1993. The Ossetians' aim is to unite South and North Ossetia into an independent state, and they have been in revolt since 1990 to achieve this goal.

THE CAPITAL

Tbilisi (or Tiflis)—meaning "hot springs" in Georgian, for the many hot springs in and around the city—is the largest and most important urban, industrial and communications center in Transcaucasia. The city, with 1,280,000 inhabitants (1991), and its surroundings account for one-quarter of Georgia's population. It is situated on the banks of the Kura River in the eastern part of the country, at an altitude of 1,325 to 1,600 feet (405 to 490 m), in a valley hedged in between a spur of the Great Caucasus and the Lesser Caucasus. Because of its enclosed position, the city is subject to comparatively climatic extremes, ranging from average minimum (January) and maximum (July) temperatures of 22.5°F (−5.3°C) to 88.4°F (31.3°C).

The city grew rapidly after it became the capital of the Transcaucasian Soviet Federated Socialist Republic (1922–1936) and later of the Georgian Soviet Socialist Republic (1936). Its population was 150,000 at the turn of the century, increasing to 519,000 by 1939, to 694,000 by 1959, to 879,000 by 1969 and to 1,260,000 by 1989. The city has large minority groups of Russians, Armenians and Azerians, who make up about 40 percent of its population. Tbilisi was founded in the fourth century. The advantages of its location at the meeting point of important north-south and east-west trade routes resulted in its growing importance as a commercial and political center. It became the capital of Karteli (ancient Iberia) in the fifth century, and was later the seat of Persian, Byzantine and Arab governors following their successive conquests. It was the capital from 1122 to 1234 of the united Georgian Kingdom, at the height of its expansion and prosperity. It was then part of the Mongol Empire. From the early fifteenth century to 1800, when it came under Russian rule, it was alternately under Persian, Turkish or Georgian suzerainty. After the annexation of Georgia by tsarist Russia, it became the administrative and military center of Transcaucasia, a position reenforced after the Transcaucasian SFSR was established in the Soviet Union (1922).

The city's historical relics include the old Metekhi Castle of Georgian kings, first built in the sixth century and rebuilt several times since; the Sion cathedral (from the fifth century) and other churches, the present buildings of which date back to the fifteenth century; and the Armenian Van cathedral (rebuilt in the fifteenth century). The older part of the city dates mainly to the eighteenth and nineteenth centuries. Most of the city is modern, with many impressive public buildings erected during the Soviet period. Large parts of the residential suburbs are typical of Soviet post–World War II architecture. Tbilisi is an important cultural center, the seat of the Georgian Academy of Sciences, a large university, many scientific institutions, technical and professional colleges and high schools, academies of art and music, museums, theaters and ballet.

Industries in and around the urban area include many large plants and a wide variety of products. The Zemo-Avchala hydroelectric power station on the Kura River, above the city, is one of the largest in the former Soviet Union. Tbilisi's industries produce machines and machine tools, agricultural machinery, iron and steel products, chemicals, electrical instruments and household goods, textiles (silk and cotton products), clothing, footwear, leather goods, furniture, timber products, building materials, processed agricultural products, foodstuffs, alcoholic beverages and tobacco products. Tbilisi is by far the busiest rail, road and air traffic center in the Caucasus and Transcaucasian region.

Education
1989–1990

	No. of Institutes	No. of Students
Primary & Secondary Schools	1,400	600,000
Higher Education	13	65,300
Technical Colleges	69	46,900

Tbilisi

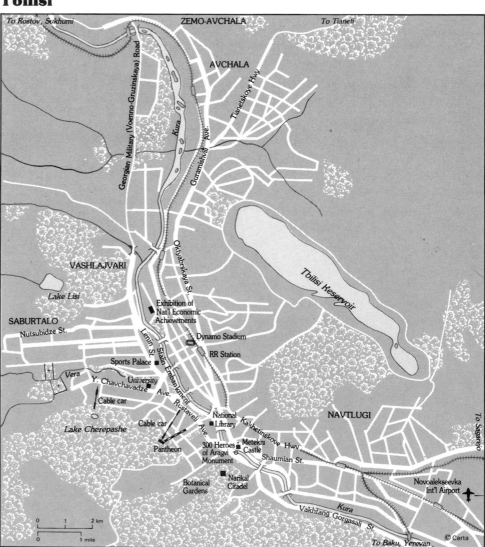

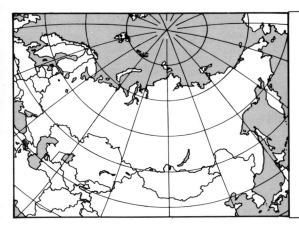

Armenia

Area: 11,490 sq. mi. (29,800 sq. km)
Population (1993 estimate): 3,500,000
Capital city: Yerevan (Erevan)

Population in Main Cities (1989 estimates):
Yerevan: 1,200,000
Karaklis (Kirovakan): 159,000
Kumairi (Leninakan): 120,000

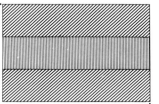

Armenia is the only landlocked country of the three Transcaucasian states of the former Soviet Union. It occupies the central part of the mountain ranges known as the Lesser (or Little) Caucasus. It is bounded on the west by Turkey, on the north by Georgia, on the southeast by Iran, and on the east and south by the two noncontiguous parts of Azerbaijan—the main part of that state and its autonomous republic, Nakhichevan. Most of the boundary with Turkey runs along the Araks (Turkish Aras, or ancient Araxes) River and its tributary, the Arpa.

NATURAL REGIONS

Armenia includes a number of natural regions, many of which extend into neighboring states. The main regions are (1) the Ararat Valley, which takes its name from the historically renowned Mount Ararat, the highest mountain (16,945 ft./5,165 m) of eastern Turkey, just south of the Turkish part of the valley; (2) the northwestern highlands, which form the highest part of the country; (3) the Sevan Depression, including Lake Sevan and the surrounding mountainous areas; and (4) the southeastern highlands, a narrow section of the eastern Lesser Caucasus, the major part of which is in neighboring Azerbaijan.

All parts of Armenia are mountainous except for the Ararat Valley. The average altitude is nearly 6,000 feet (over 1,800 m); only 8 percent of the country lies below 3,000 feet (900 m). Much of the country has a long history of volcanic activity, as shown in its extinct volcanos and large areas covered with volcanic debris and lava, and of severe earthquakes, especially in the west.

Ararat Valley

The Ararat Valley region lies at the foot of Mount Aragats and the Gegam Mountains. It comprises the northern half of a large depression cut by the Araks River, including the lower valleys of tributaries (mainly the Razdan and Kasakh) that drain into this section of the Araks. It is the lowest part of Armenia and has the most moderate relief. Much of the region is an undulating plain with rounded, low hills sloping gently toward the Araks River. It is the most developed and densely populated part of Armenia, and is the economic, cultural, political and administrative heartland of the country.

Northwestern Region

The northwestern region is made up of high mountains and volcanic plateaus dissected by deeply cut valleys. This is the most elevated part of the country, with the highest peak at Mount Aragats (13,400 ft./4,090 m), and is characterized by distinctive extinct volcanos. Economically, the region is second in importance to the Ararat Valley, both in agricultural and industrial production, concentrated in the main valleys and in the lower parts of the plateaus. The region has experienced intense seismic activity throughout its history, with disastrous earthquakes as recently as the 1980s.

Sevan Depression

The Sevan Depression contains Lake Sevan and a narrow rim of low hills and flat coastal strips (mainly where the small rivers that drain the neighboring mountains enter the lake). The mountain ranges surrounding the depression soar to a height of nearly 11,800 feet (3,598 m) in the west and to 11,000 feet (3,373 m) in the east. Lake Sevan (Turkish Gökcha), which lies at an altitude of 6,230 feet (1,902 m), is 400 feet (122 m) deep and 540 square miles (1,380 sq. km) in size. The lake drains into the Araks by the Razdan River, an important source of hydroelectric energy and of water for irrigation of the Ararat Valley. The regional population is concentrated around Lake Sevan and in the valleys of the small rivers running into it. Much of the area is farmland. The mountainous parts of the region are only sparsely populated and are used mainly for grazing.

Southeastern Region

The southeastern region is dominated by the Zangezur Mountains and other high ranges. Several of the peaks exceed 10,000 feet (3,000 m), with the highest rising to 12,800 feet (3,904 m). The ranges are cut deeply by numerous steep and narrow river valleys, some of which are small isolated strips of scattered rural habitation. This is the least populated and agriculturally utilized part of the country. It is, however, rich in some mineral resources. Access to much of this region from other parts of Armenia is largely dependent on passage through Azerbaijani territory.

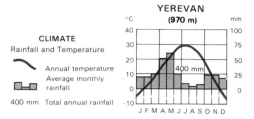

CLIMATE

Armenia's climatic conditions depend largely on geographical position and on altitude. Differences in the range of temperatures and in precipitation are often considerable over short distances. A variety of microclimate phenomena is typical of many valleys, some of which experience subtropical conditions. A continental climate prevails over much of Armenia, especially in winter, because of its location almost halfway between the Black and Caspian seas. The winter is very cold even in the lowest, southern-facing parts of the country. The average January temperature in the Ararat Valley and the neighboring foothills is 22° to 29°F (−5.6° to −1.6°C) and in the Sevan Basin (altitude, 6,300–7,000 ft./1,920–2,134 m), it is 14° to 18°F (−13° to −10°C). Lower average January temperatures are recorded at altitudes above 7,000 feet. Cold spells, when temperatures drop below −20°F (−29°C), are not uncommon even in the southern valleys.

In areas below 6,000 feet (1,800 m), the summers are especially hot, with high midday temperatures. The average temperature for August in the southern valleys is 75° to 81°F (24° to 27°C), rising occasionally to a daily maximum of over

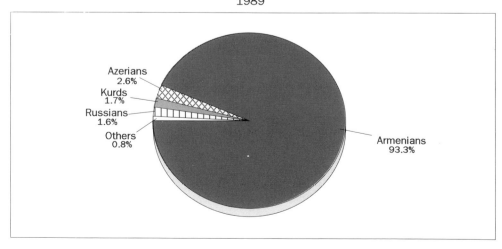

Ethnic Composition
1989

Azerians 2.6%
Kurds 1.7%
Russians 1.6%
Others 0.8%
Armenians 93.3%

105°F (40°C). The average temperature for the same month at altitudes of 6,000 to 7,000 feet (Sevan Depression) is 70° to 74°F (21° to 23°C). The average temperature for Yerevan (Erevan) (altitude, 3,170 ft./970 m) in January is 19°F (–7°C) and in July, 82°F (27°C). The average temperatures for January and July in Kumairi (formerly Leninakan), at an altitude of 5,080 feet (1,548 m), are 12°F and 76°F (–11°C and 24°C), respectively.

Precipitation falls mainly in the autumn and winter, mostly in the form of snow, in areas above 6,000 feet. Average annual precipitation varies from over 100 inches (2,500 mm) on exposed, high mountain slopes facing the humid air masses coming from the west and north, to 14 to 20 inches (350 to 500 mm) in the Ararat and some sheltered valleys. The Ararat and adjacent valleys are occasionally subject to drought, and intensive modern agriculture here depends on irrigation systems. The precipitation that falls on the high mountainous areas occupying most of Armenia abundantly feeds the many short rivers that drain the country and provides ample energy sources and water for irrigation.

POPULATION

The population was estimated at 3.5 million in 1993. It was 3,304,800 at the last census held in the USSR in 1989. The average annual increase over the decade preceding this census was 0.9 percent. There has been hardly any increase in recent years.

Some Armenians immigrated from Azerbaijan, while Azerians (Azerbaijanis) and members of other minorities emigrated. In 1989, 93.3 percent of the inhabitants were Armenians (this has now increased to 95 percent), 2.6 percent were Azerians, 1.7 percent Kurds and 1.6 percent Russians. Armenian is the official language, but Russian is widely spoken. Armenia's population was 780,000 in 1926, 1,281,600 in 1939, and has nearly doubled since 1959, when it was 1,768,000. The percentage of Armenians has gradually risen from 82 percent in 1926. Of all the Armenians in the former Soviet Union, 72 percent (1989) lived in Armenia. It is believed that this percentage has since increased slightly because of violent events, mainly in the Muslim republics of the new Commonwealth of Independent States. According to estimates, less than half of the Armenians in the world live in Armenia.

Despite seventy years of Communist rule, the great majority of the Armenian population is affiliated, at least nominally, with the Armenian church, whose world center and seat of the church's supreme authority are in Echmiadzin (near the capital Yerevan). The Azerians and Kurds are Muslims.

Only a small part of the country is densely inhabited. The average population density is 285 persons per square mile (111 per sq. km). It is, however, 1,200 persons per square mile (470 per sq. km) in the Ararat Valley, and more than 500 per square mile (195 per sq. km) in the larger, southward-facing valleys. More than half the population resides in the valleys and on slopes below 3,300 feet (1,000 m) and nearly 90 percent live in areas below 5,200 feet (1,600 m).

Armenia's population, which was predominantly rural (90 percent in the early 1920s and 80 percent in the early 1930s), has undergone a process of rapid urbanization since World War II. The urban population rose from 26 percent in 1940 to 59 percent in 1970 and to nearly 74 percent in 1989; half of the urban population is concentrated in the capital Yerevan (1.2 million). The other main urban centers are Karaklis (Kirovakan) with 159,000 inhabitants and Kumairi (Leninakan) with 120,000. The latter's population was 226,000 before the disastrous 1988 earthquake that destroyed much of the city. There are twenty smaller towns and townships, mostly in the Ararat and nearby valleys.

ECONOMY

Armenia has one of the most advanced economies of the Asian republics of the former Soviet Union. It developed a largely modern agriculture while an intensive industrialization process took place under Soviet rule.

The abundance of cheap energy produced by numerous hydroelectric power stations constructed along Armenia's many torrent streams, especially along the Razdan River, enhanced industrial development and led to the electrification and mechanization of agriculture. An atomic power station supplements the output of electricity, over 80 percent of which is provided by hydroelectric stations.

Agriculture

Approximately 25 percent of the country is under cultivation, nearly 40 percent of which is irrigated. The Ararat Valley is

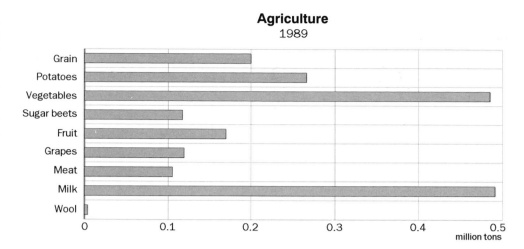

Agriculture
1989

million tons

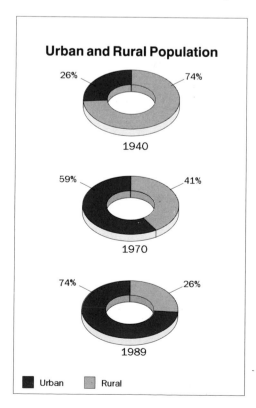

Urban and Rural Population

26% 74%
1940

59% 41%
1970

74% 26%
1989

■ Urban ▨ Rural

the chief agricultural region, most of it irrigated. Nearly 30 percent of the country is used as permanent or seasonal pasture. Raising cattle, sheep, goats and pigs is the chief occupation in much of the mountainous areas.

The main agricultural products are grain (mostly grown on the plateaus of the northwestern region), vegetables, fruit (especially subtropical fruit, such as figs, pomegranates, almonds, peaches and olives), grapes (for wine production), cotton, sugar beets, tobacco and potatoes. Livestock farms produce large quantities of milk and milk products, meat and wool. Agricultural production has grown more than fivefold over the past fifty years. Much of the vegetable and fruit crops are used for canned products. Before the breakup of the Soviet Union and Armenia's independence, 99 percent of the total cultivated area was in collective or state farms. Organization and ownership of agricultural activities have been in the process of transformation since 1991.

Mineral Resources

Armenia has large deposits of copper, zinc, molybdenum, bauxite (aluminum), marble and salt, mainly in the southeastern region. Copper is also mined in the northwestern region. Mining activity has become important since the 1970s, but was closely linked with the planning and requirements of the USSR.

Industry

Armenia today is mainly an industrialized country with a wide variety of products, most of which are exported to other republics of the former USSR. Over half the industrial activity is concentrated in the capital, Yerevan, and the surrounding area. Other main industrial centers are Kumairi and Karaklis. Industry is the leading economic activity in a number of smaller towns: Alaverdi, Kafan, Megri and Oktemberyan.

The chief industries are chemicals (mainly fertilizers), paper, mechanical engineering, machine tools, mechanical instruments, electronics, building materials, ceramics, textiles (cotton, wool, silk fabrics and other products), carpet weaving (also cottage industry) and leather products. The food industry includes fruit, vegetable and meat canning, winemaking, fruit preserves and cream-

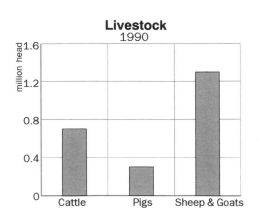

Livestock
1990

90

eries. Nearly 40 percent of the labor force is employed in industry, mines and quarries.

Trade

Armenia's exports consist of industrial products and fresh and preserved agricultural products. Until 1991, all exports went through the USSR's domestic and foreign trade systems, as did all imports. Main imports include fuel, raw materials, agricultural and industrial machinery and other equipment, vehicles, household electrical appliances and food.

HISTORY

The history of Armenia and the Armenian people goes back to biblical times. The area inhabited by the Armenians was subject to many changes in area, composition, population density and political fate. The region of what is known historically and geographically as Greater Armenia extended over most of present-day eastern Turkey, Transcaucasia and a small part of northern

Iran, an area which is more than ten times that of the present Armenian Republic. Because of its position and physical characteristics—highly mountainous and rugged—it was always a region of transition, penetration and confrontation between tribes, various ethnic groups, cultures and empires. Other people, such as the Kurds and Azerians, lived in areas of mixed ethnic habitation. For a long time the region had been an area of contention between the Roman-Byzantine Empire and the Persians. Much later (fifteenth to eighteenth centuries), the contest was between the Turks (of the Ottoman Empire) and the Persians. By the beginning of the nineteenth century, most of Greater Armenia, along with the great majority of the Armenian people, was part of the Ottoman Empire, while the northern portion, the area of present-day Armenia, came under Russian (tsarist) control.

The Armenians in Turkey experienced many tragic events during the second

half of the nineteenth and the early twentieth centuries as a result of violent clashes with their Muslim (mainly Kurdish) neighbors and punitive actions by the Turkish authorities. Large numbers of Armenians were massacred, while many others were forced to flee. These events reached their climax during World War I, when an extremely brutal evacuation was forced on the Armenians who inhabited eastern Turkey. More than 800,000 Armenians (half the Armenian population of Turkish Armenia) were driven to their death or killed during this expulsion. This resulted in the almost complete disappearance of the Armenians from eastern Armenia and to a large extent from Turkey.

An independent Armenian republic was established in 1918 in what was Russian Transcaucasia after the disintegration of a short-lived (1917) Transcaucasian Republic. This was followed by unsuccessful Armenian efforts, supported by the U.S. President Wilson, to re-

Industry and Mineral Resources

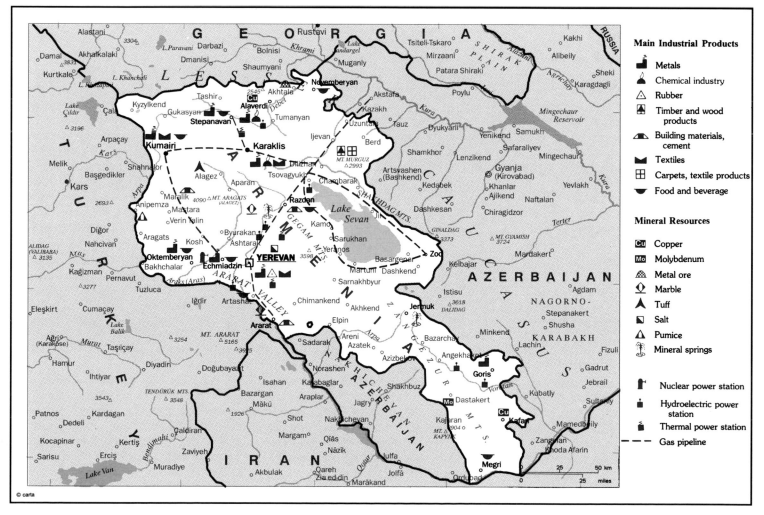

vive Greater Armenia by forcing Turkey to cede to Armenia what had been Turkish Armenia. In 1920, Armenia was incorporated into the Soviet Union as a republic. From 1922 to 1936, it formed part of the Transcaucasian Soviet Federated Socialist Republic, but from 1936 it again became a constituent republic of the USSR. Armenia proclaimed its independence in 1991 and became a member of the Commonwealth of Independent States.

GOVERNMENT AND POLITICS

The basic constitution under which the Republic of Armenia is governed was adopted in 1978, while the country was still part of the Soviet Union. Amendments enacted since the declaration of independence provide for its adaptation to the new status of the country and the government. A president with wide-ranging powers elected by popular vote for a four-year term is the head of the state. Ter Petrosyan, leader of the Armenian National Movement (MNA), was elected in 1991 by a large majority as the first president of independent Armenia. There is a 259-seat legislature in which the MNA won a large majority in the general elections held in 1990. A government, appointed in 1992, consists of leading members of this party, many of whom previously held prominent positions in the Communist party and government.

Armenia has a boundary dispute with its eastern neighbor, Azerbaijan. The Armenian parliament voted in 1990 to annex Nagorno-Karabakh, an Armenian autonomous region which is part of Azerbaijan. Hostilities have broken out in-

Education
1989–1990

	No. of Institutes	No. of Students
Primary & Secondary Schools	1,400	600,000
Higher Education	13	65,300
Technical Colleges	69	46,900

Yerevan

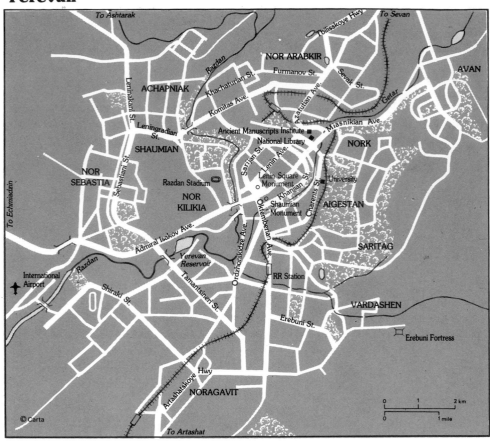

termittently between the two countries ever since.

THE CAPITAL

Yerevan (or Erevan), with a population of 1.2 million, occupies a prominent position in all aspects of Armenian life. It is built in the foothills north of the Ararat Valley, on the banks of the Razdan River where it enters this valley, at an altitude of 3,170 feet (970 m). The city, which is only 13 miles (21 km) from the Turkish boundary, overlooks Mount Ararat. The city's population has grown sixfold over the last fifty years (from 200,000 in 1939) mainly as a result of its development since World War II into a major industrial center. It also has a wide and advanced agricultural region, irrigated by a system of canals drawn mainly from the Razdan River, which is also the chief source of hydroelectric power to the city and its industries. It is a focal point for communication; its site controls the southern gate to the most convenient and used pass through the Lesser Caucasus ranges.

Remnants of a settlement and fort dating back to the eighth century B.C. in-

dicate that the site's advantages were recognized early in this part of the world. Yerevan has been one of the main urban centers of the Armenians since the seventh century A.D. An old sixteenth-century Turkish fort on a rock rising above the city and parts of an old eighteenth-century walled Persian city with narrow lanes and a beautiful mosque (the Hasan Ali Khan mosque) are the main remnants of old Yerevan. The greater of these by far is a modern city built mostly in typical Russian style. In addition to being the economic, administrative and political center of the country, it is also the core of Armenian cultural activities. It contains an Armenian university, a theological seminary, higher educational and scientific institutions, museums, an institute of Armenian music and libraries.

The large old monastery of Echmiadzin, 12 miles (19 km) west of Yerevan, is the seat of the head of the Armenian church and its supreme institutions. First built in the early fourth century, it is one of the oldest Christian monasteries and contains one of the oldest and finest libraries, including a unique collection of ancient manuscripts.

Azerbaijan

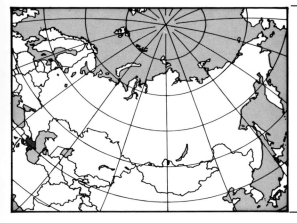

Area: 33,430 sq. mi. (86,600 sq. km)
Population (1993 estimate): 7,600,000
Capital city: Baku (Baky)

Population in Main Cities (1989 estimates):
Baku: 1,200,000
Gyanja (Kirovabad): 280,000
Sumgait: 235,000
Sheki (Nukha): 60,000
Mingechaur: 60,000
Lenkoran: 50,000

Azerbaijan is the largest, in both area and population, and the easternmost of the three Transcaucasian republics of the former Soviet Union, and the only Muslim one of the three. Its territory is not continuous. The country borders on Russia in the north, on Georgia in the northwest, on Armenia in the south-west, on Iran in the southeast and on the Caspian Sea in the east. Most of its boundary with Iran runs along the Araks River. The country includes the geographically separate Nakhichevan autonomous region, which lies beyond an intervening strip of Armenian territory. Nakhichevan is bordered on the south by Iran and on the west, for a short distance, by Turkey. The Azerbaijan republic extends over nearly half the territory inhabited by the Azeri people, approximately 60 percent of whom live in northwestern Iran (Irani Azerbaijan). Azerbaijan is rich in natural resources and has a wide variety of landscapes.

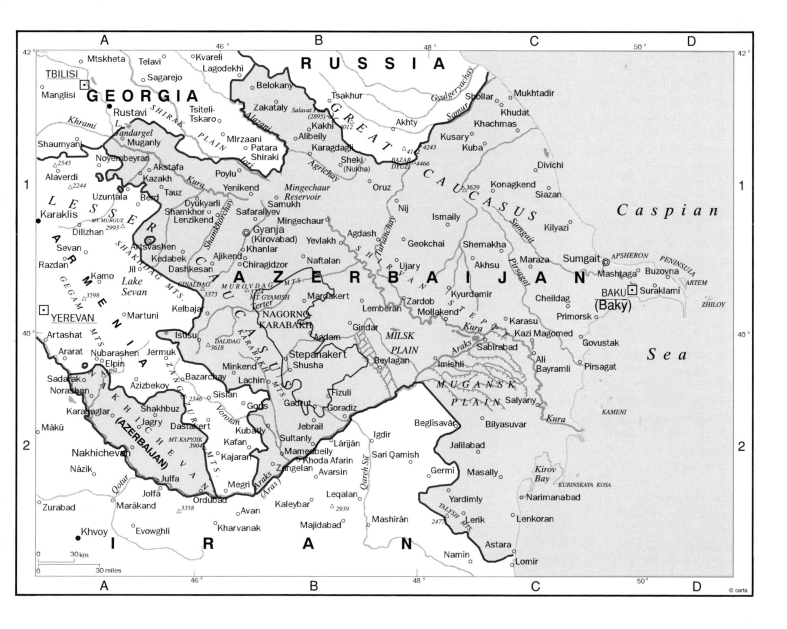

The future of areas with an Armenian majority and of the border with Armenia has been in question since Azerbaijan gained its independence in 1991, and is the source of unrest and belligerency.

NATURAL REGIONS

Three main natural regions can be distinguished: the mountain regions of the Great Caucasus and Lesser Caucasus, in the north and south, respectively, and the Kura-Araks Lowland that lies in between. The lowland with its adjoining valleys take up nearly half the area of the country. Each of the mountain regions are bounded on the east by a narrow coastal plain, much of which, like the adjoining Caspian Sea, is below sea level. The mountain regions are actually parts of much larger natural regions, extending well beyond the boundaries of Azerbaijan, while the lowland region is almost entirely within its borders.

The high mountain wall, with a long continuous line of ridges above 9,800 feet (3,000 m), of the Great Caucasus runs along the entire length of northern Azerbaijan. The highest peak, Bazar Dyuzi, is 14,650 feet (4,466 m). Several other peaks are above 13,000 feet (4,000 m). The only convenient pass through most of this region is at Salavat, at 9,490 feet (2,895 m). In the west, only the southern part of the range is included in Azerbaijan, whose boundary with Russia runs along the line of high ridges. About halfway along northern Azerbaijan the boundary turns north, along the Samur Valley, to the Caspian Sea, thus including the entire width of the easternmost part of the Caucasus range. The Caucasus is cut here by numerous deep, narrow river valleys that run almost perpendicular to the main northwest-to-southeast direction of the main range. The southward-flowing rivers are tributaries of the Kura River. Most of the region is sparsely inhabited. The population lives on the lower and gentler slopes (to an altitude of 4,600 ft./ 1,400 m) and in the valleys. Much of this part of the Caucasus is covered by forests.

A spur of hills (up to 1,150 ft./350 m in height) at the eastern end of the Caucasus forms the 47-mile- (75-km-) long Apsheron Peninsula, on which the capital, Baku, is situated. The peninsula has long been known for its oil fields and for its numerous mud volcanoes,

the largest of which is Bosdag, at an elevation of 950 feet (290 m). More than two hundred mud volcanos (mostly small, cone-shaped hills) are found on the Apsheron Peninsula and in the adjacent northeastern part of the Kura-Araks Lowland.

The natural region of Lesser Caucasus (or the southern highlands) consists of three subregions in Azerbaijani territory: (1) the northeastern part of the mountain system (the Shakhdag, Murovdag and Karabakh mountains); (2) the southeastern part of the system (the Nakhichevan autonomous region/ Zangezur Mountains); and (3) the Azerbaijan share of the Talysh Mountains, in the extreme southeast. The first two subregions are separated by the central parts of the easternmost Lesser Caucasus, in Armenian territory, including what is known as the Armenian Plateau. The third subregion is separated from the rest of the southern highlands by the Araks Valley and by Iranian territory. The Talysh Mountains are an eastern outlier of the Lesser Caucasus and a northwestern extension of the Elburz mountain system of northern Iran. The Talysh Mountains run in a northwest-southeast direction, rising to a maximum elevation of 8,127 feet (2,477 m) and sloping gently, for the most part, toward the Caspian Sea coast.

The highlands of this region are much lower than those of the main Caucasus. The highest peaks here are Mount Gyamish (12,210 ft./3,724 m) in the northern subregion and Mount Kapyjik (12,800 ft./3,906 m) in the Nakhichevan subregion. Generally, slopes are less steep and valleys are broader. The population density is also higher. The tortuous boundary with Armenia of both the northern and southern subregions, as well as that with Iran in the Talysh Mountains, follow the lines of high ridges which are also watersheds between the southward and northward flowing streams. Semiarid conditions prevail over much of the southern highlands of Azerbaijan, up to an altitude of about 4,000 feet (1,200 m), the severity of which varies considerably with geographical position and microclimatic conditions.

The Kura-Araks Lowland consists of a number of large valleys and steppes, drained by the rivers for which it is named and their tributaries. It is funnel shaped: narrow in the west, where the

valleys of the Kura River and its tributaries (Iori and Alazani) converge, and broader in the southeast, where it reaches a width of 75 miles (120 km). The eastern half of the lowlands is made up of almost flat plains (steppes) covered by a thick mantle of soft sediments. The lowlands are largely ill drained. Many streams flowing down from the highlands fail to cross these arid plains and end in swamps. Large parts of the steppes are irrigated by an extensive system of canals, making those areas the most agriculturally productive. A large dam on the Kura River, just below the confluence with its main tributary, the Alazani River, and the huge Mingechaur Reservoir (240 sq. mi./622 sq. km) which it forms, play a major role in the main irrigation system. It feeds the Upper Karabakh Canal, 109 miles (175 km) long, extending to the Araks River, and provides water for the irrigation of some 250,000 acres. The Mugansk Plain, in the southeast, is also irrigated by canals, running from the Araks to the Lower Kura rivers. Some areas in the eastern parts of the lowland are semidesert because of water scarcity and soil conditions.

CLIMATE

Climatic conditions, especially temperature and precipitation, in the northern and southern highlands depend on position and altitude and often vary considerably over short distances. The southward and southwestward-facing valleys and slopes generally experience higher temperatures and, in many cases, more precipitation. The lowlands have what is described as a subtropical, semiarid climate, with mild winters and hot summers. In the lowlands, average temperatures for the coldest month (January) are 34° to 38.5°F (1° to 3.5°C), with minimum temperatures of 26° to 32°F (−3.5° to 0°C), while the average for the hottest month (August) is 78° to 81°F (25.5° to 27°C), with a maximum of 84° to 87°F (29° to 30.5°C). Temperatures of over 100°F (38°C) are recorded in summer.

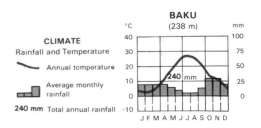

In the highlands, from 3,000 to 4,000 feet (900 to 1,200 m) in altitude, average temperatures for January are 20° to 25°F (–4° to –7°C), with minimum temperatures of 14° to 18°F (–8° to –10°C); average temperatures for August are 74° to 78°F (23.5 to 25.5°C), with a maximum of 81° to 85°F (27° to 29.5°C).

Precipitation varies to a great extent. The driest parts of the lowlands (in the extreme east and in the Araks Valley of the Nakhichevan region) receive an average annual precipitation of 8 inches (200 mm). Rain falls mostly in winter. Baku, the capital, receives an average of 9.5 inches (240 mm) of rain annually. The average annual precipitation over most of the lowlands is 12 to 16 inches (300 to 400 mm); precipitation occurs mainly in winter and spring. The wettest part of the country is the Talysh Mountains, in the extreme southeast, where an average of over 56 inches (1,400 mm) is recorded in some areas; about half of this amount falls in spring and summer. Most of the other mountain regions have an average annual precipitation of 16 to 32 inches (400 to 800 mm), with some of the more exposed parts of the Great Caucasus receiving as much as 40 to 48 inches (1,000 to 1,200 mm) a year. June and July are the wettest months. The permanent snow line is at 9,000 to 10,000 feet (2,700 to 3,000 m) on the northern slopes of the Great Caucasus, and approximately 11,000 to 12,000 feet (3,350 to 3,650 m) on the southern slopes of the Lesser Caucasus.

POPULATION

In 1993, the population was estimated at 7,600,000. It was 7,021,178 in the 1989 census, 6,028,000 in 1979 and 5,117,000 in 1970. The average annual rate of natural increase for the 1980s was nearly 1.6 percent. The population has more than tripled since 1926, when it was 2.3 million. According to the 1989 census, Azerians were 82.7 percent of the population; Russians (in the main urban areas) were 5.6 percent; Armenians, 5.6 percent; Lezgins (in the northeast), 2.4 percent; and Avars, 0.6 percent. There are also smaller minorities of Ukrainians, Georgians, Talysh (in the extreme southeast), Kurds (in the south), Tats (in the northeast) and Tsakhurs (in the north). The percentage of Azerians has risen considerably over the last forty years, mainly because of their

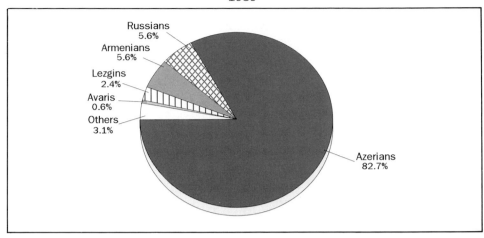

Ethnic Composition
1989

much higher birth rate. They were 57 percent of the population in 1958, 66 percent in 1960, 70 percent in 1970 and 74 percent in 1979. In the early 1950s, Russians comprised more than 15 percent of the population and Armenians, 14 percent; their share in the population had decreased to 10 and 9 percent, respectively, by 1979.

The Azerians, Lezgins, Kurds, Talysh and Tats are Muslims, who make up 87 percent of the population. Twelve percent are Christians (or of Christian descent), including Russians (Russian Orthodox), Armenians (Armenian church) and Georgians (Georgian Orthodox). The Armenians are concentrated mainly in the Nagorno-Karabakh autonomous region in the southwest.

The Azerians speak a Turkic language, which is the official language of the country. They are believed to be of mixed Caucasian, Iranian and Turkish origin. The Azerian language is presently written in the Cyrillic alphabet. The previously used Arabic alphabet was replaced under Soviet rule.

The average population density for the country as a whole is 220 persons per square mile (85 per sq. km). However, in the higher parts of the highlands and in large parts of the lowlands (especially in the east) the density does not exceed 80 persons per square mile (30 per sq. km). The density is much higher in the foothills and on the lower mountain slopes. The most densely inhabited districts are the Apsheron Peninsula and neighboring areas, the lower slopes, foothills and adjoining coastal plain of the Talysh Mountains, and parts of the central Kura Valley, where the

population density reaches more than 800 persons per square mile (300 per sq. km).

Urbanization has expanded considerably over the last fifty years. It was less than 25 percent in the 1920s, nearly 40 percent in the early 1950s, 50 percent in 1970 and over 60 percent in 1989. In addition to the capital, Baku, with 1.2 million inhabitants (1.8 million in the metropolitan area), the other main urban centers are Gyanja (Kirovabad), 280,000; Sumgait, 235,000; Sheki (Nukha), 60,000; Mingechaur, 60,000; Lenkoran, 50,000; Nakhichevan, 40,000; and Stepanakert, 33,000.

ECONOMY

The economy is based mainly on a wide variety of industries, in which the country's rich mineral resources, especially oil and natural gas, play a dominant role. The country's share in the industrial and agricultural output of the former Soviet Union considerably exceeded its share in population and arable land. Its modernized, intensive agriculture is mostly based on the extensive irrigation projects developed by the former Soviet regime and on the advantages of subtropical climate conditions. The highly developed transportation system by sea and river (the Caspian Sea and the Volga River to the internal waterway system of Russia and Ukraine), railways, roads and pipelines contributed significantly to the country's economic growth. The planning of economic development, especially since World War II, was subject to the central policies, general interests and requirements of the former Soviet Union—interests that, repeatedly, did not correspond to the potentials and local requirements of Azerbaijan. Since the country's independence in 1991, policy trends have been to reorient economic development; however, little apparent progress has yet been made.

Agriculture

Agricultural development is concentrated on subtropical crops, cotton, rice, tobacco, grayule (a rubber plant), tea, fruit (including citrus), vegetables (winter and spring), silk and winter wheat. Approximately 70 percent of the total area is agriculturally utilized, much of it as permanent grazing grounds. Cotton is grown primarily in the southeast (Mugansk and Salyany steppes) and the south (Nakhichevan). Production increased fourfold since the 1940s and reached 600,000 tons in 1989 (17 percent of Soviet output). Tea, rice and citrus fruit are mainly grown in the southeast (Talysh slopes and coastal plain). The production of grapes (mainly for wine) has risen from 10,400 tons in 1960 to 1,100,000 tons in 1989. The southern

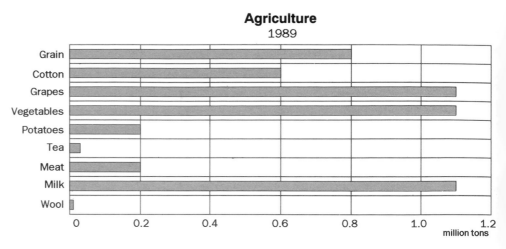

Agriculture
1989

million tons

foothills and lower slopes of the highlands and the Shirvan Steppe specialize in viticulture. Azerbaijan is also a large producer of walnuts and hazelnuts. In 1989, 1.1 million tons of vegetables and 800,000 tons of grain were produced.

Livestock is mainly bred in the highlands, where in some parts (especially the south and southwest) it constitutes, in value, the majority of agricultural production. In 1990 there were 1.9 million

cattle, 5.5 million sheep and goats and 200,000 pigs, from which 1.1 million tons of milk and milk products, 200,000 tons of meat and 10,400 tons of wool were produced.

Before the breakup of the Soviet Union, nearly all agricultural production was carried out in 608 collective farms and 800 state farms. The latter controlled most of the land that was developed and irrigated over the last forty years. The

Agriculture

© carta

Industry and Mineral Resources

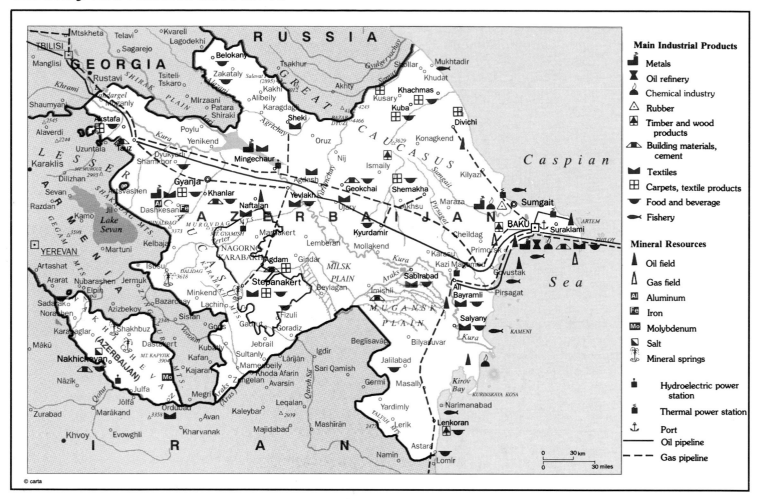

reorganization and gradual privatization of agriculture have been in progress since 1991.

Fisheries are important along the Caspian Sea coast. They are especially famous for the production of caviar (sturgeon roe).

Mineral Resources

Azerbaijan's mineral wealth derives mainly from its oil and natural gas resources. Although some oil fields have

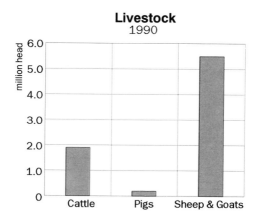

been in production for over a century, their output is the country's major source of income. Most of the oil and gas fields are on or near the Apsheron Peninsula, some of them in the Caspian Sea south and east of Baku. There are also oil fields in the central and lower Kura Valley. The Apsheron oil fields are connected by pipelines to the Black Sea port of Batumi. The gas fields are connected by pipes with the gas pipeline system of Russia. In the early twentieth century, Azerbaijan was the world's largest producer and refiner of oil. It contributed to about half the world's total output and over 90 percent of that of the Russian Empire, which was then about 12 million tons. It was still 71 percent of the Soviet Union's production in 1939 and 62 percent in 1945. Although production doubled (to over 22 million tons) by the early 1970s, it made up only 6 percent of the Soviet Union's output at that time, and less than 4 percent in 1990.

Other mineral resources include iron

ore (near Dashkesan), copper, lead, zinc, aluminum (bauxite), molybdenum, iodobromide, sulfur, salt and marble. Electric power is mostly produced by thermoelectric power stations using oil and gas, although a substantial amount is produced by hydroelectric stations on the Kura and Araks rivers.

Industry

Oil production was the initial cause of industrialization and is still an important factor in Azerbaijan's industries with large refineries, by-products, petrochemical and other products. The oil industry is mainly concentrated in and around Baku. There is also a large and varied iron, steel, nonferrous metallurgy and engineering industry, including equipment for oil drilling, pumping and refining, agricultural machinery and tools, and aluminum products. There are also industries that manufacture machine tools, electrical equipment and household appliances. The chemical industry produces fertilizers, pesticides, synthetic fibers, synthetic rubber, pharmaceutical products and various consumer goods. There is also a large textile and clothing industry, as well as leather and plastics industries. Most towns and townships throughout the country have food industries and plants for processing agricultural products.

Baku and its vicinity, including Sumgait (the main center of iron and steel products), are by far the largest and most varied industrial region. Gyanja, in the western part of the country, is second in importance, with its metal, machinery, chemical, textile and food industries. Mingechaur and its surrounding area are another industrial region in which textile, clothing and leather products are most prominent. Sheki, in the north, is another textile-producing center.

Trade

Many of the country's industrial and agricultural products are exported, mostly to Russia, Ukraine and other former republics of the Soviet Union, as well as to former Communist countries. Products (especially equipment for drilling and for oil and gas fields and industries) are also exported to various Asian and African countries. Until 1992, most of the foreign trade was handled by Soviet commercial organizations. These functions are gradually being taken over by the Azerbaijani government and private concerns. Imports consist mainly of raw materials, vehicles and transportation equipment, agricultural machinery, various industrial products and some foodstuffs (sugar).

HISTORY

The area of what is now Azerbaijan was known as Atropatene during the time of Alexander the Great (third century B.C.). It later became known as Albania, a name used as late as the tenth or eleventh century. Various peoples and tribes lived here, some of them only temporarily, mainly on their wanderings to the west or north. Much of the country was inhabited by Armenians as early as the first centuries A.D., and was repeatedly under their control. In the early medieval period, various Persian kingdoms extended their rule over the region. Arab armies gained control and brought Islam to the area in the middle of the seventh century. In the second half of the eighth century, the country came under Abbasid rule, which lasted

nearly two centuries. It was during this period that the region was repeatedly invaded by the Khazar kingdom from the north.

Turkish tribes from the east began settling the country in the eleventh century and became the predominant inhabitants. The country was part of the Mongol Empire in the early thirteenth century. After the death of Timor (1405) and the disintegration of his empire, the country was divided into a number of small local Tatar-Turkish principalities (khanates), of which Shirvan was the most powerful. After a short period under the Ottomans (1578–1603), the country was ruled by the Persians, until captured by the Russians in the early nineteenth century.

Russian penetration into what is present-day Azerbaijan actually began in the early eighteenth century, during the rule of Peter the Great. The Russians conquered parts of the country, but held them for only short periods of time. The country, up to its present boundary with Iran, officially became part of the Russian Empire in 1828, under a treaty with Persia (Iran); however, Russia gained full control of large parts of the mountain regions only in the latter half of the nineteenth century, after subduing the mountain people. An attempt to establish an independent Islamic state, with the help of Turkey, was made in 1918, following the collapse of the tsarist regime. It also became a battleground between tsarist forces (White Russians), supported by the British, and Communist forces (the Red Army). Turkish forces in support of local nationalists were also involved. The country was occupied by the Red Army in 1920 and became a Soviet republic. In 1922 it was united with Armenia and Georgia in the Transcaucasian Soviet Federated Socialist Republic, a union that came to an end in 1936, when each of the countries became a constituent republic of the Soviet Union.

Azerbaijan declared its independence and the establishment of a democratic regime in 1991, following the disintegration of the former Soviet Union. It joined the Commonwealth of Independent States (CIS) in the same year.

GOVERNMENT AND POLITICS

The country is governed by an executive

Education
1989–1990

	No. of Institutes	No. of Students
Primary & Secondary Schools	4,300	1,400,000
Higher Education	16	99,700
Technical Colleges	78	61,200

president, who is elected for a four-year term by popular vote. Presidential elections were held in 1992, in which Abdulfaz Ali Elchibey won 60 percent of the vote. The constitution adopted under Soviet rule in 1978 has been adapted to the requirements of an independent democratic state. The 360-member legislature, the People's Assembly (formerly the Supreme Soviet), was elected in 1990. It is dominated by the Popular Front (280 seats), which consists mostly of former Communists. The government is appointed by the president and is subject to the approval of the People's Assembly. There are several opposition groups. Much internal instability in 1992 and 1993 had prevented the normal functioning of the presidency. The country is also involved in hostilities with the

Nagorno-Karabakh

Armenian population of the Nagorno-Karabakh autonomous region (which declared its independence) and with Armenia, which occupied some areas in western Azerbaijan.

The country includes two autonomous regions, each with its own local legislature and autonomous administration. The Nakhichevan autonomous republic (area, 2,120 sq. mi./5,500 sq. km; population, 300,000) is a separate enclave in the south. Azerians form the large majority of the population. The region's capital is Nakhichevan. The Nagorno-Karabakh autonomous region (1,700 sq. mi./4,400 sq. km; population, 200,000) is in the southwestern part of the main territory. Armenians make up 76 percent of the population (according to the 1989 census). The region's capital is Stepanekart. Nagorno-Karabakh declared its independence from Azerbaijan in 1991 and has been in armed revolt ever since, with an aim of being incorporated into Armenia.

The town of Bashkend and its surrounding area in the extreme west are an enclave of Armenian territory in Azerbaijan. Similarly, there are two small enclaves of Azerbaijani territory inside Armenia, west of the town of Kazakh. Azerbaijan is divided into thirty-eight districts.

THE CAPITAL

The capital, Baku, with a population of 1.2 million (1992) and a metropolitan-area population of 1.8 million (nearly one-quarter of the country's inhabitants), is by far the largest and most important urban center of the country, and one of the most important cities of the former Soviet Union. It lies in a small bay on the southwestern coast of the Apsheron Peninsula, opposite the narrowest part of the Caspian Sea, a convenient landing site for boats crossing the sea. It was mentioned as Bakuya as early as the tenth-century writings of Arab geographers, who referred to the presence of crude mineral oil in the vicinity. It remained a small clustered township until the middle of the nineteenth century. It had a population of 6,000 in 1830. It was first captured by the Russians in 1723 and held for twelve years before it reverted to Persia; the town was again captured by the Russians for a short time in 1796, and finally in 1806. It owes its growth to the development of the oil industry, beginning in the 1860s, follow-

Baku

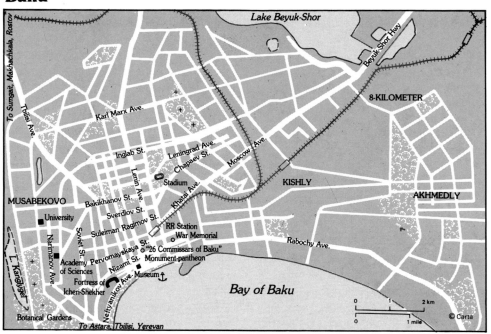

ing the invention of the refining process. It became a regional capital in 1859. Its population numbered 14,000 in 1863, grew to 86,000 by 1886 and to 112,000 by 1897. By that time it became the largest and most important oil-producing and refining center in the world. Industrialization and the development of a communications center accelerated the city's expansion, and by 1939 it had 809,000 inhabitants.

The city had suffered serious damage during the failed revolution of 1905 and even more so during the Communist Revolution (1918–1920). There were also serious outbursts of riots and massacres of the Armenian minority. More than ten thousand Armenians were murdered in the autumn of 1918. The city was taken by the Red Army in the spring of 1920 and has been the capital of Azerbaijan ever since. Industrialization was expanded and modernized after World War II, although the relative importance of Baku as an oil-producing center diminished considerably. The number of people living in the metropolitan area had increased to 968,000 by 1959 and to 1.3 million by 1970.

The growth and prosperity which the oil fields and industries brought to Baku had attracted people of various nationalities: mainly Russians, who comprised about one-third of the population, and Armenians, who were one-fifth; Azerians formed only about two-fifths of the population. The proportions have changed significantly since the declaration of in-

dependence in 1991. Many of the Armenians, numerous Russians and other non-Azerians have emigrated.

Although not much is left of the Persian town, its oriental character can still be distinguished in the old nucleus. There is a large fourteenth-century mosque, a palace that belonged to the Shirvan khanate rulers from the eleventh to fifteenth centuries, remains of palaces from the thirteenth to fifteenth centuries, and remnants of old walls, some dating to the tenth century. The modern city center, with its wide avenues and numerous large public buildings, many in typical post–World War II Soviet style, is surrounded by large residential quarters and suburbs. Some of these quarters, especially those east of the old center and built in the early twentieth century, are distinctly lower class and, along with the adjoining oil and port installations, are known as the "Black City."

Many large industries with a wide range of products are located in and around Baku. These include equipment for the oil industry, various machines and machine tools, chemicals (especially fertilizers), textiles and clothing and food products.

Baku is the seat of the Azerbaijan Academy of Sciences, many scientific institutes, a large university, several technical colleges and schools of the arts and libraries. It also has theaters, an opera house, museums, radio and television stations, film studios and a center for printing and publishing.

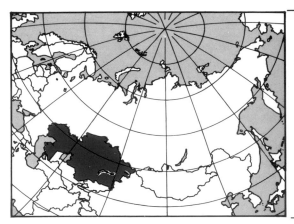

Kazakhstan

Area: 1,049,155 sq. mi. (2,717,300 sq. km)
Population (1993 estimate): 17,160,000
Natural increase (1990–1993): 0.65%
Capital city: Almaty (Alma-Ata)

Population in Main Cities (1989 estimates):

Almaty: 1,200,000 (1992)	Ust-Kamenogorsk: 324,000
Karaganda: 614,000	Jambul: 307,000
Chimkent: 393,000	Aktyubinsk: 253,000
Semipalatinsk: 334,000	Petropavlovsk: 241,000
Pavlodar: 331,000	Kustanai: 224,000

Kazakhstan is the second largest in area (after Russia) of the former Soviet republics. Although much larger in area than all the former Asian Soviet republics put together, it is the most thinly populated of them. The country extends about 1,200 miles (1,930 km) from east to west and 800 miles (1,285 km) from north to south. It borders on Russia in the north and northwest, on China in the east, on Kyrgyzstan, Uzbekistan and Turkmenistan in the south and on the Caspian Sea in the west. With the Ural River as the generally accepted boundary between Europe and Asia, Kazakhstan extends into Europe in the extreme west, where it includes a wide strip of territory between the Ural and Volga valleys, down to the northern coast of the Caspian Sea. It is a country of extremely wide-open arid and semiarid lowlands, through which, since prehistoric times, people migrated from Asia into Europe. It is also a country with a great variety of landscapes, peoples and resources, especially in its eastern and southeastern parts. The political entity of Kazakhstan, in its present extent and boundaries, is, in fact, a creation of the Soviet Union, first as one of its constituent republics and now, after its dismemberment, an independent state.

NATURAL REGIONS

The country shares a number of natural regions with neighboring states: the North Caspian Lowlands with Russia

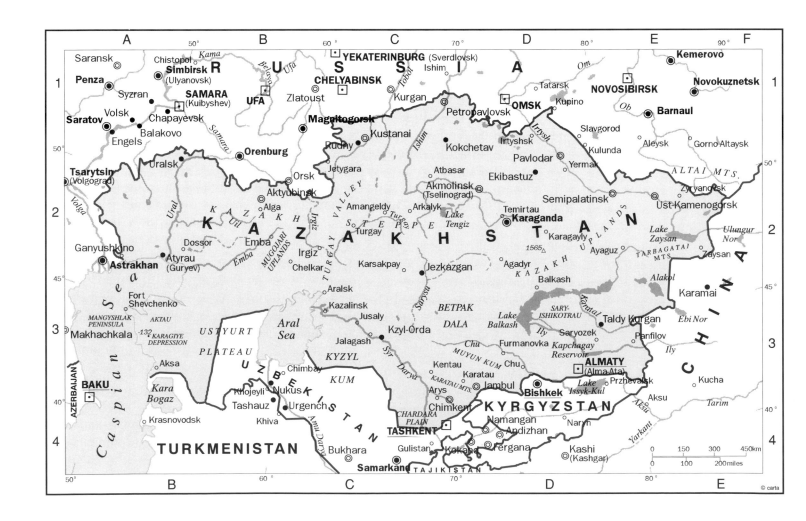

(the Astrakhan region and the Kalmyk Autonomous Republic) in the west; the Ustyurt Plateau, Aral Sea and Kyzyl Kum Desert with Uzbekistan in the southwest and south; the southern part of the West Siberian Lowlands with Russia (the Kurgan and Omsk regions) in the north; and the northern part of the Tien Shan Mountains with Kyrgyzstan and Uzbekistan in the south-southeast. A region known as the Kazakh (or Kirghiz) Steppe covers the central part of the country; although not clearly defined, it is assumed to take up most of the area. The Betpak Dala (Hunger Steppe), the Muyun Kum Desert and Lake Balkash are entirely within Kazakhstan.

The Caspian and Aral Regions

Much of the Kazakhstan part of the North Caspian Lowlands is an almost flat, ill-drained plain, at about the same level of the Caspian Sea (-92 ft./-28 m) or slightly above it. Some areas fall well below this level, and thus form small, local drainage basins. One such example is the Karagiye Depression, which includes the lowest point in what was the Soviet Union—433 feet (132 m) below sea level (340 ft. below the level of the Caspian Sea). It is drained by the Ural and Emba rivers, but numerous small rivers, probably once tributaries of these main rivers or that reached the Caspian Sea, end in swampy areas or in small, salt lakes. The area is thinly populated, except in the north, where most of the arable land is, and in the surroundings of the oil fields (along the coastal belt). Large areas are used for (mostly sheep) grazing with scattered patches of cultivation (field crops).

Kazakhstan controls the northeastern half of the shallow, shrinking Aral Sea. Part of the country, especially the catchment area of the central and lower Syr Darya, the great water artery of the south, drains into this inland sea.

The Deserts and Semideserts

From the eastern shores of the Aral Sea to the foot of the highlands in the southeast, a chain of deserts stretches, beginning with the northern part of the Kyzyl Kum, through the Betpak Dala (Hunger Steppe) and Muyun Kum, to the Sary Ishikotrau (southeast of Lake Balkash). This almost continuous belt of deserts, composed mostly of sand, gravel and bare rock, is interrupted only by the valley of the Syr Darya, a few

other, much smaller rivers (such as the Chu, Ily and Karatal) and two main spurs (Karatau and Aktau) of the Tien Shan Mountains.

Settlement and agriculture in these deserts have the character of oases, the most extensive of which is that along the Syr Darya, where large areas are under irrigation. However, with a much smaller discharge (only about one-third) than that of the Amu Darya in Uzbekistan, expansion of agricultural production here has been significantly less. Part of the wide desert areas are used as permanent or seasonal grazing grounds, where mainly sheep (including karakul sheep) are bred.

The deserts are drained by many seasonal and perennial streams, some of them ending in lakes, the larger of which are the Aral Sea (24,750 sq. mi.) in the west and Lake Balkash (7,060 sq. mi.) in the east. Others are Lake Tengiz (610 sq. mi.) in the north and Lake Alakol (1,020 sq. mi.) in the extreme east. Many of the small lakes form chains which are, in fact, residues of larger lakes. Lake Balkash has shrunk considerably in the last four decades due to the use of much of the waters from rivers flowing into it for development projects.

The Kazakh (Kirghiz) Steppe

The Kazakh Steppe is a low, much dissected plateau and a partly hilly upland, which represent outcrops of resistant old rocks—remnants of mountainous landscapes of early geological periods. Most of the hills rise no more than a few hundred feet above an undulating peneplain, generally 1,000 to 2,000 feet (300 to 600 m) high. The boldest such outcrops reach an altitude of 5,130 feet (1,565 m). The uplands slope gently northward toward the West Siberian Lowlands, where they bear some of the effects of the Ice Age, mainly with regard to good arable soils. The watershed between northern and northeastern Kazakhstan, drained by the Irtysh River (and its tributaries) to the Arctic Ocean, and the rest of the country, which drains toward inland basins—the Caspian Sea, Aral Sea, Lake Balkash and other small basins—runs across the uplands of the Kazakh Steppe. Plans to divert large quantities of water southward from the Irtysh system (that carries twice as much water as the Nile) across the watershed, to irrigate extensive areas

in the arid and semiarid parts of central Kazakhstan, have been the target of great development projects. The Karaganda Canal, in the east, is one such project.

Since the end of the nineteenth century the northern and northeastern parts of the region have attracted colonization from the European half of tsarist Russia and later the Soviet Union. These are the moderately inhabited parts of the region, most of which is only thinly populated.

Two natural features separate the Kazakh Steppe from the Caspian Lowlands: the Mugojari Uplands in the west and the Turgay Depression farther east. The Mugojari Uplands are in fact a southern extension of the Ural Mountains, a much eroded, almost undulating plateau, rising gently to 2,155 feet 656 m). The north, where dry farming is possible, is fairly well populated, becoming, however, thinner as one goes south. The Turgay Depression is a deep, narrow, north-south valley, flanked east and west by escarpments or steep slopes of the adjoining uplands. During the Ice Age, it was the furrow through which much of southwestern Siberia (Tobol and Ishim catchment areas) drained to the Aral Sea. It was then that it developed many of its natural characteristics. It is partly covered by a chain of small lakes and by swamps.

The Eastern and Southeastern Highlands

Ranges and spurs of the Altai, Tarbagatai, Alatau and Tien Shan, of the Central Asian high mountain systems, and their forelands and interspersed valleys and basins, dominate the landscape of the eastern and southeastern regions. Some of these spurs, such as the Karatau and Altai, thrust deep into Kazakhstan, forming highland wedges between parts of its sand deserts. Most of the region is well provided with water resources—through precipitation or streams fed by glaciers and snow from the neighboring high mountains. The Irtysh, the country's largest river and richest water resource, has its origins in these mountains. On entering Kazakhstan, it flows through Lake Zaysan, an important freshwater reservoir, which provides hydroelectric power and water to large, densely inhabited agricultural and industrial areas. Much of the region lies above 2,000 feet (600 m); areas above

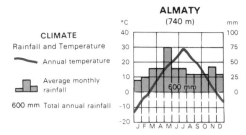

ALMATY
(740 m)

CLIMATE
Rainfall and Temperature

— Annual temperature

Average monthly rainfall

600 mm Total annual rainfall

5,000 feet (1,500 m) are small and mostly close to the border. There are a few peaks above 10,000 feet (3,000 m), the highest being 22,944 feet (6,995 m), on the border with Kyrgyzstan.

Much of this region is densely inhabited and contains several of Kazakhstan's most important centers of economic activity. This was brought about by the availability of large areas for dry farming, irrigation possibilities in the valleys and basins, mineral resources and hydroelectric resources.

CLIMATE

Typical continental climatic conditions, with varying degrees of aridity or semiaridity, prevail over Kazakhstan, except in parts of the mountainous areas in the east and southeast and on the northern fringes where average annual precipitation is above 12 inches (300 mm). There are great ranges in seasonal and diurnal temperatures, most extreme in the desert regions. Winters are very cold and midsummer temperatures are high. The average minimum and maximum temperatures for the coldest month (January) and hottest month (July), respectively, are 7°F (–14°C) and 83°F (28.3°C) in Almaty (Alma-Ata; the foothills in the southeast); –4°F (–20°C) and 87°F (30.5°C) in the Betpak Dala (Hunger Steppe); –3°F (–19.4°C) and 83°F (28°C) in Karaganda (central uplands); –5°F (–20.5°C) and 81°F (27.2°C) in Semipalatinsk (in the northeast); 4°F (–15.5°C) and 89°F (31.7°C) in Atyrau (Guryev; the Caspian Lowlands); and –2°F (–19°C) and 81°F (27.2°C) in the northwest. There are, on the average, 130 to 180 frost-free days in the coldest and warmest parts of the country, respectively.

The average annual precipitation varies from 4.5 inches (115 mm) in the deserts to 24 inches (600 mm) in the foothills in the southeast. Average annual amounts of 40 inches (1,000 mm) and more are recorded in the highlands in the east and southeast, at altitudes of above 3,000 feet (1,000 m). There is no completely dry season; in most parts of the country the comparatively wettest months are in summer and autumn. Years of serious drought are common in most of Kazakhstan, especially in areas with average annual precipitation of less than 20 inches (500 mm).

POPULATION

The number of inhabitants was estimated at 17,160,000 in 1993. It was 16,538,000 at the 1989 census and 14,685,000 at the 1979 census. The average annual increase in recent years has been 0.65 percent; during the 1980s it was 1.2 percent. The rate was much higher among the Kazakhs and other Asian ethnic groups and lower among the Russians, Ukrainians and other Europeans. The population has grown nearly threefold since 1939, when it was 6,146,000, but much of this growth was due to immigration, especially in the 1950s.

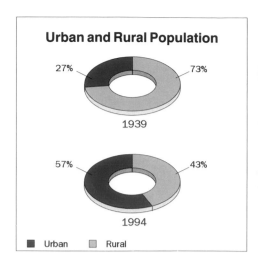

Urban and Rural Population

27%   73%
1939

57%   43%
1994

■ Urban   ▢ Rural

In 1993, 41.9 percent of the inhabitants were Kazakhs, 37 percent Russians, 5.2 percent Ukrainians, 4.7 percent Germans, 2.1 percent Uzbeks and 2 percent Tatars. There are also smaller minorities of Karakalpaks, Belorussians, Armenians, Uighurs and Kirghiz. There has been an exodus of Germans, Russians and Ukrainians since the country became independent in 1991. Immigration from the European parts of the former Soviet Union, which actually began in the second half of the nineteenth century and reached its climax in the late 1940s and in the 1950s, reduced the Kazakhs to a minority in their own country. They were still 62 percent of the population in 1939, but only 30 percent by 1960, while the Russians and Ukrainians, who were 33 percent in 1939, became a majority (51 percent) by 1960. The Russians (and other Europeans) form the majority of the population in the more fertile lands of the north and in many of the larger urban centers.

The Kazakhs, Uzbeks and other Central Asian ethnic groups are Sunni Muslims (or descendants of Muslims), among whom some revival of religious activity has recently taken place, especially in the southern and southeastern parts of the country. The Russians and other Europeans are Christians (or descendants of Christians), mostly of the Orthodox church.

The population is concentrated mostly in the northern, eastern and southeastern parts of the country, where there are several densely populated subregions. Other parts of the country are only thinly populated or, in the case of some desert areas, almost uninhabited, except for the Syr Darya Valley in the south and the Karaganda district in the Kazakh

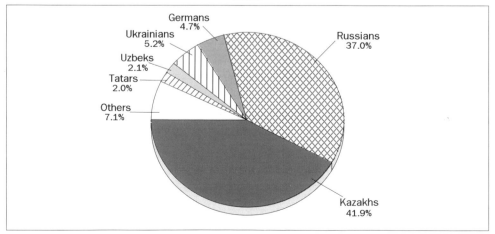

Ethnic Composition
1993

Germans 4.7%
Ukrainians 5.2%
Uzbeks 2.1%
Tatars 2.0%
Others 7.1%
Russians 37.0%
Kazakhs 41.9%

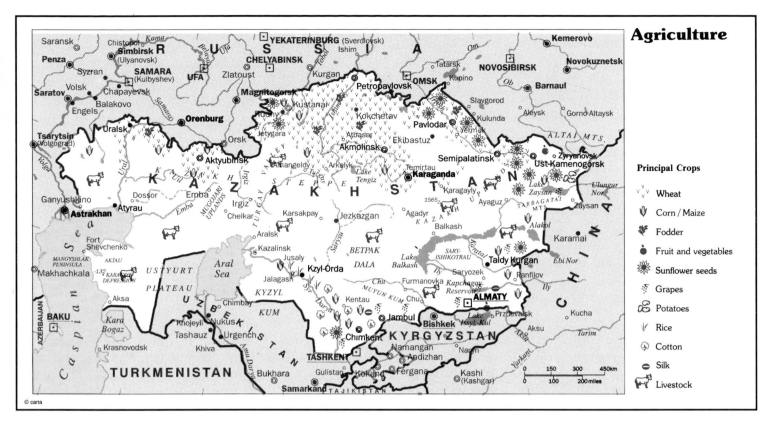

Agriculture

Principal Crops

v v v Wheat

ᵛ Corn / Maize

✿ Fodder

🍒 Fruit and vegetables

✿ Sunflower seeds

🍇 Grapes

🥔 Potatoes

✿ Rice

🌱 Cotton

○ Silk

🐄 Livestock

Steppe. The average population density for the country as a whole is 16.3 persons per square mile (6.3 per sq. km), the lowest density for any of the former republics of the Soviet Union. It is, however, 56 persons per square mile (21.6 per sq. km) in the Almaty (Alma-Ata) region and 44 persons per square mile (17 per sq. km) in the Karaganda and Chimkent regions.

Fifty-seven percent of the population is urban (27 percent in 1939). Nomadism, which was widespread up until the 1930s, has almost vanished. The main urban centers (population in 1989) are the capital Almaty (1,151,000), Karaganda (614,000), Chimkent (393,000), Semipalatinsk (334,000), Pavlodar (331,000), Ust-Kamenogorsk (324,000), Jambul (307,000), Aktyubinsk (253,000), Petropavlovsk (241,000) and Kustanai (224,000).

ECONOMY

Despite the fact that a major part of Kazakhstan is desert or dry steppe, it is economically one of the richest and most productive of the former states of the Soviet Union. Because of its natural resources in minerals (more than ninety different kinds), in arable land and in water and energy sources, it has figured prominently in Soviet development programs during and since World War II,

attaining one of the highest economic growth rates in the former USSR. This is particularly true with regard to industrial and agricultural production, and is reflected, as mentioned earlier, in the extent to which the country attracted immigrants from other parts of the Soviet Union. It was here that in the 1950s the Soviet government embarked on one of its most ambitious agricultural development projects, the utilization of the "virgin-lands," the only project that attracted large numbers of urban people to rural settlements and occupations. This project failed to achieve its targets, but it expanded Kazakhstan's arable land considerably. Industrial development surpassed that of agriculture and is the

predominant economic activity insofar as production is concerned.

Agriculture

Nominally 68 percent of the area is classified as agricultural land, but more than four-fifths of this is used for pasture only, mostly for rough grazing. Much of the cultivated land is located in the north (the black soils on the southern fringe of the West Siberian Lowlands), at the eastern and southern margins of the country, and in some river valleys, mainly the Syr Darya floodplain. Production of grains (18.8 million tons in 1989), mostly wheat, is the main activity, especially in the northern regions. Fodder, potatoes, sugar beets, vegetables, melons and fruit

Agriculture
1989

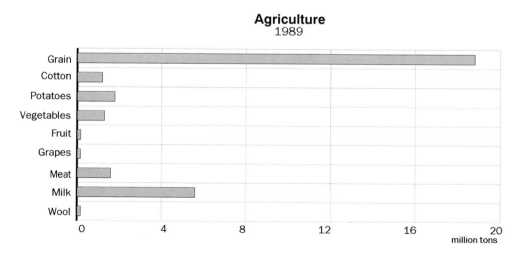

Livestock
1990

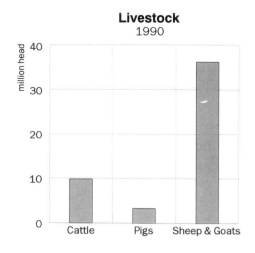

are also widely grown. Cotton, tobacco, rubber plants, rice, grapes and some types of fruit are grown in the south and southeast. Raising livestock, especially cattle (9.8 million in 1990), sheep and goats (36.2 million), pigs (3.3 million) and poultry, is the main occupation of many large farms, especially in the arid parts of the country. Production of meat, dairy products, eggs and wool are next in value and importance to grains.

State farms, which numbered 2,140 in 1989, control by far the largest part of the agricultural lands and production. This is particularly true of grains, cotton and livestock. There were also 388 collective farms. Production of vegetables and fruit on privately held land, which

existed on a limited scale, mainly in the south and east, has been expanding in recent years. The large surpluses from agriculture are exported mainly to Russia and to the European states of the former Soviet Union.

Mineral Resources

Kazakhstan is rich in a large variety of mineral resources; for some (such as copper, lead and zinc) the country was the main source for the USSR. There are rich oil fields in the Caspian region in the west (in the lower Emba Valley, south of Aktyubinsk and on the Mangyshlak Peninsula). Large coal deposits are found in the Karaganda district (in central Kazakhstan), as are iron ore

Industry and Mineral Resources

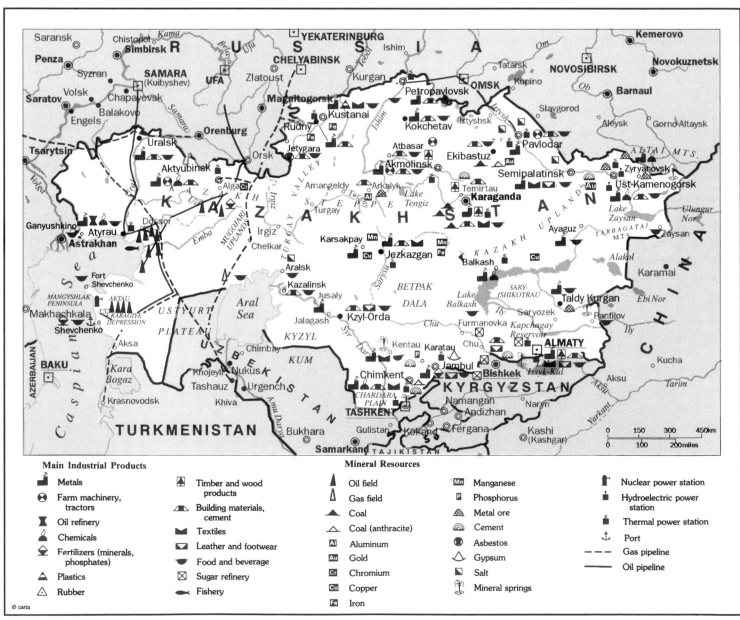

Main Industrial Products		Mineral Resources		
Metals	Timber and wood products	Oil field	Manganese	Nuclear power station
Farm machinery, tractors	Building materials, cement	Gas field	Phosphorus	Hydroelectric power station
Oil refinery	Textiles	Coal	Metal ore	Thermal power station
Chemicals	Leather and footwear	Coal (anthracite)	Cement	Port
Fertilizers (minerals, phosphates)	Food and beverage	Aluminum	Asbestos	Gas pipeline
Plastics	Sugar refinery	Gold	Gypsum	Oil pipeline
Rubber	Fishery	Chromium	Salt	
		Copper	Mineral springs	
		Iron		

© carta

and tungsten. Coal is also found in the northeast and east. Iron is mined in the northwest (near Rudny) and in the east. Large deposits of manganese and copper are in the center (Jezkazgan) and at several locations in the east. Lead, zinc, silver, nickel, cobalt, vanadium, antimony, molybdenum and chromium are found in the highland regions of the east and south, where a number of other minerals are mined. Gold mines have long been in operation in the hilly areas in the northeast (near Ust-Kamenogorsk and Ekibastuz). Nonmetallic minerals, such as asbestos, phosphorite, borates, salt and marble, are also mined, some on a large scale. There are many hydroelectric power stations, mainly in the east and south, which provide a substantial part of the electrical power.

Industry

Among the former republics of the Soviet Union, Kazakhstan ranks third (after Russia and Ukraine) in value and variety of industrial production. Mainly over the last fifty years it has been transformed from a grain-producing and livestock-breeding country (to a large extent by nomads) into a highly industrialized one. Industries are engaged in processing the minerals mined in the country and its agricultural products. There is a large and varied heavy industry, which produces iron, steel (6.8 million tons in 1989), ferrous and nonferrous metals and products, machines, industrial and agricultural equipment and tools, fertilizers, chemicals, building materials (8.7 million tons of cement in 1989), wood products, textiles and clothing, leather products (mainly footwear), various food products (sugar, a wide variety of canned foods, milk and meat products), electronics and fine instruments. Kazakhstan also has a

Employment of Labor Force

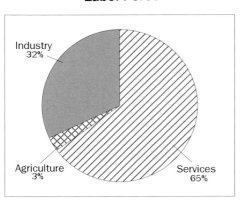

Industry 32%

Agriculture 3%

Services 65%

large and highly developed military industry, which includes the production and/or assembly of missiles, spacecraft and atomic weapons. Some of the Soviet Union's main testing stations of advanced military equipment were located in Kazakhstan.

Karaganda and its surrounding area (in central Kazakhstan) are the main industrial center. Most other industrial concentrations are located in and around the main urban areas in the northern, eastern and southern fringes. The most important of these are Almaty (the capital), Ust-Kamenogorsk, Semipalatinsk, Chimkent, Jambul (Dzhambul), Pavlodar, Akmolinsk (Tselinograd), Kustanai, Petropavlovsk, Aktyubinsk, Uralsk and Atyrau (Guryev).

Trade

Nearly all trade is still with Russia and other former Soviet republics. Efforts to develop direct trade with countries outside the former Soviet bloc are in progress. These apply mainly to industrial products and minerals. The large surpluses of agricultural products go almost entirely to Russia. China, the only neighboring state outside the former Soviet Union, is the first promising new trading partner.

HISTORY

The steppes and deserts of Kazakhstan appear to have been transit areas for people who moved westward from central and eastern Asia during most of the first millennium A.D. Nomadic tribes roamed the more hospitable parts of the country. The Kazakhs, tribes of mixed Turkish-Mongol origin, are first mentioned in eleventh-century Persian literature. Kazakh, meaning "nomad rider" in one of the Turkish dialects of Central

	Main Industrial Products 1989
Steel	6,800,000 tons
Rolled ferrous metals	5,100,000 tons
Timber	1,900,000 cu. m
Paper	3,000 tons
Cement	8,700,000 tons
Fabrics	330,000,000 sq. m
Knitwear	122,900,000 items
Hosiery	82,600,000 pairs
Footwear	35,200,000 pairs
Butter	83,000 tons
Granulated sugar	377,000 tons
Preserves	448,000,000 jars

Education
1989–1990

	No. of Institutes	No. of Students
Primary & Secondary Schools	8,600	3,200,000
Higher Education	55	285,600
Technical Colleges	244	255,400

Asia, were nomads organized in tribal groups ruled by chiefs, each of whom controlled the land of their wanderings. In the thirteenth century the country became part of the Mongol Empire of Genghiz Khan and his descendants. A state extending from the Caspian Sea to the Irtysh Valley, which was a confederation of chiefs of nomadic and semi-nomadic tribal groups, came into being in the sixteenth century. This broke up into three smaller entities known as the Great Horde (in the east in the Semipalatinsk-Alatau region), the Middle Horde (northeast of the Caspian and Aral seas) and the Little Horde (south of the Ural Mountains and along the Ural River).

Russian penetration into Kazakhstan began early in the eighteenth century. They established Semipalatinsk in 1718 and Ust-Kamenogorsk in 1719. The three Hordes came under their protection and control from 1731 to 1741. These three local Kazakh states were successively abolished in the first half of the nineteenth century, following rebellions against Russian rule. Growing Russian and Ukrainian settlement followed, against strong opposition and uprising of the Kazakhs. An attempt to establish an independent Kazakh state was made during the Communist Revolution (1918) but by 1920 the Red Army had regained full control of the country. It was at first made the Autonomous Republic of Kirghizia within the Russian SFSR, with Orenburg (Chkalov) as its capital. It was renamed the Autonomous Republic of the Kazakhs in 1925 and its capital moved to Kzyl-Orda and later (1929) to Almaty (Alma-Ata). In 1936 it became one of the constituent republics of the Soviet Union. Settlement of Russians and Ukrainians increased considerably during and after World War II within the framework of large agricultural and industrial development programs.

In 1991, following the breakup of the Soviet Union, Kazakhstan became an independent state and member of the Commonwealth of Independent States (CIS), which replaced the Soviet Union.

GOVERNMENT AND POLITICS

The country is ruled by an executive president, Nursultan Nazarbayev (a Kazakh), who was elected in 1991 by popular vote for a five-year term. He formerly held a leading position in the Communist Party and in the Soviet-controlled administration. The single-chamber legislature, which consists of 510 members, was elected in 1985 as the Supreme Soviet and became the parliament of free Kazakhstan following the declaration of independence in 1991. All delegates were members of the Communist Party, which in 1991 became the Socialist Party. There are two active opposition parties: the Azad (Liberal Movement) and the Moslem League. A new constitution was adopted in 1993.

The Council of Ministers (government) is actually appointed by the president. The prime minister, since independence, is Russian. Local government elections were held in 1989. Former Communists remained in control of all local authorities.

The country is divided into nineteen provinces, each of which is divided into a number of rural and urban districts. The official languages are Russian and Kazakh.

THE CAPITAL

Almaty (Alma-Ata), with an estimated population of 1.2 million (1992), is by far Kazakhstan's largest metropolitan area. It numbered 1,128,000 in the 1989 census and 730,000 in 1970. The city was originally called Vernyi (until 1921). It is situated in the northern foothills of the Alatau Range, at an altitude of 2,430 feet (740 m), amid a fertile agricultural region well watered by streams flowing down from the high mountains. Almaty is a mostly modern, spread-out city with wide avenues, public gardens and numerous government and public buildings, especially in its center.

It was founded by the Russian government in 1855 as a fortified settlement and garrison base. It was a small town until

it was linked to the Trans-Siberian and Trans-Turkestan railways in the 1920s. Another catalyst for development occurred in 1929, when Almaty became the country's capital. Its population almost doubled during the 1920s and 1930s, reaching 230,000 in 1939. Despite its position at the southern edge of the vast country for which it serves as capital, Almaty grew rapidly, especially after World War II, because of the topographic and comparative climatic advantages of the site, its importance as a communications (railways and roads) center and the mineral and agricultural resources of the surrounding areas. The industrialization process made it an im-

portant center for the production of heavy industry (heavy machines, engineering, agricultural equipment, chemicals), lumber, textiles, food preserves and tobacco. It is one of the most important industrial and commercial centers in Central Asia.

In addition to the capital's political and administrative functions, it is Kazakhstan's main scientific and cultural center, with a university (established in 1934), an academy of sciences, research institutes, various technical and art colleges and institutions, museums and theaters. It is a leader in the publication of books, periodicals and newspapers in the Kazakh language.

Almaty

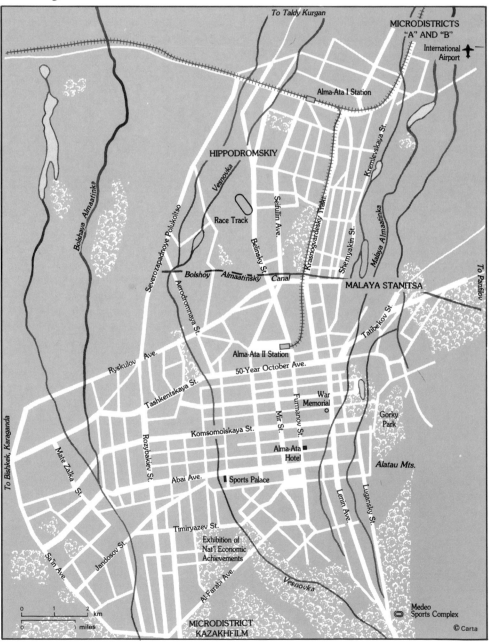

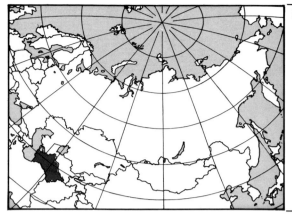

Turkmenistan

Area: 186,400 sq. mi. (488,100 sq. km)
Population (1993 estimate): 3,920,000
Natural increase (1990–1993): 2%
Capital city: Ashgabat (Ashkhabad)

Population in Main Cities (1992 estimates):

Ashgabat: 420,000	Mary (Merv): 90,000
Charjou (Chardzhou): 170,000	Nebit-Dag: 80,000
Tashauz: 115,000	Krasnovodsk: 60,000

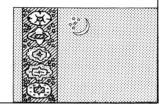

Turkmenistan is the southernmost of the former Soviet republics and the second largest in area of the CIS's Asian constituents. It is one of the five newly independent Muslim states in Central Asia, and the most arid of them, with deserts occupying nearly 90 percent of the area. It borders on the Caspian Sea in the west, on Kazakhstan in the north, on Uzbekistan in the east and on Iran and Afghanistan in the south. The main inhabited areas of Turkmenistan are drained by rivers flowing down from the high mountain ranges to the south and southeast. The largest of these rivers, the Amu Darya, is the "Nile" of Turkmenistan. Most of the cultivated areas are characteristic oases. The great majority of the population are descendants of native tribes.

NATURAL REGIONS

Turkmenistan is the southern part of the great arid region of western Central Asia known as the Turanian Lowlands. Historically, it is the western part of Turkestan, which extends into the west-

ern regions of present-day China. Four main geographical regions are distinguishable: the mountain rim in the south and southeast; the Caspian coastal region; the desert; and the oases belt in the south and east. Over the last fifty years, development projects to exploit the country's rich mineral resources and extend the land under irrigation have substantially pushed back the uninhabited desert areas.

The Mountain Rim
The mountain rim consists of the western and northern fringes of the Kopet-Dag Mountains, extending in a northwest-southeast direction. Most of this mountain range is in Iran. It is considered to be part of the mountain system that encloses the Iranian Plateau—a northeastern extension of the Elburz Range and the Paropamisus Range in Afghanistan as its eastern continuation. However, some scholars believe the Kopet-Dag is an eastern extension of the Caucasus mountain system. The Kopet-Dag's highest peak in Turkmenistan is Mount Rize, at 9,646 feet (2,942 m). The deep, narrow valley of the Tejen (Tedzhen) River marks the eastern end of the range. The Kopet-Dag is a seismically active zone. There are frequent earthquakes, some of which in the last fifty years have resulted in serious damage. The northward-facing slopes, especially their lower parts, are arid, sparsely populated and mainly used as rough grazing lands. Most of the people here live in valleys where precipitation or water resources make agriculture possible. The piedmont of Kopet-Dag belongs largely to the oases belt. At the easternmost corner of Turkmenistan, across the Amu Darya River, the southwestern spur of the Hissar Mountains (of the Pamir-Alay mountain complex) rises to an elevation of 10,283 feet (3,137 m).

The Caspian Coastal Region
The importance of the Caspian coastal region lies in its mineral wealth, mainly its rich oil and natural gas fields. The region's southern part, up to the Cheleken Peninsula, consists mostly of a low-lying plain, much of it below sea level (to −100 ft./−32 m), slightly above the level of the adjoining Caspian Sea. It is covered partly by swamps or sand dunes

and rises slowly eastward. Between the Cheleken Peninsula and the Gulf of Kara-Bogaz, the coastal lowlands are interrupted by the Balkhan Mountains, a spur rising to 6,160 feet (1,880 m) and, farther north, by a dissected low plateau (600–900 ft./180–275 m) ending in high cliffs on or near the coast. The Krasnovodsk Bay—the focus of industrial activities in this region—is enclosed by eastern outliers of the highlands and plateau. The latter occupies most of the northern part of the region and embraces the large Gulf of Kara-Bogaz (Kara-Bogaz Gol), which penetrates deep into northern Turkmenistan. This shallow gulf, connected to the main body of the Caspian Sea by a very narrow strait, is a natural producer of salt, mirabilite (Glauber's salt) and gypsum deposits because of the high evaporation from its surface.

The Desert
The Kara Kum (Black Sands), which is one of the largest continuous sand-covered areas in Asia, extends over most of Turkmenistan's deserts. It consists mostly of dunes (partly drifting dunes) and almost flat areas, covering nearly 70 percent of the country. The rest of the desert is bare rock surface or areas covered by gravel and typical desert soils. Parts of the desert are dissected by beds of sporadic streams or depressions that turn into short-lived lakes or swamps after occasional heavy rains. Natural vegetation provides extensive areas of year-round or seasonal grazing for sheep, goats, camels and even cattle. Shifting dunes cover grazing lands in some parts of the desert. Until the discovery of rich mineral resources (mainly oil and gas), the deserts had only a few permanent settlements on small oases. The Turkmen nomadic tribes, who used to roam those parts of the desert in which grazing and some water were available, have almost disappeared from the landscape.

The Oases
Narrow zones along the foothills of the mountain rim, the main rivers (Amu Darya, Murgab, Tejen) and canal systems watered by them form the densely inhabited lands in which most of the country's economic activity is concentrated. The natural attributes of these belts in the heart or margins

of the Turanian deserts justify their description as oases. Areas under irrigation have been extended considerably, especially over the last fifty years, by the building of canals and large reservoirs. These include the world's longest irrigation and shipping canal—the Kara Kum (Karakumskiy) Canal—which diverts waters of the Amu Darya to the southern part of the Kara Kum Desert, connecting the irrigation canals of the lower Murgab and Tejen rivers and extending, farther westward along the desert's edge, to the foot of the Kopet-Dag. The irrigated and settled lands broaden considerably next to the ancient delta of the Amu Darya, in the northeastern frontier zone, as well as around the deltas of the Murgab and Tejen, ending in the dunes of the Kara Kum. These zones are generally flatlands of the floodplains of the rivers or adjacent, slightly elevated, river terraces. At the foot of the Kopet-Dag they are the lower part of short streams flowing down from the mountains into the desert, alluvial fans and areas where ample groundwater resources are available.

Turkmenistan for the most part has an inland drainage system which ends in the desert sands or in depressions and swamps. Much of the western region drains into the Caspian Sea. The Amu Darya, Central Asia's largest inland river (average annual discharge of 48 billion cu. m) is, insofar as water resources are concerned, the country's main lifeline, even though it drains only a small part of the country.

CLIMATE

Turkmenistan has an arid continental climate, prevalent over large parts of Central Asia. This is expressed in extreme diurnal and seasonal ranges in temperatures, scanty precipitation (except on parts of the mountain rim) with

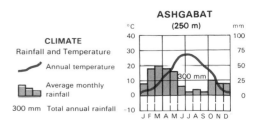

Ethnic Composition
1989

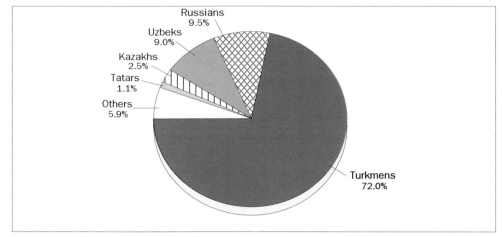

- Russians 9.5%
- Uzbeks 9.0%
- Kazakhs 2.5%
- Tatars 1.1%
- Others 5.9%
- Turkmens 72.0%

wide fluctuations from year to year, low humidity and dry, dust-carrying winds. The average minimum temperature for the coldest month (January) is 32°F (0°C) on the Caspian coast, 21°F (-6°C) in the southeast and 8°F (-13°C) in the northeast; absolute minimum temperatures in these regions are 1° to -24°F (-17° to -30°C). The average maximum temperatures for the hottest month (July) in the same regions are 90°F (32°C), 90°F (32°C) and 92°F (33°C), respectively. Temperatures of over 95°F (35°C) are often recorded during the height of the summer. In the Kara Kum Desert, an absolute maximum of 122°F (50°C) was recorded.

Spring and winter are the main seasons of precipitation. The average annual amounts range from 3 to 5 inches (75 to 120 mm) in the Caspian coastal region, 8 to 10 inches (200 to 250 mm) on the foothills of the southern mountain rim and only 2 to 3 inches (50 to 75 mm) over much of the Kara Kum.

POPULATION

Turkmenistan had one of the fastest growing populations by natural increase in the Soviet Union. It grew by 75 percent from 1970 to 1990, and has been increasing by 2 percent annually ever since. In 1993, the population was estimated at 3,920,000. According to the 1989 census, the population numbered 3,534,000, of whom 72 percent were Turkmens, 9.5 percent Russians, 9 percent Uzbeks, 2.5 percent Kazakhs and 1.1 percent Tatars. The rest were mainly Ukrainians, Belorussians, Azeri-

ans, Armenians and Karakalpaks. In the 1970 census the Turkmens were only 66 percent, while the Russians were 15 percent. Most of the Russians, Ukrainians and other Europeans settled in Turkmenistan during and after World War II. Emigration of Russians and other Europeans to Russia has been growing steadily since the country won its independence in 1991. The majority (87 percent) of the population are Sunni Muslims or descendants of Muslim parents. Approximately 11 percent are Christians (Orthodox). Muslim religious activities, with rapidly growing participation, have gained prominence since independence.

The Russians and other Europeans live mainly in the larger urban centers. The Uzbeks live in the east and southeast, and are the majority in the highlands and foothills of the country's southeastern corner. Most of the Kazakhs live in the northeast.

The population is concentrated in approximately 10 percent of the country, in the oasis region and part of the coastal region, where in some areas the density is as high as 1,400 persons per square mile (540 per sq. km). The rest of the country, especially the Kara Kum Desert and parts of the mountainous areas, is sparsely inhabited, with less than 3 persons per square mile (1 per sq. km). The average population density for the country as a whole is 20.3 persons per square mile (7.8 per sq. km). Nomadism, which was still widespread in the 1920s, has almost disappeared.

Urbanization has increased rapidly since World War II, when only about

30 percent of the population resided in towns. It reached 50 percent in the late 1970s and is approximately 60 percent at present. The main urban centers are the capital, Ashgabat (Ashkhabad), with 420,000 inhabitants; Charjou, 170,000; Tashauz, 115,000; Mary (Merv), 90,000; Menbashid (Krasnovodsk), 60,000; and Nebit-Dag (a recently developed oil and industrial town), 80,000.

ECONOMY

The growing exploitation of the wealth of mineral resources and the industrialization process, in progress since World War II, coupled with the extensive expansion and modernization of agriculture, made Turkmenistan economically one of the most prosperous of the Soviet republics. The exploitation of the geographical advantages (the southernmost area of the USSR) and the soil and water resources played an important role in developing agricultural production to meet essential requirements of the Soviet Union. To achieve this, one of the world's largest irrigation systems was built, centered on the 900-mile-long Kara Kum Canal. Although relegated to third place in the GNP, agriculture is still the main occupation of the population, an important source of raw materials for local industry and a prominent contributor to the list of exports.

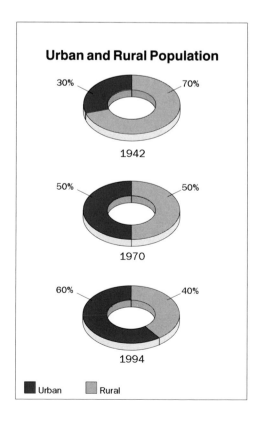

Urban and Rural Population

- 30% / 70% — 1942
- 50% / 50% — 1970
- 60% / 40% — 1994

■ Urban   ▨ Rural

Agriculture
1989

Grain	
Cotton	
Vegetables	
Fruit	
Grapes	
Meat	
Milk	
Wool	

0   0.2   0.4   0.6   0.8   10.   1.2   1.4
                                    million tons

Agriculture

With the exception of small areas on the southern mountain rim, all cultivated areas are irrigated. The area under cultivation (1990) is approximately 2.8 million acres (1.13 million hectares). Turkmenistan was the USSR's main producer of silk. Other main products are cotton (of which Turkmenistan was the USSR's second largest producer), maize, wheat, barley, fodder, rice, kenaf, vegetables and fruit.

Raising livestock, especially karakul sheep (for the production of Astrakhan and other furs), other sheep (for the production of wool), goats and cattle, has remained an important part of agriculture. Large quantities of meat, milk and their products are produced. Agricultural activities under the Soviet Union were carried out in 350 collective farms and 134 state farms. Most agricultural production has been undergoing privatization since 1991.

Mineral Resources

Turkmenistan's rich oil and natural gas fields are located mainly in the central part of the Caspian coastal region. There are additional, smaller fields near the Amu Darya Valley in the east and in the Murgab Delta in the south. Sulfur, potassium, mirabilite (Glauber's salt) and large quantities of salt are also produced in the coastal region, mainly in and around the Kara-Bogaz Gol. Deposits of magnesium and coal have been discovered.

Industry

Local mineral and agricultural raw materials are used in most industrial enterprises. These include oil refining, chemical industries, building materials (mainly cement), textiles (cotton, wool and silk products), leather products, food products (mainly preserves) and, to a lesser extent, engineering, industrial and agricultural tools. There is also traditional carpet, knitwear and clothing production, carried out to a large extent in rural settlements. Most of the industrial activity is concentrated in and around the six urban centers mentioned above.

Agriculture

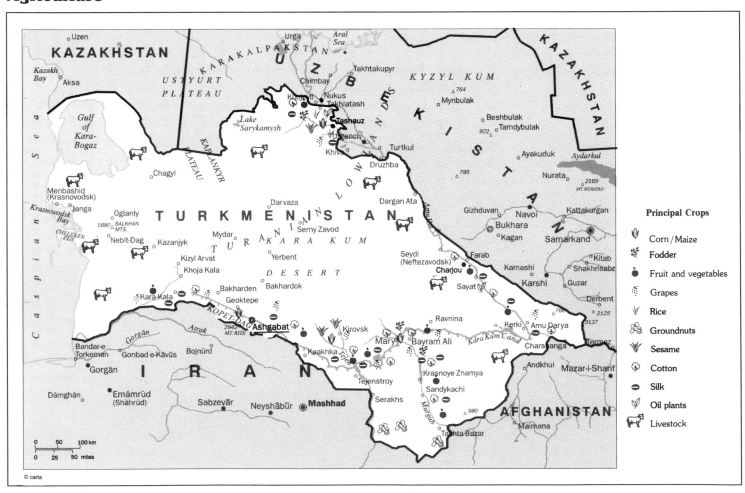

Principal Crops

- Corn / Maize
- Fodder
- Fruit and vegetables
- Grapes
- Rice
- Groundnuts
- Sesame
- Cotton
- Silk
- Oil plants
- Livestock

Industry and Mineral Resources

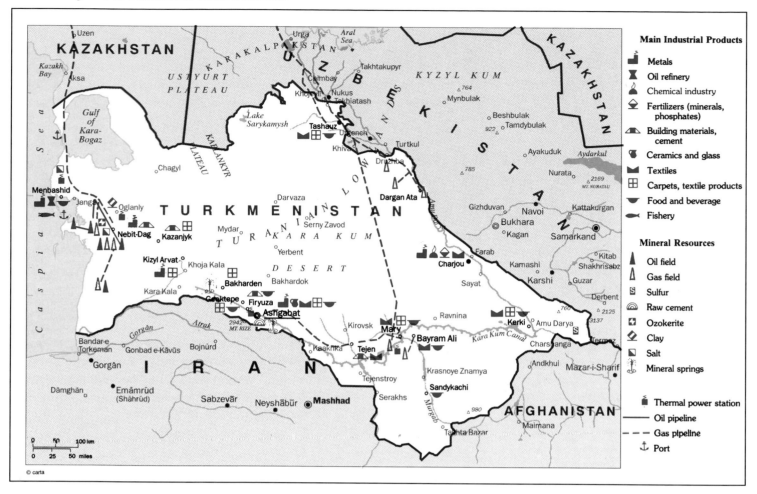

Main Industrial Products

Metals	
Oil refinery	
Chemical industry	
Fertilizers (minerals, phosphates)	
Building materials, cement	
Ceramics and glass	
Textiles	
Carpets, textile products	
Food and beverage	
Fishery	

Mineral Resources

Oil field	
Gas field	
Sulfur	
Raw cement	
Ozokerite	
Clay	
Salt	
Mineral springs	

Thermal power station
Oil pipeline
Gas pipeline
Port

© carta

Livestock
1990

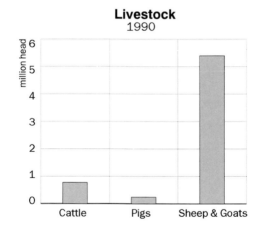

Employment of Labor Force

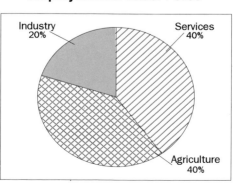

| Industry 20% | Services 40% |
| Agriculture 40% | |

Trade

Nearly all trade is still carried out with the Commonwealth of Independent States (former republics of the Soviet Union). Exports consist mainly of oil, minerals, chemicals, textiles and agricultural products. There is some direct foreign trade with Afghanistan.

HISTORY

Turkmen tribes are believed to have settled in what is today Turkmenistan during the first centuries A.D. Iranian (Aryan) tribes were already inhabiting its southern and southeastern parts at the time. Until the early part of the twentieth century, the sedentary and seminomadic population was confined to the southern and eastern rim (the oasis region) and to small isolated areas on the coastal plain. The rest of the country was only sparsely populated by nomadic tribes. The settled areas were dominated by Iranian kingdoms for long periods of time. The Arabs gained control of much of the area in the eighth century, when Islam was introduced and became prevalent. The country and its inhabitants were described by Arab geographers in the tenth century. They came under Mongol rule early in the thirteenth century. Two local kingdoms (khanates), that of Khiva in the north and of Bukhara in the south, took control of the country in the sixteenth and seventeenth centuries, following the breakup of the Mongol Empire. Most of the country was, however, dominated by large Turk-

Main Industrial Products	
1989	
Steel	2,100 tons
Timber	67,000 cu. m
Cement	1,100,000 tons
Fabrics	53,600,000 sq. m
Knitwear	11,100,000 items
Hosiery	19,900,000 pairs
Footwear	4,800,000 pairs
Butter	4,000 tons
Preserves	80,000,000 jars

men tribes—the Tekke in the south, the Ersar in parts of the Amu Darya Valley and the Yomud in the coastal region—who were often in violent confrontation among themselves and with tribes and people of neighboring territories. The Russians occupied the country (1869–1884) and annexed it along with the other Central Asian territories to their empire. They built the Transcaspian railway, from Menshabid (Krasnovodsk) to Tashkent, which became a major milestone in the development of the region.

A rebellion against Russia broke out in 1916, followed by extensive battles in which British forces took part during the Russian civil war. The Communist forces gained control over Turkmenistan in 1920. Initially the Transcaspian region of Turkestan, it became the Turkmen Soviet Socialist Republic in 1924 and a full constituent republic of the Soviet Union in 1925. It declared its independence in 1991, with the breakup of the Soviet Union, and became a member of the Commonwealth of Independent States.

GOVERNMENT AND POLITICS

A new constitution under which the country would be run by an executive president and legislature was adopted in 1992. After the declaration of independence in 1991, the Supreme Soviet, elected in 1990, became the democratic parliament of the state. It consisted of 285 members elected for a four-year term. The legislature now has 175 seats. The Presidium of the Supreme Soviet is made up of a chairman, two vice chairmen, a secretary and eleven members. The president, Saparmurad Niyazov, who was elected in 1992 by popular vote for a five-year term, had played a leading role in the previous Communist regime. The former Communist Party, now known as the Democratic Party, is still the leading political force, having won 90 percent of the votes in the last elections (1992). Opposition groups derive their support mainly from conservative Muslim religious elements. The country is divided into five administrative regions and forty-two subdistricts.

THE CAPITAL

The capital, Ashgabat (Ashkhabad, "City of Love"), formerly Poltoratsk, has a population of 420,000 (1992) and is by far Turkmenistan's largest urban and industrial center. The city, which was founded in 1883, is situated at the foot of the Kopet-Dag Mountains, at an altitude of 820 feet (250 m), in an area watered by streams and springs known as the Akkal Oasis. It is surrounded by an intensively cultivated and very productive agricultural region. It is less than 20 miles (30 km) from the Iranian border, and is within easy reach of mountain summer resorts (such as Kheyrabad, in Iran, at an altitude of 5,800 ft./ 1,770 m). The central, older part of the city is spaciously built, with wide avenues and streets, public gardens and many public buildings. Much of the city was ruined or badly damaged as a result of a severe earthquake in 1948 and had to be reconstructed. It was a small town with approximately 30,000 inhabitants in 1925, when it became the capital of the Turkmen Soviet Socialist Republic. Industrialization began here in the 1930s, when the first factory, a textile mill, was opened. The city had a population of 127,000 in 1939. Rapid growth and industrialization began in the 1950s; the city's population numbered 142,000 in 1956 and 253,000 in 1970. Its residential and industrial areas expanded mainly southward and northward into the fringes of the desert. Many of the new residential areas were built in typical Soviet urban style.

In addition to its political and administrative functions as capital, Ashgabat is the country's main economic and cultural center, the seat of the Turkmen Academy of Sciences, institutions of higher learning and scientific research, high technical schools, schools of art and music, museums, theaters and the main center of Turkmen publishing. There is a wide variety of industries: mainly textiles and clothing, food, engineering and metal products, glass and building materials.

Education
1989–1990

	No. of Institutes	No. of Students
Primary & Secondary Schools	1,800	800,000
Higher Education	9	42,000
Technical Colleges	38	35,000

Ashgabat

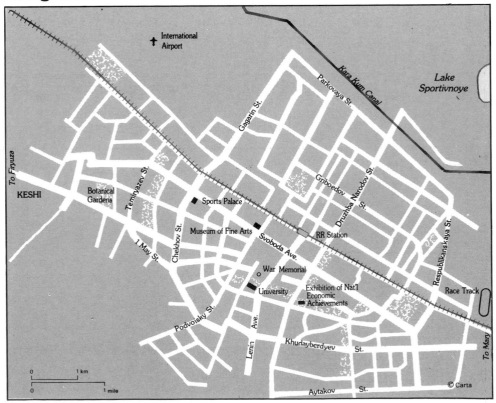

Uzbekistan

Area: 174,740 sq. mi. (447,400 sq. km)
Population (1993 estimate): 22,130,000
Natural increase (1990–1993): 2.2%
Capital city: Tashkent
Population in Main Cities (1992 estimates):

Tashkent: 2,200,000	Bukhara: 225,000
Samarkand: 370,000	Kokand: 210,000
Namangan: 308,000	Fergana: 200,000
Andizhan: 293,000	

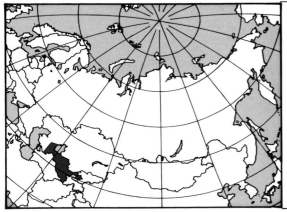

Uzbekistan is the most populous of the former Asian republics of the Soviet Union. It is generally considered to be the most politically influential of the five Muslim Asian members that joined the Commonwealth of Independent States (CIS) after the breakup of the USSR. It is bordered by Turkmenistan on the west, by Kazakhstan on the northwest and north, by Kyrgyzstan on the east, by Tajikistan on the southeast and by Afghanistan for a short distance on the south. The country's boundaries are long and tortuous, especially in the east, where its narrow projections extend deep into the high mountainous regions of Central Asia and include valleys and basins which ethnically and economically are part of the lands of the Uzbeks. Historically, it is the most interesting of the Central Asian states and the richest in relics of the past.

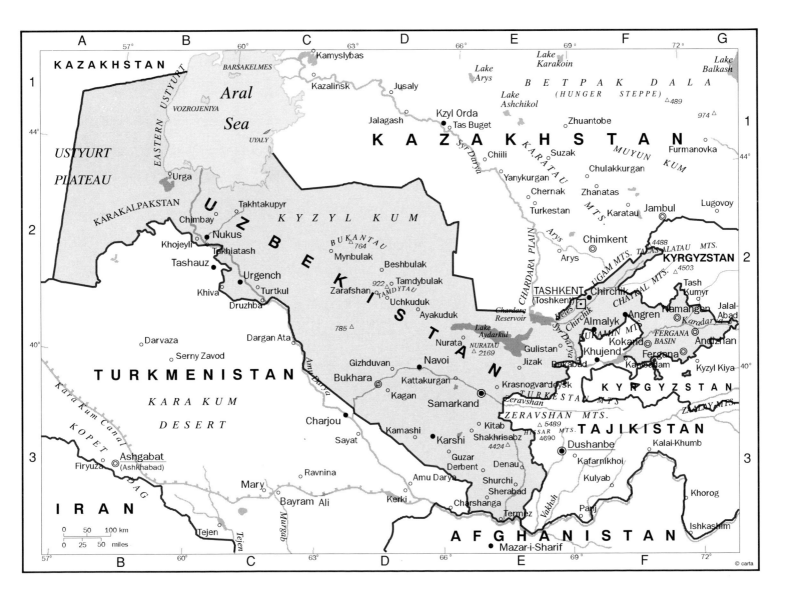

NATURAL REGIONS

Uzbekistan is a country with widely differing natural regional characteristics and a great variety of landscapes. At the same time, the great majority of its area is part of the wide, arid expanses of Central Asia, made up of deserts and dry steppes. The arid regions occupy more than 80 percent of the country's area and are almost empty of inhabitants. Only the highlands in the southeast that face rain-bearing winds or are above certain altitudes are outside these arid regions. The natural regions are the Ustyurt Plateau (Uzbeki part), west of the Aral Sea; the Kyzyl Kum (Red Sands) Desert; the Amu Darya valley and delta (Uzbeki part) and the Zeravshan Valley; the highlands and their foothills and forelands in the southeast; and the Fergana Basin in the east. Uzbekistan controls the southwestern half of the Aral Sea, Central Asia's largest lake, whose level has fallen and area shrunk considerably over the last four decades.

Ustyurt Plateau

The Ustyurt (or Ust Urt) is a low, arid, desolate plateau between the Aral and Caspian seas; its southeastern part forms most of the Karakalpak (Karakalpakstan) autonomous region (republic) of Uzbekistan. It has an undulating, flat surface to heights of 600 to 900 feet (180 to 275 m), ending in an escarpment along the shores of the Aral Sea. Much of the surface is made up of barren rock, shallow saline soils and some sandy areas. Salt pans, especially near the southeastern margins of the plateau, occur in depressions. The Aral Sea, Asia's second largest inland sea (after the Caspian), is a shallow salt lake. Its natural surface level fluctuates generally between 155 and 174 feet (48 and 53 m). However, the lake has sunk much lower since Soviet development projects diverted much of the flow of the Amu Darya and Syr Darya, the two large rivers by which it is fed.

Kyzyl Kum

The Kyzyl Kum is a sand desert stretching between the Amu Darya and Zeravshan valleys (in the south), the Syr Darya Valley (in the north) and the Aral Sea (in the west). A great portion of this desert is within Kazakhstan. It is the largest natural region of Uzbekistan,

covering more than half its area. Although largely sand-covered, the desert has only comparatively small patches of shifting dunes. Outcrops of old hard rocks form several isolated mountain ranges, the most conspicuous of which are the Tamdytau (3,023 ft./922 m) and Bukantau (2,505 ft./764 m). Some sites at the foot of these highlands have attainable water sources, providing for several oases in what is an almost uninhabited wilderness.

Amu Darya and Zeravshan Valleys

Uzbekistan includes most of the lower part and delta area of the Amu Darya, shared by neighboring Turkmenistan. Part of the middle Amu Darya runs along Uzbekistan's boundary with Afghanistan. The middle and lower Zeravshan Valley are entirely within Uzbekistan. Areas in the floodplains and neighboring flatlands of the two rivers have been irrigated since early times. They formed the core of flourishing powerful states for centuries before the Russian Empire expanded into Central Asia. The irrigated areas, especially after World War II, were greatly extended under the Soviet Union by the construction of large reservoirs, long modern canals and pumping stations. These narrow belts of irrigated land on the fringes of the Kara Kum

and Kyzyl Kum deserts belong to the small, densely populated and economically productive parts of Uzbekistan.

The Highlands and Their Forelands

This region consists mainly of spurs and outliers of several ranges of the western Tien Shan mountain system, their foothills and the valleys and basins in between. Included here are the spurs of the Zeravshan and Hissar mountains (highest peak, 14,510 ft./4,425 m) in the south; the Turkestan and Nuratau mountains in the center; and the Kuramin, Chatkal and Talas-Alatau mountains in the north. The highest peak in Uzbekistan is on its eastern frontier, at 15,380 feet (4,690 m). The valleys and parts of the foothills in this region are densely populated and to a large extent cultivated. The region is semiarid but is provided with adequate water sources, originating in the high mountains to the east. The capital, Tashkent, Samarkand (the second largest city) and many of Uzbekistan's urban centers are in this region.

The Fergana Basin

The Fergana Basin is an oval plain, with its long axis running east to west and with an average altitude of 1,300 feet (400 m); it is surrounded on all

Fergana Basin

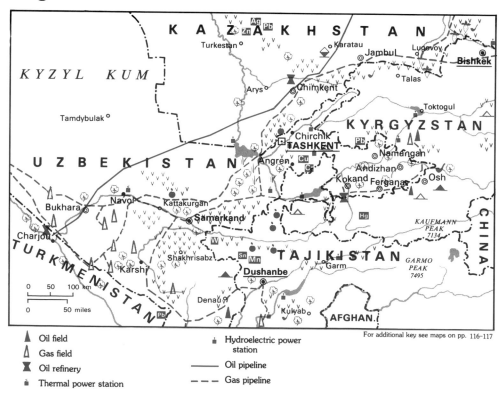

Symbol	
▲	Oil field
△	Gas field
✕	Oil refinery
🏭	Thermal power station
🏭	Hydroelectric power station
——	Oil pipeline
- - -	Gas pipeline

For additional key see maps on pp. 116–117

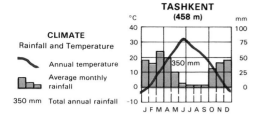

CLIMATE
Rainfall and Temperature

〜 Annual temperature

▮▮ Average monthly rainfall

350 mm Total annual rainfall

TASHKENT
(458 m)

sides by the western Tien Shan Mountains. It forms the easternmost part of Uzbekistan and is connected to the previously mentioned region by a narrow gap through which the Syr Darya, which drains this basin, flows westward. The Fergana is the largest and most densely inhabited fertile basin in Central Asia. It is abundantly watered by the Syr Darya and its tributaries, and is irrigated by a dense network of canals. Industrialization has led to much urbanization, especially on the margins of the basin.

CLIMATE

Uzbekistan has a continental arid climate typical of the lowlands of Central Asia. Only the hilly and mountainous parts of the eastern regions are semiarid or, above certain altitudes, are sufficiently fed by precipitation to make dry-farming possible. Seasonal and diurnal ranges of temperature are considerable. The average minimum temperatures for the coldest month (January) are 6°F (−14.5°C) in the extreme north, 25°F (−4°C) in the south, 21°F (−6°C) in the central foothills (Tashkent) and 18°F (−8°C) in the Fergana Basin. Absolute minimum temperatures of −20° to −36°F (−29° to −38°C) have been recorded. The average maximum temperatures for the hottest month (July) for the same regions are 90°F (32°C), 94°F (35°C), 92°F (33°C) and 95°F (33.5°C), respectively. Absolute maximum temperatures of 106° to 114°F (41° to 45.5°C) have been recorded. Rain and snow fall during the spring and winter. The average annual amounts vary from 3 inches (75 mm) in the desert areas in the west to 15 inches (375 mm) in the foothills in the east, with substantially larger amounts on some mountain slopes and peaks above 3,000 feet (915 m).

POPULATION

The population is estimated to be 22,130,000 (1992). It was 19,906,000 in the 1989 census and 15,391,000 in 1979. The average annual increase of the population in recent years has been 2.2 percent. During the 1980s it was 2.6 percent, the highest rate for any of the former republics of the Soviet Union. The population has more than tripled since 1930, when it was 6,282,000, and more than doubled since 1962, when it was 8,986,000.

At the 1989 census Uzbeks made up 71.4 percent of the population, Russians 8.3 percent, Tajiks 4.7 percent, Kazakhs 4.1 percent, Tatars 3.4 percent and Karakalpaks 2.1 percent. Central Asian people, who are Sunni Muslim, form 88 percent of the population. The Russians (and other Europeans) live mostly in the main urban centers, the Tajiks live in the southeast and the Fergana Basin, the Kazakhs in the northeast and the Kyzyl Kum region and the Karakalpaks in the northwest (the Amu Darya delta). A revival of Muslim religious activities and institutions has taken place in recent years, especially since the declaration of independence. The Europeans (Russians, Ukrainians, Belorussians) are Orthodox Christians, at least by origin.

Uzbek, the national language, belongs to the Turkic group of languages. Russian is widely used, especially in government and public services and in higher education. The Arabic script was used for many centuries. After World War I, it was replaced by the Latin and, later, Cyrillic alphabet imposed by the Soviets. In 1993 the country again adopted the Latin alphabet, in accordance with the Turkish system.

The population is concentrated in the Amu Darya and Zeravshan valleys, in the foothills, valleys and basins of the highland region and in the Fergana Basin. About 80 percent of the country is uninhabited or only sparsely so. The average population density for the country as a whole is 123 persons per square mile (48 per sq. km). It reaches 1,140 persons per square mile (440 per sq. km) in most of the river valleys mentioned above.

Urbanization has increased rapidly, partly as a result of industrial development. It was less than 25 percent in the mid-1940s, 35 percent in 1962 and 41 percent in 1989. The capital, Tashkent, with 2.2 million inhabitants, is by far the largest urban center. Several famous old cities, which played an important role in the history of Central Asia and on the trade routes between China and Europe, have returned to prominence as regional urban centers. They are Samarkand (370,000 inhabitants), Bukhara (225,000), Kokand (210,000), Fergana (200,000) and Khiva (50,000). Other main cities are Namangan (308,000), Andizhan (293,000), Karshi (156,000) and Urgench (128,000). There are 124 towns.

ECONOMY

Uzbekistan is economically the most developed and the most productive of the former Asian republics of the Soviet Union. It has a wealth of mineral resources, especially natural gas and oil. Moreover, its agriculture has utilized extensive areas under modern irrigation systems and was the Soviet Union's main source of cotton and some other essential products. The large and varied agricultural production, coupled with the mineral and energy resources, provided

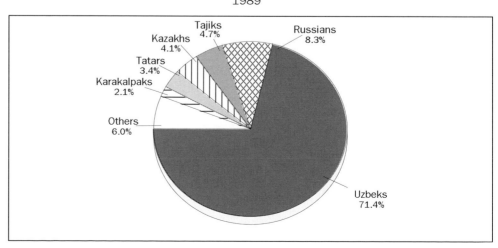

Ethnic Composition
1989

Tajiks 4.7%
Kazakhs 4.1%
Tatars 3.4%
Karakalpaks 2.1%
Others 6.0%
Russians 8.3%
Uzbeks 71.4%

the basis for much industrialization, which substantially overtook agriculture in the GNP. Under the Soviet Union, the use of resources and economic planning and development were largely subject to the policies of the central government, which often gave preference to interests other than those of the Uzbek economy. Independent Uzbekistan is heading for major changes in economic planning and ties, in order to derive more benefits from its industrial and agricultural production potentials.

Agriculture

Most of Uzbekistan's agriculture is dependent on irrigation, a system that has been greatly expanded, improved and modernized, especially over the last fifty years. It is fed by one of the world's longest (94,000 mi./151,000 km) and densest networks of irrigation canals, numerous reservoirs and other installations. The irrigated area covers approximately 9.3 million acres. Much of this land, especially in the Amu Darya, Zeravshan and Karadarya valleys and the

Fergana Basin, are, in fact, oases. The main irrigated crops are cotton (which constituted 62 percent of the ex-USSR's total output), rice, fruit, vegetables and grains. Cultivation is intensive and largely mechanized. Orchards (510,000 acres) and vineyards (330,000 acres), for which the above-mentioned valleys have been famous for centuries, cover substantial parts of the surrounding areas of the old urban centers. Grain, fodder, fruit and vegetables are also grown by dry-farming on higher ground, where average annual precipitation exceeds 12 inches (300 mm).

Semidesert areas in the western regions and parts of the Kyzyl Kum wilderness are used as seasonal or permanent grazing areas, where large numbers of karakul and other sheep and goats (nearly 9 million) and cattle (over 4 million) are bred. Uzbekistan was the USSR's main source of high-quality Astrakhan (karakul) furs of different colors and shades, that were exported to many countries. Various other furs (silver fox, blue fox and mink, bred on farms) are

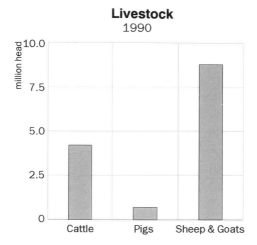

Livestock
1990

also produced, mainly for export.

Uzbekistan has for many centuries been Central Asia's main producer of silk (more than half the production of the ex-Soviet Union). Mulberry trees, on whose leaves silkworms feed, are a prominent feature in the landscape of the Fergana Basin.

Mineral Resources

Natural gas is the main resource. The country has several rich fields with vast

Agriculture

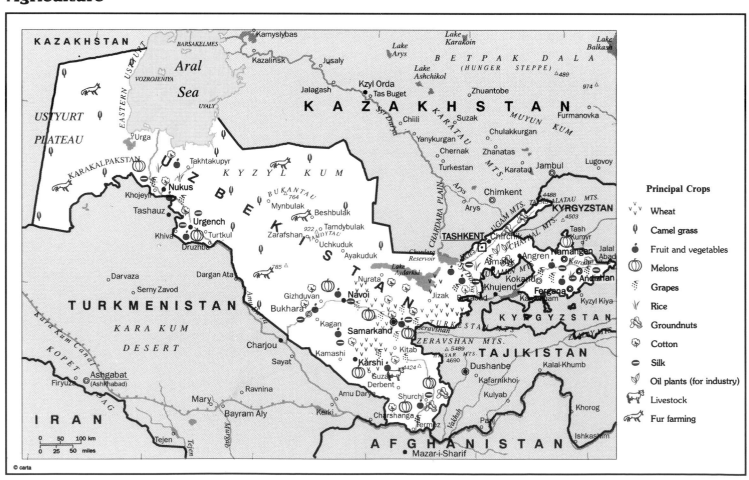

Industry and Mineral Resources

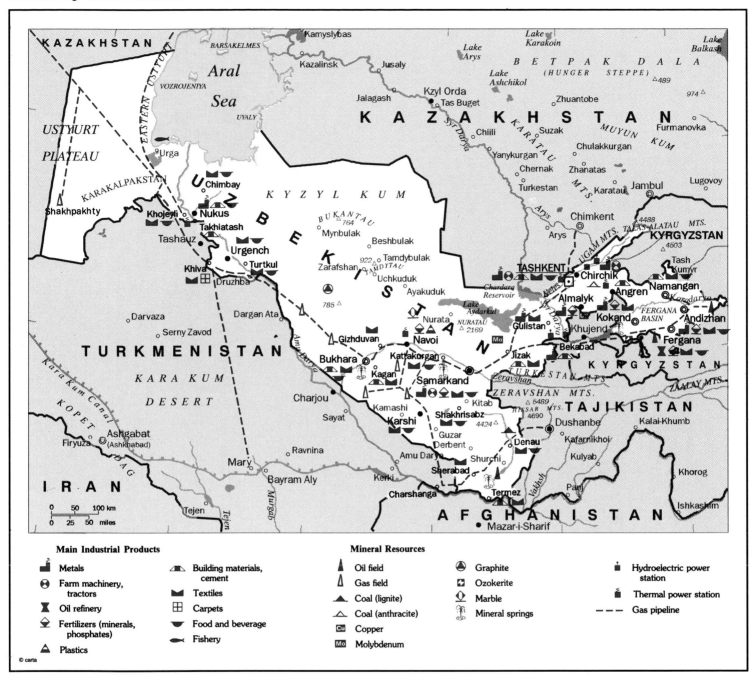

Main Industrial Products

- 🔩 Metals
- ⊖ Farm machinery, tractors
- ✕ Oil refinery
- ⬧ Fertilizers (minerals, phosphates)
- △ Plastics
- ⬔ Building materials, cement
- ⊻ Textiles
- ⊞ Carpets
- ▽ Food and beverage
- ⤳ Fishery

Mineral Resources

- ▮ Oil field
- ▯ Gas field
- ▲ Coal (lignite)
- △ Coal (anthracite)
- Cu Copper
- Mo Molybdenum
- ◉ Graphite
- ⊡ Ozokerite
- ◇ Marble
- ⚘ Mineral springs
- ▮ Hydroelectric power station
- ▮ Thermal power station
- – – – Gas pipeline

© carta

reserves, mainly in the southwest (near Bukhara). In addition to supplying local energy requirements, most of the production is piped to European Russia and to the industrial region of the southern Urals. Oil is produced from several fields in the Fergana Basin, as well as in the southwest (Bukhara district) and northwest.

Coal to meet local requirements is mined in the southeast, on a spur of the Hissar Mountains. Lignite is mined in the northeast (east of Tashkent), as are copper, zinc and lead, in the Kuramin Mountains, where tungsten and molybdenum are also found. Extensive gold

mining is taking place in the Tamdytau Mountains, the Kyzyl Kum Desert and the Kuramin Mountains. Marble is quarried at a number of sites in the hilly region. Hydroelectric power stations on the Syr Darya and several of its tributaries and on the lower Amu Darya supply a large part of the country's energy requirements.

Industry

Modern industry was initially based on local agricultural production and on the requirements of agricultural development. It was preceded by much traditional small industry in the urban centers, en-

Main Industrial Products	
1989	
Steel	1,100,000 tons
Rolled ferrous metals	900,000 tons
Timber	563,000 cu. m
Paper	26,000 tons
Cement	6,200,000 tons
Fabrics	762,000,000 sq. m
Knitwear	110,000,000 items
Hosiery	113,700,000 pairs
Footwear	44,200,000 pairs
Butter	16,000 tons
Preserves	1,163,000 jars

Agriculture
1989

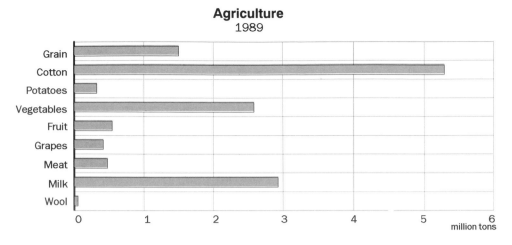

gaged in wool, silk, cotton and leather products, food products, various tools and pottery.

Over the last sixty years Uzbekistan has developed from a primitive agricultural country into a highly industrialized one. There is a wide variety of industries, some of which had a prominent place in the former Soviet Union's production requirements, both domestic and foreign. There are over 1,600 industrial enterprises, concentrated in and around the main urban centers. The largest industrial region is the Tashkent metropolitan area. Cotton, wool and silk processing and products are the largest industrial activity. This is followed by heavy industries, including iron and steel products, machinery (agricultural, cotton-processing, industrial), irrigation equipment and chemicals (fertilizers, petrochemical products). Building materials (especially cement), leather products, wood products and food products are noteworthy. Some of the traditional industries (especially carpet-weaving) are still maintained, particularly in rural areas.

Trade

Uzbekistan's trade was largely with other parts of the Soviet Union; however, a substantial part of both its industrial and agricultural products were exported through the Soviet trade organization to more than sixty countries. This included equipment for harvesting and processing cotton, for irrigation, natural gas and oil installations and for textile and food industries. Since independence, full control of exports has passed to the Uzbek authorities, who sell industrial and agricultural products directly to countries outside the former Soviet Union; how-ever, by far the greater part of trade is still with Russia, other CIS countries and former Comecon countries. This includes all exports of natural gas and other minerals.

HISTORY

Iranian (Aryan) tribes are believed to have inhabited parts of the Amu Darya (Oxus), Syr Darya (Jaxartes) and Ze-ravshan valleys and the Fergana Basin early in history. The southern and eastern parts of Uzbekistan were included in the Persian Empire by Cyrus (c. 530 B.C.) and remained so until the arrival of Alexander the Great (328 B.C.), who made them part of his empire. When this broke up, much of the area came under the kingdom of the Seleucids, the independent local Graeco-Bactrian kingdom (255 B.C.). Mongolian tribes overran the region in the second century B.C. It later reverted, in part, to the control of Iranian rulers. Arab armies (under the Umayyads), who introduced Islam, reached Central Asia toward the end of the seventh century and, by the middle of the eighth century, took control of most of what is present-day Uzbekistan. From the end of the eighth to the mid-tenth centuries, it was part of the Abbasid caliphate. The Arabs named the country Ma Wara en-Nahar (the "land beyond the river"), which to the Europeans became Transoxiana. It became an important base for Islamic religious and cultural activities. Local rulers under Seljuk sovereignty controlled the area in the eleventh and early twelfth centuries. This was followed by extensive penetration of Mongol forces and a long period of Mongol rule. It became the core of an empire that extended westward into Syria, under Timur (1369–1405). It was then that Samarkand became a center of learning, art and trade.

The Uzbeks (or Uzbeqs) are descendants of Turkish tribes, pushed westward by Mongol invasions, who settled in what is present-day Uzbekistan in the fourteenth century, and became (in the fifteenth century) the dominant ethnic group. The breakup of Timur's empire was followed by the division of the country into a number of Uzbek states (khanates), namely Khiva, Bukhara and Kokand. A period of struggle with successive Persian (Iranian) rulers for the country's sovereignty ensued. The Uzbek khanates were prosperous centers of agriculture, industry and trade during periods of political stability between the sixteenth and nineteenth centuries. Russian interest in the Uzbek khanates began toward the end of the sixteenth century; however, actual moves to control the Central Asian lands began only in the middle of the nineteenth century. Tashkent was occupied in 1864; the entire country came under Russian domination by 1873. The khanates of Bukhara and Khiva became vassal states.

During the Communist Revolution (1917–1918), both khanates attempted to revive their independence, at first with the approval of the Soviet authorities. The country became involved in the civil war, in which the Red Army had the upper hand. The khanates were made into People's Republics (1920) but were later merged into what became the Uzbek Soviet Socialist Republic (1924) and then a constituent republic of the Soviet Union (1925). In 1991, Uzbekistan declared its independence and became a member of the CIS.

Education
1989–1990

	No. of Institutes	No. of Students
Primary & Secondary Schools	8,300	4,700,000
Higher Education	44	331,600
Technical Colleges	244	277,300

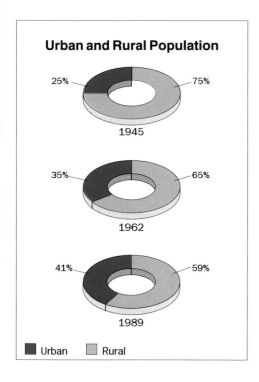

Urban and Rural Population

25% — 75%
1945

35% — 65%
1962

41% — 59%
1989

■ Urban   ■ Rural

GOVERNMENT AND POLITICS

The country is still governed, to a large extent, on lines and practices laid down over many years of Communist rule. A slow democratization and privatization process is in progress. An executive president, Islam Karimov, elected in 1991 by popular vote for a four-year term, heads the government. The single-chamber legislature is the 500-member Supreme Soviet, elected in 1990, which has been turned into a parliament run on democratic principles. The government is appointed by the president, with the approval of parliament. The former Communist Party, renamed the People's Democratic Party, is the dominant political force; it holds nearly all seats in parliament. The president and all the ministers come from this party. There is a small opposition party—Erkl (Independence Party)—and a Democratic Movement Birlik. Conservative Islamic groups are also politically active.

The country is divided into twelve administrative districts, one of which, Karakalpakstan (in the northwest), with an area of 63,670 square miles (164,900 sq. km) and a population of 1.3 million, is the autonomous republic of the Karakalpak people. In addition to 124 towns and 97 urban settlements, there are 155 rural subdistricts. Before privatization began in 1989, there were 856 collective farms and 1,085 state farms.

THE CAPITAL

The capital, Tashkent, with 2.2 million inhabitants (1992), is not only the largest Uzbeki city, but is by far the largest and most important metropolitan area in Central Asia. The city is situated on an elevated plain, at an altitude of 1,500 feet (458 m) in the western foothills of the Chatkal Mountains, on an oasis watered by two tributaries (the Chirchik and Keles) of the Syr Darya. It is surrounded by a fertile, irrigated and intensively cultivated agricultural region.

Tashkent was first mentioned in seventh-century Chinese documents. It had been for many centuries the town of the oasis and its surrounding area, but was not a main urban center of the region as Samarkand or Kokand were. It assumed its leading importance only after the Russian conquest, when it was made the Russian military and administrative center of Turkestan (1865). The Russians at the time built a new, spacious, modern town northeast of the old, native, densely clustered one. It later developed into a main communications center with its connection to the Russian railway system. By 1900 it was the largest city in Central Asia, with a population of 156,000, but its main growth began after it became the capital of the Uzbek Soviet Socialist Republic (1925) and underwent industrialization (since the 1930s). It had 585,000 inhabitants in 1939 and 1,385,000 in 1970. A large majority of the Russians (and other Europeans) of Uzbekistan live in Tashkent.

The city suffers from repeated earthquakes. In 1966, a large part of the city was severely damaged and had to be rebuilt.

The city has many modern public buildings, wide avenues and parks. In addition to its political and administrative functions, it has many scientific and cultural institutions, a university and other institutions of higher learning (technical, professional, art), museums, theaters, libraries and an academy of music.

Tashkent is the largest and most varied industrial center in Central Asia. The city and its surrounding area produce agricultural and mining machinery, various tools and industrial equipment, electrical equipment, chemicals, textiles, leather products, furniture and wood products, pottery and foodstuffs. It also has a military industry.

Tashkent

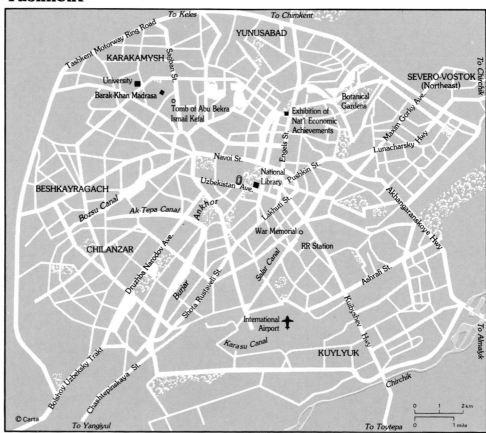

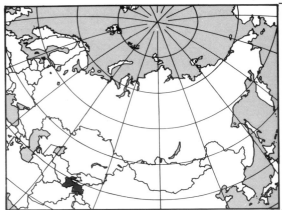

Tajikistan

Area: 55,240 sq. mi. (143,100 sq. km)
Population (1992 estimate): 5,400,000
Capital city: Dushanbe
Population in Main Cities (1992 estimates):
Dushanbe: 600,000
Khujend (Leninabad): 160,000
Kulyab: 69,000
Kurgan Tyube: 53,000

Tajikistan is the most mountainous and isolated of the former republics of the Soviet Union. It is a landlocked country in the heart of Asia with long, tortuous boundaries, most of which run through desolate or sparsely populated territories. It is bordered by Afghanistan on the south, where most of the frontier is formed by the Amu Darya River (and its upper reaches, known as the Panj, or Pyandzh), by China on the east, by Kyrgyzstan on the north and by

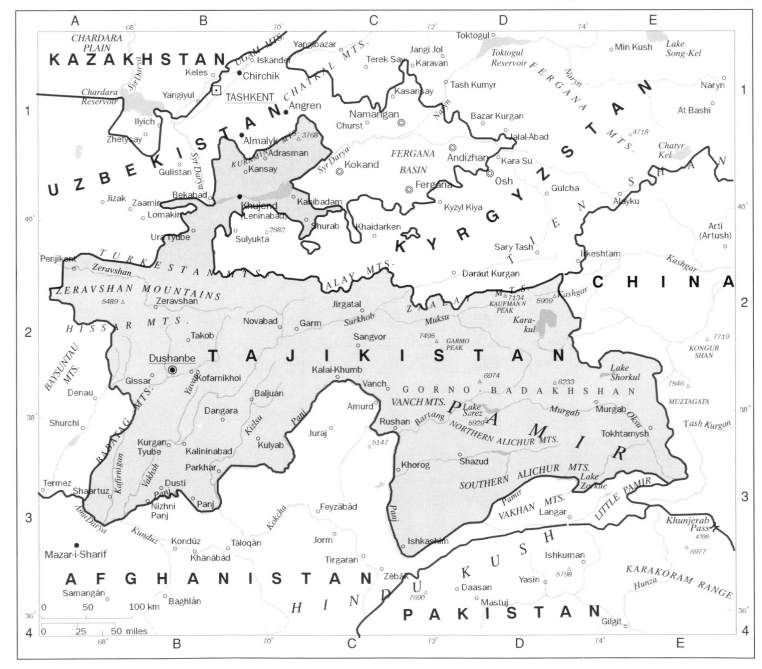

Uzbekistan on the west and northwest. It is the country where the Russian Empire, in its expansion into Central Asia, almost came in territorial contact with British India. These empires were separated by a narrow buffer zone, annexed to Afghanistan, which today separates Tajikistan from Pakistan.

More than half the country's area lies above 10,000 feet (3,000 m). Many peaks are above 20,000 feet (6,000 m), including the two highest elevations in the ex-USSR: Garmo Peak (24,585 ft./7,495 m), which was first renamed Stalin, then Communism, under Communist rule, and has now reverted to its original name; and Kaufmann Peak (23,400 ft./7,134 m), which bore Lenin's name under Soviet rule. The country is part of a seismically active region. Earthquakes in recent decades have hit some of the most inhabited valleys here. One of Tajikistan's most scenic lakes, Sarez, was formed as a result of a huge landslide caused by an earthquake. The headwaters of some of Central Asia's most important rivers—the Amu Darya, Syr Darya, Zeravshan and Kashgar—have their sources in the glaciers and high mountains of Tajikistan, the entire area of which drains into inland basins, mainly that of the Aral Sea.

NATURAL REGIONS

Tajikistan is generally divided into three main natural regions: the Pamir, in the eastern half of the country; the Tien Shan, in the northwest, including the western part of the Fergana Basin (most of which is in Uzbekistan); and the southwest, where most of the population and economic activities are concentrated. A variety of natural characteristics exists in each region, depending on altitudinal zones, topographic and microclimatic conditions, and prevalent types of rock formation and soil. Each of these natural regions extends beyond the boundaries of Tajikistan, as do the areas inhabited by the Tajiks.

Pamir

The Pamir region, also known as "the roof of the world," extends from the Hindu Kush Mountains in the south to the Zaalay Mountains in the north. It is a knot of high mountain chains and plateaus with many glaciers and permanently snow-covered peaks. The broad

valleys between the ranges are generally well over 10,000 feet (3,000 m) high and, in some cases, even more than 15,000 feet (5000 m). They are typical glacial valleys in which much of the area is covered by morainic material. There are many small lakes of glacial origin, the largest of which is Karakul, a salt lake at an altitude of 13,200 feet (4,030 m). The eastern part of Pamir is arid and desertlike, with extensive sand-covered areas. The permanent snow line is about 15,000 feet (5,000 m) on the slopes and valleys facing south and east and 1,000 to 1,200 feet (300 to 360 m) lower on other valleys and slopes. There are few good all-weather roads here, and accessibility to large parts of the region is difficult. The region is very sparsely inhabited; although it forms about half the area of Tajikistan, only 3.5 percent of the population lives here. The population is concentrated in the lower parts of the larger valleys, mainly at their fringes. Nearly the entire natural region of Pamir within the boundaries of Tajikistan forms the administrative autonomous region of Gorno-Badakhshan.

Tien Shan

The Tien Shan region of Tajikistan covers only part of the extensive Tien Shan mountain system, namely, the Turkestan and Zeravshan mountains of southwestern Tien Shan and the fringes of the Kuramin Mountains of northwestern Tien Shan. These nearly east-west ranges form a region of much lower and more fragmented relief than the Pamir, with smaller and less extensive glaciers and snow-capped areas. Several peaks rise to altitudes of 18,000 feet (5,500 m), while others never exceed 15,500 feet (4,700 m). Valleys generally below 12,000 feet (3,600 m) and lower slopes lend themselves to agricultural activities and to grazing and are much more inhabited than the Pamir region. Wedged between the northern and southern ranges of Tien Shan in this region is the narrow, western part of the Fergana Basin, which is only 6 miles (9 km) wide at this point (it reaches 90 mi./150 km in width farther east, in Uzbekistan). This 1,100-foot- (335-m-) high lowland, irrigated by the Syr Darya River and its tributaries that feed the great Fergana Canal, is one of the most densely inhabited and intensively cultivated parts of Tajikistan.

The Southwest

The southwest is a region of moderate relief with broad, southward- and southwestward-facing valleys, the largest and most important of which are the Vakhsh, Kizilsu, Yavansu and Kafirnigan valleys. It extends from the Hissar (Gissar) Mountains in the north to the Amu Darya Valley in the south. The valleys, which are generally 1,200 to 1,500 feet (400 to 500 m) high, are separated by mountain ranges that even in this region occupy most of the area. However, the slopes in many cases are moderate and, with few exceptions, do not rise above 8,000 feet (2,400 m).

The nature of the comparatively gentle landscape and the climate make this the most inviting region of Tajikistan. It is the home of more than two-thirds of the inhabitants, while occupying only about one-quarter of the total area. This is, in fact, the core of the country, where most of its economic, political and cultural activities take place, and where its capital, Dushanbe, is located. The region also has the country's densest and most advanced railway and road network. Through its valleys run some of the former USSR's main communication lines with Afghanistan.

CLIMATE

Typical extreme continental conditions and altitude dominate the climate. Winters are very cold, with prevalence of frost, even in the lower parts of the country, for at least three to four months of the year. Summers are very hot. Maximum temperatures of over 100°F (38°C) are recorded frequently in the lower valleys. The diurnal temperature range is considerable. The average temperatures for the coldest (January) and hottest (July) months are, respectively, 29°F (–1.7°C) and 82°F (27.8°C) in Khu-

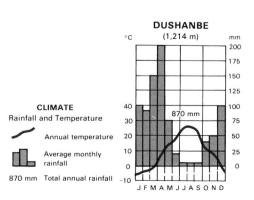

jend (formerly Leninabad) in the Fergana Basin (1,150 ft./350 m); 36°F (2.2°C) and 86.5°F (30.3°C) in Kulyab (1,200 ft./366 m) in the extreme south; 24°F (-4.5°C) and 71°F (21.5°C) in the southern Tien Shan (3,300 ft./1,000 m); 16°F (-9°C) and 67°F (19.5°C) in Khorog (6,800 ft./2,073 m) at the western foot of the Pamir Massif; and -2°F (-19°C) and 53°F (11.6°C) in the central Pamir region (12,000 ft./3,660 m). The temperature here frequently drops in winter to below -50°F (-45.5°C).

Precipitation over most of Tajikistan is scant, especially over the eastern and central parts of the Pamir range. It falls mainly in summer and, in the southwest and western Pamir, in winter and mainly in spring. The average annual precipitation ranges from 2.5 to 3.5 inches (60 to 80 mm) in eastern and central Pamir to 30 to 60 inches (750 to 1,500 mm) on the wettest slopes and valleys in southwest Pamir and Tien Shan. The precipitation falls mostly as snow on the Pamir and Tien Shan ranges. Much of the snow from winter and spring melts in summer. Rivers have high water levels in late spring and early summer.

Altitudinal zones of climate with corresponding natural vegetation vary slightly between north and south, as well as with the position and direction of slopes and valleys. Areas up to an altitude of 5,000 to 6,000 feet (1,500 to 2,000 m) are generally arid or semiarid with desert or steppe vegetation. Much of the higher reaches of this zone provide rough to good seasonal grazing. The wooded zone, at 6,000 to 9,000 feet (2,000 to 3,000 m), has deciduous and mixed forests in its lower part. The subalpine zone, at 9,000 to 12,000 feet (3,000 to 3,700 m), has mainly shrubs, meadows and good summer grazing. The high alpine zone (tundra vegetation), at 12,000 to 15,000 feet (3,700 to 4,500 m), is characterized by scanty vegetation of mosses and low shrubs. Areas above 15,000 to 16,000 feet (4,500 to 4,800 m) are permanently frozen and covered by glaciers or snow. Tajikistan's largest glacier, in northern Pamir, covers an area of 350 square miles (900 sq. km).

POPULATION

The number of inhabitants was estimated at 5.4 million in 1992. It was 5,093,000 in the 1989 census of the USSR. The figures for the 1979 and 1970

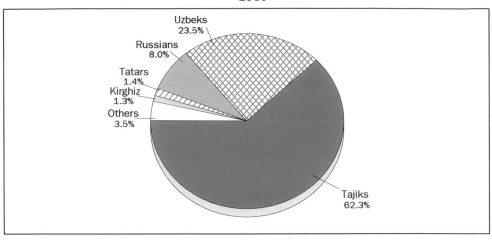

Ethnic Composition
1989

censuses were 3.8 million and 2.9 million, respectively. The natural growth of the population over the period 1979–1989 was 34.5 percent, the highest for a Soviet republic (the average for the USSR was only 9.2 percent). The population has more than doubled over the last twenty-five years. According to the 1989 census, 62.3 percent were Tajiks, 23.5 percent Uzbeks and 8 percent Russians (and other Europeans). There are also Kirghiz (1.3 percent), Kazakhs, Tatars (1.4 percent) and Turkmens. The high natural increase is among the Tajiks and other Asians, whose percentage in the population has increased considerably over that of the groups of European origin. Tajik is an Iranian language. Several different dialects are spoken. The Tajiks are believed to be of Indo-Iranian origin, although many have Mongolian features, especially those in the Pamir region. Indo-Iranian (European) features are predominant among Tajiks in the southwestern region. The Uzbeks are concentrated mainly in the northwest and southwest, the Russians (and other Europeans) in the main urban centers and the Kirghiz and Kazakhs in the north and northeast.

The Tajiks, Uzbeks and other Asians are Sunni Muslims. Conspicuous revival of religious activities and following has taken place in recent years, especially since independence. Throughout the period of Communist rule, Muslim religious services and practices had taken place mainly in rural areas.

The average population density is 97 persons per square mile (38 per sq. km). Over more than half the country—in the Pamir and part of the Tien Shan

region—the density is less than 7 persons per square mile (2.7 per sq. km). It is, however, 158 persons per square mile (62 per sq. km) in the Tajikistani part of the Fergana Basin and over 200 per square mile (80 per sq. km) in the valleys of the southwest. The majority of the population (70 percent) is rural and lives in villages organized as collective or government farms. Nearly 30 percent are urban and live in twenty-one towns and a number of townships. The capital, Dushanbe (600,000 inhabitants), and Khujend (formerly Leninabad) with a population of 160,000, are the only large towns. Other towns are Kulyab (69,000) and Kurgan Tyube (53,000).

ECONOMY

Tajikistan is still mainly agrarian, although the national income from its steadily growing industry significantly exceeds that of agriculture. Still, half the labor force is employed in agriculture, which has also made great progress in mechanization, irrigation and organization. The exploitation of the country's abundant mineral resources has made

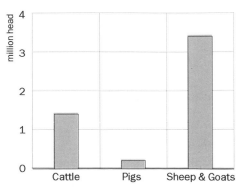

Livestock
1990

Agriculture

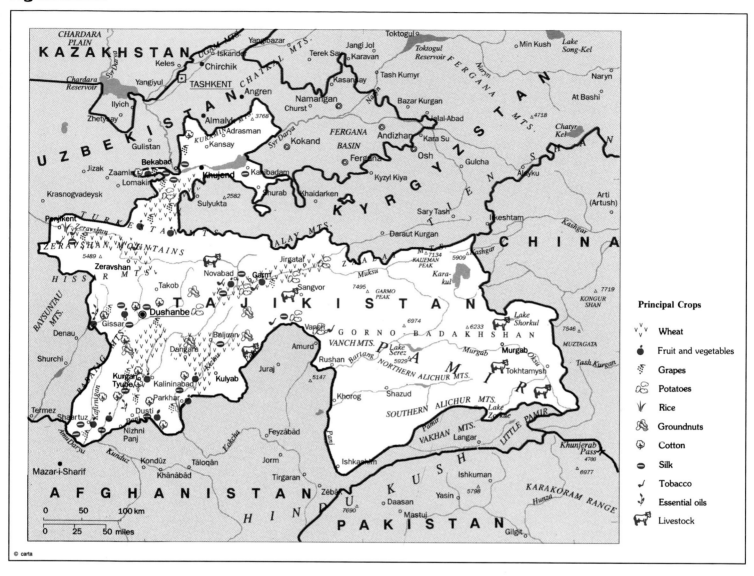

Principal Crops

- v v v   Wheat
- Fruit and vegetables
- Grapes
- Potatoes
- Rice
- Groundnuts
- Cotton
- Silk
- Tobacco
- Essential oils
- Livestock

© carta

rapid strides forward, especially over the last thirty years. The great majority of the country's economic activities and production takes place in only about 10 percent of its area.

Agriculture

Over 80 percent of the cultivated land is concentrated in the valleys of the southwestern region, in the Fergana Basin and in the Zeravshan Valley. Most of the land under cultivation is irrigated. An extensive network of irrigation canals, mainly developed over the last fifty years, is the backbone of Tajikistan's modern agriculture which, until recently, was organized to a great extent in large collective (157) and state (299) farms. The main product is cotton, of which Tajikistan was the third largest producer (about 10 percent) with the highest yield per acre in the USSR. Grains (mainly wheat but also barley, corn and rice) are next in

importance. Vegetables and fruits (apricots, pears, figs, plums and nuts) are grown over large areas, mostly for canning and dried products. They form a substantial part, second to cotton, of the agricultural exports. Grapes are also extensively grown. Cattle (1.4 million in

1989) and sheep and goats (3.4 million) are widely bred for the production of meat, milk and wool. Large areas in the highlands provide good permanent or seasonal grazing. Sericulture is widely practiced in some valleys in the west and southwest.

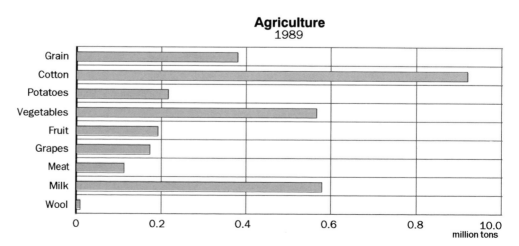

Agriculture
1989

Mineral Resources

The country is rich in mineral resources, although some minerals known to exist in the Pamir region have so far not been exploited on a commercial scale. Oil and natural gas fields are found in the north, at the edge of the Fergana Basin, and in the southwest. There are also large deposits of brown coal in the north. Lead, zinc, tin, mercury, wolfram, antimony, tungsten fluorite, arsenic and bismuth are mined. Uranium and radium deposits were worked until recently. Mica, asbestos, potassium, sulfur and semiprecious stones are produced. Most of the minerals are processed locally and exported to Russia and the other former republics of the USSR. Eighty dams and hydroelectric power stations tap the energy resources of the main rivers flowing down from the Pamir and Tien Shan mountains. They provide most of the electricity required (15,300 million kilowatts in 1989).

Industry

Modern industrialization had mainly begun during World War II. Industry produces over 40 percent of the national income. Textiles (cotton, wool and silk) and clothing are the most important industry. Carpets are produced on a large scale in factories, while the traditional cottage weaving is still maintained. Next in extent and importance is the food industry, which produces large quantities of vegetables, fruit, meat, milk and grains. The chemical industry produces fertilizers and a variety of other materials and products. Other industries include metalworking, engineering, building materials (mainly cement), sawn timber and wood products. Most industries are concentrated in and around the capital, Dushanbe, and Khujend. These include the largest silk factory in what was the USSR, as well as one of the largest textile complexes.

Main Industrial Products 1989	
Steel	4,700 tons
Timber	187,000 cu. m
Cement	1,100,000 tons
Fabrics	217,000,000 sq. m
Knitwear	16,200,000 items
Hosiery	44,600,000 pairs
Footwear	10,800,000 pairs
Butter	6,000 tons
Preserves	374,000,000 jars

Industry and Mineral Resources

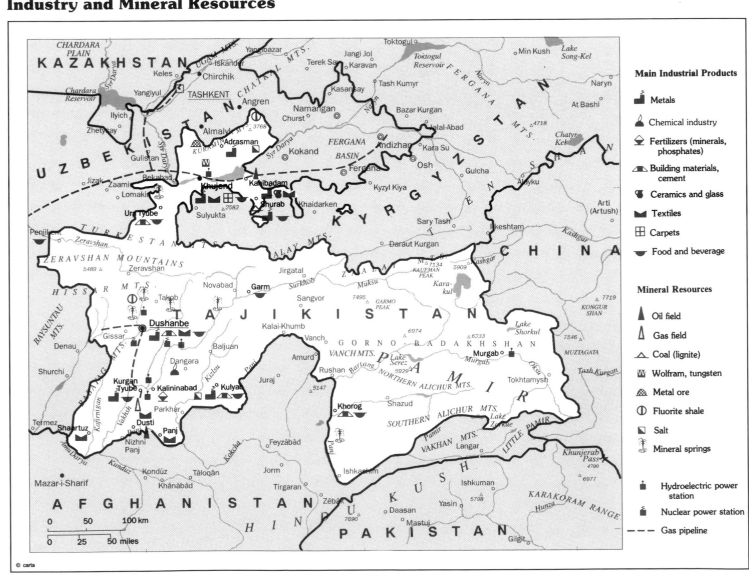

Education
1989–1990

	No. of Institutes	No. of Students
Primary & Secondary Schools	3,100	1,300,000
Higher Education	10	65,600
Technical Colleges	42	41,700

Trade

Nearly all foreign trade is still carried out with other republics of the former USSR or through Russian commercial enterprises.

HISTORY

The western regions of present-day Tajikistan were part of the Khanate of Bukhara when they came under the suzerainty of the Russian Empire (1886–1893); the empire extended its rule over the rest of the country in 1895. Tajikistan came into being as a separate political entity only under the USSR, when the regions predominantly inhabited by Tajiks were given autonomous status in 1924. In 1929, these regions were made into a constituent republic of the Soviet Union. The Gorno-Badakhshan region, which extends over most of the area of the Pamir Massif, remained an autonomous region within the Tajik Soviet Socialist Republic. Tajikistan declared its independence in August 1990 and the following year became a member of the Commonwealth of Independent States.

GOVERNMENT AND POLITICS

The country, under a constitution drawn up and adopted in 1978 and adapted to the status of a new sovereign state in 1990, was at first governed by a president with wide-ranging powers elected by popular vote. Rakhman Nabiyev was elected president in 1991 by a 56.9 percent majority. The legislature consists of 230 members. The last elections were held in 1990. The presidency, however, was abolished by parliament in 1992. The formal functions of the president were taken over by the speaker and the executive powers were vested in the government.

The country is divided into five administrative regions. The autonomous region of Gorno-Badakhshan is the largest (24,590 sq. mi./63,700 sq. km) and most sparsely populated (165,000 inhabitants in 1992), extending over nearly the entire natural region of Pamir. Its inhabitants are Tajiks (83 percent) and Kirghiz (11 percent). A local legislature and government were elected in 1989.

An internal political alignment has been in the making since independence. At present (1994) there are two main forces. One is a Socialist Democratic movement, which has taken over some of the functions and institutions of the former Communist regime. It is led by people who held key positions in the former Communist Party. These leaders have essentially taken over the running of the country and its democratization. The second force has a local conservative Muslim religious character. It is headed by Muslim religious leaders and is backed mainly by the rural population. It organized armed forces, tried to seize power by force in 1992 and has carried out violent acts against the government in some parts of the country.

THE CAPITAL

The capital, Dushanbe, with a population of over 600,000 (1992), is the largest city in Tajikistan. The capital and its surrounding area contain the country's largest and most varied concentration of industries. It is also the administrative, cultural and communications core of the country. The city is situated on the banks of the Dushanbinka River (a tributary of the Amu Darya), with a fertile agricultural region and proximity to a number of large hydroelectric stations. It was a small market township, a station on the caravan route between Samarkand and Kashgar (in China). It had a population of 50,000 in the mid-1920s, 83,000 in 1939, 101,000 in 1956 and nearly 400,000 in 1972. Formerly Dushambe, or Dyushambe, and named Stalinabad in 1929, the name reverted to Dushanbe in 1961. Although Tajiks form the majority of the population, the city has a large minority of Russians (and other Europeans, mainly Ukrainians) and Uzbeks. Much of the city is built in the typical Soviet urban residential style of the 1950s to 1970s, with large public buildings. There is very little left from the pre-Soviet period. There are a number of museums, a university, research institutes and technical colleges. It is also the main center for the publication of books, periodicals and newspapers in the Tajik language, which has been written in the Cyrillic alphabet since 1940.

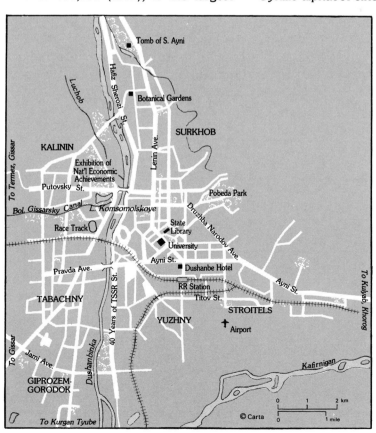

Dushanbe

Kyrgyzstan

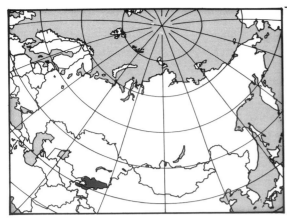

Area: 76,640 sq. mi. (198,500 sq. km)
Population (1993 estimate): 4,630,000
Natural increase (1990–1993): 1.6%
Capital city: Bishkek (Frunze)
Population in Main Cities (1992 estimates):
Bishkek: 650,000
Osh: 220,000
Jalal-Abad: 78,000
Przhevalsk: 65,000

Kyrgyzstan is the easternmost of the landlocked Central Asian republics of the former Soviet Union. It has a great variety of landscapes and physical and human geographical features. Wedged between the extensive desert areas of Turan (in Kazakhstan and Uzbekistan), in the northwest, and of Tarim (in western China), in the southeast, it is a heavily mountainous country, mostly within the high mountain systems of Central Asia.

About 85 percent of the area lies above 6,500 feet (2,000 m) and less than 5 percent below 3,000 feet (900 m). It is bounded by Kazakhstan on the north, by Uzbekistan on the west, by Tajikistan on the south and by China on the east. As in neighboring Tajikistan, penetration of modernization and sovietization was slower and less dominant than in the other former Soviet republics. The traditional native population has been better

preserved in some parts of Kyrgyzstan than elsewhere in the former Soviet Union.

NATURAL REGIONS

Kyrgyzstan is almost entirely covered by ranges of the Tien Shan mountain system and their intervening valleys and basins. The ranges, which run in a southwest-northeast or west-east direction, are generally divided into two main

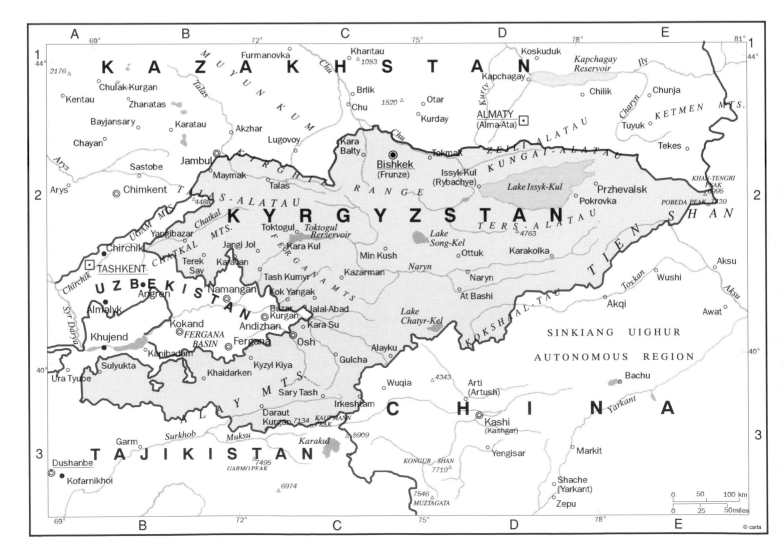

structural regions: the southern (or Middle Tien Shan) region and the northern (Northern Tien Shan) region. The long and narrow valley of the Naryn River, a tributary of the Syr Darya, is taken as the dividing line between the two regions.

The Northern Region

Two arc-shaped sets of high mountain ranges, which encompass a large, deep basin occupied by Lake Issyk-Kul, take up most of the northern region. The northern arm of these highlands consists (from west to east) of the Kirghiz, Kungai-Alatau and Zeili-Alatau ranges. They are narrow ranges, with many peaks above 13,000 feet (4,000 m) and numerous small glaciers. There are many small valleys watered by perennial streams flowing down the generally gentle, northward-facing slopes of the ranges. Some of the larger streams that originate in these mountains provide the water resources for many settlements in neighboring southern Kazakhstan. Most of Kyrgyzstan's long and tortuous boundary with Kazakhstan runs along the high ridges of these ranges.

The Talas-Alatau and Ters-Alatau form the southern arm of this system. The Ters (Terskiy) Alatau, south of the Issyk-Kul Basin, has several peaks above 16,000 feet (5,000 m) and is the most formidable part of this region, with several large glaciers. It is the main source of the Naryn River, which irrigates large areas of the Fergana Basin and is a main tributary of the Syr Darya. The ranges of both the northern and southern arms of this mountainous region are only thinly populated, except in some valleys and lower slopes at the northern fringes.

Lake Issyk-Kul fills nearly the entire area of a deep basin. It is 115 miles (185 km) long, 38 miles (61 km) wide and has a surface area of 2,425 square miles (6,280 sq. km). The lake, 5,275 feet (1,609 m) above sea level and 2,300 feet (702 m) deep, undergoes minor seasonal fluctuations and is slightly brackish (0.6 percent salt). The lake is well known for its clear waters and scenic shores. The steep slopes of the surrounding mountains leave only narrow strips of flat beaches, except in the extreme east, where the bottom of the basin is higher than the lake. The large, flat areas east of the lake are mostly irrigated and

form one of the main inhabited areas of the northern region. The lake is fed by many small streams flowing down from the surrounding mountains. The lake does not freeze in winter, except for small areas along the beach, despite the prevailing low temperatures. This is attributed to the inflow of water from hot springs. Issyk-Kul means "the warm lake" in Kirghiz.

The northern region has an extension into the foothills of the Kirghiz Range and the arid lowlands bordering the Muyun Kum Desert (in Kazakhstan), along the valleys of the Chu and Talas rivers. This subregion, which bulges from mountainous Kyrgyzstan into the lowlands of Kazakhstan, is the most populated and economically active part of Kyrgyzstan and includes its capital, Bishkek. This is a land of low, rounded hills, broad valleys, river terraces and floodplains covered by deposits of fertile soils brought down from the mountains by rivers and glaciers. Much of this area has the characteristics of oases; it is a transitional zone between the adequately rain-fed mountain slopes and the sands of the Muyun Kum Desert. Like other regions of Central Asia, earthquakes in Kyrgyzstan are a frequent occurrence. The basins and some of the valleys have experienced several strong, destructive quakes over the past century.

The Southern Region

The southern region is the least accessible and the most thinly inhabited part of the country. Several high mountain ranges, the most prominent of which is the Kokshaal-Tau, take up nearly the entire area. The Kokshaal-Tau, a formidable physical barrier with many peaks above 16,000 feet (5,000 m) and several large glaciers, formed the frontier zone between the ex-Soviet Union and China. Its highest part, in the extreme east, has several peaks above 22,000 feet (6,700 m), including Pobeda (Victory) Peak (24,400 ft./7,440 m) and Khan-Tengri Peak (22,950 ft./6,995 m). The large glaciers here are the source of several rivers on which the population of neighboring valleys depends. The largest of these, the Inylchek Glacier, is 36 miles (57 km) long, with an area of 280 square miles (720 sq. km) descending from an altitude of 23,000 feet (6,990 m) to 9,400 feet (2,870 m). The Aksu River Valley,

running south into the Tarim Basin (in China), is one of the few high passes in this region through the Tien Shan.

The region includes the eastern and southern fringes of the Fergana Basin (most of which is in Uzbekistan), one of the two small, but highly important, lowland areas of Kyrgyzstan. It is an area of low, rounded hills with broad, flat valleys, where much of the country's economic activity and urban life are concentrated. The densely inhabited Kyrgyzian part of the Fergana Basin extends into some of the valleys and lower slopes of the adjoining highlands (the Alay Mountains in the south and the Fergana Mountains in the east).

CLIMATE

Situated in the heart of Asia, approximately 1,400 miles (2,200 km) from the nearest open sea, Kyrgyzstan experiences an extremely arid continental climate, varied and moderated with altitude due to its highly mountainous nature. A wide diurnal and seasonal range of temperatures is one of the characteristics of this climate. The winter is very cold, with average minimum temperatures for January ranging from 10°F (−12°C) in the northern lowland areas to 7°F (−14°C) in the eastern part of the Fergana Basin, and to −7°F (−22°C) in the Naryn Valley (altitude, 6,800 ft./2,070 m). The summers are hot in the basins, the northern foothills and lowlands, with average maximum temperatures for July of 84°F (29°C), 86°F (30°C) and 64°F (18°C), respectively. Maximum July and August temperatures of 95° to 100°F (35° to 38°C) are frequently recorded in the lower parts of the country.

Precipitation (which falls mainly in winter and spring) varies greatly with position and altitude—from 5 to 8 inches (120 to 200 mm) in parts of the basins and some valleys, to 16 to 24 inches (400 to 610 mm) on some westward- and northward-facing lower

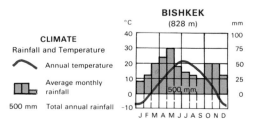

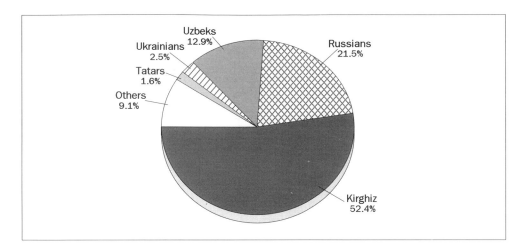

Ethnic Composition
1989

Uzbeks 12.9%
Ukrainians 2.5%
Tatars 1.6%
Others 9.1%
Russians 21.5%
Kirghiz 52.4%

slopes and foothills. Larger amounts are recorded on some slopes with altitudes above 6,000 feet (1,800 m). The greater part of the country receives less than 12 inches (300 mm), mostly in the form of snow. The perpetual snow line is highest on the southward-facing slopes of the Kokshaal-Tau Range (13,000–14,000 ft./4,000–4,300 m) and lowest on the northward-facing slopes of the Kirghiz and Kungai-Alatau ranges (10,000–11,500 ft./3,000–3,500 m).

POPULATION

In 1993, the population was estimated at 4,630,000. It was 4,258,000 in 1989, at the last census carried out by the Soviet Union. It was 3,529,000 in 1979 and has tripled since 1939, when it was 1,459,000. The average annual natural increase in recent years has been 1.6 percent; during the 1980s it was 1.9 percent. The Kirghiz and other Asiatic ethnic groups have an average annual natural increase of 2.5 percent, while the Russian and European ethnic groups have less than 1 percent.

According to the 1989 census, the Kirghiz were 52.4 percent of the population, Russians 21.5 percent, Uzbeks 12.9 percent, Ukrainians 2.5 percent and Tatars 1.6 percent. On the eve of World War II, the Kirghiz (67 percent), Uzbeks and other native Central Asian ethnic groups made up over 90 percent of the population. During and after the war, large numbers of Russians, Ukrainians and other people from the European parts of the Soviet Union settled in Kyrgyzstan, mainly in the urban areas,

the northern lowlands and the Fergana Basin. By the early 1960s, they formed well over 40 percent of the population, a majority in some of the urban centers. In the early 1970s, the Kirghiz were only 40 percent of the population and the Uzbeks 11 percent, while the Russians were 30 percent, Ukrainians 6.6 percent and other Europeans 4.1 percent. The balance has since shifted considerably in favor of the Kirghiz because of their higher rate of natural increase. The Uzbek minority is mainly concentrated in the southwestern part of the country.

The Kirghiz and the other Central Asian ethnic groups are Sunni Muslims (or of Muslim descent). The Russians and Ukrainians are Christian Orthodox (or of Christian descent). Nearly 90 percent of Kyrgyzstan is thinly populated or virtually uninhabited. The average population density of the country as a whole is 60 persons per square mile (23 per sq. km) and over large parts of the mountainous areas, less than 10 persons per square mile (4 per sq. km). The northern foothills and lowlands (lower Chu and Talas valleys) are the most densely inhabited areas, with an average density of 240 persons per square mile (92 per sq. km). The Kyrgyzstan areas of the Fergana Basin have a slightly lower density. Kyrgyzstan has undergone rapid urbanization over the last fifty years. While only 12 percent of the population resided in towns in the late 1920s and 18.5 percent in 1939, half of the population had become urbanized by 1989, living in eighteen towns and thirty-one settlements officially clas-

sified as urban. The capital, Bishkek (650,000 inhabitants), is the only large city. It is followed by Osh (220,000) and Jalal-Abad (78,000), both in the Fergana Basin, and Przhevalsk (65,000) in the Issyk-Kul Basin.

ECONOMY

Kyrgyzstan is still largely an agricultural land that specializes in livestock breeding; about 90 percent of the economically utilized lands are used as pasture or for growing fodder. Only a small percentage of the land is under cultivation, but substantial surpluses in agricultural products have been produced as a result of extensive development projects in recent decades. The country is rich in mineral resources, only part of which is exploited. Difficulties in accessibility are delaying the development of some known mineral deposits in remote mountainous areas. The country is also rich in energy resources (mainly coal). Industry, which has mostly developed since World War II and has become the country's prime economic activity, is based largely on Kyrgyzstan's agricultural, mineral and energy resources. However, as in other former Asian republics of the Soviet Union, it was designed to a great extent to fit into the economic plans and targets of the Soviet empire.

Agriculture

Cultivation, largely under irrigation, is mainly concentrated in the Chu and Talas valleys and neighboring foothills and slopes, in the Fergana Basin and adjoining valleys and slopes, in the eastern part of the Issyk-Kul Basin, and in some of the larger valleys (such as the Naryn) between the main ranges. Most of the area is devoted to cereals. Kyrgyzstan is

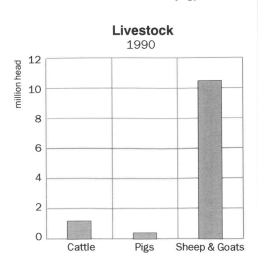

Livestock
1990

million head

12
10
8
6
4
2
0

Cattle   Pigs   Sheep & Goats

more than self-sufficient in wheat. Other important crops are sugar beets (mainly in the north), cotton (in the Fergana Basin), tobacco, rice, vegetables, fruit, medicinal plants and hemp.

Sheep and goats (10.5 million in 1990), cattle (1.2 million) and pigs (411,000) are widely bred, while at altitudes above 8,000 feet (2,500 m) a type of yak is raised. Horses are also widely bred, especially in the highlands. Stock breeding is the main occupation of many of the farms in the mountainous, thinly populated parts of the country. Large quantities of meat, milk and wool are produced. Kyrgyzstan is also known for its sericulture, an activity which is concentrated in the Fergana Basin. Fishing is important in Lake Issyk-Kul.

Forests cover only 4 percent of the country. They extend over large, continuous areas only on the northward-facing slopes of the northern mountain region.

The great majority of agricultural activities and production is carried out in the 176 collective and 290 state farms. Reorganization and partial privatization of agriculture has been in slow progress

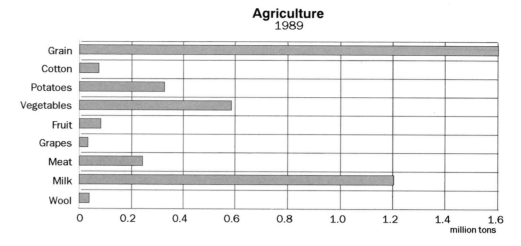

Agriculture
1989

since 1992. In 1989, Kyrgyzstan produced 1.6 million tons of grain (mostly wheat), 1,202,000 tons of milk and milk products, 585,000 tons of vegetables, 324,000 tons of potatoes, 241,000 tons of meat, 74,000 tons of cotton and 39,000 tons of wool.

Mineral Resources

Kyrgyzstan has the largest coal deposits in Central Asia. Coal is mined in two areas: on the eastern fringes of the Fergana Basin and in the eastern part of the Issyk-Kul Basin. Deposits exist in other parts of the country. Oil and natural gas for local requirements and for neighboring areas in Uzbekistan are produced in the northeastern part of the Fergana Basin. Mercury (the main source for the former USSR) and antimony are mined in the Alay Mountains (south of the Fergana Basin). Deposits of several nonferrous metals are known to exist in the Chatkal Mountains (north of the Fergana Basin). Hydroelectric power stations, mainly along the Naryn River,

Agriculture

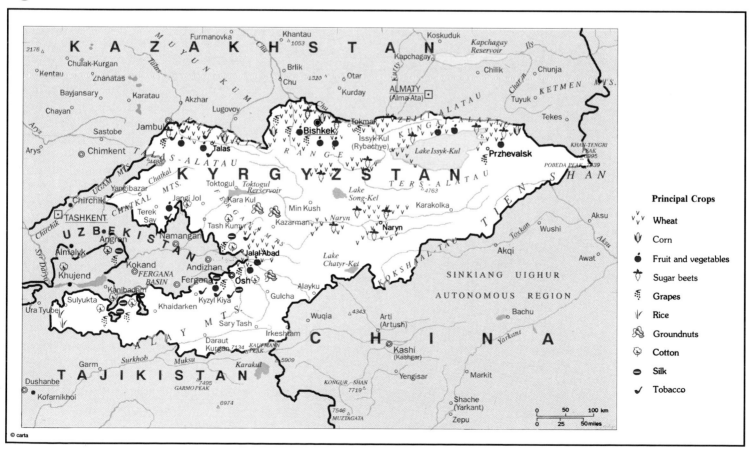

Principal Crops

- Wheat
- Corn
- Fruit and vegetables
- Sugar beets
- Grapes
- Rice
- Groundnuts
- Cotton
- Silk
- Tobacco

© carta

Industry and Mineral Resources

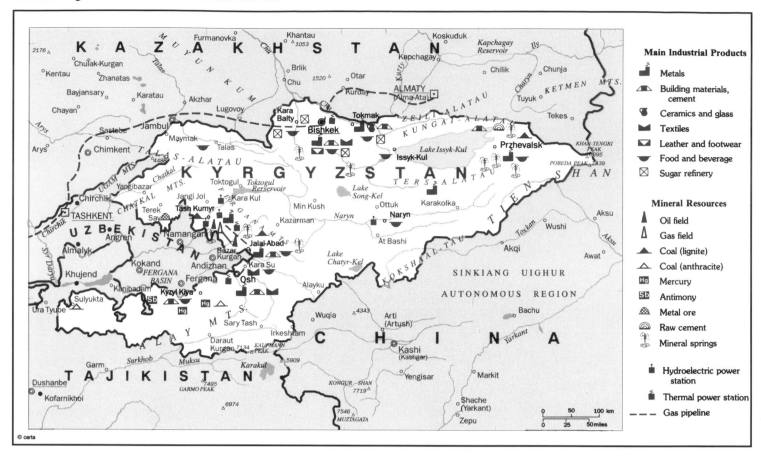

Main Industrial Products

- ⚒ Metals
- ⛰ Building materials, cement
- 🍷 Ceramics and glass
- ✂ Textiles
- 👞 Leather and footwear
- ⚗ Food and beverage
- ⊠ Sugar refinery

Mineral Resources

- ▲ Oil field
- △ Gas field
- ▲ Coal (lignite)
- △ Coal (anthracite)
- Hg Mercury
- Sb Antimony
- ⬡ Metal ore
- ⌂ Raw cement
- ⚘ Mineral springs
- ■ Hydroelectric power station
- ▮ Thermal power station
- --- Gas pipeline

provide most of the electricity requirements.

Industry

Local industries are mainly engaged in the processing of agricultural and mineral raw materials and the utilization of these materials for a wide variety of products. These industries produce cotton, wool, silk and artificial fiber products, leather and leather products, various food products (sugar, edible oils, canned meat, vegetables, fruit and milk products), building materials (mainly cement), chemicals, agricultural machinery (mainly for mountainous lands), various metal and engineering products, and timber and wood products.

Industries are concentrated in two areas: the northern lowlands and foothills (the Chu Valley), with the capital, Bishkek, as the main core; and in and around the eastern part of the Fergana Basin, with the towns of Osh and Jalal-Abad as the chief centers. There is also a much smaller industrial center in the eastern part of the Issyk-Kul Basin in and around Przhevalsk. These main industrial areas are almost contiguous with those of southeastern Kazakhstan in the north and of the Uzbeki parts of the Fergana Basin in the south.

Trade

Trade was and still is almost entirely with Russia, other former republics of the Soviet Union, or through Soviet trade channels. Efforts are underway to reduce the country's large dependence on the transportation systems of the former USSR by developing independent trade links.

HISTORY

The Kirghiz, who speak a Turkish language, are believed to be of Mongol-Tatar origin. They were nomadic tribes who, probably as early as the tenth century, began migrating from lands farther northeast to the high mountain regions that make up the present state. These tribes were in control of most of the country by the thirteenth century, when they came under the suzerainty of the Mongol Empire. Following the collapse of the empire, the history of the country was very similar to that of the neighboring regions of present-day Uzbekistan and Kazakhstan, although control of most of the mountainous parts of the country was practically in the hands of local tribal chiefs. The Russians began their penetration into the region in the middle of the nineteenth century. In 1864 they officially extended their rule over the country and made it part of their Turkestan province. The majority of the population was at that time nomads or seminomads. Russians began to settle in Kyrgyzstan toward the end of the nineteenth century.

Main Industrial Products	
1989	
Steel	3,200 tons
Timber	7,000 cu. m
Cement	1,400,000 tons
Fabrics	150,000,000 sq. m
Knitwear	20,500,000 items
Hosiery	32,900,000 pairs
Footwear	11,900,000 pairs
Butter	14,000 tons
Granulated sugar	415,000 tons
Preserves	161,000,000 jars

Education
1989–1990

	No. of Institutes	No. of Students
Primary & Secondary Schools	1,800	900,000
Higher Education	9	59,300
Technical Colleges, Teachers' Training	48	46,000

After the Communist Revolution, Kirghizia (as it was known then) was included in the Turkestan Autonomous Republic that was part of the Russian Soviet Federated Socialist Republic (1921). In 1924 it was separated from Turkestan to become first an autonomous region and then, in 1926, an autonomous republic in the RSFSR. In 1936, it was proclaimed a constituent republic of the Soviet Union. Nomadism has been in retreat since the 1920s. Vertical seasonal movements of herdsmen still occur, on a limited scale, in some inland valleys. Large numbers of Russians and Ukrainians were encouraged during and after World War II to settle in Kyrgyzstan. Large numbers of Germans (who for generations lived in European Russia) and Tatars were forcibly moved to Kyrgyzstan during the war. Many of them have since left or plan to do so. Kyrgyzstan declared its independence in 1991 and shortly afterward became a member of the Commonwealth of Independent States (CIS).

GOVERNMENT AND POLITICS

In general elections held in 1990, the Supreme Soviet became the single-chamber legislature of independent, democratic Kyrgyzstan. It is composed of 350 members—335 former Communists and 15 opposition members (of the Democratic Movement)—elected for a four-year term. The country is headed by a president with executive powers, Askar Akayev, who was elected in 1991 by popular vote for a four-year term; he was a leading member of the local Communist Party. The government is appointed by the president. The country is divided into six administrative regions that are subdivided into urban and rural districts.

THE CAPITAL

Bishkek (Frunze, 1926–1991), with a population of 650,000 (1992), is by far Kyrgyzstan's largest urban and industrial center. It is built on the lower northern slope of the highest part of the Kirghiz Range, backed by permanently snow-capped peaks of more than 15,000 feet (4,600 m). Built on the banks of two small tributaries of the Chu River, it is spread over altitudes of 2,200 to 3,000 feet (670 to 900 m) in the agriculturally rich region of the Chu Valley. Russians, Ukrainians and other European ethnic groups form about half of its population. Except for a small, older nucleus, Bishkek is a modern city with wide, tree-lined main streets, parks and numerous government and public buildings. Most of the city is built in typical post–World War II Soviet style.

The town was founded by the Russians in 1878, next to a small fort built toward the end of the eighteenth century or in the early nineteenth century by the Khanate of Kokand as a base against Kirghiz nomads. The fort, whose name (Pishkek) the town adopted, fell into Russian hands in 1862. It was at first a small administrative and garrison center mainly inhabited by Russians. In 1924, it became the capital of the Kirghiz Autonomous Region and, in 1926, of the Kirghiz Autonomous Republic. It was then named Frunze in memory of Mikhail Frunze, a prominent Communist leader and one of the founders of the Red Army, who was born there. The population increased from 30,000 in the mid-1920s to 93,000 in 1939, but the city's main growth came after World War II, when it more than tripled, reaching 431,000 in 1970. It has since increased by more than 50 percent. In 1936, it became the capital of the Kirghiz Soviet Socialist Republic. Rapid industrialization has been the main cause of growth.

The city and its surrounding area have a wide variety of industries that are the main source of occupation for its inhabitants. The industries range from processing local agricultural raw materials into food, textile, clothing and leather products to producing heavy machinery, engineering products, agricultural machinery and tools and building materials.

In addition to its political, administrative and economic functions, Bishkek is Kyrgyzstan's main cultural center. It is the seat of the Kirghiz Academy of Sciences (founded 1954), a university (founded 1951), research institutes, high-level training institutes in various technical professions and arts, theaters, museums and the main source of publications in Kirghiz. It is also Kyrgyzstan's main center of rail and road communication with neighboring countries and other parts of the former Soviet Union.

Bishkek

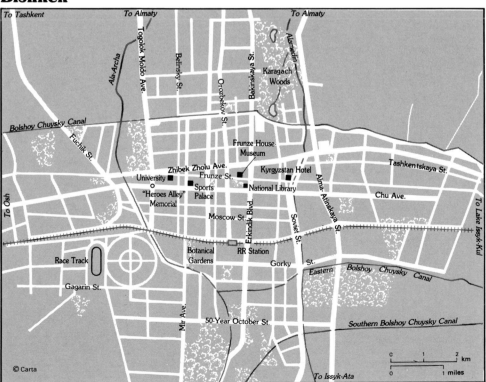

List of Sources

Akiner, S., *The Islamic Peoples of the Soviet Union*. London, 1986.

Bater, J. H., *The Soviet Scene: A Geographical Perspective*. London, 1989.

Belkindas, M. V., and M. J. Sagers, *Preliminary Analysis of Economic Relations among Union Republics of the USSR: 1970–1988*. Soviet Geography, Vol. 31/9. New York, 1990.

Bilmanis, A. A., *A History of Latvia*. Princeton, N.J., 1951.

Bolshaya Sovetskaya Entsiklopaedia (Great Soviet Encyclopedia). Moscow, 1959–1978, and Annual Supplements.

Bradshaw, M. J., *The Soviet Union: A New Regional Geography*. London, 1991.

Bremner, I., and R. Taras, *Nations and Politics in the Soviet Successor States*. Cambridge, 1992.

Cambridge Encyclopedia of Russia and the Soviet Union. Cambridge, 1982.

Dienes, L., *Soviet Asia*. Boulder, Colo., 1987.

Hooson, D. J. M., *The Soviet Union: A Systematic Regional Geography*. London, 1966.

Kubiojovyc, V., *Encyclopedia of Ukraine*. Toronto, 1984.

Lang, D. M., *The Georgians*. London, 1966.

Lavigne, M., *The USSR and East Europe in the Global Economy*. Cambridge, 1991.

Lewis, R. A., *Geographical Studies on Central Asia*. London, 1990.

Lubachko, I. S., *Belorussia under Soviet Rule: 1917–1957*. Lexington, Ky., 1972.

Lydolph, P., *Geography of the USSR*. 5th ed. Elkhart Lake, Wis., 1990.

Medvedev, Z., *Soviet Agriculture*. New York, 1987.

Medvedkov, O. L., *Soviet Urbanization*. London, 1990.

Motyl, A. A., *The Post-Soviet Nations*. New York, 1992.

Narodnoe Khozyaistvo SNG. Moscow, 1992.

Narodnoe Khozyaistvo SSSR. Annual. Moscow, 1985–1991.

Office of the Geographer, U.S. Department of State: *Ethnicity and Political Boundaries in the Soviet Union*. Washington, D.C., 1990.

Olcott, M. B., *The Kazakhs*. Stanford, Calif., 1987.

Pockney, B. P., *Soviet Statistics Since 1945*. New York, 1991.

Raun, T. U., *Estonia and the Estonians*. Stanford, Calif., 1987.

Rodgers, A., *The Soviet Far East: Geographical Perspective and Development*. London, 1990.

Shabad, T., *Basic Industrial Resources of the USSR*. New York, 1969.

Shaw, W., and D. Pryce, *Encyclopaedia of the USSR*. London, 1990.

Smith, G., *The Nationalities Question in the Soviet Union*. London, 1990.

Walker, C. J., *Armenia*. 2d ed. London, 1990.

Wheeler, G., *The Peoples of Soviet Central Asia*. London, 1966.

Annotated Bibliography
prepared by Linda S. Vertrees

IMPERIAL RUSSIA. Interest in Russia continues to grow because of recent events. The fastest way to get an overview of the country and people is to rent *The Rise and Fall of the Soviet Union* (2 vols.; VCII Home Entertainment, 1993) or *Inside Russia* (2 vols.; Library Distributors of America, 1992). Both are excellent pictorial introductions to the history, culture, and current affairs of Russia. *Inside Russia Today* by John Gunther (Harper & Brothers, 1958) is an old but still good introduction to the people and geography of this region. James H. Billington's *The Icon and the Axe* (Knopf, 1966) provides an introduction to the cultural development of the Russian peoples from 1300 to 1960, during which time Russia emerged as a powerful, destructive, and creative civilization. Paul Dukes's *A History of Russia: Medieval, Modern, Contemporary* (2d ed.; Duke University Press, 1990) and *A History of Russia* by Nicholas V. Riasanovsky (5th ed.; Oxford University Press, 1993) are excellent general histories that include information on recent events. *Encyclopedia of Russian History* by John Paxton (ABC-CLIO, 1993) provides a chronology of events from about 900 to 1989 and includes information on the independent republics.

See *Prehistoric Russia* by Tadeusz Sulimirshi (Humanities Press, 1970) for a well-illustrated presentation of archaeological artifacts in Eastern Europe prior to the end of the seventh century B.C. M. Tikhomirov's *The Towns of Ancient Rus* (Foreign Language Publishing House, 1959) provides insight into how the towns of the ninth and tenth centuries functioned, as well as short histories of individual towns (e.g., Kiev and Novgorod). *The Influence of the Mongols on Russia* by Paul H. Silfen (Exposition Press, 1974), *The Tatar Yoke* (Slavica Publishers, 1985), and *Russia and the Golden Horde* (Indiana University Press, 1985) both by Charles J. Halperin complement each other with descriptions of the invasion by the Mongols, sacking of Kiev (twice in the twelfth century), and the eventual rise of Moscovy during the middle ages. *The Formation of the Great Russian State* by A. E. Presniakov (Quadrangle Books, 1970) is an excellent interpretation of the rise of Moscow during the thirteenth to fifteenth centuries. W. Bruce Lincoln's *The Conquest of a Continent: Siberia and the Russians* (Random House, 1994) describes the expansion of Moscovy east through Siberia and discusses current problems with the exploitation of natural resources. *The History of Siberia* edited by Alan Wood (Routledge, 1991) is a series of essays on the European Cossack's conquest of the Mongolian empire in Siberia.

Ivan the Terrible by Ruslan G. Skrynnikov (Academic International Press, 1981) is a short scholarly biography of Ivan the Terrible. Another excellent biography is *Ivan the Terrible* by Robert Payne and Nikita Romanoff (Thomas Y. Crowell, 1975). *Boris Godunov* (Academic International Press, 1982), a good biography, and *The Time of Troubles* (Academic International Press, 1988) both by Ruslan G. Skrynnikov present the chronology of the political unrest, social upheaval, and economic disruption of the times of Boris Godunov and the False Dmitry.

W. Bruce Lincoln's *The Romanovs* (Dial Press, 1981) is a collective biography of the fifteen men and four women who ruled Russia from 1613 to 1917. *The Rise of the Romanovs* by Vasili Klyuchevsky (Macmillan, 1970) presents an analysis of seventeenth-century Russia and the social, political, economic, and religious changes that took place. *Russian Expansion on the Pacific, 1641–1850* by F. A. Golder (Peter Smith, 1960) deals with the exploration of Siberia, the Pacific coast of Asia, and North America with emphasis on Vitus Bering's voyages. *Peter the Great: His Life and World* by Robert K. Massie (Knopf, 1981) is a well-written, enjoyable biography. *Peter the Great Transforms Russia* edited by James Cracraft (D. C. Heath, 1991) is an excellent collection of essays on Peter the Great and his many reforms. *Elizabeth and Catherine, Empresses of All the Russias* by Robert Coughlan (G. P. Putnam's Sons, 1974) is the story of two remarkable women and their era. Carol S. Leonard's *Reform and Regicide: The Reign of Peter III of Russia* (Indiana University Press, 1992) is a scholarly analysis of the short reign of Peter III, the grandson of Peter the Great; he was overthrown by his wife, who ruled as Catherine the Great. Gladys S. Thomson's *Catherine the Great and the Expansion of Russia* (Greenwood Press, 1985) is a good biography of Catherine. *The German Colonies on the Lower Volga* by Gottlieb Beratz (American Historical Society of Germans from Russia, 1991) is a history of the 150-year-old German settlement established by Catherine II in 1764. *Years of the Golden Cockerel: The Last Romanov Tsars, 1814–1917* by Sidney Harcave (Macmillan, 1968) is a collective biography of the last five tsars and the events that overtook them.

The Shadow of the Winter Palace by Edward Crankshaw (Viking, 1976) and Adam B. Ulam's *Russia's Failed Revolutions* (Basic Books, 1981) provide an analysis of events from the Decembrists in 1825 through the Crimean War, the Russo-Japanese War, and the Revolution of 1917. *The Crimean War* by Andrew D. Lambert (Manchester University Press, 1990) discusses the strategy of the British against Russia. *The War against Russia: 1854–1856* by A. J. Barker (Holt, Rinehart and Winston, 1970) is a good history of the war that Russia fought against the British and French. W. Bruce Lincoln's *The Great Reforms* (Northern Illinois University Press, 1990) brings into focus the importance of the social and economic reforms of the 1860s, including freeing the serfs, restructuring the court system, and establishing local governments. *Perestroika under the Tsars* by W. E. Mosse (I. B. Tauris, 1992) shows the similarities of the 1860 reforms to the actions taken by Gorbachev. *School and Society in Tsarist and Soviet Russia* edited by Ben Eklof (St. Martin's Press, 1993) is a collection of essays dealing with nineteenth-century educational

systems; also discussed is the use of textbooks for Soviet propaganda purposes. *Road to Power* by Steven G. Marks (Cornell University Press, 1991) is a history of the construction of the Trans-Siberian Railway, including maps showing the route. Benson Bobrick's *East of the Sun* (Poseidon Press, 1992) describes Siberia's rich resources, subjugation of the natives, and establishment of the penal colonies, as well as the building of the railway. *The Island: A Journey to Sakhalin* by Anton Chekhov (Washington Square Press, 1967) is the fascinating account of his journey around 1890 to the most notorious of the tsar's penal colonies. John J. Stephan's *Sakhalin* (Clarendon Press, 1971) presents the history of the contested frontier between Russia and Japan. *In War's Dark Shadow* by W. Bruce Lincoln (Dial Press, 1983) tells the story of Russia's attempt to industrialize at the beginning of the twentieth century. *The Origins of the Russo-Japanese War* by Ian H. Nish (Longmans, 1986) describes the events in both Japan and Russia that led up to the Russo-Japanese War. *The Tide at Sunrise* by Denis and Peggy Warner (Charterhouse, 1974) is an excellent history of the Russo-Japanese War. *The Short Victorious War* by David Walder (Harper & Row, 1973) describes the military and political aspects of the Russo-Japanese War.

Leon Trotsky's *1905* (Random House, 1971) is the official Communist view of the 1905 Revolution. *The Crisis of Russian Autocracy* by Andrew M. Verner (Princeton University Press, 1990) explains the role autocrats and Nicholas II as tsar played in the 1905 Revolution. *Before the Revolution* by Kyril Fitzlon and Tatiana Browning (Overlook, 1993) is an excellent pictorial representation of Russia at the turn of the century. *Nicholas and Alexandra: The Family Album* by Prince Michael of Greece (Tauris Parke Books, 1992) is an outsized book with wonderful black-and-white photos of the last Romanovs from their marriage to their imprisonment. Robert K. Massie's *Nicholas and Alexandra* (Atheneum, 1967) is an excellent, readable biography. A more recent biography is *The Last Tsar: The Life and Death of Nicholas II* by Edvard Radzinsky (Doubleday, 1992); it contains information recently made available by the opening of the records at the national archives. *The Secret Letters of the Last Tsar* edited by Edward J. Bing (Longman, Green, 1938) is a collection of the correspondence between Tsar Nicholas II and his mother presenting the daily activities of the tsar's family after the 1905 Revolution. *Rasputin: The Man behind the Myth* by Maria Rasputin and Patti Barham (Prentice Hall, 1977) is the personal recollections of his daughter and others who knew him. For a more historical and objective view see *Rasputin: Satyr, Saint or Satan* by Douglas Myles (McGraw-Hill, 1990).

Miriam Kochan's *The Last Days of Imperial Russia* (Macmillan, 1976) is an objective presentation of life and society before the war and revolution began. *The Octoberists in the Third Duma, 1907–1912* by Ben-Cion Pinchok (University of Washington Press, 1974) is a good history of the Third Duma, a crucial testing of the constitutional monarchy as established after the 1905 Revolution. *St. Petersburg between the Revolutions* by Robert B. McKean (Yale University Press, 1990) is a scholarly work on the industrial unrest that existed in St. Petersburg before the Revolution. *Black Night, White Snow* by Harrison E. Salisbury (Doubleday, 1978) is an excellent history of the 1905 and 1917 Revolutions and the people who made them. *The Bolsheviks* by Adam B. Ulam (Macmillan, 1965) analyzes the political and intellectual development of the Bolsheviks.

Richard Abraham's *Alexander Kerensky* (Columbia University Press, 1987) is a comprehensive analysis of the politics of the premier of the Provisional Government; also described are his activities in exile after being overthrown by the Bolsheviks. *The Russian Revolution of 1917: The Origins of Modern Communism* by Leonard Schapiro (Basic Books, 1984) deals with the consolidation of power by the Bolsheviks from the Provisional Government. Richard Pipes's *The Russian Revolution* (Knopf, 1990) is an excellent comprehensive history of the political and military struggle for power in Russia. The gradual decay of the tsarist regime led to the establishment of Soviet Russia between 1917 and 1920. *Comrades: 1917—Russia in Revolution* by Brian Moynahan (Little, Brown, 1992) is an excellent history emphasizing social and cultural life as well as political changes. *Untimely Thoughts* by Maxim Gorky (Paul S. Eriksson, 1968) is an interesting collection of essays written by Gorky in 1917–1918 on the Revolution, culture, and the Bolsheviks. W. Bruce Lincoln's *Passage through Armageddon* (Simon & Schuster, 1986) describes the events of World War I and the Revolution. This story is continued in Lincoln's *Red Victory: A History of the Russian Civil War* (Simon & Schuster, 1989), a presentation of the civil war in which millions of Russians died.

Notes of a Red Guard by Eduard M. Dune (University of Illinois Press, 1993) is the memoir of a participant in the Revolution, but also a lifelong opponent of Stalin and his regime. *The Mensheviks after October* by Vladimir N. Brovkin (Cornell University Press, 1991) analyzes the Mensheviks during the first year of the Revolution and how the Bolsheviks consolidated their power. Also edited by Vladimir N. Brovkin is *Dear Comrades* (Hoover Institution Press, 1991), a presentation of actual documents of the Mensheviks that analyze the social and political process during the civil war. William G. Rosenberg's *Liberals in the Russian Revolution* (Princeton University Press, 1974) is a history of the Constitutional Democratic Party (Kadets) from 1917 to 1921.

SOVIET UNION. *Soviet Civilization: A Cultural History* by Andrei Sinyavsky (Arcade Publishers, 1990) is an introduction to the Soviet world through its literature, society, and politics. *Russia Speaks* by Richard Lourie (HarperCollins,

1991) is an oral history of many individuals across Russia from the Revolution to glasnost. M. K. Dziewanowski's *A History of Soviet Russia* (4th ed.; Prentice Hall, 1993) is a single-volume history through the 1991 attempted coup. *The Soviet Tragedy* by Martin E. Malia (Free Press, 1994) is another good history of the Soviet Union. *Claws of the Bear* by Brian Moynahan (Houghton, 1989) is a balanced history of the Soviet military. *Red Bread* by Maurice Hindus (Indiana University Press, 1988) is the story of farm collectivization and how village life changed. *Steeltown U.S.S.R.* by Stephen Kotkin (University of California Press, 1991) is a short history of the building of steel works and people's sacrifices during the 1930s.

Behind the Urals by John Scott (Indiana University Press, 1982), originally published in 1942, is the absorbing story of an American's life during the 1930s in the new industrial city of Magnitogorsk. *Black on Red* by Robert Robinson (Acropolis Books, 1988) is the personal experiences of a black in the Soviet Union from the 1930s to the mid-1970s and his constant fear of the KGB. A more positive American experience in the Soviet Union is *Fifty Russian Winters* by Margaret Wettlin (Pharos Books, 1992). This is the autobiography of the author who moved to the Soviet Union in 1932 for one year, and who stayed for fifty.

Philip Pomper's *Lenin, Trotsky, and Stalin: The Intelligencia and Power* (Columbia University Press, 1990) is a collective biography of three important revolutionaries from 1905 to Lenin's death in 1924. For an excellent biography of Lenin see Robert Service's *Lenin: A Political Life* (Indiana University Press, 1991–), a projected three-volume set, the first two of which have been published. *The Life and Death of Lenin* by Robert Payne (Simon & Schuster, 1964) is a good one-volume biography of Lenin. *My Life* by Leon Trotsky (Thornton Butterworth, 1930) is well written; it ends with his exile in Mexico. *The Life and Death of Trotsky* by Robert Payne (McGraw-Hill, 1977) is another good biography. Three books by Robert Conquest provide a fascinating view of Joseph Stalin and the formation of Stalinism. *The Great Terror: Stalin's Purge of the Thirties* (Macmillan, 1968) describes the immense scale of the purge. *Inside Stalin's Secret Police: NKVD Politics, 1936–1939* (Hoover Institution Press, 1985) is an interesting study of the police-state politics of that era. *Stalin: Breaker of Nations* (Viking, 1991) is an excellent biography. *Stalin: The Man and His Era* by Adam B. Ulam (Beacon Press, 1989) is another excellent biography. *The Trial of Bukharin* by George Katkov (B. T. Batsford, 1969) is the story of Nikolai Bukharin, a leading member of the Communist Party, who was charged, convicted, and executed by Stalin for "crimes against the state." *This I Cannot Forget: The Memoirs of Nikolai Bukharin's Widow* by Anna Larina (W. W. Norton, 1993) tells the story of her internal exile and persecution.

The Soviet Union and the Threat from the East, 1933–41 by Jonathan Haslam (University of Pittsburgh Press, 1992) is a well-written analysis of Japanese-Soviet relations before the start of World War II. William R. Trotter's *A Frozen Hell* (Algonquin Books, 1991) is a well-balanced description of the Russo-Finnish War in 1939–40. The joint biography *Hitler and Stalin: Parallel Lives* by Alan Bullock (Knopf, 1992) describing the similarities between the two men makes for fascinating reading. *The Great Patriotic War* by Peter G. Tsouras (Greenhill Books, 1992) is an excellent photo history of World War II as seen by the Soviets. *The Big Three* by Robin Edmonds (W. W. Norton, 1991) presents the wartime relationship between Churchill, Roosevelt, and Stalin. *FDR & Stalin* by Amos Perlmutter (University of Missouri Press, 1993) discusses the relationship between Roosevelt and Stalin from 1943 to 1945. *Marshal Zhukov's Greatest Battles* by Georgi K. Zhukov (Harper & Row, 1969) is the personal reminiscences of the Soviet general. William Craig's *Enemy at the Gates* (Reader's Digest Press, 1973) and *199 Days* by Edwin P. Hoyt (Tor Books, 1993) are both excellent and highly readable histories of the battle for Stalingrad. *900 Days* by Harrison E. Salisbury (Harper & Row, 1969) is an excellent history of the siege of Leningrad. Vera Inber's *Leningrad Diary* (St. Martin's Press, 1971) tells the same story from the perspective of a resident of Leningrad. *Moscow: 1941* by Janusz Piekalkiewicz (Presidio, 1981) is the history of the battle of Moscow. *Red Storm on the Reich* by Christopher Duffy (Atheneum, 1991) describes the Soviet assault on Germany during 1945, but it does not include the assault on Berlin. Vasili I. Chuikov's *The Fall of Berlin* (Holt, Rinehart & Winston, 1967) recounts the battle of Berlin from the Soviet perspective. *Katyn* by Allen Paul (Scribner's, 1991) is a well-researched description of the massacre of Polish Army officers by the Soviet Army at the beginning of World War II.

Soviet Foreign Policy since World War II by Alvin Z. Rubinstein (HarperCollins, 1992) is a broad comprehensive presentation of the Soviet Union as a participant in world affairs; the growing importance of domestic affairs is also mentioned. *Molotov Remembers* by Viacheslav M. Molotov and Felix Chvev (Ivan R. Dee, 1993) reveals the inner workings of the Soviet system; the book is divided into four sections: "International Affairs," "With Lenin," "With Stalin," and "Since Stalin." Andrei Gromyko's *Memoirs* (Doubleday, 1989) is a fascinating look at the behind-the-scenes operations of the Kremlin and its leaders. *Beria: Stalin's First Lieutenant* by Amy Knight (Princeton University Press, 1993) is an interesting biography of Lavrenty Beria. After Stalin's death, Beria was arrested and executed in a coup led by Khrushchev.

Soviet Intellectuals and Political Power by Vladimir Shlapentokh (Princeton University Press, 1990) analyzes the relationship between the political regime and the creative thinkers' movement toward modernization. *The Spy Who Saved the World* by Jerrold L. Schecter and Peter S. Deriabin (Scribner's, 1992) tells the important story of a CIA agent at the time of the Cuban missile crisis and the information he provided. Georgi Arbatov's *The System* (Times Books, 1992) provides an insider's look at Soviet politics and decision making

as well as the decision makers. *The Communists: The Story of Power and Lost Illusions, 1948–1991* by Adam B. Ulam (Scribner's, 1992) is a fascinating account of the disintegration of Communism; the comparison of Gorbachev to Khrushchev is especially interesting. *Khrushchev Remembers* (Little, Brown, 1970) and *Khrushchev Remembers: The Last Testament* (Little, Brown, 1974) are interesting and insightful books based on tapes dictated by Khrushchev during his retirement. *Khrushchev Remembers: The Glasnost Tapes* (Little, Brown, 1990) is a sequel and fills in many of the gaps in the first two books. *From Brezhnev to Gorbachev* edited by Hans-Joachim Veen (St. Martin's Press, 1987) is a series of essays on domestic and foreign policy issues from the 1960s through the 1980s. Vladislav Tamarov's *Afghanistan: Soviet Vietnam* (Mercury House, 1992) is a personal account of the author's experiences; the similarity to Vietnam is striking. *Holy War, Unholy Victory* by Kurt Lohbeck (Regnery Gateway, 1993) is told by an American journalist from the Afghan perspective. *The Fateful Pebble* by Anthony Arnold (Presidio, 1993) is a comprehensive analysis of the Soviet invasion of Afghanistan and its effect on the Soviet Union.

Why Gorbachev Happened by Robert G. Kaiser (Simon & Schuster, 1991) is an analysis of Gorbachev, his rise and decline. *Gorbachev: Heretic in the Kremlin* by Dusko Doder and Louise Branson (Penguin Books, 1991) is another good biography of Gorbachev. See Urda Jurgens's *Raisa* (Summit Books, 1990) for a well-written biography of Raisa Gorbachev. *The New Russians* by Hedrick Smith (Random House, 1990) is based on hundreds of interviews and provides new insights into the Soviet Union and its people. *Chronicle of a Revolution* edited by Abraham Brumberg (Pantheon Books, 1990) is a unique collection of essays of Western and Soviet scholars discussing perestroika and glasnost. *Gorbachev & Glasnost* edited by Isaac J. Tarasulo (Scholarly Resource Books, 1989) translates thirty-three articles from the Soviet press in 1987–88 covering perestroika. Continuing this theme is *Perils of Perestroika* edited by Isaac J. Tarasulo (Scholarly Resource Books, 1991) with articles from 1989 to 1991. Walter Laqueur's *The Long Road to Freedom: Russia and Glasnost* (Scribner's, 1989) is an interesting examination of glasnost in the context of Russian history. *What Went Wrong with Perestroika* by Marshall I. Goldman (W. W. Norton, 1991) analyzes the repression and economic stagnation of the Soviet Union under Gorbachev. *Russia's Secret Rulers* by Lev Timofeyev (Knopf, 1992) presents a series of revealing interviews with leaders of the new Russia. *The Fate of Marxism in Russia* by Alexander Yakovlev (Yale University Press, 1993) assesses the long-range effects of Marxism and Bolshevism on the Soviet Union and its current state. James H. Billington's *Russia Transformed* (Free Press, 1992) presents an eyewitness account of the 1991 coup attempt and its aftermath on the Russian people. *The End of the Cold War* edited by Michael J. Hogan (Cambridge University Press, 1992) is a series of interesting essays presenting many different points of view on the beginning and end of the Cold War.

RUSSIA. *Boris Yeltsin* by Vladimir Solovyov and Elena Klepikova (G. P. Putnam's Sons, 1992) is an interesting personal and political biography of the Russian president. John Morrison's *Boris Yeltsin: From Bolshevik to Democrat* (Dutton, 1992) is an excellent biography. *End of the Empire* edited by G. R. Urban (American University Press, 1993) is a series of essays on what leading Soviet scholars expected to happen as the Soviet Union collapsed. *Russia beyond Communism* by Vladislav Krasnov (Westview Press, 1991) is a scholarly analysis of the changes occurring in the new Russian state. John B. Dunlop's *The Rise of Russia and the Fall of the Soviet Union* (Princeton University Press, 1993) examines the causes of the breakup of the Soviet Union, including economic problems and ethnic nationalism, as well as the failed coup of 1991 and Boris Yeltsin. *The End of the Soviet Empire* by Helene Carrere d'Encausse (Basic Books, 1993) analyzes the nationalist movements that contributed to the breakup of the Soviet Union; also discussed are the problems currently facing Boris Yeltsin. *The Soviet Military and the Future* edited by Stephen J. Blank and Jacob W. Kipp (Greenwood Press, 1993) is a collection of articles dealing with the Russian military and the changes currently under consideration. *Russia 2010* by Daniel Yergin and Thane Gustafson (Random House, 1993) presents a series of four "what if" scenarios concerning Russia's future over the next twenty years.

Soviet Disunion by Bohdan Nahaylo and Victor Swoboda (Free Press, 1990) is a general history of the nationalist problems facing the Soviet state. Miron Rezun edited *Nationalism and the Breakup of an Empire* (Praeger, 1992), a collection of essays dealing with ethnicity and the breakup of the Soviet Union. *Who's Who in Russia and the New States* edited by Leonard Geron and Alex Pravda (I. B. Tauris, 1993) is an excellent overview of each state including a listing of all government and ministry officials. *Russia and the Independent States* edited by Daniel C. Diller (Congressional Quarterly, 1993) reflects all changes to mid-1992, and includes individual profiles of each republic. *The Newly Independent States of Euroasia* by Stephen K. and Sandra L. Batalden (Oryx, 1993) is a comprehensive analysis of each state's economic, political, social, and religious issues. Walter Laqueur's *Black Hundred: The Rise of the Extreme Right in Russia* (HarperCollins, 1993) is a comprehensive study of the ultranationalists in Russia. The title refers to a right-wing movement that flourished between 1904 and 1917. *Ethnicity and Conflict in a Post-Communist World* edited by Kumar Rupesinghe (St. Martin's Press, 1992) is a series of essays on the Soviet Union after its dissolution and how it is dealing with a variety of ethnic problems. *New Nations Rising* by Nadia Diuk and Adrian Karatnycky (John Wiley, 1993) analyzes the rise of nationalism within the independent states and how they are coping with these problems.

Distant Friends: The United States and Russia, 1763–1867 by Norman E.

Saul (University Press of Kansas, 1991) is a history of the relations between the two countries through the purchase of Alaska. *Alternative Paths* by David W. McFadden (Oxford University Press, 1993) studies the first three years after the Revolution and the beginning of American-Soviet relations. Betty M. Unterberger's *America's Siberian Expedition, 1918–1920* (Greenwood Press, 1969) tells the story of one of the strangest adventures in American military history. This intervention initiated a trend in America's attitude toward the Soviet Union, specifically, and the Far East, in general. *Culture, Conflict and Coexistence* by J. D. Parks (McFarland, 1983) is the history of American and Soviet cultural relationships from 1917 to 1958. *Herbert Hoover and Famine Relief to Soviet Russia: 1921–1923* by Benjamin M. Weissman (Hoover Institution Press, 1974) is the fascinating account of the American Relief Administration and its efforts to feed the starving throughout the Soviet Union for almost two years. *Mission to Moscow* by Joseph E. Davies (Simon & Schuster, 1941) is a personal account of the relations between the United States and the Soviet Union just before the beginning of World War II. *The Cold War Begins* by Lynn E. Davis (Princeton University Press, 1974) is a history of the Soviet and Western leaders' conflict over the political future of Eastern Europe; the Yalta Conference is discussed in detail. Adam B. Ulam's *The Rivals: America and Russia since World War II* (Viking, 1971) studies the causes of America's and Russia's policies toward each other as well as the personalities of the two countries' leaders. *Soviet-American Relations in Asia, 1945–1954* by Russell D. Buhite (University of Oklahoma Press, 1981) analyzes policies toward Asian countries and how they changed during this period. *The Crisis Years: Kennedy and Khrushchev, 1960–1963* by Michael R. Beschloss (Burlingame Books, 1991) is an excellent history of a very turbulent time. *The Missiles of October* by Elie Abel (Macgibbon & Kee, 1969) is the classic narrative of the events of the Cuban missile crisis. *Cuba on the Brink* by James G. Blight, Bruce J. Allyn, and David A. Welch (Pantheon, 1993) studies the role Cuba and Castro played in the missile crisis. *Detente and Confrontation* by Raymond L. Garthoff (Brookings Institution, 1985) studies the relations between the United States and the Soviet Union from Nixon to Reagan. Don Oberdorfer's *The Turn* (Poseidon, 1991) discusses the changes in relations between the United States and the Soviet Union from 1983 to 1990. *At the Highest Levels: The Inside Story of the End of the Cold War* by Michael R. Beschloss and Strobe Talbott (Little, Brown, 1993) is the fascinating story of negotiations between George Bush and Mikhail Gorbachev. *The Cold War Is Over—Again* by Allen Lynch (Westview Press, 1992) discusses the revolutionary events of 1989 and explores the complexities of East-West relations. *The Limited Partnership* edited by James E. Goodby and Benoit Morel (Oxford University Press, 1993) is a collection of essays on the changing relationship of the United States and Russia.

The Long Pretense by Arnold Beichman (Transaction Publishers, 1991) discusses diplomacy from Lenin to Gorbachev and what it will take to reform the system. *The Soviet Union and Cuba* by W. Raymond Duncan (Praeger, 1985) is a history of Soviet-Cuban relations since Castro's revolution in 1959. *The Soviet Union in Asia* by Geoffrey Jukes (University of California Press, 1973) is a history of the development of Soviet Asia and its interests in other Asian countries. *The Japanese Thrust into Siberia, 1918* by James W. Morley (Books for Libraries Press, 1972) analyzes why the Japanese intervened in Siberia in 1918. Pedro Ramet's *The Soviet-Syrian Relationship since 1955* (Westview Press, 1990) discusses the Soviet interests in Syria and Syria's changing importance in the Third World. *The Soviet Policy toward Turkey, Iran, and Afghanistan* by Alvin Z. Rubinstein (Praeger, 1982) assesses Soviet policy under Khrushchev and Brezhnev toward these countries. *The USSR and Iraq* by Oles and Bettie M. Smolansky (Duke University Press, 1991) examines the relationship between the Soviet Union and Iraq. *The Forgotten Friendship* by Arnold Krammer (University of Illinois Press, 1974) is a history of the Soviet Union's relationship with Israel from 1947 to 1953. The Soviet Union was the second country after the United States to recognize Israel. *Soviet Policy toward Israel under Gorbachev* by Robert O. Freedman (Praeger, 1991) analyzes the improving relations between the Soviet Union and Israel since 1987.

ECONOMY. *History of the National Economy of Russia to the 1917 Revolution* by Peter I. Lyashchenko (Octagon Books, 1970) is an excellent history of the Russian economy from primitive through feudal systems, industrialization, and the Revolution. There are chapters on the colonial policy of the tsars as it relates to Central Asia. *Landscape and Settlement in Romanov Russia, 1613–1917* by Judith Pallot and Denis J. B. Shaw (Clarendon Press, 1990) is a good historical geography dealing primarily with the European section of Imperial Russia. *The Origins of Capitalism in Russia* by Joseph T. Fuhrmann (Quadrangle Books, 1972) deals with the development of manufacturing, industrial growth, and technology during the sixteenth and seventeenth centuries. *The Plow, the Hammer and the Knout* by Arcadius Kahan (University of Chicago Press, 1985), an excellent economic history of the eighteenth century, includes discussions of population, agriculture, industry, foreign trade, fiscal systems, the political order, etc. Continuing this analysis for the nineteenth century is *Russian Economic History* also by Arcadius Kahan (University of Chicago Press, 1989). William L. Blackwell's *The Beginnings of Russian Industrialization, 1800–1860* (Princeton University Press, 1968) is concerned with the economic aspects of modernization including transportation of goods, private enterprise, growth, and technology. *Russian Economic Development from Peter the Great to Stalin* edited by William L. Blackwell (New Viewpoints, 1974) is a collection of essays that provide historical continuity in the development of the economy.

Planning for Economic Growth in the Soviet Union, 1918–1932 by Eugene Zaleski (University of North Carolina Press, 1971) is an excellent history of the early Soviet economy, dealing with the goals and fulfillment of the first five-year plan, as well as enumerating the goals of the second five-year plan. *Russia's Last Capitalists* by Alan M. Ball (University of California Press, 1987) is the story of the NEP (New Economic Policy) men in the 1920s. Private business activity was allowed because of the inability of the government to stabilize the economy. *Stalin's Industrial Revolution* by Hiroaki Kuromiya (Cambridge University Press, 1988) is the history of the rapid industrial transformation that took place during the first five-year plan. Timothy Dunmore's *The Stalinist Command Economy* (St. Martin's Press, 1980) analyzes the post–World War II economy. *Perestroika and East-West Economic Relations* edited by Michael Kraus and Ronald D. Liebowitz (New York University Press, 1990) is a collection of essays providing insight into the economy of the late 1980s and the direction of the economy in the future. *Milestones in Glasnost and Perestroika* edited by Ed A. Hewett and Victor H. Winston (Brookings Institution, 1991) is a series of essays on how glasnost and perestroika have opened up the economy and contributed to a restructured society. *From Stagnation to Catastroika* by Philip Hanson (Praeger, 1992) presents key economic issues for the 1990s as they relate to the end of the Soviet Union. *A Study of the Soviet Economy* (3 vols.; International Monetary Fund, 1991) is a highly technical analysis of the Soviet economy since 1985 dealing with general issues as well as foreign trade and other economic and environmental issues. *The Emerging Russian Bear* edited by Josef C. Brada and Michael P. Claudon (New York University Press, 1991) is a series of essays examining the Soviet economy of Gorbachev and what needs to be done to energize it. *Soviet Market Economy: Challenge and Reality* edited by Boris Z. Milner and Dmitry S. Lvov (North Holland, Elsevier, 1991) is a collection of scholarly and technical essays analyzing the measures taken since 1985 to transform the economy.

Open for Business by Ed A. Hewett and Clifford G. Gaddy (Brookings Institution, 1992) documents the complex Soviet economy that Russia and the other independent states must reform before they can integrate into the global economy. *What Is to Be Done?* edited by Merton J. Peck and Thomas J. Richardson (Yale University Press, 1991), a collection of essays by Western economists discussing the problems of economic reform in Russia, presents a series of proposals for the transition period. *Russia and the World Economy* by Alan Smith (Routledge, 1993) examines the historic, economic, and political obstacles facing Russia during the transition to a market economy. *Changing the Economic System in Russia* edited by Anders Aslund and Richard Layard (Pinter Publishers, 1993) is a series of essays concentrating on the key issues in the transition to a market economy. *Red Tape: Adventure Capitalism in the New Russia* by Bill Thomas and Charles Sutherland (Dutton, 1992) is a good study of the problems of foreign investment in Russia. *How to Profit from the Coming Russian Boom* by Richard Poe (McGraw-Hill, 1993) is a good guide to doing business in Russia. It provides information on culture and etiquette as well as economic data from all the independent republics and Russia.

NATURAL RESOURCES/ENVIRONMENT. *Siberia: Problems and Prospects for Regional Development* edited by Alan Wood (Croom Helm, 1987) is a collection of essays describing the historical, geographical, and environmental developments during the 1980s in Siberia. *Siberia and the Soviet Far East* edited by Rodger Swearingen (Hoover Institution Press, 1987) is a series of essays on Siberia's enormous natural resources. *The Soviet Far East* edited by Allan Rodgers (Routledge, 1990) analyzes the feasibility of Gorbachev's long-range development plans in a region with many environmental problems. Peter Matthiessen's *Baikal: Sacred Sea of Siberia* (Sierra Club, 1992) is a beautifully illustrated story of Lake Baikal, the oldest, largest, and deepest freshwater lake in the world.

Environmental Misuse in the Soviet Union edited by Fred Singleton (Praeger, 1976) is a series of essays analyzing the problems of misuse of natural resources. *Environmental Management in the Soviet Union* by Philip R. Pryde (Cambridge University Press, 1991) analyzes the changes in environmental policy brought about by glasnost. Environmental issues are presented as an opportunity for cooperation between East and West. D. J. Peterson's *Troubled Lands* (Westview Press, 1993) summarizes the widespread neglect and abuse of the environment during the seventy years of Soviet rule. *Ecocide in the USSR* by Murray Freshbach and Alfred Friendly, Jr. (Basic Books, 1992) details the constant misuse of the environment and the horrible conditions the people were forced to live under during the Communist regime.

RELIGION. *Icons and Their History* by David and Tamara T. Rice (Overlook Press, 1974) is a well-illustrated book on the history of icons from Byzantium to Russia. Kurt Weitzmann's *The Icon: Holy Images—Sixth to Fourteenth Century* (George Braziller, 1978) is a short excellent history of the Eastern Orthodox Church and the veneration of icons, illustrated with mostly color plates. *Christianity and the Arts in Russia* edited by William Brumfield (Cambridge University Press, 1991) is a series of essays on the history of the art of the medieval church, Russian folk beliefs, Christianity, and religious traditions. *Religious Revolt in the XVIIth Century* by Nicholas Lupinin (Kingston Press, 1984) is an excellent history of the internal problems of the Russian church in 1666. *The Church Reform of Peter the Great* by James Cracraft (Stanford University Press, 1971) continues the discussion of religious problems in Russia that led to Peter the Great's reforms, which established the Eastern Orthodoxy in Russia. *Antireligious Propaganda in the Soviet Union* by David C. Powell (MIT Press, 1975) is a scholarly study of the attempt by the Communist Party to reeducate the people away from religion. Included are many of the cartoons printed in the Communist papers. *Religion and Modernization in the Soviet Union* edited by Dennis J. Dunn (Westview Press, 1977) is a collection of essays dealing with religion, old believers, and modern Soviet society. *Gorbachev, Glasnost and the Gospel* by Michael Bourdeaux (Hodder & Stoughton, 1990) explains the Communist attempt to erase religion from society and Gorbachev's decision to reverse that attempt. *Religious Policy in the Soviet Union* edited by Sabrina P. Ramet (Cambridge University Press, 1993) is a collection of essays on a broad range of subjects about both the historical and contemporary aspects of religion. Jim Forest's *Religion in the New Russia* (Crossroad, 1990) is an excellent account of the emerging religious freedom in the Soviet Union.

The Tsars and the Jews by Heinz-Dietrich Lowe (Harwood Academic Publishers, 1993) is an interesting account of the image of Jews in Russia created by the tsarist government and used for their own political ends. *A Jewish Life under the Tsars* by Chaim Aronson (Allanheld, Osmun, 1983) is the autobiography of the author chronicling his life in the 1800s in Imperial Russia; he emigrated to the United States in 1888. *The Jews in the Soviet Union since 1917: Paradox of Survival* by Nora Levin (2 vols.; New York University Press, 1988) is an excellent comprehensive history of Soviet Jewry from the Revolution to Gorbachev. Louis Rapoport's *Stalin's War against the Jews* (Free Press, 1990) is a good history of Stalin and his relationship with Jews. *From Moscow to Jerusalem* by Rebecca Rass (Shengold Publishers, 1976) is the story of the problems encountered in the Soviet Union by the Jews who wanted to emigrate to Israel. *Soviet Jewry in the 1980s* edited by Robert O. Freedman (Duke University Press, 1989) is a collection of essays on the Soviet Union's policies on anti-Semitism and emigration of Jews during the 1980s. *Jews in Soviet Culture* edited by Jack Miller (Institute of Jewish Affairs, 1984) is a collection of essays dealing with Jews in the arts, philosophy, literature, and educational aspects of Soviet culture.

The U.S.S.R. and the Muslim World edited by Yaacov Ro'i (Allen & Unwin, 1984) deals with the Soviet attitude toward the Muslims and the Central Asian attitude toward the Soviet Union. *Muslims of the Soviet Empire* by Alexander Bennigsen and S. Enders Wimbush (Indiana University Press, 1986) is a short history of the spread of Islam throughout the region and an analysis of the Muslim influence in the area.

ARTS AND LETTERS. *A History of Russian Architecture* by William C. Brumfield (Cambridge University Press, 1993) is an excellent, beautifully illustrated history covering all aspects of Russian architecture. *Russian Houses* by Elizabeth Gaynor and Kari Haavisto (Stewart, Tabori & Chang, 1991) is an interesting, well-illustrated history of houses throughout Russian society, showing many different styles. *Imperial Splendor: Palaces and Monasteries of Old Russia* by Prince George Galitzine (Viking, 1992) is a beautiful picture book of palaces and monasteries, with a brief introduction to each area. *Imperial Palaces of Russia* by Prince Michael of Greece (Tauris Parke Books, 1992) is a beautifully illustrated book of the twenty-five imperial palaces in Russia. *Fabergé* by G. Lothringen and A. von Solodkoff (Rizzoli, 1979) is a well-written history of the House of Fabergé and includes color illustrations of his most famous pieces. *Carl Fabergé* by A. Kenneth Snowman (Greenwich House, 1983) is another well-illustrated history of the House of Fabergé. *Red Women and the Silver Screen* edited by Lynne Attwood (HarperCollins, 1993) is a collection of scholarly essays on the role of women in film making under the Soviet regime.

The Sun Maiden and the Crescent Moon (Interlink Books, 1991) is a collection of Siberian folk tales, including an excellent ethnographic introduction to them. *Russian Gypsy Tales* collected by Yefim Druts (Interlink Books, 1993) is a collection of folk tales about the Gypsy life in old Russia. Leonid Grossman's *Dostoevsky* (Bobbs-Merrill, 1975) is a good biography of the nineteenth-century author of *The Brothers Karamazov*. *Tolstoy* by A. N. Wilson (W. W. Norton, 1988) is an excellent biography of Tolstoy as a soldier in the Crimean War and author of *War and Peace*. Henri Troyat's *Chekhov* (Dutton, 1986) is a fine biography of the author of *The Cherry Orchard*. Brian Boyd's *Vladimir Nabokov: The Russian Years* Volume 1 (Princeton University Press, 1990) and *Vladimir Nabokov: The American Years* Volume 2 (Princeton University Press, 1991) are excellent, comprehensive biographies of the author of *Lolita*. *Boris Pasternak, His Life and Art* by Guy de Maliac (University of Oklahoma Press, 1981) is an excellent biography of the Nobel prize-winning poet and author of *Dr. Zhivago*. *Solzhenitsyn* by Michael Scammell (W. W. Norton, 1984) is an excellent biography of the twentieth-century author of *A Day in the Life of Ivan Denisovich* and *Gulag Archipelago*, both of which deal with the Soviet prison system.

Soviet Civilizaton: A Cultural History by Andrei Sinyavsky (Arcade Publishing, 1988) is a good introduction to the Soviet society through its literature by an early dissident author. *Dangerous Thoughts* by Yuri Orlov (Morrow, 1991) is the autobiography of a human rights activist in the Soviet Union. His story of exile and imprisonment and eventual freedom in the United States is fascinating. *Shcharansky* by Martin Gilbert (Macmillan, 1986) is a good biography of the leader of the Refuseniks and his struggle to leave the Soviet Union. He was finally allowed to emigrate to Israel in 1986. Two very interesting books by Andrei Sakharov are *Memoirs* (Knopf, 1990), an account of his years as a physicist and leader of the dissident movement, and *Moscow and Beyond, 1986–1989* (Knopf, 1991) about his return to Moscow after seven years of internal exile in Gorky and his election to the First Congress of People's Deputies. Elena Bonner wrote *Alone Together* (Knopf, 1986), the story of her seven years of exile with Andrei Sakharov in Gorky. Also by Elena Bonner is *Mothers and Daughters* (Knopf, 1992), a vivid portrait of three generations of her family and the life in the 1920s and 1930s of a privileged Communist family, and

their downfall after her parents were arrested in 1937. *Under a New Sky* by Olga A. Carlisle (Ticknor & Fields, 1993) tells the interesting story of the author's Russian literary heritage and her many trips to the Soviet Union to visit family, as well as her concerns for the new Russia.

The New Grove Russian Masters (2 vols.; W. W. Norton, 1986) is an excellent collection of biographies of nineteenth-century composers. *Tchaikovsky* by Alexander Poznansky (Schirmer Books, 1991) is an excellent biography of the composer of *Sleeping Beauty* and *The Nutcracker*. Harlow Robinson's *Sergei Prokofiev* (Viking, 1987) is an interesting biography of the composer of *Peter and the Wolf* and *Romeo and Juliet*, including the years he lived in the West. *Soviet Diary 1927 and Other Writings* by Sergei Prokofiev (Northeastern University Press, 1992) presents the literary side of Prokofiev with the two-month diary of his visit to the Soviet Union as well as his short stories.

TRAVEL. *Russian Journal, 1965–1990* by Inge Morath (Aperture, 1991) is a well-illustrated travelogue through Russia, Armenia, Georgia, and other republics. *Red Odyssey* by Marat Akchurin (HarperCollins, 1992) describes life in the southern republics after the collapse of the Soviet Union. Richard Lourie's *Russia Speaks* (HarperCollins, 1991) is an interesting oral history. The author traveled from Moscow to Central Asia to Lithuania to Georgia and interviewed many different people. *Epics of Everyday Life* by Susan Richards (Viking, 1990) is the interesting account of the people and problems encountered by the author while traveling through the Soviet Union as it falls apart. *Stalin's Nose* by Rory MacLean (Little, Brown, 1993) is the humorous account of the author's trip visiting relatives throughout Eastern Europe.

The Volga by Marvin Kalb (Macmillan, 1967) is the well-illustrated story of a TV journalist's journey down the river. *Down the Volga* by Marq de Villiers (Viking, 1992) is the interesting account of the author's trip down the Volga in 1990; the people he met and talked with present a skepticism about their future.

Siberian Man and Mammoth by E. W. Pfizenmayer (Blackie & Son, 1939) is the story of two expeditions in the early 1900s to bring back mammoth carcasses, with fascinating descriptions of the natives and nature. *Off the Map* by Mark Jenkins (Morrow, 1992) is the story of the author's bicycle trip from Vladivostok to Leningrad in 1989. *Red Express: The Greatest Rail Journey from the Berlin Wall to the Great Wall of China* by Michael Cordell (Prentice Hall, 1991) is the well-illustrated story of the world's longest train route and the people along the way. Frederick Kempe's *Siberian Odyssey* (G. P. Putnam's Sons, 1992) is the story of his journey along the Ob and Om rivers from the Altai mountains to above the Arctic Circle and the people he meets.

Pskov: A Guide by Yelena Morozkina (Raduga Publishers, 1984) is a nicely illustrated travel book of one of the better known ancient Russian cities. *Moscow, 1900–1930* edited by Serge Fauchereau (Rizzoli, 1989) is a coffee table–sized book with excellent illustrations of turn-of-the-century Moscow. *Moscow, Leningrad, Kiev: A Guide* by Lydia Dubinskaya (Progress Publishers, 1981) provides short histories of the three cities with basic travel information. *Before the Revolution* by Mikhail P. Iroshnikov, Yury B. Shelayev, and Liudmila A. Protsai (Abrams, 1992) includes many photographs never before published, concentrating on Nicholas II from 1890 to World War I. *St. Petersburg, Portrait of an Imperial City* by Boris Ometev and John Stuart (Vendome Press, 1990) is a wonderfully illustrated outsized book that includes an excellent short history of the city. Laurence Kelly's *St. Petersburg* (Atheneum, 1983) is a well-illustrated travel book with good maps. *Russiawalks* by David and Valeria Matlock (Henry Holt, 1991) is one of the better travel books with seven walking tours of Moscow and Leningrad; additionally, it provides general tourist information.

UKRAINE. *Ukraine: A History* by Orest Subtelny (University of Toronto Press, 1988) is an excellent general history. *The Ukrainian Impact on Russian Culture, 1750–1850* by David Saunders (University of Atlanta Press, 1985) analyzes the Ukrainian contribution through integration to the cultural identity of early nineteenth-century Russia. *The Mazepists* by Orest Subtelny (Columbia University Press, 1981) is the history of followers of Hetman Ivan Mazepa, an early eighteenth-century proponent of separatism from Russia. *The Shaping of a National Identity: Sub-Carpathian Rus, 1848–1948* by Paul R. Magocsi (Harvard University Press, 1978) is a scholarly analysis of a national identity, with emphasis on 1918–1948. *The Sovietization of Ukraine, 1917–1923* by Jurij Borys (Canadian Institute of Ukrainian Studies, 1980) analyzes the Soviet influence from 1917 to 1923. *The Harvest of Sorrow* by Robert Conquest (Oxford University Press, 1986) is an excellent history of agricultural collectivization and the resulting famine in the Ukraine. Miron Dolot's *Execution by Hunger: The Hidden Holocaust* (W. W. Norton, 1985) is the story of a great famine which struck several areas of the Soviet Union in 1932–1933, during which an estimated 5 to 7 million people died; the author was a boy in a Ukrainian village. *Ethnocide of Ukrainians in the U.S.S.R.* by Maksym Sahaydak (Smoloskyp Publishers, 1991) is an interesting collection of articles from underground periodicals dealing with repression from Moscow. For an excellent history of the collectivization in the Ukraine see David R. Marples's *Stalinism in Ukraine in the 1940s* (St. Martin's Press, 1992). *Soviet Ukrainian Dissent* by Jaroslaw Bilocerkowycz (Westview Press, 1988) is a scholarly study of political dissent as practiced in the Ukraine. *Essays in Modern Ukrainian History* by Ivan L. Rudnytsky (Harvard University Press, 1987) is a series of essays by the author covering the political and intellectual history of the Ukraine from the seventeenth century; of special interest are the essays on the relations with Imperial Russia and Poland. *Dilemmas of Independence* by Alexander J. Motyl (Council on Foreign Relations, 1993) analyzes the post–Communist struggle in the politics and economy of the Ukraine.

Ukrainian-Jewish Relations in Historical Perspective edited by Howard Aster and Peter J. Potichnyj (Canadian Institute of Ukrainian Studies, 1990) is a collection of essays discussing the history of Jewish relations from the sixteenth century through the Russian Revolution. *The Millennium of Ukrainian Christianity* (Philosophical Library, 1988) and *A Thousand Years of Christianity in the Ukraine* (Smoloskyp Publishers, 1988) are both well-illustrated histories of religion in the Ukraine from 988 when Grand Prince Volodymyr the Great brought Christianity to Kiev to 1988.

The Ukraine within the USSR: An Economic Balance Sheet edited by I. S. Koropeckyj (Praeger, 1977) is a series of essays on the economy of the Ukraine as it relates to the rest of the Soviet Union. *Ukraine under Perestroika* by David R. Marples (St. Martin's Press, 1991) focuses on the social and economic events from 1985 to 1990, but also exposes the years of economic exploitation from Moscow. *The Ukrainian Economy: Achievements, Problems, Challenges* edited by I. S. Koropeckyj (Harvard University Press, 1992) analyzes the economy in the late 1980s and presents some possible paths the economy might take in the 1990s. *The Truth about Chernobyl* by Grigori Medvedev (Basic Books, 1991) is a dramatic account of the meltdown at Chernobyl and some of the immediate aftermath. Also by Grigori Medvedev is *No Breathing Room* (Basic Books, 1993) recounting the author's attempts to publicize nuclear hazards in the Soviet Union. Another excellent book about the Chernobyl disaster is *Ablaze: The Story of Chernobyl* by Piers Paul Read (Random House, 1993).

Kiev: A Portrait, 1800–1917 by Michael F. Hamm (Princeton University Press, 1993) emphasizes the relationship among Kiev, Moscow, and Odessa in the nineteenth century, including a short history of early Kiev. Solomea Pavlychko's *Letters from Kiev* (St. Martin's Press, 1992) is the personal account of the shifting political forces in the Ukraine in 1990–1991. *Kiev* by Boris Andreyev and Pavel Poznyal (Hippocrene Books, 1991) is a very good guide book with some historical highlights. *Odessa: A History, 1794–1914* by Patricia Herlihy (Harvard University Press, 1986) is a good history of Odessa and its importance to Russia because of its location on the Black Sea. Maurice Friedberg's *How Things Were Done in Odessa* (Westview Press, 1991) is an interesting profile of Odessa with information on the ethnicity, religion, educational institutions, etc., that are part of this city. *Soviet Laughter, Soviet Tears* by Christine and Ralph Dull (Stillmore Press, 1992) details the personal experiences of an American couple's stay in a Ukrainian village.

BELARUS. *Belorussia: The Making of a Nation* by Nicholas P. Vakar (Harvard University Press, 1956) is a good general history of Belarus. Ivan S. Lubachko's *Belorussia under Soviet Rule, 1917–1957* (University Press of Kentucky, 1972) is a scholarly study of the history of Belarus since World War I with emphasis on the Stalin era. *Belarus* by Jan Zaprudnik (Westview Press, 1993) is an excellent history of modern Belarus covering politics, economics, ethnic revival, etc., as well as a section on its early history. *The Minsk Ghetto* by Hersh Smolar (Holocaust Library, 1989) tells the story of the struggle and eventual destruction of the largest Soviet Jewish ghetto during World War II. *Children of Chernobyl* by Michelle Carter and Michael J. Christensen (Augsburg, 1993) is the story of some of the rescue efforts to save the children affected by the Chernobyl disaster. See also Ukraine for additional books on Chernobyl. *Belarus* by John Odling-Smee, Peter Hole, and James Blalock et al. (International Monetary Fund, 1992) is a good analysis of the changing economy and prospects of Belarus.

MOLDOVA. *From Moldavia to Moldova* by Nicholas Dima (Columbia University Press, 1991) presents a history of the area bordering Romania, Ukraine, and the Soviet Union, including a discussion of socioeconomic development under the Soviet regime. *Moldavia: A Guide* by M. Shukhat (Reduga Publishers, 1986) is a travel book on the area published in Moscow. *Moldavia* (Chelsea House, 1990) is a good travel book with a short history of Moldova.

BALTIC STATES. *The Baltic Nations and Europe* by John Hiden and Patrick Salmon (Longman, 1991) is a short history from the middle ages to World War I showing the similarity and diversity of the three countries. *The Baltic States: Estonia, Latvia, and Lithuania* (Clio, 1993) is an annotated guide to materials on the three republics compiled by Inese A. Smith and Marita V. Grunts. *Russification in the Baltic Provinces and Finland, 1855–1914* edited by Edward C. Thaden (Princeton University Press, 1981) is a collection of scholarly essays showing the complexity of Russian relationships with the western borderlands. *The Baltic States in Peace and War, 1917–1945* edited by V. Stanley Vardys and Romuald J. Misiunas (Pennsylvania State University Press, 1978) is a collection of essays dealing with the Baltic States between the World Wars. *Soviet Policy toward the Baltic States, 1918–1940* by Albert N. Tarulis (University of Notre Dame Press, 1959) analyzes the Soviet need for expansion and its attempts to incorporate the Baltic area into the Soviet sphere of influence. *Baltic Independence and the Russian Empire* by Walter C. Clemens, Jr. (St. Martin's Press, 1991) presents a modern history of the Baltic States' relationship with the Soviet Union. David M. Crowe's *The Baltic States and the Great Powers* (Westview Press, 1993) explores the historical and ethnic differences of the area and their relations with the major powers between the World Wars. *Toward Independence: The Baltic Popular Movements* edited by Jan A. Trapans (Westview Press, 1991) is a collection of essays describing the development, strategy, and political aims of the movements working for independence from the Soviet Union. Anatol Lieven's *The Baltic Revolution* (Yale University Press, 1993) analyzes the events after each state's independence and the political direction they are headed. For an excellent travel guide to the area see *A Guide to the Baltic States* by Ingrida Kalnins (Inroads, 1990). *Ticket to Latvia* by Marcus Tanner (Henry Holt, 1990) is a personal story about traveling through the Eastern Bloc countries, and is especially informative about Lithuania.

ESTONIA. *Estonia and the Estonians* by Toivo U. Raun (Hoover Institution Press, 1987) is an excellent general history of Estonia with an emphasis on the Soviet period. Villem Raud's *Developments in Estonia, 1939–1941* (2d ed.; Tallinn, 1987) presents a detailed history of the time when Estonia was caught between Germany and the USSR. *War in the Woods: Estonia's Struggle for Survival, 1944–1956* by Mart Laar (Compass Press, 1992) is the story of partisan warfare in Estonia by the guerrillas called Forest Brothers. *A Case Study of a Soviet Republic: The Estonian SSR* edited by Tonu Parming and Elmar Jarvesoo (Westview Press, 1978) is a collection of scholarly essays dealing with the political, economic, and social process as well as educational and cultural issues. Rein Taagepera's *Estonia: Return to Independence* (Westview Press, 1993) offers an overview of the country's history and an insider's account of the reestablishment of independence. *Tallinn* by H. Gustavson and R. Pullat (Progress Publishers, 1980) is a travel guide with a short history of Tallinn.

LATVIA. *The 1917 Revolution in Latvia* by Andrew Ezergailis (Columbia University Press, 1974) provides a short but excellent history of the area prior to 1917. *Latvia* by Visvaldis Mangolis (Cognition Books, 1983) is the story of Latvia's struggle to survive between Germany and the Soviet Union after World War I. *The Unfinished Road* edited by Gertrude Schneider (Praeger, 1991) is a collection of scholarly essays dealing with the Nazi occupation during World War II, the persecution and the survival of the Latvian Jews. *Entrepreneur in a Small Country* by Nicholas Balabkins and Arnold Aizsilnieks (Exposition Press, 1975), an excellent economic history from 1919 to 1940, analyzes the function of entrepreneurship in a small country. *Riga* by Maria Debrer (Progress Publishers, 1982) is a travel book with a short history of Riga.

LITHUANIA. *Lithuania: Years and Deeds* by Antanas Barkauskas (Mintis Publishers, 1982) is a good general history of Lithuania. Alfred E. Senn's *The Emergence of Modern Lithuania* (Greenwood Press, 1975) is the story of the establishment of Lithuania in 1918 and how it developed. Leonas Sabaliunas's *Lithuania in Crisis* (Indiana University Press, 1972) analyzes the political and economic developments in Lithuania between the World Wars. *Surviving the Holocaust: The Kovno Ghetto Diary* by Avraham Tory (Harvard University Press, 1990) is the story of life in the eighth largest Jewish ghetto run by the Nazis from 1941 to 1943 and describes many mass executions. *Fighting Back* by Dov Levin (Holmes & Meier, 1985) summarizes the roles played by the Lithuanian Jews during World War II; only 40,000 out of appromimately 250,000 Jews remained at the end of World War II. *My Lithuania* by Aleksandras Macijauskas (Thames & Hudson, 1991) is a collection of photographic essays documenting the daily activity of the countryside. *Lithuania: The Transition to a Market Economy* (The World Bank, 1993) is a highly technical comprehensive assessment of the recent developments in the Lithuanian economy. *Vilnius* by Antanas Papsys (Progress Publishers, 1981) is a travel book containing a short history of Vilnius.

CAUCASIAN STATES. *Transcaucasia and Ararat* by James Bryce (Arno Press and The New York Times, 1970), a reprint of an 1896 publication, is an 1876 account with engravings of a trip down the Volga River and through the Caucasus mountains to Armenia. *The Crimea and Transcaucasia* by J. Buchan Telfer (2 vols.; Henry S. King, 1876) is a classic story of a personal journey through the greater Transcaucasia area including many line drawings of the area. *Studies of Greek Pottery in the Black Sea Area* by Jan Bouzek (Charles University, 1990) is a survey of the archaeological finds around the southern part of the Black Sea area. *To Caucasus* by Fitzroy Maclean (Little, Brown, 1976) is an illustrated short history of the area that emphasizes resistance to tsarist Russia. *The North Caucasus Barrier* edited by Marie B. Broxup (Hurst, 1992) is a collection of scholarly essays highlighting the almost continuous struggle with Russia since the end of the eighteenth century. Alan W. Fisher's *The Russian Annexation of the Crimea, 1772–1783* (Cambridge University Press, 1970) is a history of the relationship between Russia and Turkey and the eventual invasion of the Crimea by Russia in 1771. *Tatars of the Crimea* edited by Edward Allworth (Duke University Press, 1988) is a collection of scholarly essays on the history of the Crimean Tatars. *The Black Sea Coast of the Caucasus* by G. Khutsishvili (Progress Publishers, 1980) is a well-illustrated guide book which also includes a short history of the area.

GEORGIA. *The Georgians* by David M. Lang (Praeger, 1966) presents an archaeological and anthropological history of ancient Georgia, including photos, line drawings, and a chronological timetable. *A History of the Georgian People* by W. E. D. Allen (Barnes & Noble, 1971) is an excellent history from ancient times through the Russian conquest in the nineteenth century. David M. Lang's *A Modern History of Soviet Georgia* (Grove Press, 1962) is an excellent history dealing with tsarist Russia from the early 1800s through the Soviet Union and especially Stalin. *The Making of the Georgian Nation* by Ronald G. Suny (Indiana University Press, 1988) is another excellent history of Georgia dealing with the Georgian monarchies, the Russian Empire, and Soviet Georgia. *Please Don't Call It Soviet Georgia* by Mary Russell (Serpent's Tail, 1992) is the interesting story of the author's two-month journey through Georgia. *The Georgian Republic* by Roger Rosen (Passport Books, 1991) is a well-illustrated guide to Georgia.

ARMENIA. *History of the Armenians* by Moses Khorenats'i (Harvard University Press, 1978) is the classic on ancient legend and history concerning the origins of the Armenian people. *The Kingdom of Armenia* by M. Chahin (Croom Helm, 1987) is a short history of a civilization that was discovered on the eastern shores of Lake Van in eastern Turkey. This civilization begins in 1275 B.C. and ends early in the sixth century. *History of the Armenian People: Pre-History to A.D. 1500* by George A. Bournoutian (Mazda Publishers, 1993–) is volume one of a two-volume set; volume two is not yet published. It is a history of Armenia and its people in relation to the rest of the world. *Armenia: The Survival of a Nation* by Christopher J. Walker (2d ed.; St. Martin's Press, 1990) is an excellent history of greater Armenia, extending into eastern Turkey and other areas of Asia Minor. *Armenian Village Life before 1914* by Susie H. Villa and Mary K. Matossian (Wayne State University Press, 1982) attempts to capture the myriad details of daily life in rural Armenia before World War I. *Survivors: An Oral History of the Armenian Genocide* by Donald E. and Lorna T. Miller (University of California Press, 1993) is the personal story of survivors of the Turkish attempt to exterminate the Armenians. The authors interviewed more than 100 of the survivors. Arthur Tcholakian's *Armenia* (Paradon Publishing, 1975) is a beautiful book with many photo essays on Armenia; also included is a short, comprehensive history of Armenia.

AZERBAIJAN. *Russian Azerbaijan, 1905–1920* by Tadeusz Swietochowski (Cambridge University Press, 1985) is a short history of Azerbaijan and Transcaucasia. Azerbaijan was greatly influenced by Iran and converted to Islam in the seventh century. *The Azerbaijani Turks* by Audrey L. Alstadt (Hoover Institution Press, 1992) is a comprehensive history of Azerbaijan, including an analysis of the disputed Nagorno-Karabakh region. *Azerbaijan: Economic Review* (International Monetary Fund, 1992) is an analysis of current economic conditions and policies. *Let's Visit Azerbaijan* (Chelsea House, 1989) is an excellent travel book with many illustrations and a short history of the region.

CENTRAL ASIAN STATES. A. H. Dani and V. M. Masson's *History of Civilizations of Central Asia: The Dawn of Civilization—Earliest Times to 700 B.C.* (UNESCO Publishing, 1992–), volume one of a projected six-volume set, is an excellent introduction to the earliest times in Central Asia; heavily illustrated with line drawings and photos. *A History of Asia* by Rhoads Murphy (HarperCollins, 1992) is an excellent overview of Asian history showing the relationships among the many countries of Asia. *History of the Mongols* by Henry H. Howorth (3 vols.; Longmans, 1876) is the first major western history of the Mongols, covering the Mongols, the Tartars of Russia and Central Asia, and the Mongols of Persia. *A History of the Moghuls of Central Asia* by N. Elias (Curzon Press, 1972), originally published in 1895, is one of the first attempts to preserve the history of the Mongols and their Khans. *Genghis Khan: His Life and Legacy* by Paul Ratchnevsky (Blackwell, 1991) is a scholarly biography of Genghis Khan who united the scattered Mongol tribes into one nation. *Storm from the East* by Robert Marshall (University of California Press, 1993) is an excellent overview from Genghis Khan to his grandson Kublai Khan. The book is based on the TV series of the same name. Walter Heissig's *A Lost Civilization* (Basic Books, 1966) is a history of the 700 years of the Mongols and includes archaeological information; it brings the Mongols into the twentieth century. *Historie of the Great Emperour Tamerlan* by Jean Du Bec-Crespin (DaCapo Press, 1968), originally published in 1597, is a facsimile edition of this account of the early life of Tamerlane and times. *The Rise and Rule of Tamerlane* by Beatrice F. Manz (Cambridge University Press, 1989) is an excellent biography of Tamerlane.

The Partition of the Steppe by Fred W. Bergholz (Peter Lang, 1993) examines the history of the relations between Russia and China and their expansion into Central Asia in the seventeenth and eighteenth centuries. *Central Asia: 120 Years of Russian Rule* edited by Edward Allworth (Duke University Press, 1989) is a series of essays dealing with the changes in the Central Asian countries due to the influence of Russia. *The Great Game* by Peter Hopkirk (Kondansha International, 1992) is the story of Russian attempts at influence in Central Asia, as well as the British attempts from India; many of the individual stories are very interesting. *Soviet Central Asia: The Failed Transformation* edited by William Fierman (Westview Press, 1991) is a collection of essays concerned with the attempted development of the area from Stalin to Gorbachev and the aftermath of perestroika. *Geographic Perspectives on Soviet Central Asia* edited by Robert A. Lewis (Routledge, 1992) is a collection of essays providing general information on the social and economic geography of the region. *Cultural Change and Continuity in Central Asia* edited by Shirin Akiner (Kegan Paul International, 1991) is a series of essays highlighting the similarities of Central Asian cultures.

Travels in Central Asia by Arminius Vambery (Harper & Brothers, 1865) is a classic nineteenth-century account of the author's journey from Teheran through Turkoman to Bukhara and Samarkand, with wonderful tales of adventure throughout Central Asia. *On the Other Side* by Geoffrey Moorhouse (Henry Holt, 1990) is the account of a two-month journey from Alma-Ata to Samarkand and Tashkent. *Red Odyssey* by Marat Akchurin (HarperCollins, 1992) is the story of a 10,000-mile car trip across the non-Russian republics and the interesting people the author met along the way. *In Search of Genghis Khan* by Tim Severin (Atheneum, 1992) recounts the author's interesting experiences as he travels with the Mongols following some of Genghis Khan's trails throughout Central Asia. *Fabled Cities of Central Asia* by Robin Magowan (Abbeville, 1990) presents beautiful photographic essays on the architecture, people, and sights of Samarkand, Bukhara, and Khiva. Philip Glazebrook's *Journey to Khiva* (Kodansha International, 1994) presents a fascinating look at modern-day Tashkent, Bukhara, Samarkand, and Khiva and how they have and have not changed.

Painting of Central Asia by Mario Bussagli (Skira, 1963) is a short analysis of the art history of Turkmenistan, Tajikistan, and Uzbekistan, including a map of the caravan routes of the area. *Turkoman Studies I: Aspects of the Weaving and Decorative Arts of Central Asia* edited by Robert Pinner and Michael Franses (Oguz Press, 1980) is an interesting study of the parallel development of the Turkoman carpet to the classic Oriental carpet.

The Soviet Model and Underdeveloped Countries by Charles K. Wilber (University of North Carolina Press, 1969) is a history of the economy of Central Asia under the Soviet Union. *Soviet Asia* by Leslie Dienes (Westview Press, 1987) examines the position of Soviet Asia in the overall economy of the Soviet Union, and analyzes the impact of the Soviet Union's economic decisions on the development of the Central Asian economy. Boris Z. Rumer's *Soviet Central Asia* (Unwin Hyman, 1989) is a good introduction to the regional economic policy of the Soviet Union in Central Asia; also discussed is the impact of the Gorbachev reforms on Central Asia. *Central Asia in World History* by S. A. M. Adshead (St. Martin's Press, 1993) is a concise history of Central Asia in the context of world events, especially events in the 1990s.

KAZAKHSTAN. *The Kazakhs* by Martha B. Olcott (Hoover Institution Press, 1987) is an excellent history, describing the rise and fall of the Khanate, the conquest by the Russians, and Soviet rule. *Kazakhstan* by John Odling-Smee and Ishan Kapur et al. (International Monetary Fund, 1992) is an excellent history of the economic conditions in Kazakhstan and the economic policies of the 1990s. See the books listed under Central Asian States for more information on Kazakhstan.

TURKMENISTAN. *The Turks of Central Asia* by M. A. Czaplicka (Curzon Press, 1973), originally published in 1918, provides a good general history especially of archaeology, Iranian Turks, and religion. *Journey to Khiva* by Nikolay Murav'yov (Oguz Press, 1977), originally published in 1822, is the interesting story of a Russian soldier's two-year adventure through the mysterious Turkoman country with its famous nomads. *Bolshevism in Turkestan, 1917–1927* by Alexander G. Park (Columbia University Press, 1957) is an interesting study of Bolshevism at work, providing insight into the actual operation of policy. *Turkmenistan* (International Monetary Fund, 1992) is an excellent history of the economic conditions in Turkmenistan and the economic policy of the 1990s. See the books listed under Central Asian States for more information on Turkmenistan.

UZBEKISTAN. *Russia's Protectorates in Central Asia: Bukhara and Khiva, 1865–1924* by Seymour Becker (Harvard University Press, 1968) is the interesting history of how both cities retained their native rulers and political autonomy under the tsars, as well as how the khanates were brought under the influence of the Soviet Union. *Soul to Soul* by Yelena Khanga (W. W. Norton, 1992) tells the story of an American Communist family's move in 1931 to Uzbekistan to develop the cotton industry; the author's personal experiences of being black and Jewish in Uzbekistan are interesting. *The Modern Uzbeks* by Edward Allworth (Hoover Institution Press, 1990) is an excellent cultural history from the fourteenth century, concentrating on twentieth-century Uzbekistan. *Nationalism in Uzbekistan* by James Critchlow (Westview Press, 1991) is a good history of the nationalist movement that resulted in the independence of Uzbekistan. *Uzbekistan* by John Odling-Smee (International Monetary Fund, 1992) is an excellent history of the economic policy of the 1990s. See the books listed under Central Asian States for more information on Uzbekistan.

TAJIKISTAN. *Russia and Nationalism in Central Asia* by Teresa Rakowska-Harmstone (Johns Hopkins University Press, 1970) is a good history of the area after the Russian Revolution, with emphasis on 1946–1956. See the books listed under Central Asian States for more information on Tajikistan.

KYRGYZSTAN. *In the Kirghiz Steppes* by John W. Wardell (The Galley Press, 1961) is the account of the personal experiences of a small isolated British community in Russia to help modernize a smelting plant; the descriptions of their experiences in the countryside, and with the climate and inhabitants are fascinating. *Turkestan Solo* by Ella K. Maillart (G. P. Putnam's Sons, 1935) is the interesting story of one woman's solo journey from Tien Shan to Kyzyl Kum. See the books listed under Central Asian States for more information on Kyrgyzstan.

Index of Place Names

Charjou (Chardzhou) (Turk.) 107 F3
Charshanga (Turk.) 107 H4
Charyn R. (Kaz.) 126 E2
Chashniki (Bel.) 49 D2
Chatkal Mts. (Uzb., Kyr.) 113 F2; 126 B2
Chatkal R. (Kyr.) 126 B2
Chatyr-Kel, L. (Kyr.) 126 D2
Chausy (Bel.) 49 E3
Chayan (Kaz.) 126 B2
Cheboksary (Rus.) 24 D4
Chechenia see Checheno-Ingush
Checheno-Ingush Aut. Rep. (Rus.) 37
Cheildag (Azer.) 93 C1
Chelekhen Pen. (Turk.) 107 A3
Chelkar (Kaz.) 100 B2
Chelyabinsk (Rus.) 24 F4
Cherek R. (Rus.) 80 B1
Cheremkhovo (Rus.) 32
Cherepovets (Rus.) 24 C4
Cherkassy (Ukr.) 40 C2
Cherkessk (Rus.) 24 D5
Cherkovo (Ukr.) 40 D2
Chernak (Kaz.) 113 E2
Chernevo (Rus.) 62 E2
Chernigov (Ukr.) 40 C2
Chernobyl (Ukr.) 40 C2
Chernovtsy (Ukr.) 40 B3
Chernyakhovsk (Rus.) 74 A2
Cherski Mts. (Rus.) 25 M-N3
Cherven (Bel.) 49 D3
Chervono, L. (Bel.) 49 C3
Chiatura (Geo.) 80 B1
Chiili (Kaz.) 113 E1
Chilik (Kaz.) 126 E2
Chimankend (Arm.) 87 C3
Chimbay (Uzb.) 113 B2
Chimishliya (Mol.) 56 C2
Chimkent (Kaz.) 100 C3
Chiragidzor (Azer.) 93 B1
Chirchik (Uzb.) 113 F2
Chirchik R. (Uzb.) 113 F2
Chişinău (Mol.) 56 C2
Chistopol (Rus.) 100 B1
Chita (Rus.) 25 K4
Chu (Kaz.) 100 D3
Chu R. (Kaz.) 100 D3
Chudskoye see Peipsi, L.
Chugush, Mt. (Rus.) 80 A1
Chukot Nat. Okr. (Rus.) 37
Chukot Pen. (Rus.) 25 R3
Chulak-Kurgan (Kaz.) 113 F2; 126 B2
Chunja (Kaz.) 126 E2
Churst (Uzb.) 120 C1
Chuvash Aut. Rep. (Rus.) 37
Communism Peak see Garmo Peak
Crimea (Ukr.) 40 C3
Crimean Mts. see Yaila Range

D

Dagda (Lat.) 68 D2
Dagestan Aut. Rep. (Rus.) 37
Dainegorsk (Rus.) 33
Dalidag, Mt. (Azer.) 93 B2
Dangara (Taj.) 120 B2
Danube R. 40 B3
Darasun (Rus.) 32
Daraut Kurgan (Kyr.) 126 C3
Darbazi (Geo.) 80 C2
Dargan Ata (Turk.) 107 F2
Darvaza (Turk.) 107 D2
Daryal Pass (Geo.) 80 C1
Dashkend (Arm.) 87 D2
Dashkesan (Azer.) 93 B1
Dastakert (Arm.) 87 E3
Daugava R. (Lat.) 68 C-D2 (see also Dvina R., Western)
Daugavpils (Lat.) 68 D3
David Horodok (Bel.) 49 C4
Demidov (Rus.) 49 E2
Denau (Uzb.) 113 E3
Derbent (Uzb.) 113 E3
Desna R. (Ukr.) 40 C2
Dieveniškes (Lith.) 74 C2

Diklosmta, Mt. (Rus.) 80 C1
Dikson (Rus.) 24 H2
Dilizhan (Arm.) 87 D2
Disna (Bel.) 49 D2
Disna R. (Bel.) 49 C2
Divichi (Azer.) 93 C1
Dmanisi (Geo.) 80 C2
Dnepr (Dnieper) R. 24 C4; 40 C2-3; 49 E2-4
Dnepr-Bug Canal (Bel.) 50
Dnepropetrovsk see Yekaterinoslav
Dnestr (Dniester) R. 40 A2; 56 C2
Dobele (Lat.) 68 B2
Dokshitsy (Bel.) 49 C2
Dolginovo (Bel.) 49 C2
Dolinskoye (Ukr.) 40 B3
Domanevka (Ukr.) 56 D2
Don R. (Rus.) 24 D4
Donetsk see Yuzovka
Donets R. (Ukr.) 40 D2
Donets Upland (Ukr.) 40 D2
Dorpat see Tortu
Dossor (Kaz.) 100 B2
Dotnuva (Lith.) 74 B2
Drogobych (Ukr.) 40 A2
Drokiya (Mol.) 56 B1
Druskininkai (Lith.) 74 C3
Drut R. (Bel.) 49 D3
Druya (Bel.) 49 C2
Druzhba (Uzb.) 113 C2
Dubna R. (Lat.) 68 D2
Dubossary (Mol.) 56 C2
Dubrovno (Bel.) 49 E2
Dubysa R. (Lith.) 74 B2
Dudinka (Rus.) 24 H3
Dukhovshchina (Rus.) 49 F2
Dukstas (Lith.) 74 D2
Dulovka (Rus.) 62 E3
Dundaga (Lat.) 68 B2
Durbe (Lat.) 68 A2
Dushanbe (Taj.) 120 B2
Dusheti (Geo.) 80 C1
Dusti (Taj.) 120 B3
Dvina R., Northern (Rus.) 24 D3
Dvina R., Western (Bel.) 49 C2 (see also Daugava R.)
Dvinsk see Daugavpils
Dyatlovo (Bel.) 49 B3
Dykhtau, Mt. (Rus.) 80 B1
Dyukyarli (Azer.) 93 A1
Dzerzhinsk (Bel.) 49 C3
Dzhugdzhur Mts. (Rus.) 25 M4

E

East Siberian Sea (Rus.) 25
Echmiadzin (Arm.) 87 C2
Egris Mts. (Geo.) 80 B1
Eišiškes (Lith.) 74 C2
Ekaterinburg see Yekaterinburg
Ekaterinodar see Krasnodar
Ekibastuz (Kaz.) 100 D1
Elbrus, Mt. (Rus.) 80 B1
Eleja (Lat.) 68 B2
Elista (Rus.) 24 D5
Elpin (Arm.) 87 D3
Elva (Est.) 62 D2
Emajõgi R. (Est.) 62 D2-3
Emba (Kaz.) 100 B2
Emba R. (Kaz.) 100 B2
Emmaste (Est.) 62 B2
Engels (Rus.) 100 A1
Engure (Lat.) 68 B2
Engure, L. (Lat.) 68 B2
Erevan see Yerevan
Ērgļi (Lat.) 68 C2
Essei (Rus.) 24 J3
Evenki Nat. Okr. (Rus.) 37

F

Farab (Turk.) 107 F3
Feodosiya (Ukr.) 40 C3
Fergana (Uzb.) 113 F2
Fergana Basin (Uzb.) 113 F2; 114
Fergana Mts. (Kyr.) 126 C2

Firyuza (Turk.) 113 D3
Fisht, Mt. (Rus.) 80 A1
Fizuli (Azer.) 93 B2
Floreshty (Mol.) 56 C2
Fort Shevchenko (Kaz.) 100 B3
Franz Josef Land (Rus.) 24 E1
Frunze see Bishkek
Frunzovka (Ukr.) 56 C2
Furmanovka (Kaz.) 100 D3

G

Gadrut (Azer.) 93 B2
Gagra (Geo.) 80 A1
Gali (Geo.) 80 A1
Gantsevichi (Bel.) 49 C3
Ganyushkino (Kaz.) 100 A2
Gargždai (Lith.) 74 A2
Garliava (Lith.) 74 B2
Garm (Taj.) 120 C2
Garmo Peak (Taj.) 120 D2
Gauja R. (Lat.) 68 C-D2
Gayvoron (Ukr.) 56 C1
Gdov (Rus.) 62 D2
Gegam Mts. (Arm.) 87 C2
Geokchai (Azer.) 93 B1
Geoktepe (Turk.) 107 C3
George Land (Rus.) 24 D1
Georgiu-Dezh see Liski
Ginaldag, Mt. (Azer.) 93 A1
Gindar (Azer.) 93 B1
Gissar (Taj.) 120 B2
Gissar Mts. see Hissar Mts.
Gizhduvan (Uzb.) 113 D2
Glubokoye (Bel.) 49 C2
Gogland I. (Rus.) 62 C1
Golovanevsk (Ukr.) 56 D1
Gomel see Homel
Goradiz (Azer.) 93 B2
Gori (Geo.) 80 C1
Goris (Arm.) 87 E3
Gorki (Bel.) 49 E2
Gorki (Rus.) see Nizhniy Novgorod
Gorlovka (Ukr.) 40 D2
Gorno-Altai Aut. Obl. (Rus.) 37
Gorno-Altaisk (Rus.) 24 H4
Gorno-Badakhshan Aut. Obl. (Taj.) 120 D3
Gorodenka (Ukr.) 56 A1
Gorodishche (Bel., nr. Baranovichi) 49 B3
Gorodishche (Bel., nr. Mohilev) 49 D3
Gorodnya see Horodnya
Gorodok see Horodok (Bel.)
Goryn R. (Ukr.) 40 B2
Govustak (Azer.) 93 C1
Graham Bell I. (Rus.) 24 F1
Grigoryopol (Mol.) 56 C2
Grobiņa (Lat.) 68 A2
Grodno see Horodno
Grozny (Rus.) 24 D5
Gruzdžiai (Lith.) 74 B1
Gryazi (Rus.) 40 D1
Gudauta (Geo.) 80 A1
Gudermes (Rus.) 80 D1
Gukasyan (Arm.) 87 B1
Gulbene (Lat.) 68 D2
Gulcha (Kyr.) 126 C2
Gulistan (Uzb.) 113 E2
Guryev see Atyrau
Gusev (Rus.) 74 B2
Guzar (Uzb.) 113 E3
Gvandra, Mt. (Geo.) 80 B1
Gvardeisk (Rus.) 74 A2
Gyamish, Mt. (Azer.) 93 B1
Gyanja (Azer.) 93 B1
Gyda Pen. (Rus.) 24 G2
Gyulagaran (Arm.) 87 C2
Gyulgeryachay R. (Rus.) 93 C1

H

Häädemeeste (Est.) 62 C3
Haapsalu (Est.) 62 B2
Halliste R. (Est.) 62 C2
Hargla (Est.) 62 D3

Hiiumaa I. (Est.) 62 B2
Hissar Mts. (Uzb., Taj.) 113 E3; 120 A2
Homel (Bel.) 49 E3
Horodno (Bel.) 49 A3
Horodnya (Ukr.) 40 C2
Horodok (Bel.) 49 D2
Horodok (nr. Minsk) see Logoisk
Hoverla, Mt. (Ukr.) 40 B2
Hullo (Est.) 62 B2
Hunger Steppe see Betpak Dala

I

Iecava (Lat.) 68 C2
Iecava R. (Lat.) 68 C2
Igarka (Rus.) 24 H3
Iisaku (Est.) 62 D2
Ijevan (Arm.) 87 D2
Ilūkste (Lat.) 68 D3
Ily R. (Kaz.) 100 D2
Ilyich (Kaz.) 120 B1
Imishli (Azer.) 93 C2
Indigirka R. (Rus.) 25 N3
Ingul R. (Ukr.) 40 C3
Ingulets R. (Ukr.) 40 C3
Inguri R. (Geo.) 80 B1
Ingushetia see Checheno-Ingush
Ionava (Lith.) 74 C2
Iori R. (Geo., Azer.) 80 C2; 93 B1
Irbe Strait 62 A3; 68 B2
Irgiz (Kaz.) 100 C2
Irgiz R. (Kaz.) 100 C2
Irkeshtam (Kyr.) 126 C3
Irkutsk (Rus.) 24 J4
Irsha R. (Ukr.) 40 B2
Irtysh R. (Rus., Kaz.) 24 G4; 100 D1
Irtyshsk (Kaz.) 100 D1
Ishim (Rus.) 24 F4
Ishim R. (Rus., Kaz.) 24 G4; 100 C1
Ishkashim (Taj.) 120 C3
Iskandar (Uzb.) 120 B1
Ismaily (Azer.) 93 C1
Issyk-Kul (Kyr.) 126 D2
Issyk-Kul, L. (Kyr.) 126 D2
Istisu (Azer.) 93 A2
Ivangorod (Rus.) E2
Ivano-Frankovsk (Ukr.) 40 B2
Ivanovka (Ukr.) 56 D2
Ivanovo (Bel.) 49 B3
Ivanovo (Rus.) 24 D4
Ivdel (Rus.) 32
Ivenets (Bel.) 49 C3
Ivye (Bel.) 49 B3
Izhevsk (Rus.) 24 E4
Izmail (Ukr.) 40 B3

J

Jaama (Est.) 62 D2
Jäärja (Est.) 62 C3
Jagry (Azer.) 93 A2
Jalagash (Kaz.) 100 C2
Jalal-Abad (Kyr.) 126 C2
Jalilabad (Azer.) 93 C2
Jambul (Kaz.) 100 D3
Jandargel, L. (Geo.) 80 C2
Janga (Turk.) 107 A2
Jangi Jol (Kyr.) 126 C2
Järva-Jaani (Est.) 62 C2
Järvakandi (Est.) 62 C2
Jaunjelgava (Lat.) 68 C2
Jaunpiebalga (Lat.) 68 D2
Java (Geo.) 80 B1
Jebrail (Azer.) 93 B2
Jekabpils (Lat.) 68 C2
Jelgava (Lat.) 68 B2
Jelgavkrasti (Lat.) 68 C2
Jermuk (Arm.) 87 D3
Jetygara (Kaz.) 100 C1
Jewish Region Aut. Obl. (Rus.) 37
Jezkazgan (Kaz.) 100 C2
Jieznas (Lith.) 74 C2
Jil (Arm.) 87 D2
Jirgatal (Taj.) 120 C2
Jizak (Uzb.) 113 E2

140

Jogeva (Est.) 62 D2
Joniškis (Lith.) 74 B1
Julfa (Azer.) 93 A2
Juminda, C. (Est.) 62 C2
Juodupe (Lith.) 74 C1
Jūra R. (Lith.) 74 A2
Jurbarkas (Lith.) 74 B2
Jūrmala (Lat.) 68 B2
Jusaly (Kaz.) 100 C2
Juuru (Est.) 62 C2

K

Kaakhka (Turk.) 107 D4
Kabardino-Balkar Aut. Rep. (Rus.) 37
Kačergine (Lith.) 74 B2
Kachanovo (Rus.) 62 D3; 68 D2
Kafan (Arm.) 87 E3
Kafirnigan R. (Taj.) 120 B3
Kagan (Uzb.) 113 D3
Kagul (Mol.) 56 C3
Kaišiadorys (Lith.) 74 C2
Kajaran (Arm.) 87 E3
Kakhi (Azer.) 93 B1
Kalai-Khumb (Taj.) 120 C2
Kalarash (Mol.) 56 C2
Kalinin see Tver
Kalininabad (Taj.) 120 B3
Kaliningrad (Rus.) 24 B4
Kallaste (Est.) 62 D2
Kalmyk Aut. Rep. (Rus.) 37
Kalnciems (Lat.) 68 B2
Kaluga (Rus.) 24 C4
Kalvarija (Lith.) 74 B2
Kama R. (Rus.) 24 E4
Kamashi (Uzb.) 113 D3
Kambja (Est.) 62 D2
Kamchatka Pen. (Rus.) 25 O4
Kamenets Podolski (Ukr.) 40 B2
Kameni I. (Azer.) 93 C2
Kamenka (Mol.) 56 C1
Kamo (Arm.) 87 D2
Kamyslybas (Kaz.) 113 C1
Kandalaksha (Rus.) 24 C3
Kandava (Lat.) 68 B2
Kanibadam (Taj.) 120 C1
Kansay (Taj.) 120 B1
Kansk (Rus.) 24 I4
Kapchagay (Kaz.) 126 D2
Kapchagay Res. (Kaz.) 100 D3
Kaplankyr Plateau (Kaz., Turk.) 107 C2
Kapsukas see Marijampole
Kapyjik, Mt. (Azer.) 93 A2
Karabaglar (Azer.) 93 A2
Karabakh Mts. (Azer.) 93 B2
Kara Balty (Kyr.) 126 C2
Kara-Bogaz, Gulf of (Turk.) 107 A2
Karachayevo-Cherkess Aut. Obl. (Rus.) 37
Karachayevsk (Rus.) 80 A1
Karadarya R. (Uzb.) 113 G2
Karaganda (Kaz.) 100 D2
Karagayly (Kaz.) 100 D2
Karagdagli (Azer.) 93 B1
Karagiye Depression (Kaz.) 100 B3
Kara-Kala (Turk.) 107 C3
Karakalpakstan Aut. Rep. (Uzb.) 113 A-B2
Karaklis (Arm.) 87 C2
Karakoin, L. (Kaz.) 113 E1
Karakolka (Kyr.) 126 D2
Kara Kul (Kyr.) 126 C2
Karakul, L. (Taj.) 120 D2
Kara Kum Canal (Turk.) 107 F4
Kara Kum Desert (Turk.) 107 D3
Karaman R. (Kaz.) 100 D2
Kara Sea (Rus.) 24 F2
Kara Su (Kyr.) 126 C2
Karasu (Azer.) 93 C1
Karatau (Kaz.) 100 D3
Karatau Mts. (Kaz.) 100 C3
Karavan (Kyr.) 126 B2
Karelia Aut. Rep. (Rus.) 24 C3; 37
Karkinit Bay (Ukr.) 40 C3
Karpineni (Mol.) 56 C2

Karsakpay (Kaz.) 100 C2
Kārsava (Lat.) 68 D2
Karshi (Uzb.) 113 D3
Kasakh R. (Arm.) 87 C2
Kasansay (Uzb.) 120 C1
Kasari R. (Est.) 62 C2
Kaspi (Geo.) 80 C2
Kattakurgan (Uzb.) 113 E3
Kaufmann Peak (Taj.) 120 D2
Kaunas (Lith.) 74 C2
Kavacha (Rus.) 25 Q4
Kazakh (Azer.) 93 A1
Kazakh Bay (Kaz.) 107 A1
Kazakh Steppe (Kaz.) 100 B-C2
Kazakh Uplands (Kaz.) 100 D2
Kazalinsk (Kaz.) 100 C2
Kazan (Rus.) 24 D4
Kazanjyk (Turk.) 107 B3
Kazarman (Kyr.) 126 C2
Kazbegi (Geo.) 80 C1
Kazbek, Mt. (Geo.) 80 C1
Kazi Magomed (Azer.) 93 C1
Kazlu Rūda (Lith.) 74 B2
Keda (Geo.) 80 A2
Kedabek (Azer.) 93 A1
Kedainiai (Lith.) 74 C2
Kehra (Est.) 62 C2
Kelbajar (Azer.) 93 B1
Keles (Kaz.) 120 B1
Keles R. 113 E2
Kelme (Lith.) 74 B2
Kem (Rus.) 24 C3
Kemerovo (Rus.) 24 H4
Kentau (Kaz.) 100 C3
Kerch (Ukr.) 40 D3
Kerch Strait 40 D3
Kerki (Turk.) 107 G4
Ketmen Mts. (Kaz.) 126 E2
Kezhma (Rus.) 24 J4
Khabarovsk (Rus.) 25 M5
Khabarovsk Krai (Rus.) 37
Khachmas (Azer.) 93 C1
Khaidarken (Kyr.) 126 B3
Khaishi (Geo.) 80 B1
Khakass Aut. Obl. (Rus.) 37
Khanchali, L. (Geo.) 80 B2
Khanka, L. (Rus.) 25 M5
Khanlar (Azer.) 93 B1
Khantau (Kaz.) 126 C1
Khan-Tengri Peak (Kyr.) 126 E2
Khanty-Mansi Nat. Okr. (Rus.) 37
Khanty-Mansiysk (Rus.) 24 F3
Kharagauli (Geo.) 80 B1
Kharkov (Ukr.) 40 D2
Khasavyurt (Rus.) 80 D1
Khashuri (Geo.) 80 B2
Khatanga (Rus.) 24 J2
Khatyrka (Rus.) 25 Q3
Kherson (Ukr.) 40 C3
Khiva (Uzb.) 113 C2
Khmelnitski (Ukr.) 40 B2
Khoja Kala (Turk.) 107 C3
Khojeyli (Uzb.) 113 B2
Kholopenichi (Bel.) 49 D2
Khomi (Geo.) 80 C1
Khoni (Geo.) 80 B1
Khorog (Taj.) 120 C3
Khotimsk (Bel.) 49 F3
Khotin (Ukr.) 56 B1
Khozapini, L. (Geo.) 80 B2
Khrami R. (Geo.) 80 C2
Khudat (Azer.) 93 C1
Khujend (Taj.) 120 B1
Kiev (Ukr.) 40 C2
Kihelkonna (Est.) 62 A2
Kihnu I. (Est.) 62 B2
Kilingi-Nõmme (Est.) 62 C2
Kiliya (Ukr.) 56 C3
Kilyazi (Azer.) 93 C1
Kingisepp (Rus.) 62 E2
Kirbla (Est.) 62 B2
Kirensk (Rus.) 24 J4
Kirghiz Range (Kaz., Kyr.) 126 C2
Kirghiz Steppe see Kazakh Steppe

Kirov (Rus.) 24 D4
Kirovabad see Gyanja
Kirovakan see Karaklis
Kirov Bay (Azer.) 93 C2
Kirovograd see Yelizavetgrad
Kirovsk (Turk.) 107 E4
Kishinev see Chişinău
Kislovodsk (Rus.) 80 B1
Kitab (Uzb.) 113 E3
Kitai, L. (Ukr.) 56 C3
Kivioli (Est.) 62 D2
Kizilsu R. (Taj.) 120 B3
Kizyl Arvat (Turk.) 107 C3
Klaipėda (Lith.) 74 A2
Klintsy (Rus.) 40 C1; 49 E3
Klukhor Pass (Geo.) 80 A1
Klyuchevskaya, Mt. (Rus.) 25 P4
Klyuchi (Rus.) 33
Kobrin (Bel.) 49 B3
Kobuleti (Geo.) 80 A2
Kodori R. (Geo.) 80 A1
Kodry Mts. (Mol.) 56 B-C2
Kodyma (Ukr.) 56 C1
Kodyma R. (Ukr.) 56 C2
Kofarnikhoi (Taj.) 120 B2
Kohtla (Est.) 62 C2
Kohtla-Järve (Est.) 62 D2
Kokand (Uzb.) 113 F2
Kokchetav (Kaz.) 100 C1
Kokshaal-Tau Mts. (Kyr.) 126 D2
Kok Yangak (Kyr.) 126 C2
Kola Pen. (Rus.) 24 C-D3
Kolga-Jaani (Est.) 62 C2
Kolka (Lat.) 68 B2
Kolkhida Plain (Geo.) 80 A-B1
Kolomyya (Ukr.) 40 B2
Kolosnoye (Ukr.) 56 C2
Kolyma Mts. (Rus.) 24 D3
Kolyma R. (Rus.) 25 O3
Komi Aut. Rep. (Rus.) 37
Komi-Permyak Nat. Okr. (Rus.) 37
Komrat (Mol.) 56 C2
Komsomolets I. (Rus.) 24 I1
Komsomolsk (Rus.) 25 M4
Konagkend (Azer.) 93 C1
Kõngesaare (Est.) 62 B2
Konotop (Ukr.) 40 C2
Koosa (Est.) 62 D2
Kopet-Dag Mts. (Turk.) 107 C3
Kopyl Ridge (Bel.) 50
Korneshty (Mol.) 56 B2
Korosten (Ukr.) 40 B2
Koryak Mts. (Rus.) 25 P-Q3
Koryak Nat. Okr. (Rus.) 37
Kose (Est.) 62 C2
Kosh (Arm.) 87 C2
Koskolovo (Rus.) 62 E2
Koskuduk (Kaz.) 126 D1
Kossovo (Bel.) 49 B3
Kostopol (Ukr.) 40 B2
Kostyukovichi (Bel.) 49 E3
Kotelny I. (Rus.) 25 M2
Kotlas (Rus.) 24 D3
Kotovsk (Mol.) 56 C2
Kotovsk (Ukr.) 40 B3
Kotyuzhany (Mol.) 56 C2
Kovarskas (Lith.) 74 C2
Kovel (Ukr.) 40 B2
Kovno see Kaunas
Krāslava (Lat.) 68 D3
Krasnaya Polyana (Rus.) 80 A1
Krasnodar (Rus.) 24 C5
Krasnodar Krai (Rus.) 37
Krasnograd (Ukr.) 40 C2
Krasnogvardeysk (Uzb.) 113 E3
Krasnovodsk see Menbashid
Krasnovodsk Bay (Turk.) 107 A3
Krasnoyarsk (Rus.) 24 I4
Krasnoyarsk Krai (Rus.) 37
Krasnoye Znamya (Turk.) 107 F4
Krasnoznamensk (Rus.) 74 B2
Krasny Bazar (Azer.) 98
Krasnye Okny (Ukr.) 56 C2
Kremenchug (Ukr.) 40 C2

Kretinga (Lith.) 74 A2
Krichev (Bel.) 49 E3
Krivichi (Bel.) 49 C2
Krivoi Rog (Ukr.) 40 C3
Krivoye Ozero (Ukr.) 56 D2
Krupki (Bel.) 49 D2
Kuba (Azer.) 93 C1
Kuban R. (Rus.) 40 D3; 80 B1
Kubatly (Azer.) 93 B2
Kuchurgan R. (Ukr.) 56 C2
Kudirkos Naumiestis (Lith.) 74 B2
Kudymkar (Rus.) 24 E4
Kuibyshev see Samara
Kuldīga (Lat.) 68 A2
Kulunda (Rus.) 24 G4
Kulyab (Taj.) 120 B3
Kuma R. (Rus.) 80 B1
Kumairi (Arm.) 87 B2
Kunda (Est.) 62 D2
Kungai-Alatau Mts. (Kyr.) 126 D2
Kupcin (Mol.) 56 B1
Kupino (Rus.) 24 G4
Kupiskis (Lith.) 74 C2
Kura R. (Geo., Azer.) 80 B2; 95
Kuramin Mts. (Uzb., Taj.) 113 E2; 120 B1
Kurday (Kaz.) 126 D2
Kuressaare (Est.) 62 B2
Kurgan (Rus.) 24 F4
Kurgan Tyube (Taj.) 120 B3
Kurian Lagoon (Lith., Rus.) 74 A2
Kurian Spit (Lith., Rus.) 74 A2
Kuril Is. (Rus.) 25 N-O5
Kurinskaya Kosa (Azer.) 93 C2
Kuršenai (Lith.) 74 B2
Kursk (Rus.) 24 C4
Kurta (Geo.) 80 B1
Kurty R. (Kaz.) 126 D2
Kusary (Azer.) 93 C1
Kustanai (Kaz.) 100 C1
Kutaisi (Geo.) 80 B1
Kuyalinik R. (Ukr.) 56 D2
Kuznetsk Basin (Rus.) 24 H4
Kvareli (Geo.) 80 C2
Kvemo Azhara (Geo.) 80 A1
Kyakhta (Rus.) 24 J4
Kybartai (Lith.) 74 B2
Kyurdamir (Azer.) 93 C1
Kyyiv see Kiev
Kyzyl (Rus.) 24 I4
Kyzylkend (Arm.) 87 B1
Kyzyl Kiya (Kyr.) 126 C2
Kyzyl Kum Desert (Kaz., Uzb.) 100 C3; 113 C-D2
Kzyl-Orda (Kaz.) 100 C3

L

Lachin (Azer.) 93 B2
Ladoga, L. (Rus.) 24 C3
Ladyzhinka (Ukr.) 56 D1
Lagodekhi (Geo.) 80 D2
Lan R. (Bel.) 50
Lanchkhuti (Geo.) 80 B1
Laptev Sea (Rus.) 24-25
Lata (Geo.) 80 A1
Latgale Upland (Lat.) 68 D2
Laudona (Lat.) 68 D2
Lavassare (Est.) 62 C2
Lazdijai (Lith.) 74 B2
Lebedin (Ukr.) 40 C2
Lehtse (Est.) 62 C2
Lelchitsy (Bel.) 49 D4
Lemberan (Azer.) 93 B1
Lena R. (Rus.) 24-25 J4-L2
Leninabad see Khujend
Leninakan see Kumairi
Leningrad see St. Petersburg
Lenin Peak see Kaufmann Peak
Lenkoran (Azer.) 93 C2
Lensk (Rus.) 25 K3
Lenzikend (Azer.) 93 B1
Leovo (Mol.) 56 C2
Lepel (Bel.) 49 D2
Lerik (Azer.) 93 C2
Lesna R. (Bel.) 50

Petropavlovsk Kamchatskiy (Rus.) 25 O4
Petrovsk-Zabaykalskiy (Rus.) 32
Petrozavodsk (Rus.) 24 C3
Pevek (Rus.) 25 Q3
Piltene (Lat.) 68 A2
Pina R. (Bel.) 50
Pinsk (Bel.) 49 C3
Pirita R. (Est.) 62 C2
Pirsagat (Azer.) 93 C2
Pirsagat R. (Azer.) 93 C1
Plaviņas (Lat.) 68 C2
Pleshchenitsy (Bel.) 49 C2
Pluci (Lat.) 68 C2
Plungė (Lith.) 74 A2
Plyussa R. (Rus.) 62 E2
Pobeda, Mt. (Rus.) 25 N3
Pobeda Peak (Kyr.) 126 E2
Pochinok (Rus.) 49 F2
Pokrovka (Kyr.) 126 D2
Polessk (Rus.) 74 A2
Polesye Lowland (Ukr., Bel.) 40 B2;
    49 B-D4; 50
Polotsk (Bel.) 49 D2
Poltava (Ukr.) 40 C2
Põltsamaa (Est.) 62 C2
Põltsamaa R. (Est.) 62 C2
Polva (Est.) 62 D3
Pomoshnaya (Ukr.) 56 D1
Ponoi (Rus.) 24 D3
Poronaysk (Rus.) 33
Postavy (Bel.) 49 C2
Poti (Geo.) 80 A1
Poylu (Azer.) 93 B1
Prangli I. (Est.) 62 C2
Pregradnaya (Rus.) 80 A1
Preiļi (Lat.) 68 D2
Priazov Upland (Ukr.) 40 D3
Priekule (Lat.) 68 A2
Priekulė (Lith.) 74 A2
Priluki (Ukr.) 40 C2
Primorsk (Azer.) 93 C1
Primorskoye (Ukr.) 40 B3
Primorye Krai (Rus.) 37
Pripet (Pripyat) R. 40 B2; 49 C3-D4
Prokhladnyy (Rus.) 80 C1
Prut R. 40 B3; 56 B2-C3
Pruzhany (Bel.) 49 B3
Przhevalsk (Kyr.) 126 E2
Pskhu (Geo.) 80 A1
Pshish, Mt. (Rus.) 80 A1
Pskov (Rus.) 24 B4
Pskov, L. (Est., Rus.) 62 E3
Ptich R. (Bel.) 49 D3
Pumpenai (Lith.) 74 C2
Purikari, C. (Est.) 62 C2
Pustoshka (Rus.) 49 D1
Putorana Mts. (Rus.) 24 I3
Puurmani (Est.) 62 D2
Pyatigorsk (Rus.) 80 B1
Pyatlovo (Rus.) 68 D2
Pyvesa R. (Lith.) 74 C2

R
Raasiku (Est.) 62 C2
Rachin Mts. (Geo.) 80 B1
Radun (Bel.) 49 B3
Radviliškis (Lith.) 74 B2
Rakov (Bel.) 49 C3
Rakvere (Est.) 62 D2
Ramygala (Lith.) 74 C2
Räpina (Est.) 62 D2
Rapla (Est.) 62 C2
Raseiniai (Lith.) 74 B2
Ravnina (Turk.) 107 F3
Raychikhinsk (Rus.) 33
Razdan (Arm.) 87 C2
Razdan R. (Arm.) 87 C2
Razdelnaya (Ukr.) 56 C2
Rechitsa (Bel.) 49 E3
Reut R. (Mol.) 56 C2
Reval see Tallinn
Rēzekne (Lat.) 68 D2
Rēzekne R. (Lat.) 68 D2
Rezna, L. (Lat.) 68 D2

Rietavas (Lith.) 74 A2
Riga (Lat.) 68 C2
Riga, Gulf of 64, 70
Riisipere (Est.) 62 C2
Rioni R. (Geo.) 80 B1
Risti (Est.) 62 B2
Ristna, C. (Est.) 62 A2
Ritsa (Geo.) 80 A1
Rize, Mt. (Turk.) 107 D4
Rogachev (Bel.) 49 E3
Roja (Lat.) 68 B2
Rokiškis (Lith.) 74 C2
Roman Kosh, Mt. (Ukr.) 40 C3
Rootsi (Est.) 62 B2
Roslavl (Rus.) 49 F3
Rossony (Bel.) 49 D2
Rossosh (Rus.) 40 D3
Rostov (Rus.) 24 C5
Rovno (Ukr.) 40 B2
Rozhka (Rus.) 80 A1
Rubtsovsk (Rus.) 24 H4
Rūdiškės (Lith.) 74 C2
Rudnitsa (Ukr.) 56 C1
Rudnya (Rus.) 49 E2
Rudolph I. (Rus.) 24 E1
Ruhnu I. (Est.) 62 B3
Rūjiena (Lat.) 68 C2
Rushan (Taj.) 120 C3
Rustavi (Geo.) 80 C2
Ryazan (Rus.) 24 C4
Rybachye see Issyk-Kul
Rybinsk (Rus.) 24 C4
Rybnitsa (Mol.) 56 C2
Ryshkany (Mol.) 56 B2

S
Säare (Est.) 62 A3
Saaremaa I. (Est.) 62 B2
Sabile (Lat.) 68 B2
Sabirabad (Azer.) 93 C1
Sadarak (Azer.) 93 A2
Safaraliyev (Azer.) 93 B1
Safonovo (Rus.) 49 F2
Sagarejo (Geo.) 80 C2
St. Petersburg (Rus.) 24 C4
Sakha Aut. Rep. (Rus.) 37
Sakhalin I. (Rus.) 25 N4
Šakiai (Lith.) 74 B2
Salaca R. (Lat.) 68 C2
Salacgrīva (Lat.) 68 C2
Salantai (Lith.) 74 A1
Salavat Pass (Azer.) 93 B1
Šalčininkai (Lith.) 74 C2
Saldus (Lat.) 68 B2
Salekhard (Rus.) 24 F3
Salyany (Azer.) 93 C2
Samara (Rus.) 24 E4
Samara R. (Rus.) 100 B1
Samarkand (Uzb.) 113 E3
Samogitian Upland (Lith.) 74 B2
Samolva (Rus.) 62 D2
Samro, L. (Rus.) 62 E2
Samtredia (Geo.) 80 B1
Samukh (Azer.) 93 B1
Samur R. (Azer.) 93 C1
Sandykachi (Turk.) 107 F4
Sangvor (Taj.) 120 C2
Saransk (Rus.) 24 D4
Sarata (Ukr.) 56 C2
Saratov (Rus.) 24 D4
Sarez, L. (Taj.) 120 D2
Sarnakhbyur (Arm.) 87 D2
Sarny (Ukr.) 40 B2
Sarukhan (Arm.) 87 D2
Sary-Ishikotrau Desert (Kaz.) 100 D2
Sarykamysh, L. (Turk.) 107 C2
Saryozek (Kaz.) 100 D3
Sarysu R. (Kaz.) 100 C2
Sary Tash (Kyr.) 126 C3
Sastobe (Kaz.) 126 B2
Sasyk, L. (Ukr.) 56 C3
Saulkrasti (Lat.) 68 C2
Savran (Ukr.) 56 C1
Sayat (Turk.) 107 F3
Sebezh (Rus.) 49 D1

Seda (Lat.) 68 C2
Seda (Lith.) 74 A1
Seda R. (Lat.) 68 C2
Seduva (Lith.) 74 B2
Semipalatinsk (Kaz.) 100 E1
Senaki (Geo.) 80 B1
Senno (Bel.) 49 D2
Serakhs (Turk.) 107 E4
Seredka (Rus.) 62 E2
Serny Zavod (Turk.) 107 D3
Serov (Rus.) 24 F4
Seskar I. (Rus.) 62 E1
Šešupe R. (Lith.) 74 B2
Šėta (Lith.) 74 C2
Sevan (Arm.) 87 C2
Sevan, L. (Arm.) 87 D2
Sevastopol (Ukr.) 40 C3
Severnaya Zemlya I. (Rus.) 24 I1-J2
Severo-Kurilsk (Rus.) 33
Seydi (Turk.) 107 F3
Seym R. (Ukr.) 40 C2
Shaartuz (Taj.) 120 B3
Shakhbuz (Azer.) 93 A2
Shakhdag Mts. (Arm., Azer.) 87 D2,
    93 A1
Shakhpakhty (Uzb.) 117
Shakhrisabz (Uzb.) 113 E3
Shamkhor (Azer.) 93 A1
Shamkhorchay R. (Azer.) 93 B1
Shantar Is. (Rus.) 25 M4
Shargorod (Ukr.) 56 B1
Sharkovshchina (Bel.) 49 C2
Shatili (Geo.) 80 C1
Shaumyani (Geo.) 80 C2
Shaviklde, Mt. (Geo.) 80 C1
Shazud (Taj.) 120 D3
Shchara R. (Bel.) 49 B3
Sheki (Azer.) 93 B1
Shemakha (Azer.) 93 C1
Sherabad (Uzb.) 113 E3
Shereshevo (Bel.) 49 B3
Shirak Plain (Geo.) 80 D2
Shirvan Steppe (Azer.) 93 B-C1
Shkhara, Mt. (Geo.) 80 B1
Shklov (Bel.) 49 E2
Shollar (Azer.) 93 C1
Shorkul, L. (Taj.) 120 E2
Shostka (Ukr.) 40 B2
Shpola (Ukr.) 40 C2
Shroma (Geo.) 80 B1
Shumilino (Bel.) 49 D2
Shurab (Taj.) 120 C1
Shurchi (Uzb.) 113 E3
Shusha (Azer.) 93 B2
Šiauliai (Lith.) 74 B2
Siazan (Azer.) 93 C1
Siberia (Rus.) 24
Signakhi (Geo.) 80 C2
Sigulda (Lat.) 68 C2
Sikhote Alin Mts. (Rus.) 25 M5
Šilalė (Lith.) 74 B2
Sillamäe (Est.) 62 D2
Šilutė (Lith.) 74 A2
Simbirsk (Rus.) 24 D4
Simferopol (Ukr.) 40 C3
Simnas (Lith.) 74 B2
Sindi (Est.) 62 C2
Sinyuka R. (Ukr.) 40 C2-3
Širvinai (Lith.) 74 C2
Sisian (Arm.) 87 E3
Skaudvilė (Lith.) 74 B2
Skidel (Bel.) 49 B3
Skriveri (Lat.) 68 C2
Skrunda (Lat.) 68 A2
Skuodas (Lith.) 74 A1
Slantsy (Rus.) 62 E2
Slavgorod (Bel.) 49 E3
Slavgorod (Rus.) 24 G4
Slavyansk (Ukr.) 40 D2
Sloboda (Bel.) 49 C3
Slonim (Bel.) 49 B3
Slovechna R. (Bel.) 50
Sluch R. (Ukr.) 40 B2
Slutsk (Bel.) 49 C3
Smalininkai (Lith.) 74 B2

Smela (Ukr.) 40 C2
Smiltene (Lat.) 68 C2
Smolensk (Rus.) 24 C4
Smorgon (Bel.) 49 C2
Sochi (Rus.) 24 D5
Soligorsk (Bel.) 49 C3
Somerpalu (Est.) 62 D3
Song-Kel, L. (Kyr.) 126 D2
Soroki (Mol.) 56 C1
Sõrve, C. (Est.) 62 A3
Sõrve Pen. (Est.) 62 A2
Southern Bug R. (Ukr.) 40 C3
South Ossetia Aut. Obl. (Geo.)
    80 B-C1
Sovetsk (Rus.) 74 A2
Sovetskaya Gavan (Rus.) 33
Sozh R. (Bel.) 49 E3
Srednekolymsk (Rus.) 25 O3
Stanovoi Mts. (Rus.) 25 L4
Starobelsk (Ukr.) 40 D2
Starodub (Rus.) 49 F3
Starokazachye (Ukr.) 56 C2
Stavropol (Rus.) 24 D5
Stavropol Krai (Rus.) 37
Stende (Lat.) 68 B2
Stende R. (Lat.) 68 B2
Stepanakert (Azer.) 93 B2
Stepanavan (Arm.) 87 C1
Sterlitamak (Rus.) 24 E4
Stochod R. (Ukr.) 50
Stolbtsy (Bel.) 49 C3
Strasheny (Mol.) 56 C2
Strenči (Lat.) 68 C2
Styr R. (Ukr., Bel.) 50
Subačius (Lith.) 74 C2
Sukhumi (Geo.) 80 A1
Sula R. (Ukr.) 40 C2
Sultanly (Azer.) 93 B2
Sulyukta (Kyr.) 126 B3
Sumgait (Azer.) 93 C1
Sumgait R. (Azer.) 93 C1
Sumy (Ukr.) 40 C2
Suntar Khayata Mts. 24 M-N3
Sunzha Range (Rus.) 80 C1
Sunzha R. (Rus.) 80 C1
Suraklami (Azer.) 93 D1
Surame (Geo.) 80 B1
Suram Mts. (Geo.) 80 B1
Surazh (Rus.) 49 F3
Surgut (Rus.) 24 G3
Surkhob R. (Taj.) 120 C2
Susēja R. (Lat.) 68 C2
Susuman (Rus.) 25 N3
Sušve R. (Lith.) 74 B2
Suure-Jaani (Est.) 62 C2
Suur Pakri I. (Est.) 62 B2
Suvorovo (Ukr.) 56 C3
Suzak (Kaz.) 113 E1
Svanet Mts. (Geo.) 80 B1
Svatovo (Ukr.) 40 D2
Švenčioneliai (Lith.) 74 D2
Švenčionys (Lith.) 74 D2
Sventoji R. (Lith.) 74 C2
Sverdlovsk see Yekaterinburg
Svetlogorsk (Bel.) 53
Svir, L. (Bel.) 49 C2
Svisloch R. (Bel.) 50
Svobodny (Rus.) 33
Syktyvkar (Rus.) 24 E3
Syr Darya R. 100 C3; 113 E2
Syzran (Rus.) 100 A1

T
Tabatskuri, L. (Geo.) 80 B2
Taganrog (Rus.) 24 C5
Taganrog, Gulf of 40 D3
Tagiloni (Geo.) 80 A1
Tahkuna, C. (Est.) 62 B2
Taimyr, L. (Rus.) 24 J2
Taimyr Nat. Okr. (Rus.) 37
Taimyr Pen. (Rus.) 24 H-K2
Takhiatash (Uzb.) 113 C2
Takhta Bazar (Turk.) 107 F5
Takhtakupyr (Uzb.) 113 C2
Takob (Taj.) 120 B2

Talas (Kyr.) 126 C2
Talas-Alatau Mts. 113 F-G2; 126 B-C2
Talas R. (Kaz., Kyr.) 126 B2
Taldy Kurgan (Kaz.) 100 D2
Tallinn (Est.) 62 C2
Talsi (Lat.) 68 B2
Talysh Mts. (Azer.) 93 C2
Tambov (Rus.) 24 D4
Tamdybulak (Uzb.) 113 D2
Tamdytau Mts. (Uzb.) 113 D2
Tannu Ola Mts. (Rus.) 24 I4
Tara (Rus.) 24 G4
Tarakliya (Mol.) 56 C2
Tarbagatai Mts. (Kaz.) 100 E2
Tartu (Est.) 62 D2
Tarutino (Ukr.) 40 B3
Tas Buget (Kaz.) 113 D1
Tashauz (Turk.) 107 D2
Tashir (Arm.) 87 C1
Tashkent (Uzb.) 113 F2
Tash Kumyr (Kyr.) 126 C2
Tatarbunary (Ukr.) 40 B3
Tatarsk (Rus.) 24 G4
Tatarstan Aut. Rep. (Rus.) 37
Tauragė (Lith.) 74 B2
Tauz (Azer.) 93 A1
Taz R. (Rus.) 24 H3
Tbilisi (Geo.) 80 C2
Teberda (Rus.) 80 A1
Teberda R. (Rus.) 80 A1
Teenuse R. (Est.) 62 C2
Tejen (Turk.) 107 E4
Tejen R. (Turk.) 107 E4
Tejenstroy (Turk.) 107 E4
Tekes (Kaz.) 126 E2
Telavi (Geo.) 80 C2
Teleneshty (Mol.) 56 C2
Telšiai (Lith.) 74 B2
Temirtau (Kaz.) 100 D1
Temirtau (Rus.) 24 H4
Tengiz, L. (Kaz.) 100 C1
Teplik (Ukr.) 56 C1
Terek R. (Geo., Rus.) 80 C1
Terek Say (Kyr.) 126 B2
Termez (Uzb.) 113 E3
Ternopol (Ukr.) 40 B2
Ters-Alatau Mts. (Kyr.) 126 D2
Terter R. (Azer.) 93 B1
Teterev R. (Ukr.) 40 B2
Tien Shan Mts. 120 D2; 126 E2
Tiksi (Rus.) 25 L2
Tiligul R. (Ukr.) 56 D2
Tiraspol (Mol.) 56 C2
Tisza R. (Ukr.) 40 A2
Tkvarcheli (Geo.) 80 A1
Tobol R. (Rus., Kaz.) 24 F4; 100 C1
Tobolsk (Rus.) 24 F4
Togliatti (Rus.) 24 D4
Tokhtamysh (Taj.) 120 E3
Tokmak (Kyr.) 126 D2
Toktogul (Kyr.) 126 C2
Toktogul Res. (Kyr.) 126 C2
Tolochin (Bel.) 49 D2
Tomsk (Rus.) 24 H4
Torva (Est.) 62 C3
Toshkent see Tashkent
Tõstamaa (Est.) 62 B2
Trakai (Lith.) 74 C2
Tremlya R. (Bel.) 50
Troskunai (Lith.) 74 C2
Tsageri (Geo.) 80 B1
Tsakhur (Rus.) 93 B1
Tsaritsyn (Rus.) 24 D5
Tsebrikovo (Ukr.) 56 C2
Tselinograd see Akmolinsk
Tsiteli-Tskaro (Geo.) 80 D2
Tskhenis Tskali R. (Geo.) 80 B1
Tskhinvali (Geo.) 80 B1
Tsna R. (Bel.) 50
Tsovagyukh (Arm.) 87 C2
Tsulukidze see Khoni
Tuapse (Rus.) 40 D3
Tukums (Lat.) 68 B2
Tula (Rus.) 24 C4
Tulchin (Ukr.) 56 C1
Tulun (Rus.) 32
Tumanyan (Arm.) 87 C2
Tunguska R., Lower (Rus.) 24 I3
Tura (Rus.) 24 J3
Turanian Lowlands 107 C3

Turgay (Kaz.) 100 C2
Turgay R. (Kaz.) 100 C2
Turgay Valley (Kaz.) 100 C2
Türi (Est.) 62 C2
Turia R. (Ukr.) 50
Turianchay R. (Azer.) 93 B1
Turkestan (Kaz.) 113 E2
Turkestan Mts. (Uzb., Taj.) 113 E3; 120 B2
Turmantas (Lith.) 74 D2
Turtkul (Uzb.) 113 C2
Turukhansk (Rus.) 24 H3
Tuva Aut. Rep. (Rus.) 37
Tuyuk (Kaz.) 126 E2
Tver (Rus.) 24 C4
Tynda (Rus.) 25 L4
Tyruliai (Lith.) 74 B2
Tytuvėnai (Lith.) 74 B2
Tyumen (Rus.) 24 F4

U
Ubort R. (Bel.) 50
Uchkuduk (Uzb.) 113 D2
Udmurt Aut. Rep. (Rus.) 37
Uelen (Rus.) 25 R3
Ufa (Rus.) 24 E4
Ufa R. (Rus.) 100 B1
Ugāle (Lat.) 68 A2
Ugam Mts. (Kaz., Uzb.) 113 F2; 126 B2
Uil R. (Kaz.) 100 B2
Ujary (Azer.) 93 B1
Ukhta (Rus.) 24 E3
Ukmergė (Lith.) 74 C2
Ulan-Ude (Rus.) 24 J4
Ulla (Bel.) 49 D2
Ulyanovsk see Simbirsk
Uman (Ukr.) 40 C2
Ungeny (Mol.) 56 B2
Ural Mts. (Rus.) 24 E3-4
Ural R. (Kaz.) 100 B2
Uralsk (Kaz.) 100 B1
Ura Tyube (Taj.) 120 B2
Urengoi (Rus.) 24 G3
Urga (Uzb.) 113 B2
Urgench (Uzb.) 113 C2
Urukh R. (Rus.) 80 C1
Ushachi (Bel.) 49 D2
Ushachi R. (Bel.) 49 D2
Ushba, Mt. (Geo.) 80 B1
Usmas, L. (Lat.) 68 B2
Ussuri R. (Rus.) 25 M5
Ussuriysk (Rus.) 33
Ust-Ilimsk (Rus.) 24 J4
Ustinov see Izhevsk
Ust-Kamchatsk (Rus.) 25 P4
Ust-Kamenogorsk (Kaz.) 100 E1
Ust-Kut (Rus.) 24 J4
Ust-Luga (Rus.) 62 E2
Ust-Ordyn-Buryat Nat. Okr. (Rus.) 37
Ust-Ordynsk (Rus.) 24 J4
Ustyurt Plateau (Kaz., Uzb.) 100 B3; 113 A2
Utena (Lith.) 74 C2
Uulu (Est.) 62 C2
Uyaly I. (Kaz.) 113 C1
Uzda (Bel.) 49 C3
Uzen (Kaz.) 100 B3
Uzhgorod (Ukr.) 40 A2
Uzuntala (Arm.) 87 D2
Užventis (Lith.) 74 B2

V
Vaguaz (Azer.) 98
Väike-Maarja (Est.) 62 D2
Vainameri Strait (Est.) 62 B2
Vainode (Lat.) 68 A2
Vakhsh R. (Taj.) 120 B3
Valdemārpils (Lat.) 68 B2
Valga (Est.) 62 D3
Valge R. (Est.) 62 C2
Valka (Lat.) 68 C2
Valmiera (Lat.) 68 C2
Valuyki (Rus.) 40 D2
Vanch (Taj.) 120 C2
Vanch Mts. (Taj.) 120 C2
Vändra (Est.) 62 C2
Vāne (Lat.) 68 B2
Vapnyarka (Ukr.) 56 C1
Varakļāni (Lat.) 68 D2

Varėna (Lith.) 74 C2
Varniai (Lith.) 74 B2
Vasalemma (Est.) 62 C2
Vasilishke (Bel.) 49 B3
Veisiejai (Lith.) 74 B2
Velikaya R. (Rus.) 62 E3
Velikiye Luki (Rus.) 49 E1
Velizh (Rus.) 49 E2
Venta R. (Lat., Lith.) 68 A2; 74 B2
Ventspils (Lat.) 68 A2
Veretski Pass (Ukr.) 40 A2
Verin Talin (Arm.) 87 B2
Veriora (Est.) 62 D3
Verkhovani (Geo.) 80 C1
Verkhoyansk Mts. (Rus.) 25 L3
Veselinovo (Ukr.) 56 D2
Vidzeme Upland (Lat.) 68 C2
Viekšniai (Lith.) 74 B1
Viļaka (Lat.) 68 D2
Viļāni (Lat.) 68 D2
Vileika (Bel.) 49 C2
Viliya R. (Bel.) 49 C2 (see also Neris R.)
Viljandi (Est.) 62 C2
Vilkaviškis (Lith.) 74 B2
Vilkija (Lith.) 74 B2
Vilkovo (Ukr.) 56 C3
Vilnius (Vilna) (Lith.) 74 C2
Vilsandi I. (Est.) 62 A2
Vilyui R. (Rus.) 25 L4
Vilyuysk (Rus.) 32
Vinnitsa (Ukr.) 40 B2
Vireši (Lat.) 68 D2
Virtsu (Est.) 62 B2
Virvyte R. (Lith.) 74 B2
Vit R. (Bel.) 50
Vitebsk (Bel.) 49 E2
Vitim R. (Rus.) 25 K4
Vladikavkaz (Rus.) 24 D5
Vladimir (Rus.) 24 D4
Vladivostok (Rus.) 25 M5
Vohandu R. (Est.) 62 D3
Võhma (Est.) 62 B2
Võhma (Est.) 62 C2
Volga R. (Rus.) 24 D4
Volgograd see Tsaritsyn
Volkovysk (Bel.) 49 B3
Volkovysk Plateau (Bel.) 50
Vologda (Rus.) 24 C4
Volozhin (Bel.) 49 C2
Volsk (Rus.) 100 A1
Volyn-Podolsk Plateau (Ukr.) 40 B2
Võnnu (Est.) 62 D2
Vorkuta (Rus.) 24 F3
Vormsi I. (Est.) 62 B2
Voronezh (Rus.) 24 C4
Voronezh R. (Rus.) 40 D1-2
Voropayevo (Bel.) 49 C2
Voroshilovgrad see Lugansk
Vorotan R. (Arm., Azer.) 87 E3; 93 B2
Vorskla R. (Ukr.) 40 C2
Võrts, L. (Est.) 62 C2
Voru (Est.) 62 D3
Vosu (Est.) 62 C2
Voznesensk (Ukr.) 40 C3
Vozrojeniya I. (Uzb.) 113 B1
Vyatka R. (Rus.) 24 E4
Vygonovsko, L. (Bel.) 49 B3
Vysokaya, Mt. (Mol.) 56 B1
Vysokopolye (Ukr.) 40 C3
Vysokoye (Bel.) 49 A3

W
Western Dvina R. see Dvina R., Western
White Sea (Rus.) 24 C-D3
Wilczek Land (Rus.) 24 F1
Wrangel I. (Rus.) 25 R2

Y
Yablonitsa Pass (Ukr.) 40 B2
Yaila Range (Ukr.) 40 C3
Yakutia see Sakha
Yakutsk (Rus.) 25 L3
Yalpug R. (Mol.) 56 C3
Yalpukh, L. (Ukr.) 56 C3

Yalta (Ukr.) 40 C3
Yamalo-Nenets Nat. Okr. (Rus.) 37
Yamal Pen. (Rus.) 24 G2
Yaminsk (Bel.) 49 D3
Yamm (Rus.) 62 E2
Yampol (Ukr.) 56 C1
Yana R. (Rus.) 25 M3
Yangibazar (Kyr.) 126 B2
Yangiyul (Uzb.) 120 B1
Yanykurgan (Kaz.) 113 E2
Yardimly (Azer.) 93 C2
Yaroslavl (Rus.) 24 C4
Yartsevo (Rus.) 49 F2
Yaselda R. (Bel.) 49 B3
Yavan (Taj.) 120 B2
Yedintsy (Mol.) 56 B1
Yekaterinburg (Rus.) 24 F4
Yekaterinodar see Krasnodar
Yekaterinoslav (Ukr.) 40 C2
Yelets (Rus.) 40 D1
Yelizavetgrad (Ukr.) 40 C2
Yelnya (Rus.) 49 F2
Yenikend (Azer.) 93 B1
Yeniseisk (Rus.) 24 I4
Yenisey R. (Rus.) 24 H3-I4
Yeranos (Arm.) 87 D2
Yerbent (Turk.) 107 D3
Yerevan (Arm.) 87 C2
Yermak (Kaz.) 100 D1
Yevlakh (Azer.) 93 B1
Yevpatoriya (Ukr.) 40 C3
Yoshkar Ola (Rus.) 24 D4
Yuzhno-Sakhalinsk (Rus.) 25 N5
Yuzovka (Ukr.) 40 D3

Z
Zaalay Mts. (Taj., Kyr.) 120 C2
Zaamin (Uzb.) 120 B1
Žagarė (Lith.) 74 B1
Zakataly (Azer.) 93 B1
Zanga R. see Razdan R.
Zangelan (Azer.) 93 B2
Zangezur Mts. (Arm., Azer.) 87 D-E3; 93 A2
Zaporozhye (Ukr.) 40 C3
Zarafshan (Uzb.) 113 D2
Zarasai (Lith.) 74 D2
Zardob (Azer.) 93 B1
Zasa (Lat.) 68 C2
Zaysan (Kaz.) 100 E2
Zaysan, L. (Kaz.) 100 E2
Zeili-Alatau Mts. (Kaz., Kyr.) 126 D2
Žeimelis (Lith.) 74 B1
Zelenchukskaya (Rus.) 80 A1
Želva (Lith.) 74 C2
Zeravshan (Taj.) 120 B2
Zeravshan Mts. (Uzb., Taj.) 113 E3; 120 B2
Zeravshan R. (Uzb., Taj.) 113 E3; 120 A2
Zestafoni (Geo.) 80 B1
Zeya (Rus.) 33
Zhanatas (Kaz.) 113 F2; 126 B2
Zhashkov (Ukr.) 40 B2
Zhdanov see Mariupol
Zhelaniya, C. (Rus.) 24 F2
Zheleznodorozhny (Rus.) 74 A2
Zheleznogorsk (Rus.) 40 C1
Zhetysay (Kaz.) 120 B1
Zhiloy I. (Azer.) 93 D1
Zhitomir (Ukr.) 40 B2
Zhlobin (Bel.) 49 E3
Zhmerinka (Ukr.) 40 B2
Zhuantobe (Kaz.) 113 E1
Zilupe (Lat.) 68 E2
Zima (Rus.) 24 J4
Zlatoust (Rus.) 100 B1
Zlynka (Rus.) 49 E3
Zlynka (Ukr.) 56 D1
Zod (Arm.) 87 D2
Zorkue, L. (Taj.) 120 D3
Zugdidi (Geo.) 80 A1
Zyryanka (Rus.) 25 O3
Zyryanovsk (Kaz.) 100 E1